THE POLICE

Powers, Procedures and Proprieties

Related Titles of Interest

BENYON, J.
Scarman and After: Essays reflecting on Lord Scarman's Report, the riots and their aftermath

BOUZA, A. V.
Police Administration: Organization and Performance

KATZMAN, G. S.
Understanding the Criminal Process: The Abscam Case

KING, M.
Psychology In and Out of Court: A Critical Examination of Legal Psychology

MOORE, G.
Social Work and Criminal Law in Scotland

PRIESTLY, P.
Community of Scapegoats: The Segregation of Sex Offenders and Informers in Prison

SHEPHERD, J. W. *et al.*
Identification Evidence: A Psychological Evaluation

Related Pergamon Journals of Interest

International Journal of Law and Psychiatry*

Journal of Criminal Justice*

*Free specimen copies available on request

THE POLICE
Powers, Procedures and Proprieties

Edited by

JOHN BENYON

and

COLIN BOURN

with a foreword by
LORD SCARMAN

PERGAMON PRESS
OXFORD · NEW YORK · BEIJING · FRANKFURT
SÃO PAULO · SYDNEY · TOKYO · TORONTO

U.K.	Pergamon Press, Headington Hill Hall, Oxford OX3 0BW, England
U.S.A.	Pergamon Press, Maxwell House, Fairview Park, Elmsford, New York 10523, U.S.A.
PEOPLE'S REPUBLIC OF CHINA	Pergamon Press, Qianmen Hotel, Beijing, People's Republic of China
FEDERAL REPUBLIC OF GERMANY	Pergamon Press, Hammerweg 6, D-6242 Kronberg, Federal Republic of Germany
BRAZIL	Pergamon Editora, Rua Eça de Queiros, 346, CEP 04011, São Paulo, Brazil
AUSTRALIA	Pergamon Press Australia, P.O. Box 544, Potts Point, N.S.W. 2011, Australia
JAPAN	Pergamon Press, 8th Floor, Matsuoka Central Building, 1-7-1 Nishishinjuku, Shinjuku-ku, Tokyo 160, Japan
CANADA	Pergamon Press Canada, Suite 104, 150 Consumers Road, Willowdale, Ontario M2J 1P9, Canada

First edition 1986

Library of Congress Cataloging in Publication Data

Main entry under title:
The police: powers, procedures, and proprieties.
Bibliography: p.
Includes index.
1. Criminal procedure—Great Britain. 2. Criminal investigation—Great Britain.
I. Benyon, John. II. Bourn, C. J.
KD8329.P65   1986   345.41'052   344.10552   85-29783

British Library Cataloguing in Publication Data

The Police.
1. Great Britain. Police and Criminal Evidence Act 1984.
2. Police—England.
I. Benyon, John, *1951–*   II. Bourn, Colin
344.205'52   KD4834.5/

ISBN 0-08-032697-8 (Hardcover)
ISBN 0-08-032696-X (Flexicover)

The essays in this book reflect the views of the individual authors and not necessarily those of the organisations with which they are connected, nor those of the editors or publisher.

Printed in Great Britain by A. Wheaton & Co. Ltd. Exeter

For **Coleen, Joseph** and **Danielle** and **Jill, Johanna** and **Robert**

There is still in England, in one important sense at least, a greater sense of *personal freedom* than in any other country in the world that I know. It comes, I believe, from a sense of the security of the citizen from arbitrary interference by servants of the Crown, however exalted. This feeling of freedom has been remarked with admiration by visitors to England over the centuries, and it has always seemed to me the contribution most precious and of most enduring value which the English character has made to the still unfinished process of civilising the human animal into a free man, walking upright in spirit as well as in body.

The conduct of the police is a sound measure of the health of this freedom. That the police must have powers, and adequate powers, to perform their many duties, to maintain law and order, protect the weak, prevent crime and apprehend malefactors is self-evident. But because the police represent the State and are invested with special powers it is imperative that these powers be vigilantly watched and controlled by checks against abuse or misuse. The notion, attractive to those who find more responsibility oppressive, that one should delegate this power to the police, giving them a wellnigh blank cheque and trusting to their benevolence not to overdraw, is an insidiously dangerous form of complacency. Our police are not good because they are inherently good but because they have been shaped and defined within our liberal traditions by men who have appreciated both the value and the vulnerability of freedom. There is inevitably among the police a perfectly natural tendency to acquire power; it makes them feel stronger, more competent, more in control. Thus a conscientious officer, in exceeding his authority, may feel quite genuinely that it is, in that useful phrase, 'in the public interest' for him to do so, and act with the best of intentions. . . .

Freedom is eroded little by little, and the only really effective protection is the standard and vigilance of public opinion . . . the heritage of English freedom is unique and precious but destructible, and unless ordinary men and women are prepared to stand up and at the price of criticism and inconvenience defend their freedom from unnecessary encroachments, they will lose them inch by inch.

John Chandos, 'Constabulary Duty' in
C. H. Rolph (ed), *The Police and the Public*, London: Heinemann, 1962

Contents

viii   *Contents*

Part 5   In Perspective: the Police, the Acts and the Public

Preface

On 23 June 1977 the Government announced that the Royal Commission on Criminal Procedure was to be established to examine the powers and duties of the police to investigate crime, and the rights and duties of suspected or accused people. The impetus for this review of the system of criminal procedure came from a continuously rising level of recorded crime, together with a widespread concern about the way in which the police were said to have handled certain types of suspects — a concern which came to a head in the famous Maxwell Confait murder case. The Report of the Philips Commission (Cmnd. 8092), which was published in January 1981, was the precursor for the Police and Criminal Evidence Act 1984, and the Prosecution of Offences Act 1985.

These Acts are intended to strike a balance between the powers needed to investigate and prosecute crime effectively, and the safeguards necessary for the protection of the civil liberties of suspected persons. As the essays in this book show, many people do not consider that the balance has been found. This book examines the provisions in the new Acts, and reviews police practice and the system of criminal procedure in the light of the legislation. It is a book about police powers and procedures, and also about policing proprieties and the consequent relations between members of the public and police officers.

The book arises from three one-day conferences which were held in 1985 at the University of Leicester on the theme: *After the Act — Implementing the Police and Criminal Evidence Act*. The conferences were organised by the Continuing Education Unit of the Department of Adult Education, and during the three days an audience of over 350 heard the views of twenty different speakers. Both the speakers and the audience were drawn from many different groups and interests, including police and probation officers, councillors, community and voluntary organisations, social services, the legal profession and academics. The conferences benefited greatly from the chairmanship of Sir Cyril Philips, who presided over the deliberations of the Royal Commission on Criminal Procedure.

Since the appointment of the Philips Commission by the Labour Government, debate on crime and police powers and effectiveness has continued unabated. Indeed, law and order seems to be moving ever closer to the centre of the political stage. In the debate on the Queen's Speech, in the second week of November 1985, the Opposition launched a blistering attack on the Conservative Government's record on crime and disorder. The Shadow Home Secretary, Gerald Kaufman, pointed out that since Mrs. Thatcher came to power in May 1979, burglary had risen by 59 per cent, firearms crimes by 48 per cent, criminal damage by 63 per cent, and violent crimes against individuals by 31 per cent. He said: 'Thatcher's Britain is the most crime-ridden country in Europe'.

There is of course nothing new about public concern at apparent growing crime and lawlessness, and fears about the effectiveness of the police. Indeed, as Geoffrey Pearson has shown in his book *Hooligan*, there scarcely seems to have been any period when law and order has not been a source of public anxiety. In 1958, for example, the Conservative Party Conference discussed the 'sudden increase in crime and brutality' and delegates concurred with the speaker who said

> Over the past 25 years we in this country, through misguided sentiment, have cast aside the word 'discipline', and now we are suffering from it.

And yet the annual crime figures then were a mere 626,000 indictable offences. By 1974, the total number of notifiable offences had risen to 1,963,400 and Sir Keith Joseph was asserting

> For the first time in a century and a half, since the great Tory reformer Robert Peel set up the Metropolitan Police, areas of our cities are becoming unsafe for peaceful citizens by night, and some even by day.

Similarly eccentric views of the history of order in Britain's cities were evident during the 1979 election campaign, when law and order was a major theme of the Conservatives. By then, notifiable criminal offences had risen to 2,377,000 and yet in 1984, after five years of Conservative government, the figure had increased by over 39 per cent to 3,314,000 (excluding 'other criminal damage of value £20 and under'). By 1984, Sir Keith Joseph's remarks of ten years earlier had begun to look increasingly embarrassing.

Under the Conservative Government there has not only been a huge rise in the amount of reported crime. It has also been a period in which serious public disorder occurred, not only in the cities in 1980, 1981 and 1985 but also in various areas during the coal dispute of 1984–85. The police, of course, have been at the centre of these events and on 6 October 1985 Police Constable Keith Blakelock was stabbed to death during the riot at Broadwater Farm Estate in Tottenham. He thus became, it seems, the first policeman to be killed in a riot since Constable Culley was stabbed at Cold Bath Fields on 13 May 1833 in what came to be known as the 'Clerkenwell Riot'. A total of four people died in the 1985 riots, and many more were seriously injured. These events focused attention even more closely on law and order, so that opinion polls in November 1985 showed the issue as the second most important political concern behind unemployment.

In her speech, on 6 November, the Queen announced that police powers for combatting disorders would be strengthened, and Mrs. Thatcher made it clear that additional resources would be forthcoming. In the aftermath of the riots, controversy raged over the role of the police in triggering the events, and in contributing to the underlying causes. Naturally, police officers argued that the complaints made about them were unjust, and that the riots were essentially an outbreak of criminal behaviour, fostered by drugs dealers and agitators. Some officers accepted that social grievances were a major factor, highlighting particularly high unemployment among young people. However, many people in the areas affected voiced strong criticism of police tactics, such as stop and search, and allegations were also frequently made about harassment, abuse and assault. In 1981, Lord Scarman reported that the disorders in Brixton were 'essentially an outburst of anger and resentment by young black people against the police', and in 1985, too, this argument was often put forward.

The disorders illustrated all too vividly many of the dilemmas which face the police service today. On the one hand, inner city residents expect and require police assistance, and action against crime, on the other hand, many people complain about, and resent, tough police tactics to catch criminals. In certain areas, the police must act with great caution for, it appears, they are in danger of igniting a social explosion, and yet it is often in these areas where complaints about crime and assaults are the greatest, and where police officers themselves are likely to be provoked by abuse, or perhaps even assault. It is here more than anywhere that the General Instructions, first issued by Rowan and Mayne in 1829, should be rigorously applied. The orders to every constable required that:

> He will be civil and obliging to all people of every rank and class.

> He must be particularly cautious not to interfere idly or unnecessarily in order to make a display of his authority; when required to act, he will do so with decision and boldness; on all occasions he may expect to receive the fullest support in the proper exercise of his authority. He must remember that there is no qualification so indispensable to a police officer as a perfect command of temper, never suffering himself to be moved in the slightest degree by any language or threats that may be used; if he does his duty in a quiet and determined manner, such conduct will probably excite the well-disposed of the bystanders to assist him, if he requires them.

> In the novelty of the present establishment, particular care is to be taken that the constables of the police do not form false notions of their duties and powers.

This book is concerned with the powers of the police and how they are put into effect. Is sufficient care still taken that officers 'do not form false notions of their duties and powers'; do constables never suffer themselves to be moved 'in the slightest degree' by language or threats; are the police sufficiently cautious 'not to interfere idly or unnecessarily'? These are some of the questions which Lord Scarman raised in his report on the Brixton disorders in 1981, which were also being asked in the aftermath of the 1985 riots and which the authors in this book consider. But this book also examines in detail the new powers and procedures which have been introduced in the Police and Criminal Evidence Act 1984, and the Prosecution of Offences Act, 1985. How do these provisions measure up to the needs of society, how are they likely to affect policing practice, and what impact may they have on police relations with the public?

We would like to express our appreciation to Sir Cyril Philips for playing such an important part in the smooth running of the conferences, and indeed in their organisation. We would also like to thank someone who did not attend the meetings, but whose influence on the discussions was nevertheless considerable. Lord Scarman's seminal report on the Brixton disorders (Cmnd. 8427) was frequently cited, and we are most grateful to him for writing the foreword to this book. Many of the essays which it contains are based on contributions made at the Leicester Conferences, and our thanks are due to all who participated and helped to make the discussions so lively and stimulating. We are especially grateful to the authors of the chapters which follow who, despite the considerable demands on their time, willingly revised and updated their essays.

It is a pleasure to pay tribute to all the members of the Department of Adult Education who took part in the organisation of the conferences. We would particularly like to thank the Department's Secretary, John Cunningham, who played such an important part in the administration, and the Conference Secretary, Kate Penny, who smoothly and efficiently handled the bookings and other detailed arrangements. Without them there would have been no conferences, and hence no book.

We would also like to express our appreciation to other colleagues in the University of Leicester for their help and encouragement. It is not possible to name them all, but in particular we wish to thank Professor William Forster, Director and Head of the Department of Adult Education, Professor Edward Griew of the Faculty of Law, and Mr. A. R. Siddiqui, Assistant Librarian, who is always exceedingly helpful in locating government publications and other sources. We would also like to thank Pauline Maniscalco, of the Department's secretarial staff, for her help and hard work with the conferences. We are especially grateful to Grace Belfiore, of Pergamon Press, for her advice and helpful comments on the production of the book.

One of our greatest debts is to Liz Kemp, who produced the transcript of the conferences, and the revised and edited chapters. This was a very large undertaking, and we greatly appreciated her speed and accuracy, and her ability to interpret all manner of writing that was set before her. Without her efforts, producing this book would have been a very difficult operation.

Finally, we would like to thank our respective families for their support, good humour and forbearance while we have been putting the book together.

Leicester, 10 March 1986   JOHN BENYON
                                                             COLIN BOURN

Acknowledgements

The editors and publishers wish to thank the following for permission to reproduce material:

Julian Bradley, Head of Publicity at the Metropolitan Police, New Scotland Yard, for permission to reproduce the advertisements on pages 47 and 100.

'Jedd', and **Tony Judge**, Editor of *Police*, the magazine of the Police Federation, for permission to use the cartoon on page 178.

Eric Davies, Senior Advertising and Publicity Officer at the Metropolitan Police, New Scotland Yard, for permission to reproduce the advertisement shown on page 12.

Mark Collyer, of the Home Office Public Relations Branch, for permission to reproduce the advertisement entitled 'Brothers in Law' which is shown on page 29.

The BBC, and **Mrs Jack Warner**, for permission to use the photograph of Jack Warner as George Dixon in *Dixon of Dock Green*, which appears on the cover.

The editors and publishers also wish to express their appreciation to **Angela Chorley**, graphic artist in the Audio-Visual Centre at the University of Leicester, for drawing the three-day clocks, which appear on pages 155 and 156.

Foreword

Lord Scarman

The Police and Criminal Evidence Act 1984 and the Prosecution of Offences Act 1985 are landmarks in the progressive development of the English and Welsh system of criminal justice. The two Acts will in due course work great changes in the way the criminal law is enforced. They will re-structure the whole criminal process from arrest or summons up to the moment at which the trial begins. Our police and prosecution services will be changed irreversibly: the old pattern will fade into history.

This symposium of views, forecasts and prophecies, orchestrated and led by John Benyon and Colin Bourn and developed by authors who are distinguished in their special fields, serves many purposes. It is a valuable explanation of the reforms introduced by the two Acts; it provides a view of the new policing and prosecution processes from widely different vantage points; and it includes a discussion, as profound as any that I have read, of the principles and policies which in truth guide policing and prosecuting methods but are seldom admitted, even if they be consciously recognised, by the policemen, lawyers, and administrators who run the system.

The symposium is not only a thinking response to the reforms now enacted, but is itself evidence of the truth of some of the propositions enunciated. A careful comparison of David Smith's almost philosophical contribution, designed to elicit the truth as distinct from accepted beliefs as to the nature of policing, with the admirable contributions from George Greaves (how the public of the inner city sees the police) and from Leslie Curtis (how the young policeman on the beat sees his challenges and his problems) will explain my meaning. Analysis will show that Smith, Greaves and Curtis are all developing the same theme.

Writers of forewords slip happily into using epithets such as 'thoughtful', 'stimulating', 'challenging'. The essays in this collection really do merit these adjectives. But I would add that they are also original, encouraging a new look at policing and prosecuting. And Part 4, where my professional brethren of the law take over, contains some refreshing insights into the impact upon the trial process itself of the reforms enacted in the two statutes.

All in all, John Benyon, Colin Bourn and their team of essayists are to be congratulated — and thanked. Their work will encourage clear thinking and a new approach to a problem as old as civilisation itself — how to maintain the public tranquillity of a free society.

10 March 1986   SCARMAN

The Contributors

David Ashby, MP, is Conservative Member for Leicestershire North-West, and is a Barrister-at-Law. He was a member of the Greater London Council serving as chairman of the legal and parliamentary committee and the housing committee and was a member of the Inner London Education Authority. He played a vigorous part in debates in Parliament on the Police and Criminal Evidence Bill.

John Benyon is Lecturer in Politics and Public Administration in the Department of Adult Education and the Department of Politics at the University of Leicester. He was previously at the University of Warwick and was a member of Warwick District Council, 1979–1983. He edited *Scarman and After* (Pergamon, 1984), and his publications include articles in *Public Administration*, *New Scientist*, *Local Government Studies* and *Parliamentary Affairs*.

Colin Bourn is Senior Lecturer in Law and Head of the Continuing Education Unit, Department of Adult Education, University of Leicester. He is a Barrister-at-Law and his publications on aspects of the English legal system include *Redundancy Law and Practice* (Butterworths, 1983), *Job Security* (Sweet and Maxwell, 1980) and articles in *Human Relations, Local Government Chronicle* and *New Law Journal*.

Maurice Buck, OBE, QPM is the Chief Constable of Northamptonshire and represented the Association of Chief Police Officers in consultations about the Police and Criminal Evidence Bill. He joined the Metropolitan Police in 1949 and served for twenty-three years, after which he became Assistant Chief Constable (Crime) in Birmingham, and then the West Midlands. He was Deputy Commandant of the Police Staff College at Bramshill before his appointment as Chief Constable in 1981.

Gabrielle Cox was Chairperson of the Greater Manchester Police Authority and served on the Police and Fire Committee of the Association of Metropolitan Authorities. She has been involved for some time in the Manchester police station lay visitors scheme, and she took an active role in the debate on the new policing legislation.

Leslie Curtis, BEM has been Chairman of the Police Federation of England and Wales since 1982. He became a member of the joint central committee of the Federation in 1947 and represented police officers in a number of capacities before becoming chairman. He has been active in consultations about the Police and Criminal Evidence Bill and other policing legislation.

George Greaves, MBE is Principal Community Relations Officer of the Council for Community Relations in Lambeth. He gave evidence to Lord Scarman's Inquiry into the Brixton Disorders, and has written a number of articles on police–community relations, including a chapter in *Scarman and After* (Pergamon, 1984). He is a member of the Lambeth Community–Police Consultative Group.

Clive Grenyer is Undersecretary of the Association of County Councils and is Head of Police Consumer Services and Fire and Emergency Planning for the Association. He has been involved in detailed consideration of the proposals for an independent prosecution service.

Ole Hansen is a solicitor and was Director of the Legal Action Group until 1985, and presented evidence to the Royal Commission on Criminal Procedure. He was editor of *Legal Action*, regularly writes and lectures on criminal procedure and civil liberties and was an active participant in the debate on the Police and Criminal Evidence Bill, and the Prosecution of Offences Bill.

Michael Hill, QC was formerly Treasury Counsel at the Old Bailey. As Chairman of the Criminal Bar Association he took a leading role in putting forward the views of the Bar on the Police and Criminal Evidence Bill and the proposals for an independent prosecution service.

Barrie Irving is Director of Studies at The Police Foundation in London and has made a special study of the interrogation process, carrying out research in this area for the Royal Commission on Criminal Procedure. He previously worked at the Tavistock Institute.

Tony Judge is Editor of *Police* and has served the Police Federation for over two decades. He served on the Greater London Council as a Labour Member and is the author of many books and articles on policing issues and police history, including *A Man Apart* (Baker, 1972) and *The Night the Police Went on Strike* (with G. Reynolds: Weidenfeld, 1968).

Walter Merricks was a member of the Royal Commission on Criminal Procedure. He is Professional and Public Relations Secretary at the Law Society and, as a solicitor and legal journalist, he has written extensively in the field of criminal procedure and the prosecution process. He was the editor of the journal, *Policing*, published by Sweet and Maxwell.

Kenneth Oxford, CBE, QPM has been Chief Constable of Merseyside since 1976 and was President of the Association of Chief Police Officers (1982–1983). He is chairman of the Association's crime committee and represented ACPO in consultations about the Police and Criminal Evidence Bill. He was member of the Home Office working party on the prosecution service and has contributed articles and chapters to many publications, including *Scarman and After* (Pergamon, 1984).

The Rt. Hon. Lord Scarman, OBE, was a Lord of Appeal in Ordinary from 1977 until 1986. He was Chairman of the Law Commission, 1965–1973, and he chaired the Tribunal of Inquiry into the violence and civil disturbances in Northern Ireland in August 1969. He conducted the inquiry into the 1974 Red Lion Square disorders (Cmnd. 5919) and three years later he chaired the Court of Inquiry into the Grunwick dispute (Cmnd. 6922). In 1981 he conducted the inquiry into the Brixton riots, the seminal report of which, *The Brixton Disorders 10–12 April 1981* (Cmnd. 8427), has greatly influenced recent policing developments and legislation. His books include *Law Reform: the New Pattern* (Routledge and Kegan Paul, 1968) and *English Law — the New Dimension* (Stevens, 1974).

Paul Sieghart is Chairman of the Executive Committee of Justice, the British Section of the International Commission of Jurists, and is active in law reform. Called to the Bar in 1953, he was a member of the Committee on Data Protection and is a governor of the British Institute of Human Rights and a trustee of the European Human Rights Foundation. He is a noted writer and broadcaster and among his many publications are *Privacy and Computers* (Latimer New Dimensions, 1976) and *The International Law of Human Rights* (Oxford University Press, 1983).

David Smith is a Senior Fellow at the Policy Studies Institute and has carried out extensive research into policing methods, powers and procedures. He undertook the research commissioned by the Metropolitan Police, published as *Police and People in London* (Policy Studies Institute, 1983), which is the most detailed investigation and evaluation of a police force and its community yet to have appeared. He is also the author of studies on unemployment and racial disadvantage, including *Racial Disadvantage in Britain* (Penguin, 1977).

Professor John Smith, CBE, QC, FBA has held a Chair in Law at the University of Nottingham since 1958. He was called to the Bar in 1950 and has served on the Criminal Law Revision Committee. He is a foremost authority on criminal law and has published many articles and books including (with Brian Hogan) *Criminal Law* (Butterworths, 1965), *Law of Theft* (Butterworths, 1968) and *Criminal Law, Cases and Materials* (Butterworths, 1975).

Richard Stone is a Lecturer in Law at the University of Leicester and has written many articles on aspects of the English legal system. Among his recent publications is *Entry, Search and Seizure* (Sweet and Maxwell, 1985), which considers in detail the role of the police.

Ron West, QPM, is a Chief Superintendent and full-time Assistant Secretary of the Police Superintendents' Association of England and Wales. Amongst other Association duties he has been involved with training and represented the Association on the Home Office working party on the proposals for an independent prosecutions service.

Robin White is Senior Lecturer in the Department of Law at the University of Leicester and has published extensively on criminal law and judicial procedure. His most recent book is entitled *The Administration of Justice* (Blackwell, 1985).

Clive Woodcock is Chief Prosecuting Solicitor for Cheshire and is a past President of the Prosecuting Solicitors' Society of England and Wales. He has taken an active role in the debate following the Royal Commission on Criminal Procedure, particularly on the proposals for an independent prosecution service.

Professor Michael Zander has held a Chair in Law at the London School of Economics since 1977 and has been legal correspondent of *The Guardian* since 1963. He has published extensively on the English legal system and among his books are *A Bill of Rights?* (Rose, 1975), *Legal Services for the Community* (Temple Smith, 1978), *The Law-Making Process* (Weidenfeld and Nicolson, 1980), and *Cases and Materials on the English Legal System* (Weidenfeld and Nicolson, 4th edition: 1984).

PART 1

In the Limelight: the Changing Context of Policing

CHAPTER 1

Policing in the limelight: citizens, constables and controversy

JOHN BENYON

The recorded levels of serious crime have risen apace since the inception of Mrs. Thatcher's Government. In 1979 the recorded number of notifiable offences in England and Wales was 2,536,700 and the *Criminal Statistics* for 1984, published in October 1985 (Cmnd. 9621), put the figure at 3,499,100: a rise of 962,400 or 37.9 per cent in just five years.

In the 1970s the Conservative Party campaigned vigorously on law and order issues and it may be seen as ironic that, since its election to office in May 1979, that party has presided over such a visible rise in crime and disorder. However, it is probably not surprising as the Government's inexorable economic and social policies have without doubt contributed to the increased levels of crime and disorder which are being reported. Research suggests that the property crime rate is more sensitive to the levels of unemployment and deprivation than to the number of police officers.

Judging the police and assessing the Acts

Clearly any new legislation on policing, criminal evidence and prosecutions will be judged by its effectiveness in combating crime and its success in promoting justice. As many have pointed out it is not only morally reprehensible to convict an innocent person of a crime, it is also singularly ineffective as the guilty culprit remains at large to commit further offences. The Police and Criminal Evidence Act 1984 and the Prosecution of Offences Act 1985 have been justified in terms of effectiveness, efficiency and justice, although as contributions in this book show many people are sceptical about these claims.

Leon Brittan, then the Home Secretary, frequently stressed these themes during the passage of the Bills through Parliament. He said the police needed effective *powers* and as a *quid pro quo* suitable *procedures* were needed to ensure that *proprieties* are observed; a Crown Prosecution

Service, he claimed, will promote efficiency and justice. Three themes of this book are *powers, procedures* and *proprieties*, and the contributors consider how the legislation and codes of practice measure up to the requirements.

This first chapter, though, seeks to examine whether the legislation, important and contentious as it is, really grapples with the central problems and questions of policing and crime control. It is suggested that the Home Secretary's premise that the police are able '*to conduct the fight against crime on our behalf*' is false, is contradicted by research evidence and is antithetical to the central tenets upon which British policing was founded and developed. In addition to *effectiveness* and *justice* there are four other policing criteria which can be identified against which the legislation must be evaluated; these are *identity, participation, legitimacy* and *consent*. They are interrelated, and each factor impinges upon effectiveness and justice.

Furthermore, this chapter suggests that during the last two decades the *image* of policing has adversely changed as the police have become *more remote* from many people. Eight areas of development are considered — centralisation, professionalisation, specialisation, methods, equipment, conduct, fairness and politicisation — and it appears that various changes have affected the image and remoteness of policing, and the six policing factors. It is argued that the Police and Criminal Evidence Act and the Prosecution of Offences Act should be examined with these factors in mind — does the legislation increase perceptions of identity, participation, legitimacy and justice, and hence effectiveness and consent, do the Acts diminish the remoteness of policing and criminal procedure, do they reverse the undesirable trends, or compensate for them, in the eight areas of development?

The police are now at the centre of the political stage, to an extent that would have been barely conceivable thirty years ago. In 1950 *The Blue Lamp* introduced P.C. Dixon who, in the long-running television series *Dixon of Dock Green*, came to epitomise the popular image of the friendly, firm and fatherly local policeman. In the same year that George Dixon made his entrance a postal survey found that 73·5 per cent of the respondents were 'appreciative' of the police, with just 5 per cent who were 'hostile'.[1]* A typical view was that the police were

> overworked, underpaid men with a high sense of duty; one of the chief reasons why this is such a pleasant country to live in.

In 1960, the rather more representative survey of the Royal Commission on the Police revealed that nearly 83 per cent of the sample said they had 'great respect' for the police,[2] and the Willink Commission concluded

> the findings of the survey constitute an overwhelming vote of

*Superscript numbers refer to Notes at end of chapters.

confidence in the police . . . relations between the police and the public are on the whole very good, and we have no reason to suppose that they have ever, in recent times, been otherwise. This is a finding which we believe will give great satisfaction to Your Majesty, to the police, and to the public.[3]

The development of British policing: the handyman cometh?

The account presented by Willink suggested that policing had indeed come a long way since its inception, for the first proposals to establish police in England met with stiff resistance. In 1785, five years after the infamous Gordon Riots, the Solicitor General in Pitt's Government, Sir Archibald Macdonald, presented a bill to Parliament to enable the establishment of a metropolitan police force. It was bitterly opposed and was withdrawn, although a similar bill was enacted the following year by the Dublin Parliament, which laid the foundations for the Royal Irish Constabulary. During the next forty years, further attempts to create professional police in London were rejected as incompatible with British liberty and as 'odious and repulsive', in the words of the Parliamentary Committee of 1818.

This resolute opposition to the establishment of police in England seems to have come from various classes and interests: 'a curious blend of parochial defensiveness, Whig theory and popular resistance'.

> Tories feared the over-ruling of parochial and chartered rights, and of the powers of local J.P.s; Whigs feared an increase in the powers of Crown or of Government; . . . the radical populace until Chartist times saw in any police an engine of oppression.[4]

However, by 1829 the fears of disorder, political agitation and crime — concern about the 'dangerous classes' in general — had grown sufficiently widespread to persuade a majority of parliamentarians to give their assent to Robert Peel's Metropolitan Police Act.

The new police were at first very unpopular amongst large sections of the population. The continuing opposition was illustrated by the behaviour of the jurors at the inquest into the death of P.C. Culley at the 'Battle of Cold Bath Fields' in 1833. They returned a verdict of justifiable homicide, and in their honour a medal was struck.[5] Pamphlets circulated calling for the removal of 'Peel's bloody gang', and anti-police riots took place in various parts of England, as policing was introduced elsewhere. It is a matter of debate how long serious opposition lasted to 'the plague of blue locusts'. Reith and Critchley, for example, suggest that in London the police were accepted remarkably quickly by the vast mass of the population, whereas others such as Storch and Brogden claim that hostility amongst much of the working class has continued to the present time, and is manifest in events such as the 1981 and 1985 riots and the 1984–85 coal dispute.[6]

Both views are probably overstated in that the police did acquire widespread support among many working class people, while in some areas opposition continued which varied from sullen dislike to intense hostility. In any event, the predominant *image* of policing as consensual and generally accepted was established early; in 1856, for example, the *London Quarterly Review* described how 'amid the bustle of Piccadilly or the roar of Oxford Street, P.C.X.59 stalks along, an institution rather than a man'.[7] By the turn of the century, the impression in the media was of a police service closely tied to the people, giving assistance where necessary, upholding the law in a firm but good natured fashion and, indeed, the envy of the world. On Christman Eve 1908 *The Times* positively enthused about the police and their relations with

> the people whom they serve by ties of intimate personal association which are not to be found in any other country in the world. The policeman in London is not merely guardian of the peace; he is an integral part of its social life. In many a back street and slum he not merely stands for law and order; he is the true handyman of our streets, the best friend of a mass of people who have no other counsellor or protector.[8]

As many people have pointed out, this comforting view was wildly romantic for in many 'back streets and slums' the police were resented and unloved. In *The Classic Slum* Roberts describes how nobody 'ever spoke in fond regard' of the policeman, let alone viewing him as the 'handyman of the streets'

> like their children, delinquent or not, the poor in general looked upon him with fear and dislike . . .[9]

The existence of areas in which many of the inhabitants continued to be hostile to the police is confirmed by a number of accounts. Basil Griffiths, for example, who until 1982 was Vice-Chairman of the Police Federation, stated

> there exists and has existed since the days of the industrial revolution hard core urban areas where a positive hatred is maintained towards the police by a sizable minority of the people who live there. And this hatred is matched by a belligerence displayed towards any form of authority.[10]

Griffiths' 'no nonsense' approach to such people, and his view that there is no doubt where the blame lies, is representative of the views of many police officers and members of the wider public, and perhaps a reciprocation of this antipathy helps to explain some of the enduring anti-police opinion in certain areas.

A 'Golden Age' of public acceptance?

It is surely wrong, however, to claim, as some have done, that this evidence of opposition represents a more general aversion to the police amongst working class people. Opinion polls consistently have shown the police as one of the most highly assessed groups, confirming the findings of the Willink Commission in the early 1960s. Then, concluded the most recent Royal Commission on the Police, relations between the public and the police were 'on the whole very good' and augured well for the future. According to Reiner:

> As far as police acceptance by the public is concerned, the 1950s seem a 'Golden Age' of tranquillity and accord, with only hesitant harbingers of coming crisis.[11]

As Reiner himself stresses, one must be wary of accepting unquestioningly the myth that policing in the post-war period, or at any time, was characterised by harmonious relations with all and sundry. The police are key agents of social control and in a society which is profoundly unequal and divided, the control of some of its members is bound to be intrinsically conflictual. People like those described above by Griffiths are likely to be treated rather differently by police officers than are people who they perceive to be respectable and law-abiding. Those who are arrested by the police are unlikely to have as high opinions of them as people whose views are based on media images, or whose contacts with the police are as victims of crime.

The 1950s may have been the 'Golden Age' of policing but the survey for the Willink Commission revealed that nearly one in five of the sample did *not* have 'great respect' for the police, 42 per cent thought some policemen took bribes, and 35 per cent thought that unfair methods were used on occasions to get information. The survey of police officers showed that 89 per cent wanted their relations with the public improved and over two-thirds felt these relations had changed for the worse.[12] It should also be remembered that the 1950s experienced the 'moral panic' of teddy-boys and youth violence, a rise in crime from the middle of the decade and racial attacks and anti-black riots in August 1958 in Nottingham and north Kensington (not Notting Hill as inaccurately reported in the press at the time).

Despite these provisos it does seem reasonable to argue that British policing reached its zenith in the 1950s and early 1960s. As Reiner puts it, 'by the 1950s "policing by consent" *was* achieved in Britain to the maximal degree it is ever attainable'.[13] The positive relationship between the police and a large proportion of the public, and the subsequent support which flowed from it, became known as 'the British police advantage', and this was reported to be a topic of envious comment by police officers in the United States and elsewhere.

The success of the development of British policing has been attributed to a number of factors. It was, of course, partly the result of social and economic policies which decreased the amount of overt conflict, and partly the consequence of political action which enabled the working class to articulate grievances through formal channels[14] such as elections, trade unions and the Labour Party. It was also a result of the successful extension of the hegemonic set of values and attitudes, and the creation of various agencies of social control. However, policing in Britain also succeeded in its own right, so that by the end of the 1950s a large majority of the public — 83 per cent according to the Willink survey — afforded the police respect and support. Six related factors may help to explain how policing reached its 'Golden Era'; these are *effectiveness, identity, participation, legitimacy, justice* and *consent.*

Securing public support 'in a quiet and determined manner'

Two recurring themes in an examination of these six factors are the importance of the *image* of policing and the significance of the apparent *distance* between police and public. The image that many people have of the police may be based on myth rather than reality but can nevertheless considerably affect the practicalities of policing. The perceptions of the closeness, or the remoteness, of the police may also be important in determining how policing is conducted. The first Metropolitan Police Commissioners were well aware of the need to create a positive image for the new police, and to build a relationship between them and the public which was as close and intimate as possible. In the summer of 1829, Colonel Charles Rowan and Richard Mayne, operating from their headquarters at 4 Whitehall Place (which was soon known by the name of the rear lane — Scotland Yard), decided upon their instructions to the new police and they stressed the importance of politeness, civility and a friendly disposition. The General Instructions informed each policeman that

> he must be particularly cautious not to interfere idly or unnecessarily in order to make a display of his authority; when required to act, he will do so with decision and boldness. . . . He must remember that there is no qualification so indispensable to a police officer as a perfect command of temper, never suffering himself to be moved in the slightest degree by any language or threats that may be used; if he does his duty in a quiet and determined manner, such conduct will probably excite the well-disposed of the bystanders to assist him, if he requires

them. In the novelty of the present establishment, particular care is to be taken that the constables of the police do not form false notions of their duties and powers.[15]

Peel was convinced that the new police must be free of any association with the army, and so an innocuous non-military uniform was chosen. The police were recruited from the working class and by 1 June 1830 men from the following backgrounds had been taken on[16]: butchers (135), bakers (109), shoemakers (198), tailors (51), soldiers (402), labourers (1154), servants (205), carpenters (141), weavers (51), bricklayers (75), black-smiths (55), clerks (152), shopmen (141), mechanics (141), sailors (101), plumbers (46), turners and stonemasons (28). It has been often commented that the British policing tradition has been based on recruiting the working class to control the working class, and perhaps this is one reason why white-collar, middle class crime has been afforded such a low priority. The original police had a high turnover, partly because of the stresses of the job and partly because of the insistence by Rowan and Mayne on high standards of police conduct in public. By the end of 1831, out of a total strength of 4,000, some 1,250 officers had resigned and 1,989 had been dismissed mainly for drunkenness. Incidentally, the Policy Studies Institute study of the Metropolitan Police carried out in 1980 and 1981 found that heavy drinking continues to be prevalent and indeed it appears that 'alcoholism is a serious occupational hazard for police officers'.[17]

The six policing factors are to a considerable extent dependent upon the *image* of the police, and on the *distance* between policing and the public. They are also *interrelated* and so, for example, a high level of perceived effectiveness is likely to increase consent, legitimacy, identity and so on. It is worth briefly examining these factors, and how each was enhanced by policing policies and structures, at least up to the early 1960s.

Effectiveness, identity and participation: 'a body in tune with the people'

1. Effectiveness refers to the extent to which the police are *perceived* to be successfully tackling crime, coping with disorder, enforcing the law and responding to calls for assistance. It is notoriously difficult to measure, and perceptions of police effectiveness are likely to be determined largely by media coverage, the views of opinion leaders such as politicians, and individual citizens' personal observations of, and contact with, the police. Judgements on police effectiveness are also likely to vary from place to place, and from time to time, depending upon public expectations of what the police can achieve, and on people's views on what the police ought to be concentrating their efforts.

It does seem that police effectiveness was judged favourably in many areas quite soon after their establishment, as cities became less disorderly and streets appeared to be safer. As remarked earlier, this trend may well have been the result of other factors, but the police were seen by many as an important cause. The *methods* adopted by the police also seem to have been regarded as effective. The image of low profile policing, making use of persuasion rather than coercion, or if necessary using minimal force, appears to have contributed to the widespread approval — although, of course, this image did not reflect reality in many areas. The *service role* of the constable was also favourably judged, whether it was the officer seeing school children across the road, or giving directions, or acting in a broker role in a neighbour dispute. As Brogden points out 'these duties provide concrete rewards for members of all social classes',[18] and have helped to show the police as effective and valuable public servants.

The favourable impression of police effectiveness was also furthered by the image of efficiency and discipline. The constable was seen in many areas as a man of the community, as well as 'a man apart',[19] so he was viewed as accessible and available, which strengthened the impression of an effective service. The question of effectiveness in the 1950s was by no means universally answered positively, for in some inner city areas the police were still viewed with hostility, and more generally, from the mid-1950s, notice began to be drawn to the steady rise in crime and the fall in the proportion of offences solved. The establishment of the Willink Royal Commission in January 1960 was also evidence of some unease with Metropolitan Police effectiveness, although primarily it was concerned with accountability, complaints and police pay. It was also one of the first indications of what was to become a dominant concern of the 1960s and early 1970s — that is the desire to carry out political and social modernisation of key institutions. Nevertheless, while it should not be overstated, it does seem that by the 1950s the police were widely regarded by the public as valuable, worthwhile and effective.

2. *Identity* involves the extent to which citizens identify with the police, and see a concurrence of their interests and values. It concerns perceptions of common interests, as well as identification and support with police officers, and again is largely dependent on the *image* of policing and the impressions of its closeness or remoteness. It is also likely to be affected by a person's standing, and investment, in the existing social order. In the 1950s, the archetypal image of the policeman was one with which many people could identify: it was, according to Bowden, that of 'a senior Boy Scout' and of course was represented by George Dixon of Dock Green 'the silver-haired, moderate, wise, kindly patrician and community figurehead'.[20] In fact rather than patrician he was plebeian — a commoner, a member of the working class, but one who had risen to a position of

responsibility and power; and a man who was held in respect, even by the 'villains' of Dock Green.

It was a magnificent image for the police, even though many officers grumbled that it did not reflect reality. The image of the local bobby as someone to look up to, but also a wise and friendly man of the people, was reinforced in other fictional presentations, in the mass news media (which might be regarded as another form of fiction) and even in children's literature. Reiner draws attention to Morrison's research in this area, and the example of Mr. Plod's relationship with the other folk in Toytown. When Mr. Plod is injured the Toytowners are most concerned, not least because it leaves them bereft of their protector and guardian of order: 'Who is going to protect us against robbers?' asks Miss Fluffy Cat, and Mr. Wobbly Man is similarly anxious.[21]

The identification of people with the police was facilitated by the policy of recruiting from the working class, by training and disciplinary policies and by the visibility of the police on the beat performing their service role. The *image* of the demeanour of officers — their politeness, friendliness and helpfulness stressed by Rowan and Mayne — was also an important means of developing this identity, although no doubt this varied considerably from officer to officer, and place to place. The identity of interests and values with the police was also an important aspect, and conversely in those areas where people tended to be policed *against* a clash of interests precluded a common identity. In these sorts of areas police officers felt isolated and set apart in the 1950s, just as a hundred years earlier. In some areas the predominant view of the police has been that of an alien presence, but more generally the development of British policing seems to have been characterised by a widespread public identity with them.

3. Participation should be understood in its wider sense — that is to include the availability of formal and informal means of articulating opinions about, and being involved in, policing. Dahrendorf has pointed out that 'in the normal course of events, participation is nice but not indispensable. What is important is the possibility of participation in order to veto developments, to express dissent'.[22] By the 1950s policing at least *appeared* to provide opportunities for citizens to express their views, both positively and negatively, and formally and informally.

The watch committees provided formal mechanisms, and the complaints procedure was available to afford a means of formal dissent about methods and behaviour. Informally, the pedestrian constable was available to be contacted and consulted — he was the force's 'listening post' in the community.

Again the image was probably at least as important as the reality, and at a time when many towns had their own police force, the police appeared to be quite accessible. Perhaps another aspect of this accessibility was that the

Seven and a half million people of 199 nationalities in half a million acres. Is it any wonder London's a handful to police?

It can't be done by blue serge robots. It can only be done by individuals.

They wear the same colour uniform, true, but that doesn't mean their opinions are a similar shade. It doesn't make their personalities match.

There is no such thing as a uniform police officer in London.

And it certainly doesn't produce exactly the same approach to the job.

Listen:

"I wondered if I'd become just another boy in blue when I joined" says PC Paul Edwards, "but I soon discovered that such a thing is almost against the rules! It's got to be a more individualistic and demanding job than selling tiles for a living which I did after leaving grammar school with 5 'O' levels.

It's also, of course, much more responsible. You're directly involved with people's lives.

On my beat in Chelsea I deal with everyone from scrap dealers to duchesses, so I've got to be flexible, understanding and able to see the funny side of things.

Except, of course, when I'm face to face with a hot-headed and violent villain."

WPC Linda Evans was once a beauty consultant to a French cosmetic company. She has an honours degree and enjoys learning Cantonese.

"Is being a police officer no job for a lady? Well, common sense is more important than muscle so the question's invalid.

The uniform only makes us superficially alike. I've yet to meet two coppers who fit the same description.

Same with crime. No two situations are ever exactly similar. You deal with every incident individually, so you have to develop a broad view of human affairs.

If you don't, you'd be a lousy bobby."

Cricket, jazz and photography take up the spare time of PC Henry Curniffe, along with a wife and a baby son. His parents were both born in Jamaica but he says he thinks of himself as primarily a Londoner.

"I thought I'd have a tougher time than I did when I told my friends I was going to join the Metropolitan Police. I still have lots of friends who are not cops, so I guess people take me at face value when I'm off duty.

I feel it is very important for people from immigrant backgrounds to actively participate in this society. Okay, so it's a predominantly white society, but if we don't join in we'll always be outsiders.

It's hard for a lot of people, I know. But I'm optimistic for the future.

London is a magical place to live and work for me. I hope to sit my Sergeant's exams soon."

That's what these three Metropolitan Police Officers feel. Take another three and you'd hear something different.

Certain things, however, all coppers in London have in common.

The men are all at least 172 cm (5' 8") tall and the women are 162 cm (5' 4"). And they're all very fit physically.

(You certainly won't get to meet our Selection Board if you're anything less.)

They also go through the same tough 15-week training programme. And the two year probationary period.

They all start out at the same salary, too. £5,610 a year if you're under 22 or £6,699 if you're older.

You also get London Allowances of £1,599 on top.

We'll also provide you with somewhere to live if you need it. (Or give you a tax-paid rent allowance of up to £1,980 a year.)

As for age, you need to be over 18½ for a start.

If you're into your twenties we'd still like to hear from you. We value recruits who've seen something of the world before seeing us.

May we suggest you contact us and find out more?

You can write: to the Chief Inspector at the Metropolitan Police Careers Information Centre, Dept. MD 528, New Scotland Yard, London SW1H 0BG.

You can phone: on 01-725 4575.

You can visit: our Careers Information Centre in Victoria Street.

Choose your own way to approach the job.

London needs people like you in the Metropolitan Police.

What would Rowan and Mayne make of it? The advertisement stresses diversity, but is the image of the police still one of 'a democratic body in tune with the people'?

police, at least at the lower levels, had not yet in the 1950s acquired the pretensions of a profession. The Police Federation told the Willink Commission that there 'could be nothing more disastrous for relationships between police and public' than to make the police a profession.[23] Professions tend to become exclusive, self-regulating and unaccountable and the Federation was concerned about the adverse effects this would have.

The criterion of participation can also be applied to the composition of the police, and the policy of recruitment appeared to give ordinary people the possibility of participation in it. Thus, wrote Critchley:

> From the start, the police was to be a homogeneous and democratic body, in tune with the people, understanding the people, belonging to the people, and drawing its strength from the people.[24]

It is readily apparent how this image was able to reinforce the public's identity with the police, and their acceptance of its legitimacy and their consent to, and support of, its actions. To many people Critchley's statement would have appeared ridiculous in the 1950s (and would continue to appear so), but the image of 'our police under our control' seems to have been widely accepted.

A further aspect of participation and policing should be mentioned, and perhaps this is the most important of all. A community largely polices itself and, as the police know very well, without public cooperation they can achieve little. Participation in this sense is closely tied to effectiveness. The historical basis of policing — frankpledge and watch and ward — was one of citizen participation in keeping peace and order. Private citizens retain the right to apprehend offenders, which could include the arrest of a police officer, although it is not known when this was last attempted! By law ordinary citizens must respond to a call for assistance from a police officer and a Londoner was fined for not doing so in 1976.

Accountability, control and the Willink Commission

Once more one must be wary of overstating the position in the 1950s. After all, the genesis of the Willink Commission was primarily unease about the control and accountability of the police. A number of incidents prompted the concern, including allegations about the improper administration of the Cardiganshire force in 1956, and during the next year serious charges against senior officers in Brighton and in Worcester. Another allegation which prompted considerable comment was that a boy in Thurso had been beaten by a policeman, and that the complaint had not been properly investigated.

The Popkess affair in 1959 was also a celebrated case. This involved the refusal of the Chief Constable of Nottingham to report to the Watch Committee on an investigation into alleged corruption by members of the City Council, on the grounds that he had the duty to enforce the law independently. He cited *Fisher v. Oldham Corporation* (1930) and *The Attorney General for New South Wales v. Perpetual Trustee Company* (1955)[25] to support his constabulary independence, whereas the Watch Committee cogently argued that they had the power under the Municipal Corporations Act 1835 to suspend him, as he was 'unfit' — and this they did. The Home Secretary intervened, and the Chief Constable was reinstated, but retired at the end of the year.

The Popkess affair focused attention on the accountability and control of the police,[26] and this was given added impetus by the *Garratt v. Eastmond* case. In December 1958 Mr. Brian Rix, of Whitehall farce fame, was stopped by P.C. Eastmond for allegedly speeding, and a civil servant, Mr. Garratt, also became involved. The outcome was that Garratt sued Eastmond, claiming damages for assault and battery and false imprisonment, and received £300 in an out-of-court settlement from the Commissioner without admission of liability. It was also announced that no disciplinary action would be taken against P.C. Eastmond. In the parliamentary debate on the case,[27] in November 1959, MPs wanted to know why public money had been paid out unless Eastmond had done wrong, and why if he had done wrong he was not being disciplined. The Home Secretary, as the police authority for London, was in a rather difficult position and so to extricate himself, but ostensibly to investigate the issues raised in this and the earlier cases, he announced the Royal Commission.

It is not clear that the outcome of the Willink inquiry, or the Police Act 1964, changed the position on constabulary independence, or indeed exactly what that position was, or is. Professor Wade, in evidence to the Commission, suggested that

> since anyone can normally start a prosecution on his own initiative . . . there is nothing exceptional in a local police authority requiring the police to carry out this duty since each has an equal responsibility for it.[28]

Hence the chief constable was not answerable to the law alone, and in some matters of law enforcement policy it would be quite proper for the watch committee to issue instructions to the police. The Commission appeared to agree in a section entitled 'subordination of chief constables to democratic supervision'. Here Willink argued that certain enforcement policies, such as for example those involving political demonstrations, strikes, processions, and general public order

> do not require the immunity from external influences that is generally thought necessary in regard to the enforcement of the law in particular cases.[29]

These remarks are especially interesting in light of the 1984–1985 coal dispute, and court rulings in the case of the attempt by South Yorkshire Police Authority to instruct its chief constable on methods, behaviour and expenditure. This aspect of public participation and policing also relates closely to the fourth factor mentioned earlier, that is *legitimacy*.

Legitimacy, justice and consent: 'the British political genius'

4. Legitimacy is the quality of being right or proper according to fundamental rules and principles, and the legitimacy of the police depends upon the extent to which they are judged as behaving properly, in accord with basic rules and values. The notion of legitimacy is related to effectiveness, identity and participation, so that if the police are seen to perform effectively, and if citizens identify with them and their values, the legitimacy which the public ascribe to the police is likely to be strengthened. Participation is a means of realising identity and effectiveness, but it is also directly a source of legitimacy as a prevailing cultural value is that state agencies, such as the police, should be responsive and amenable to democratic government.

A further, and central, aspect of legitimacy is the rule of law. If the police behave, and are seen to behave, strictly according to the law then the legitimacy ascribed to them by the public will be enhanced. This is the form of accountability stressed by police officers, although perhaps it should be added that *everyone* is accountable to the law. A central notion is that the law is a neutral set of rules to which all are subject:

> The law in its majestic equality, forbids the rich as well as the poor to sleep under bridges, to beg in the streets, and to steal bread.[30]

Be that as it may, the police argument has been that it is their duty to enforce the law fearlessly and without favour in an impartial, independent way. Hence their insistence on an absence of direct political control and the avoidance in the past of any serious charge of partisanship. The Metropolitan Police seems to have managed to achieve this image soon after its inception, and according to Bowden:

> The British political genius was to make this police force, clearly taking part in a class struggle, appear to be an independent, non-partisan agency simply enforcing the law.[31]

By the 1950s the legitimacy of the police was widely accepted, partly because they were seen as impartially upholding the law and partly because they were regarded as non-partisan. However, it should be remembered that 42 per cent of the public surveyed by the Royal Commission thought some policemen took bribes. Nonetheless, over four out of five people had 'great respect' for the police, confirming the widespread perception of their legitimacy.

5. Justice refers to the extent to which police actions are seen as fair, and warranted by the circumstances. It is clearly related closely to legitimacy, although it is quite possible to behave legitimately but unjustly. Police officers claim that their duty is to enforce the law impartially and independently but for a number of reasons they do not do so. These include the prioritisation of certain offences by particular chief officers, the selective enforcement of the law due to the lack of resources to investigate *all* infringements, stereotyping of, and prejudice towards, certain groups, and the injustice of rigorously applying the law in some circumstances. This last point has been stressed by the Director of Public Prosecutions, and so, for example, it might be considered unjust to prosecute an elderly or ill person for a trivial offence: *de minimis non curat lex*.[32]

In their detailed discussion of accountability and justice in *Controlling the Constable*, Jefferson and Grimshaw argue that besides *individual* justice policing is also concerned with *public* justice. The former requires the fair and impartial application of the law in individual cases, but also involves the complicating notion of special treatment, that is *just deserts*. Public justice demands that policing practices must 'guard the rights and common interests of all', which includes the requirement that all citizens gain a fair share of limited police resources in order to ensure equal protection by the law and equal subjection to it.[33]

Two key aspects of whether policing is perceived to be just are *first*, how individual police officers behave and exercise their powers and *second*, the extent to which policing policies appear to treat different groups and individuals equitably. An important element in both aspects, particularly the former, is how the police apply their extensive discretionary powers. As Lord Scarman lucidly stressed:

> Successful policing depends on the exercise of discretion in how the law is enforced. The good reputation of the police as a force depends upon the skill and judgement which policemen display in the particular circumstances of the cases and incidents which they are required to handle. Discretion is the art of suiting action to particular circumstances. It is the policeman's daily task.[34]

It is clear from many studies and accounts that since their inception, police activity has discriminated in favour of certain groups and against others, and so has on occasions not been just at either the individual or public level. For example, higher levels of crime have been accepted in some areas, and certain offences have been more rigorously pursued than others. In the post-war period young 'unconventional' men seem to have been a particular target for police attention, but then there was little novel about that. Similarly, there is evidence that black people were sometimes unfairly treated in the 1950s by the police, which was also not a new departure.[35] Nevertheless, the popular *image* appears to have been one of police behaviour which was generally just, and of a police service which responded equally readily to assist citizens from different walks of life.

6. *Consent* has been regarded as a central factor in 'the British police advantage' and appears to be related to, and largely dependent upon, the

other five policing factors. The consent of citizens is more likely to be forthcoming if policing is perceived to be effective, and if expectations are being met. A high level of identity with the police, and the satisfactory provision of means for participation, will increase the likelihood of consent. If the legitimacy of the police is widely recognised, and if they are perceived as acting with justice, consent amongst citizens will be enhanced. Consent may be forthcoming in an *active* sense as positive agreement and support or in a more *passive* sense as grudging compliance. The former is obviously the more desirable, but compliance, even grudging, is preferable to defiance and refusal to cooperate, which is likely to necessitate coercion.

Until recently, it had been accepted that the police secured widespread consent soon after their establishment, although hostility and opposition continued in some urban areas. Some recent studies have repudiated this view, stressing rather that there was frequent conflict and even where overt 'resistance' faded, dissent remained. One of the propositions derived from this evidence[36] is summarised by Brogden as the view that where

> overt conflict disappeared, it was replaced not by consent but by a kind of 'grumbling dissent'. The police institution was accepted in lower class areas, not because it had become any more popular, but because of its organisational superiority.[37]

Brogden produces evidence to support the view that relations in some areas were inherently conflictual, with periods of uneasy truces, but it is by no means clear that this seriously challenges the conventional view of policing and consent. After all, it was not claimed that there was *universal* consent amongst the public although some police historians may have exaggerated its extent. It is also not evident that 'grumbling dissent', whereby the police were 'accepted' or tolerated, differs significantly from the grudging compliance form of consent. Any kind of consent, even the most supportive, may be withdrawn from the police if for some reason people become alienated.

The development of consent depended on the other five factors: effectiveness, identity, participation, legitimacy and justice. It was furthered by Rowan and Mayne's insistence on an image of politeness and courtesy, impartiality and independence, and the minimum use of force. Reality, of course, was rather different for many who experienced police behaviour, particularly in some inner urban areas, but it seems that elsewhere the popular perception was of a low-key service, quietly but effectively keeping the peace. Consent was furthered by the service role of the police, and by their image of closeness to local communities. By the 1950s it does seem that the public's view of the police was one of general approval, and the six policing factors had reached a high level.

The wane sets in: the Police Act 1964

Public consent and cooperation are recognised as vital to successful policing. This was reaffirmed in October 1983 by the newly-appointed Home Secretary Leon Brittan who said 'we and the police now realise that effective policing is only possible with the implicit consent of individual communities'.[38] However, experience and research show that in order to tackle crime effectively, *implicit* consent is not sufficient: *explicit* cooperation is needed. Consequently, public participation in policing is directly linked to effectiveness. The majority of crimes that *are* solved — and of course the majority *are not* — are cleared up through information received from the public, not because of police detective work.[39] And yet, as Chief Superintendent Pike of Hampshire Police has stressed:

> Too much emphasis is placed on the fanatical pursuit of the impossible — a high level of detection.[40]

This 'pursuit of the impossible' reflects an accelerated trend during the last twenty years or so towards increased specialisation in policing, and this in turn seems to be one aspect of a process which has resulted in the *distancing* of the police from many members of the public. Once again the *image* is important, but there have been various developments, which the changed image reflects, which have meant that *in practice* the police have become more remote.

Some people have argued that the mass ownership of motorcars began the distancing of police and public; between 1954 and 1964 the number of vehicles doubled, and consequently more people were having 'negative' contacts with the police for traffic offences. It was, though, the Police Act 1964 and its provisions, and the subsequent 'modernising' innovations in policing, which gave impetus to the distancing trend. The 1964 Act did not implement the lamentable proposals of Dr. Goodhart, in his memorandum of dissent, for a 'centrally controlled police force' but it did take steps in this direction. The Home Secretary was given powers to promote efficient policing by developing common arrangements and by enforcing amalgamations. The successors to the watch committees, one-third of the members of which were to be magistrates, were given the responsibility to maintain 'an adequate and efficient' force (section 4), but the powers with which they were vested to carry out this duty essentially only entailed the right to call for reports and to appoint the chief constable. Furthermore, the power, provided in section 12 of the Act, to call for reports is subject to confirmation by the Home Secretary, if the chief constable wishes to challenge the request.

Experience has shown that most police authorities are extremely tame and timid creatures, unwilling to bark let alone bite. With some notable exceptions, such as those authorities in Greater Manchester, Merseyside,

South Yorkshire and to some extent the West Midlands, police committees do not appear to have performed more than a minimal watchdog role. They have tended to defer to the 'professional expertise' of the police, they have rarely ventured to comment on general law enforcement policy — despite Willink's views that this was part of their role — and they have, in short, provided a means neither for police answerability nor for public participation.[41] Incidentally, it is interesting to note that, despite opposition from within the police service as well as without, the Conservative Government's Local Government Act 1985 has abolished those police authorities that *have* attempted a more effective role.

The Police Act 1964 is a vague, ambiguous and unsatisfactory piece of legislation, but it provided the statutory basis for policing developments during the last two decades — and in the future. It curtailed participation, which it has been suggested is one of the six central policing factors, it increased the central influence of the Home Office, and enhanced the position of chief constables at the expense of the third leg of the tripartite arrangement — the local authorities. Following the Act, which removed limits on the Home Secretary's compulsory powers, a series of force amalgamations took place continuing the post-war trend. In 1939 there were 183 police forces in England and Wales, and by 1960 this had fallen to 125. On 18 May 1966 it was announced that the number of forces was to be dramatically reduced to 49, and following local government reorganisation in 1974 — another disastrous legacy of the 1960s vogue for bigness — the number reached its present level of 43. As Critchley prosaically commented in the aftermath of the 1966 amalgamations, 'a programme on this scale, it is evident, will weaken, at all events temporarily, the link between the police and local government'.[42] However, the weakening at least in some areas did not turn out to be temporary and indeed the mergers continued the trend away from local accountability, participation and identification.

From artisans to professionals: the handyman goeth?

One of the results of the larger police forces has been that officers tend to be stationed in one area for a few years and then, perhaps because of promotion or for organisational reasons, they move to another district. Local councillors and community leaders have complained that they just get to know their police (and their police them), and then they are replaced by new officers. This high turn-over of personnel, particularly in some areas of towns and cities and outlying residential estates, has not proved conducive to good police–community relations, or high levels of participation and identity between public and police.

From the early 1960s onwards a number of other developments also adversely affected the six policing criteria: effectiveness, identity, participation, legitimacy, justice and consent. As a result of these changes, and the change in the image of the police, policing became more remote from many people. The developments can be broadly listed under the headings *centralisation, professionalisation, specialisation, methods, equipment, conduct, fairness* and *politicisation*.

1. Centralisation was a tendency accentuated by the 1964 Act, as discussed above. The reduction in the number of forces, the increase in the role of the Home Office and the inspectors of constabulary, and the increasingly prevalent central arrangements for all manner of functions may be seen as evidence of the trend. During the 1984–1985 coal dispute, the National Reporting Centre was the subject of considerable comment. It was established in the wake of the miners' strike in 1972 as a means for coordinating mutual aid between forces and has been cited as another example of centralisation.

2. Professionalisation is another trend which is evident during the period since 1964. As mentioned earlier, in 1961 the Police Federation told the Willink Commission that making policing a profession would have 'disastrous' consequences for relations with the public. The Federation was aware that implicit in the notion of a profession is autonomy, self-regulation and *separateness*. One of the strengths of British policing has been the image that its officers are ordinary citizens: identity, participation and consent were consequently reinforced. In 1975, though, the Metropolitan Police Commissioner commended the changing status:

> The police are abandoning their artisan status and are achieving by our ever-increasing variety of services, our integrity, our impartiality, our accountability and our dedication to the public good, a status not less admirable than that of the most learned and distinguished professions. The constable of 1829 and 1929 would have regarded that objective as a dream as unattainable as the climbing of Everest.[43]

But the portrayal of policing as a separate and expert profession may create a gulf between those who do it and the public. Margaret Simey, Chairman of Merseyside Police Authority since 1981, discussed the implications for both police and public of the claim to professional status and concluded that a new partnership must be forged, in which the police accept professional obligations as well as advantages, and which reinforces the principle that control of any public service must ultimately be vested in the people.[44]

Policing of course is a vocation, and it is surely right that high standards of recruitment, training and conduct should be attained. However, the dangers of professionalisation ought to be recognised and, where possible, overcome. Baldwin and Kinsey found in their study of a large police force that professionalism represents a real problem; they note that for the 'professional'

> the need to rely upon outside, lay or amateur opinion or resources is a mark of failure and a challenge to the status of the job itself. Increasingly, within senior police circles, the idea predominates of a professional force, in control of its own resources with expert or 'scientific' knowledge in the field, upon which the public should rely.[45]

The danger of this trend is that the police become more remote, and consequently effectiveness, identity, participation, legitimacy and consent may diminish.

Specialisation, policing methods and 'the human factor'

3. Specialisation is a development closely related to professionalisation. During the last two decades the formation of specialist squads, and the pressure on officers to concentrate on particular skills, has been increasingly evident. Lord Scarman summarised the trend and the dangers:

> They are now professionals with a highly specialised set of skills and behavioural codes of their own. They run the risk of becoming, by reason of their professionalism, a 'corps d'elite' set apart from the rest of the community. Technological advances have offered new ways of preventing and fighting crime, of protecting life and property, and of quelling disorder without the necessity of maintaining close personal relations with the community. Indeed, not the least of the problems the police now face is how to take advantage of their technological aids without destroying the human factor, so essential if policing is to command public support.[46]

Any large organisation, especially one handling a huge variety of difficult problems, will entail specialisation and it is no surprise that the Metropolitan Police, by far the largest force, shows the greatest development of differentiation. What may come as a surprise is the sheer extent of this specialisation, with a vast array of different squads, branches and sections. The Metropolitan Police Commissioner, Sir Kenneth Newman, has undertaken a major reorganisation of Scotland Yard and this began on 'block change day' which was 11 March 1985. Few details were made public, but it is understood that the existing departments, A (operations), B (traffic) and C (crime) have been redesignated territorial policing, specialist operations and management support, while department D, personnel and training, has remained intact. There is no evidence of a reduction in specialist units.

The development of extensive specialisation has reinforced the trend to professionalism, both of which are to some extent necessary for modern policing, and indeed there is strong evidence that the police are still not sufficiently specialised in some areas, for example the investigation of 'white collar' crimes, such as fraud.[47] However, these tendencies also seem to have accentuated the trend towards separateness and remoteness, and specialisation in particular seems to have led to a down-grading of the role of the uniformed beat officer. Lord Scarman commented on the low status of home beat officers — 'regarded by other policemen as outside the mainstream of operational policing' — and he considered that they should 'be seen not as occupying the bottom of the police pecking-order (after the CID and specialist units have creamed off the best), but at its apex, in the forefront of the police team'.[48]

The Policy Studies Institute (PSI) study similarly found a low opinion of home beat officers amongst other policemen: it was quite common for them to be dismissed as 'useless' as they don't make arrests (although of course in practice some of them do); however, they were also widely regarded as providing 'valuable information'. The study observed that moving from a uniformed relief to a specialist group is regarded as career progress, as the former is seen as a job with low status.[49] A consequence of the drive to specialise is that many officers patrolling on foot in uniform are young and inexperienced, and a significant proportion are probationers. Lord Scarman noted that in 1980 36 per cent of police constables in England and Wales were aged between 18½ and 25 years, and the PSI study reported that 35 per cent of time spent patrolling on foot in uniform is put in by probationers.[50] As the incident outside the S & M Car Hire office on 11 April 1981 showed, young officers may act unwisely or provocatively when under pressure: Lord Scarman concluded that 'they acted without the discretion and judgement which maturer years might have brought'.[51]

4. *Methods* of policing are affected by the three trends already mentioned — centralisation, professionalisation and specialisation. One of the most significant innovations was the introduction of unit beat policing and panda cars, in the mid-1960s. Although the basic idea appeared sound, and was much in tune with the contemporary fashion for specialisation, rationalisation and increased efficiency, the new system did not work well in practice. Response times to calls were improved, but as most offences are not reported until some time after they occurred[52] this did not bring an appreciable improvement in effectiveness. The system did, though, tend to cut the police off from the community thus accentuating the tendency to appear remote and set apart, and thereby reducing cooperation, 'positive' personal contact and communication between public and police.[53]

The panda car system has generally been reduced or phased out, but the image of 'fire brigade policing' persists, particularly in cities where patrol cars moving at high speed with sirens wailing are a regular occurrence. Simon Holdaway has pointed out that many policemen are drawn by the excitement and thrill of a car chase (as are many members of the public), and this was strongly confirmed by the PSI study.[54] On one occasion a car chase as dawn broke continued at very high speed for over fourteen miles, and at the end of it seven area cars, four panda cars and two vans were involved. Many of the police vehicles were many miles from their home patch, but they had been unable to resist 'the magnetic attraction' of the chase. It seems likely that fire brigade policing is inefficient and may damage the image of the police, especially when deaths result from these chases. In May 1985, for example, a police car on its way to join a chase after a stolen vehicle, collided with a private car killing the passenger, and the next day the *Sunday Mirror* launched a campaign against 'Starsky and Hutch style chases'; it was reported that 30 people had been killed in police chases during the previous three and a half years in London alone.[55]

Many police officers are aware of the adverse impact that these sorts of incidents have on police standing and public relations, and various attempts, such as command and control systems, are being made to reduce over-reaction to calls. Fire brigade policing, and the prevalence of patrol cars screaming through city streets,[56] may heighten the image of remoteness, and when accidents occur may undermine the view of police legitimacy, without bringing any apparent benefits in terms of effectiveness.

Similar charges have been laid against the use of so-called 'hard' policing methods, of which the infamous Operation Swamp '81 was an example.[57] Lord Scarman reported that 'hard' vigorous policing, involving the Special Patrol Group (SPG), the 'sus' law and the exercise of stop and search powers, had 'caused offence and apprehension to many' in the Borough of Lambeth. He considered there was a 'lack of flexibility' in the application of hard policing, which he nevertheless accepted was sometimes necessary. However,

> when a community becomes resentful and restless and there is widespread loss of confidence in the police, the particular circumstances may require a review of police methods.[58]

The Special Patrol Group, which was employed in Lambeth and elsewhere for periodic saturation exercises to tackle the problem of street crime, came in for particular criticism.[59] The SPG was also prominently involved in a number of violent clashes, and it has frequently been alleged that an officer from the SPG was responsible for the death of Blair Peach at Southall on 23 April 1979.[60] It should be noted that there seem to be few countries in the world, with which comparisons can be made, where less people are injured or killed on public demonstrations, but that does not diminish the tragedy of Blair Peach's death, or of the other fatalities which have occurred. 'Hard, vigorous policing' does seem to have led to a decrease in perceptions of police legitimacy and justice, and a decline in consent, by members of the public, particularly in certain areas.

'We treat crowd control like cricket': equipment and conduct

5. *Equipment*, since the early 1960s, has changed and developed. In the 'Golden Age' of policing the image was of police officers armed only with a truncheon and a whistle. The symbolic significance of the baton was recognised by the *London Quarterly Review* in 1870:

> The mob quails before the simple baton of a police officer, and flies before it, well knowing the moral as well as the physical force of the Nation whose will, as embodied in law, it represents.[61]

The development of equipment is evident in panda cars and personal radios and it is also obvious in the increased use of computers and surveillance technology. The British police have made use of all manner of scientific advances and have been 'transformed into one of the most technically sophisticated forces in the world'.[62]

It is, though, in the field of public order and crowd control that the change in equipment has been most visible. In 1969 it could be reported that

> London's men in blue have no tear gas, no water cannons and no guns. 'We have no riot helmets or visors either' says Chief Inspector James Hargadon . . . 'We don't think they are necessary, and if we did put on riot helmets it might work the crowd up a bit and cause a spot of trouble.' British police, ever polite, refuse to comment on the violence in Chicago or Paris, but they tend to look smug when they are asked about it. 'We wouldn't consider such methods here.' says Hargadon, 'We treat crowd control like cricket. . . .'[63]

Despite the gentlemanly conduct implicit in cricket, it can be an aggressive and intimidating game although players seldom come to physical blows. Throughout the history of policing there have been violent demonstrations and clashes and police officers' truncheons were frequently used in ways other than the symbolic manner referred to by the *London Quarterly Review*. In the 1950s and 1960s there were large demonstrations, such as that on 27 October 1968 in Grosvenor Square against the Vietnam War. This was a generally peaceful protest by about 40,000 people, but it involved a bloody clash between some people and the police although it ended with a joint police and demonstrator rendition of 'Auld Lang Syne'!

However, during the latter part of the 1970s and the 1980s police equipment for crowd control changed, first to include shields and protective helmets and then CS gas, used for the first time in Britain for riot control in Liverpool 8 on 6 July 1981. Since then plastic bullets — or baton rounds as they are more euphemistically called — have been obtained by many police forces and water cannon are available. If the image of the police has changed in this respect from that described in 1969 by Chief Inspector Hargadon, so too has the reputation for being unarmed. British police remain one of the very few forces anywhere in the world which are not armed,[64] although in London alone it is estimated that over 200 armed policemen are on the streets at any one time.

Public concern about the use of guns by police was voiced after the shooting in Kensington of Stephen Waldorf in January 1983. Two police officers were subsequently acquitted of a series of charges including attempted murder, but the incident attracted widespread publicity and at the trial the Attorney General revealed that 14 shots were fired and Waldorf with several bullets in him was 'pistol whipped'.

The Police Federation reaction appeared to be the quite incredible suggestion that 'armed officers should have a form of legal protection or indemnity from prosecution'.[65] Criticism of the police use of guns rose to a crescendo after two serious incidents in 1985. In Birmingham, on 24 August, five-year-old John Shorthouse was shot dead in his bed by a policeman. Five weeks later, Mrs. Cherry Groce was permanently paralysed by a bullet from a policeman's gun, during a raid on her house in Brixton, and this led to violent disorder in the area. It was revealed that *this was the 51st armed raid in Lambeth in 1985*, and it seems inevitable that other tragic events will occur if the police use of guns continues to increase. Overall, the damage to the image of British policing caused by these shootings, and the impact of the sight of police officers heavily-equipped in an 'un-British' fashion for crowd control, is difficult to calculate. These developments, though, have most probably affected adversely the policing factors of identity, legitimacy, justice and consent.

6. *Conduct* of police officers has doubtless always varied according to the particular circumstances and individuals involved, but the founders of the police were insistent on the need for a good public image. This has been somewhat eroded in the last two decades by allegations of corruption and misbehaviour, and by the resort to heavy-handed policing on some occasions. The series of corruption scandals which emerged from Scotland Yard after 1969 have been extensively documented.[66] These involved detectives in crimes, and perjury and planting of evidence, and in the mid-1970s further scandals were revealed. In 1978 it was alleged that some detectives were implicated in armed robberies and Commissioner McNee established 'Operation Countryman' to probe more deeply. After four years' investigation of more than 200 policemen, two convictions resulted and the Dorset Chief Constable, Arthur Hambleton, retired making a number of allegations of obstruction.

The Policy Studies Institute research revealed some of the impact of these revelations and allegations. 55 per cent of the Londoners surveyed thought police officers accepted goods or favours sometimes and 51 per cent believed they took bribes 'occasionally' or 'often', while 14 per cent said 'hardly ever' and 26 per cent 'never'. In the survey of police officers the respondents were asked how many officers in every thousand they thought had taken bribes. 32 per cent said 'none' for uniformed officers, and 21 per cent thought no members of the CID had taken bribes; a further 30 per cent thought it was less than 10 in 1000 uniformed police, although a substantial minority of respondents thought that corruption in the CID was fairly common.[67]

The survey also revealed that 81 per cent of the Metropolitan Police who were sampled thought that some officers *often* behaved rudely to members of the public, and 60 per cent said they knew such officers. Nearly half the respondents thought the proportion of those who were persistently rude was under 10 per cent (in addition to the 19 per cent who thought none behaved like this). However, nearly one in ten of the respondents considered that the figure for rude officers was at least 20 per cent. Furthermore, two-thirds believed that some officers *often* used more force than necessary and 35 per cent said they knew colleagues who behaved like this. The survey of the public suggested that one in ten had 'a complete lack of confidence in the police' and 'about half have serious doubts about the standards of police conduct' though in most cases they did not think misconduct was frequent. The study also revealed 'overwhelming evidence' that those 'who have been stopped by the police (the great majority of whom are not found to have committed any offence) become much more hostile to the police as a result'.[68]

The British Crime Survey found a marked variation in the views of different sorts of people on police behaviour. Of those *who approached the police*, four out of five found them helpful and pleasant; however, whereas 80 per cent of elderly women in rural areas said they had been 'very pleasant', for young men in inner cities the figure fell to 20 per cent. Of those who were *approached by the police* 52 per cent of young men said that they had received impolite treatment.[69] Some of these reactions may be due to the preponderance of young, inexperienced officers who undertake uniformed foot patrols — a point mentioned earlier. It may prove difficult for young officers to deal with young men of a similar age in circumstances of conflict, whereas older officers may be more effective.

Another aspect of police conduct concerns the apparent low priority within the forces afforded to the traditional service role. Whether or not police officers were ever the 'handymen of the streets' in some inner city areas, the image of them as public servants helping people with all manner of problems and requests appears to have been particularly persistent. The change in image of police conduct, but also the continuing notion of performing service and helpful acts, was summed up by Alexei Sayle who said that round his way they've now got community policing: 'You're walking along the street, a police van pulls up, a squad of coppers leap out, they pin you to the ground and tell you the time'.[70] The police service of course is one of the few public agencies always available to be called for help (some social services also have 24-hour standby), however, evidence shows that many police officers have a very low opinion of the service role and do not regard it as 'real police work'.[71]

Police conduct seems also to have changed in terms of an increased willingness to use 'heavy-handed' tactics on certain occasions. This relates to the points mentioned earlier about 'hard' policing methods and the increased visibility of riot-control equipment. The conduct of some police officers during the 1984–1985 coal dispute was a very long way from 'treating crowd control like cricket'. In 1972, at the Saltley Gate picket Clutterbuck states that 'without question' the police could have kept the depot open, but they judged that the impact on the public image of policing of the measures necessary would have been too adverse to merit the policy. They 'would have unleashed far greater violence and sacrificed public sympathy'.[72] In 1984 police conduct was rather different, and for week upon week television, radio and newspaper coverage reported violent scenes and on occasions disreputable conduct by individual officers, such as that which occurred at the Orgreave coking depot in late May and early June. The behaviour of many pickets was violent and provocative, but so too it seems was that of some police officers.[73] Perhaps the most incredible and quite sensational police misconduct occurred at the village of Armthorpe and the Markham Main Colliery on 22 August 1984.[74] The full story of this sorry tale remains to be told.

The changes in police conduct during the last twenty years or so may be more imagined than real, for there is evidence that police conduct varied considerably before this period. There does though seem to have been a change in the *image* of police conduct with respect to corruption, politeness, the helpful service role and the manner whereby public order is controlled. There appears to have been some effect on public opinion but perhaps the biggest impact has been on those who have experienced the misconduct and on certain opinion leaders. The policing factors of identity, legitimacy, consent and justice are likely to have been adversely affected, and in turn this will impair participation and effectiveness.

Fairness, race and 'a crude equation'

7. *Fairness* is closely related to justice and is affected by changes in conduct and methods. Lord Scarman found evidence of racially prejudiced behaviour and harassment in Brixton and 'whether justified or not, many in Brixton believe that the police routinely abuse their powers and mistreat

fenders'. The result of these perceived injustices and impro-
~as the 'loss of confidence of significant sections' of the Lambeth
' There is a great deal of evidence that, before its repeal in 1981,
the ~~spected person' charge under section 4 of the Vagrancy Act 1824
was unfairly used against young black people. A study in 1976 found that of
2112 people arrested under this legislation in London an unduly high
proportion, 42 per cent, was black and a Home Office study showed that a
black person was *fifteen times* more likely to be arrested for 'sus' than a
white person.[76]

Many of the charges of unfairness concern police treatment of black
people.[77] In 1976 a member of the Select Committee on Race Relations
and Immigration, which was conducting an inquiry into 'the West Indian
community', commented:

> There has been a consistent, continuous allegation on the part of many
> of the witnesses appearing before us that they are discriminated against
> by the police.[78]

As the evidence submitted to the inquiry shows there was indeed
accusation after accusation, many of them extensively documented, of
unfair, prejudiced behaviour by police officers. The chairman of the
Committee's inquiry in 1971–1972 into 'Police/Immigrant Relations'
described some of the evidence as presenting 'a case almost akin to civil
war between the West Indians and the police'.[79]

There is considerable evidence that police stop and search powers have
been disproportionately applied to young people, men and Afro-
Caribbeans. The most detailed data come from the Policy Studies Institute
research in London, and these show that young black people are likely to
be stopped *repeatedly* and are far more likely to be stopped on foot than
young whites: *45 per cent* of West Indians aged 15–24 had been stopped
during the previous year compared to 18 per cent of whites in this age
group. Afro-Caribbeans were 'markedly less happy' than other groups with
the behaviour of the police who stopped them. The researchers reported:

> The cost of the present policy, in terms of the relationship between the
> police and certain sections of the public, is shown to be substantial, and
> most stops are wasted effort . . .[80]

Similar findings have been reported from Liverpool, Birmingham and
Manchester, and Willis' 1982 study broadly confirmed the PSI data.[81]

Black people are also disproportionately arrested and there is no doubt
that this is partly explained by police prejudice and discrimination. It also
seems to be partly due to socio-economic and demographic factors, and
partly caused by a higher rate of involvement of young black people in
certain sorts of crime, to which the police have directed particular
attention.[82] The PSI study reported that 'officers tend to make a crude

BROTHERS IN LAW.

As you can see, the Police have changed in recent years.

But the way they've changed is simply a reflection of the way Britain itself has changed.

Just as the individuals who make up our society come from every imaginable background, from every walk of life, so do our Police Officers.

But where some communities may be divided, the Police are not. And it's not just the uniforms they wear that unites them.

They share the same basic principles. Otherwise they would never have wanted to join in the first place.

And those are the same principles of law and order that existed twenty years ago and more.

Ask any Policeman or Police-woman why they applied for the job, and you'll get the same answer. "To get involved with people." To get involved with the community they

patrol. To understand it. Safeguard it. Unarmed, remember.

And what all Officers have in common is that they are dealing daily with human problems.

With different sorts of people. Who rarely behave predictably.

There are few situations in which an Officer has a textbook solution to the difficulties he faces.

For example, he's called in to sort out a rumpus on a housing estate.

It has been reported that a man is beating up his neighbour.

He discovers that there's only been a slanging match. Even so, the peace has been disturbed.

Technically he could arrest either or both of them. But a better solution might well be to talk the problem out.

You see, it's a grey area with no easy answer.

And every Officer will tell you that it's like that time and time again.

He needs to be something of a social worker on the one hand.

Yet, on the other, he is invested with the authority of the law.

He sees the seamy side of life, the sordid and the unpleasant.

Yet he'll also see human nature at its best.

When members of the public are helpful, kind and selfless.

The two Officers we've pictured here both have a breadth of experience few of us could match.

And it's the experience that makes them mates. Knowing they can rely on each other in times of crisis.

If you think you are the kind of man or woman who could cope with the rigours as well as the rewards, write to: Police Careers (England & Wales), Dept. CEC/82, 40 Craven St., London WC2N 5NG.

POLICE  OFFICER

Despite the implication, there are still very few black police officers — just 726 (0.6%) in the whole of England and Wales in late 1985. The marked reluctance of black people to join is likely to continue while the police, particularly in London, are widely regarded as racially discriminatory, abusive and unjust.

etween crime and black people, to assume that suspects are *ad* it was found that 'racialist language and racial prejudice were *ent* and pervasive' although the study stressed that thought was not *ssarily* carried into action and indeed the researchers were 'fairly confident' that there was 'no widespread tendency for black or Asian people to be given greatly inferior treatment'.[83]

Another charge which has been made is that the police have not responded sufficiently vigorously to racial attacks and abuse. Asians, in particular, it has been claimed, do not believe that they are offered equal protection under the law. The extent of racial attacks has been docu-mented in a number of recent studies which make horrifying reading.[84] Besides the view that the police do not take these attacks sufficiently seriously — a charge rebutted by the police — a number of court cases have occurred in which the defendants have pleaded self-defence against racial attackers. In Bradford twelve young Asians successfully argued this in 1982, and a year later the 'Newham Eight' were acquitted of serious charges; four were sentenced to 50 hours community service for affray, and, in one case, common assault. In this case it was alleged that the 8 young Asian men had attacked three plain clothes policemen, while the defence maintained that the Asians had been attacked by the three men, who they assumed were racialists.

Cases such as these have been widely reported, and the general impression that the police have not been as vigilant in tackling crimes against Asians has gained currency. A recent detailed and extensive survey of the British black population revealed that 30 per cent of Asians believed that they were treated worse than white people by the police; 26 per cent didn't know. The belief that the police discriminate against them was far more widespread than the belief that any other group or institutions do so, with the exception of employers. Among West Indians the findings were overwhelming: 64 per cent say they are treated 'worse' than whites by the police, with just 16 per cent saying 'the same'; 19 per cent didn't know. This figure was far higher than for any other group or institution.[85]

The PSI study reported 'a dangerous lack of confidence in the police among substantial numbers of young white people and a disastrous lack of confidence among young people of West Indian origin'.[86] However, the research also revealed that they do not wholly reject the present policing system although they resent what they see as its unfairness and discrimination. Derek Humphry, writing in 1972, explained that he was critical of police unfairness and misconduct because he wished to respect the police force:

> The rule of law in Britain should be a rule which is firm and just (and seen to be such) to peoples of all colours, appearances and incomes.[87]

Unfortunately many people believe that police treatment of black people is not just, and each instance of prejudiced language, or harassment, or immature action, reinforces this view. If the police are believed not to behave fairly it undermines each of the six policing factors — effectiveness, identity, participation, legitimacy, justice and consent — with potentially critical consequences, as the riots in 1981 and 1985 demonstrated.

Moving centre stage: policing in the limelight

8. *Politicisation* of policing has occurred during the period since 1964, particularly in the last decade, and the process has been documented by Reiner and others.[88] To some extent it can be seen as a reflection of other tendencies, such as centralisation, professionalisation, specialisation and the demand for more equipment and technology. Policing has always been political of course, in so far as politics is concerned with rules and procedures and the resolution of conflict, either through compromise or coercion. Policing was political at its inception, in the sense that it was vigorously opposed, and it has remained political in that it has inevitably supported and furthered certain interests at the expense of others. Social control is inherently political, but one of the reasons for the successful evolution of British policing, it was argued earlier, was that it appeared to be impartial and independent.

Sir Robert Mark's Dimbleby Lecture in November 1973 signalled the end of low profile lobbying by the police and his general approach was spelled out in a lecture at Bramshill in 1975:

> We who alone see the reality and the whole of recorded crime should not be reluctant to speak about it. We who are the anvil on which society beats out the problems and abrasions of social inequality, racial prejudice, weak laws and ineffective legislation should not be inhibited from expressing our views, whether critical or constructive.[89]

In the same year the Police Federation began to put Mark's injunction into effect. It launched a law and order campaign with the declared intention of bringing pressure on politicians to support 'the silent majority's' concern at growing crime and disorder. When criticised for entering the political arena the Federation responded by asking 'what is "political" about crime?'. The campaign was revamped in 1978, and culminated in advertisements headed 'Law and Order' which appeared in national newspapers a fortnight before polling day on 3 May 1979.[90]

Reiner has drawn attention to the considerable similarity between the Federation's demands and the Conservative Party's promises during the election campaign in 1979. Robert Mark also entered the fray with a speech two weeks before election day which likened the trade unions' relationship with the Labour Party to 'the way the National Socialist German Workers Party achieved unrestricted control of the German state'. The media eagerly took up the stricture, and the response by the Prime Minister, James Callaghan, was reported in typically elevated fashion by the *Evening News* as 'JIM PUTS IN THE JACKBOOT'.[91] The regular involvement of chief police officers and the Federation in political debate continued after the election and was of course a central feature of the media's coverage of the recent riots. In 1982 the Federation argued strongly and publicly for the restoration of capital punishment, and James Anderton, Chief Constable of Greater Manchester, proclaimed 'we are now witnessing the domination of the police service as a necessary prerequisite of the creation in this country of a society based on Marxist Communist principles'.[92]

Anderton's rather extreme remarks perhaps represented his feelings of isolation, which were also manifest in a number of clashes with the Greater Manchester Police Authority. They may also have reflected more general feelings of concern amongst the police that their traditional image of political impartiality was in jeopardy: hence Anderton's rather desperate assertion that

> A police service, immune from the ideological pressures of any single political party, provides the surest and only guarantee of the people's individual freedom.[93]

However, as the evidence shows, it was members of the police service themselves who contributed to the erosion of the image of non-partisanship. The close affinity between the Federation campaign in 1978–1979 and the Conservative Party's statements, the explicit criticisms of the Labour Government's record and the comments of Mark and others, all served to identify the police service with one particular political viewpoint. After the 1979 election the Police Federation broke with its convention of appointing an opposition MP as parliamentary consultant, and retained Sir Eldon Griffiths, whose contribution to discussions on crime, policing and criminal justice have in general been partial and not overly trenchant.

> Some members were distressed that the Federation had 'nailed its flag for all to see to the Conservative Party mast' but the Federation justified the move by 'his commitment to the policies which the Police Federation had been putting forward on law and order'.[94]

The politicisation of the police was carried a stage further during the prolonged dispute in the coal industry from March 1984 until March 1985. It was inevitable that in such a major strike, in which the tactic of mass picketing was a central feature, the police would be fundamentally involved. However, the dispute itself was politicised, by the miners' leaders, the media and the Government and so, equally inevitably, the role of the police became political. The Government must accept a large measure of responsibility for the harm done to the image of policing, for it permitted the dispute to continue for a year, and Mrs. Thatcher's references to 'the enemy within' merely succeeded in polarising opinion yet further. The extent of the politicisation of the police was manifest at the party conferences in October 1984. At the Conservatives' gathering there was a deep unwillingness to countenance any criticisms of the police whatsoever, while at the Labour Party Conference there was a sustained barrage of anti-police invective and some of what was said was frankly lunatic and irresponsible. Leslie Curtis, Chairman of the Federation, was sufficiently provoked to make a speech at Hull on 3 October 1984 which was an outspoken attack on 'the increasingly anti-police stance' of the Labour Party; he stated:

> Six times in the last forty years the political complexion of Her Majesty's Government has changed as a result of a general election. Until now, the police service has been able to offer Labour and Conservative Home Secretaries precisely the same loyal service. Successive governments have adopted a virtually bipartisan policy towards the police and the question of the rule of law. Now, for the first time in history, that system, which has been a major factor in ensuring the political neutrality of the police service, is under threat.[95]

Curtis' considered outburst was an understandable reaction to some of the things said at the Labour Party conference, although his own speech contained a number of dubious assertions. The manner in which it was reported, though, and the Home Secretary's immediate support, merely served to confirm in the eyes of many the political partiality of the police. And indeed Leslie Curtis did not appear to appreciate the role his own organisation had played, particularly under the regime of his predecessor James Jardine, in the process of politicisation. Policing in England and Wales does seem to have come a long way since Sir Harold Scott, Metropolitan Police Commissioner, could write

> I was fortunate that during my eight years at Scotland Yard, there were never any serious differences of opinion between myself and Mr. Chuter Ede or Sir David Maxwell-Fyfe. Their different political views were never allowed to influence their approach to police questions and we in this country can count ourselves very lucky that the police have always stood right outside the political scrimmage.[96]

However, during the last two decades policing has become a political rugby ball and the police themselves have been increasingly participating in the scrum, contributing to the politicisation of their role.

'Crime-fighters on our behalf': the false assumption?

The developments in the eight areas — centralisation, professionalisation, specialisation, methods, equipment, conduct, fairness and politicisation — have had various effects on the six policing criteria of effectiveness, identity, participation, legitimacy, justice and consent. Much of the impact has been detrimental to the image of policing and the distance between police and public. In many respects policing has become more remote, and the survey data which have been cited, such as that from the PSI study and the British Crime Survey, reveal that at least a significant minority of the population rate the police poorly for some or all of the six policing factors.

The difficulties of achieving and maintaining these six policing criteria were illustrated by the Confait case. Maxwell Confait was found dead in his blazing home on 22 April 1972, and on the basis of their confessions three teenaged boys were convicted respectively of murder, manslaughter and arson. In October 1975 the Court of Appeal quashed the verdicts after scientific evidence showed they could not have been guilty. An official inquiry was established under Sir Henry Fisher and when he reported in 1977 he found that although the police had not assaulted the boys or falsified statements, the suspects' rights had not been properly observed. Among the improprieties he outlined were unfair and oppressive questioning, interrogation of the boys, one of whom was mentally retarded, in the absence of any independent adult and failure to inform them of their right to telephone someone. This last provision, which was covered by Direction 7 of the Judges' Rules and Administrative Directions, was not known to senior officers and was 'not observed' in the Metropolitan Police. Fisher made a number of recommendations but generally suggested that there ought to be a Royal Commission.[97]

The outcome of the Confait case was the Royal Commission on Criminal Procedure under the chairmanship of Sir Cyril Philips, and of course it was the Report of the Philips' Commission[98] which provided the impetus for both the Police and Criminal Evidence Act 1984 and the Prosecution of Offences Act 1985. Both statutes introduce important changes the effects of which are not easy to gauge. It is clear from the chapters in this book that many of the authors are sceptical about a number of the provisions, and in some cases those directly involved in implementing the innovations are concerned about their practicality and their adverse impact.

The justifications for the changes have been summed up on a number of occasions by the Home Secretary as providing the police with 'adequate and clear powers to conduct the fight against crime on our behalf' while ensuring that the public 'have proper safeguards against any abuse'. It is claimed that this will lead to increased police effectiveness and public confidence, and the Crown Prosecution Service is justified in similar terms — as improving consistency, accountability, efficiency and effectiveness.[99] It remains to be seen whether these justifications are in practice realised, but they appear to be based on the premise that the police *are able* to fight crime effectively *'on our behalf'*. Evidence cited in this chapter and elsewhere suggests that this is a false assumption, for although the police achieve notable and vital successes, they depend upon public information, involvement and cooperation to solve the great majority of those crimes which are cleared up. As Reiner cogently argues

> crime fighting has never been, is not, and could not be the prime activity of the police. To see it as such is a part of the mythology of media images and cop culture, but presents a stumbling-block to sensible discussion or policy-making. The core mandate of policing, historically and in terms of concrete demands placed upon the police, is the more diffuse one of order maintenance.[100]

This entails settling conflicts, dealing with threatening contingencies, preventing disorder and violent disputes and generally maintaining the Queen's peace. As Lord Scarman argued succinctly and powerfully, the primary duty of the police is 'to cooperate with others in maintaining "the normal state of society". . . : the maintenance of public tranquillity comes first'.[101]

Facilitators of citizen policing or 'visible irritants'?

The new legislation does not appear to address questions such as 'what are the police for?' and 'what can society expect the police to achieve?' It assumes that they are 'crime-fighters', and thus must be equipped with powers to do this 'on our behalf' although procedures must be tightened to guard against improprieties. Research evidence, though, and experience, tends to show that the police are best regarded as *facilitators* for order maintenance and crime control. They are vested with authority, and as a final resort coercive powers, to enable them to mediate in social conflict and to promote the preservation of public tranquillity and the prevention and detection of crime. Essentially, though, order and crime control in a community seems to depend upon the behaviour and cooperation of its members and the role of the police should be to facilitate and assist citizen responsibility and involvement in the administration of order and crime control.

It is clear that there are some areas where 'citizen-policing' is likely to be problematic. In some inner urban areas, for example, where deprivation and disadvantage are widespread there may be weak and ineffective cultural controls, an absence of accepted norms of behaviour and social disintegration. In such areas the six policing factors of effectiveness, identity, participation, legitimacy, justice and consent may exist at low levels, and according to Waddington

> Here, most of all, what is required is impartial, impersonal authority and restrained use of force. In these areas the police may indeed be

seen as a visible irritant. It is even more essential, therefore, that they be seen as representatives of the law, above considerations of class and race.[102]

But while the police may be a 'visible irritant' for some people, in order to be effective here, most of all, they need to facilitate citizen support to further public tranquillity. It is essential that their actions should be seen as fair and just, but also, here most of all, the other policing factors need to be promoted.

Policing inner city areas can be difficult and depressing. As Harrison points out

> police working in the inner city are under constant stress of a degree that would drive most people to the verge of nervous breakdown. They would not be human if they did not on occasion over-react.[103]

The police have to cope with the results of social and economic deprivation and the consequent personal and inter-personal problems and community disintegration. But it is the local citizens who have to *live* with these burdens and with the high rates of crime. The British Crime Survey reported that burglary is 'a phenomenon of the inner city', and the chances of being a victim of other crimes are much greater in these areas than elsewhere.[104] However, when the six policing criteria, of effectiveness, identity, participation, legitimacy, justice and consent, are considered it appears that a gulf exists between many of the inhabitants of the inner cities and the police:

> We have, in Hackney as in other inner city areas, a police force that is largely isolated from the majority of people it serves, with a low detection rate and therefore a low deterrent effect.[105]

And yet it is in such areas that a number of the eight trends in policing have been the most evident. Centralisation, professionalisation, specialisation, methods, equipment, conduct, fairness, and politicisation have developed in ways which have made the police *remote* and have adversely affected effectiveness, identity, participation, legitimacy, justice and consent. On 1 July 1985 the results of a survey of Merseyside Police undertaken by Richard Kinsey were published and these showed that although 56 per cent of constables are formally deployed as patrol officers only 20 per cent reported that they had been out on foot on their last working day. On an average working day patrol officers spend about five-and-a-half hours outside the station, with just half that time on 'uncommitted patrol' and available to respond to public requests. The area has the second highest crime rate per capita in the country, and the highest burglary rate, but in a force of 4,593 officers the average number on uncommitted patrol at any one time is only 126 — that is one officer available for 12,000 people.[106]

One is left wondering whether the Police and Criminal Evidence Act 1984 and the Prosecution of Offences Act 1985 have really grappled with the central issues facing policing and the criminal justice procedures. They incorporate a number of changes, which may exacerbate the eight trends, and some improvements, but it is doubtful, as David Smith argues so powerfully in this book, whether *rules* alone can ensure policing proprieties. It seems that the new safeguards will prove irksome and time-consuming, and will probably result in even less police officers being available on the streets to facilitate order and citizens' involvement.

The legislation seems unlikely to reverse, and may accelerate, the trends in policing which have been identified. It appears improbable that the Acts will in total enhance the six policing criteria of effectiveness, identity, participation, legitimacy, justice and consent. Consequently there is little reason to suppose that the legislation will have the effect of halting the rise in recorded crime — changes in economic and social policies would probably be more effective and efficient in this regard. The essays in this book help to clarify some of the central aspects of the legislation, but few come to optimistic conclusions. Ultimately only experience will show whether the Acts' provisions facilitate public cooperation and involvement, and whether the legislation helps or hinders the men and women who undertake policing — a public service increasingly in the limelight.

Notes

The author acknowledges with gratitude the award by the Leverhulme Trust of a Research Fellowship, and financial support towards the production of this chapter.

1. Geoffrey Gorer, *Exploring English Character*, London: Cresset Press, 1955. The unrepresentative sample was self-selected and obtained by means of an advertisement placed in *The People* newspaper in 1950. 11,000 replies were received and from these Gorer concluded that 'the most significant factor in the development of a strict conscience and law-abiding habits in the majority of urban men and women was the invention and development of the institution of the modern English police force', *ibid.*, p. 294.
2. Royal Commission on the Police (Chairman: Sir Henry Willink), *Final Report*, London: HMSO, 1962 (Cmnd. 1728), paras. 339–343, pp. 103–104.
3. *Ibid.*, para. 338, pp. 102–103.
4. E. P. Thompson, *The Making of the English Working Class*, Harmondsworth: Pelican, 1970, p. 89.
5. G. Thurston, *The Clerkenwell Riot: the Killing of Constable Culley*, London: Allen and Unwin, 1967.
6. C. Reith, *British Police and the Democratic Ideal*, Oxford: Oxford University Press, 1943; C. Reith, *A New Study of Police History*, London: Oliver and Boyd, 1956; T. A. Critchley, *A History of Police in England and Wales 900–1966*, London: Constable, 1967; T. A. Critchley *The Conquest of Violence*, London: Constable, 1970; R. Storch, 'The plague of blue locusts: police reform and popular resistance in Northern England 1840–57', *International Review of Social History*, 20, 1975; R. Storch, 'The policeman as domestic missionary', *Journal of Social History*, Vol. 9, No. 4, 1976; M. Brogden, *The*

Police: Autonomy and Consent, London: Academic Press, 1982; M. Brogden, 'The myth of policing by consent', *Police Review*, 22 April 1983. For an excellent discussion of the various views of the history of policing see Robert Reiner, *The Politics of the Police*, Brighton: Wheatsheaf, 1985, chs 2 and 3.

7. 'The police and the thieves', *London Quarterly Review*, July 1856, p. 93; cited by Allan Silver, 'The demand for order in civil society' in David J. Bordua, *The Police: Six Sociological Essays*, New York: John Wiley, 1967, p. 13.

8. 'The Metropolitan Police' (leading article), *The Times*, 24 December 1908, p. 7; see also article on p. 6 of this issue.

9. R. Roberts, *The Classic Slum*, Harmondsworth: Penguin, 1971, p. 100; see also Brogden, *The Police: Autonomy and Consent, supra*, note 6; R. Samuel, *East End Underworld*, London: Routledge and Kegan Paul, 1981; S. Humphries, *Hooligans or Rebels?*, Oxford: Blackwell, 1981.

10. Basil Griffiths, 'One-tier policing' in John Benyon (ed.), *Scarman and After: Essays Reflecting on Lord Scarman's Report, the Riots and their Aftermath*, Oxford: Pergamon Press, 1984, p. 128.

11. Reiner, *The Politics of the Police, supra* note 6, p. 49; see also Ian Taylor, *Law and order: Arguments for Socialism*, London: Macmillan, 1981.

12. Royal Commission on the Police, *Final Report, supra* note 2, paras. 344–348, p. 104; see also *Minutes of Evidence*, Appendix 4.

13. Reiner, *The Politics of the Police, supra* note 6, p. 51.

14. Not that the articulation of grievances necessarily has much effect of course, but the provision of opportunities for institutional participation does seem to lead to decreased violent protest, helps to reinforce predominant values and facilitates integration:
    In any institutionalised society the participation of new groups reduces tensions; through participation, new groups are assimilated into the political order.
See Samuel Huntingdon, *Political Order in Changing Societies*, New Haven: Yale University Press, 1968, p. 198. However, repeated frustration of aims via formal participation may lead to other forms of participation, such as disobedience or perhaps recourse to violent protest.

15. Quoted by Critchley, *A History of Police in England and Wales 900–1966, supra* note 6, p. 53.

16. David Ascoli, *The Queen's Peace*, London: Hamish Hamilton, 1979, p. 89.

17. *Police and People in London*, Vol. 4: David J. Smith and Jeremy Gray, *The Police in Action*, London: Policy Studies Institute, 1983 (PSI No. 621), pp. 81–87.

18. Brogden, *The Police: Autonomy and Consent, supra* note 6, p. 208.

19. Anthony Judge, *A Man Apart*, London: Barker, 1972.

20. Tom Bowden, *Beyond the Limits of the Law*, Harmondsworth: Penguin, 1978, p. 37.

21. Reiner, *The Politics of the Police, supra* note 6, fn. 4, p. 219; C. Morrison, 'Why PC Plod should come off the beat', *The Guardian*, 30 July 1984, p. 8. Although the treatment of Plod is not invariably sympathetic, and sometimes he appears quite frightening to young children, he is often shown mediating as a broker in disputes and generally performing a service role in the Toytown community. For a full and interesting discussions of the treatment of policing in fiction see Reiner, *The Politics of the Police*, ch. 5 'Mystifying the police'.

22. Ralf Dahrendorf, 'Effectiveness and legitimacy: on the "governability" of democracies', *The Political Quarterly*, Vol. 51, No. 4, 1980, p. 397.

23. Cited by Ben Whitaker, *The Police*, Harmondsworth: Penguin, 1964, p. 22.

24. Critchley, *A History of Police in England and Wales 900–1966, supra* note 6, p. 52.

25. [1930] 2 KB 364; [1955] AC 477.

26. For discussion of the case and the issues which it raised see Bryan Keith-Lucas, 'The independence of chief constables', *Public Administration*, Vol. 38, 1960; Geoffrey Marshall, 'Police responsibility', *Public Administration*, Vol. 38, 1960; G. Marshall, *Police and Government*, London: Methuen, 1965; G. Marshall, 'Police accountability revisited', in D. Butler and A. Halsey, *Policy and Politics*, London: Macmillan, 1978, pp. 51–65.

27. House of Commons Official Report, Parliamentary Debates (*Hansard*), Session 1959–60, Fifth Series, Vol. 613, 18 November 1959, cols. 1239–1303.

28. Royal Commission on the Police, *Minutes of Evidence*, London: HMSO, 1962 (Cmnd. 1728) Appendix 11, pp. 33–34.
29. Royal Commission on the Police, *Final Report, supra* note 3, para. 91.
30. Anatole France, *Le Lys Rouge*, Paris, 1894, cited by Reiner, *The Politics of the Police, supra* note 6, p. 3.
31. Bowden, *Beyond the Limits of the Law, supra* note 20, p. 21.
32. 'The law is not concerned with trifles'. See interview with the Director of Public Prosecutions, Sir Thomas Hetherington, *Daily Mirror*, 1 November 1979, and article by him in *The Guardian*, 5 June, 1980; see also Tony Jefferson and Roger Grimshaw, *Controlling the Constable: Police Accountability in England and Wales*, London: Muller, 1984, pp. 146–147.
33. Jefferson and Grimshaw, *Controlling the Constable, supra* note 32, pp. 157–161; see their chapter 5, 'Legal accountability — a critical analysis of the doctrine and a review of alternatives', pp. 136–169, for an interesting discussion of legal and democratic police accountability, and the centrality of the notions of individual and public justice.
34. *The Brixton Disorders 10–12 April 1981: Report of an Inquiry by the Rt. Hon. the Lord Scarman, OBE*, London: HMSO, November, 1981 (Cmnd. 8427), para. 4.58.
35. For accounts of relations between young people and the police see: Geoffrey Pearson, *Hooligan: A History of Respectable Fears*, London: Macmillan, 1983; P. Jephcott, *Some Young People*, London: Allen and Unwin, 1954; T. R. Fyvel, *The Insecure Offenders*, Harmondsworth: Penguin, 1961; S. Hall and T. Jefferson (eds.), *Resistance through Rituals*, London: Hutchinson, 1976; D. Chapman, *Sociology and the Stereotype of the Criminal*, London: Tavistock, 1968. For accounts of relations between black people and the police in the 1950s and before, see for example Peter Fryer, *Staying Power: The History of Black People in Britain*, London: Pluto, 1984; James Wickenden, *Colour in Britain*, Oxford: Oxford University Press, 1958; Anthony Richmond, *Colour Prejudice in Britain*, London: Routledge and Kegan Paul, 1954; Ruth Glass and Harold Pollins, *Newcomers: The West Indians in London*, London: Allen and Unwin, 1960; A Sivanandan, *A Different Hunger*, London: Pluto, 1982; Nicholas Deakin, *Colour, Citizenship and British Society*, London: Panther, 1970.
36. Storch, 'The plague of blue locusts', *supra* note 6; Storch, 'The policeman as domestic missionary', *supra* note 6; R. Storch, 'Crime and justice in nineteenth century England', *History Today*, 30, 1980; C.D. Robinson, 'The deradicalisation of the policeman: a historical analysis', *Crime and Delinquency*, 24, 2, 1978; W.R. Miller, *Cops and Bobbies*, Chicago: University of Chicago Press, 1977.
37. Brogden, *The Police: Autonomy and Consent, supra* note 6, pp. 180–181.
38. Speech to the Howard League on 26 October 1983, quoted in Home Office, *Criminal Justice: A Working Paper*, London: HMSO, 1984, p. 7.
39. For example see John Burrows and Roger Tarling, *Clearing up Crime*, London: HMSO, 1982 (Home Office Research Study No. 73); Ronald V. Clarke and Mike Hough, *Crime and Police Effectiveness*, London: HMSO, 1984 (Home Office Research Study No. 79); R. Mawby, *Policing the City*, Aldershot: Gower, 1979.
40. Michael S. Pike, *The Principles of Policing*, London: Macmillan, 1985, p. 184.
41. See for example M. Brogden, 'A police authority — the denial of conflict', *Sociological Review*, Vol. 25, 1977; B. Loveday, 'The role of the police committee', *Local Government Studies*, Vol. 9, 1983; P. A. J. Waddington, 'The role of the police committee: constitutional arrangements and social realities', *Local Government Studies*, Vol. 10, 1984; B. Loveday, 'The role of the police committee: a reply to P. A. J. Waddington', *Local Government Studies*, Vol. 10, 1984; D. Regan, *Are the Police Under Control?* London: Social Affairs Unit, 1983; Marshall, *Police and Government, supra* note 26; Marshall, 'Police accountability revisited', *supra* note 26; Jefferson and Grimshaw, *Controlling the Constable, supra* note 32.
42. Critchley, *A History of Police in England and Wales 900–1966, supra* note 6, p. 312.
43. Robert Mark, 'Liberty without responsibility' in *Policing a Perplexed Society*, London: Allen and Unwin, 1977, p. 42; Sir Kenneth Newman, the current Commissioner, is also enthusiastic about policing becoming professional — see for example *Report of the Commissioner of Police of the Metropolis for the year 1984*, London: HMSO, June 1985 (Cmnd. 9541).

44. Margaret Simey 'Partnership policing' in J. T. Benyon (ed.), *Scarman and After*, Oxford: Pergamon, 1984, pp. 135–142.
45. Robert Baldwin and Richard Kinsey, *Police Powers and Politics*, London: Quartet, 1982, p. 98.
46. *The Brixton Disorders, supra* note 34, para. 5.3
47. Ben Whitaker, *The Police in Society*, London: Sinclair Browne, 1982, ch. 3, pp. 73–126.
48. *The Brixton Disorders, supra* note 34, paras. 5.48–5.51.
49. *Police and People in London*, Vol. 4: Smith and Gray, *The Police in Action, supra* note 17, pp. 34–44; see also Pike, *The Principles of Policing, supra* note 40, pp. 184–186.
50. *The Brixton Disorders, supra* note 34, paras. 5.34–5.35; *Police and People in London*, Vol. 3: David J. Smith, *A Survey of Police Officers*, London: Policy Studies Institute, 1983 (PSI No. 620) pp. 40–41.
51. *The Brixton Disorders, supra* note 34, para. 3.79.
52. Clarke and Hough, *Crime and Police Effectiveness, supra* note 39, pp. 8–9; Pauline Morris and Kevin Heal, *Crime Control and the Police*, London: HMSO, 1981 (Home Office Research Study No. 67), pp. 19–21.
53. Baldwin and Kinsey, *Police Powers and Politics, supra* note 45, pp. 26–58; Simon Holdaway (ed.), *The British Police*, London: Edward Arnold, 1979; Simon Holdaway, 'Changes in urban policing', *British Journal of Sociology*, Vol. 28, 1977.
54. Holdaway, 'Changes in urban policing' *supra*, note 53; Simon Holdaway, *Inside the British Police*, Oxford: Blackwell, 1983; *Police and People in London*, Vol. 4: Smith and Gray, *The Police in Action*, supra note 17, pp. 51–56.
55. 'Police car in death crash on way to chase', *The Guardian*, 11 May 1985; 'STOP this chase of death', *Sunday Mirror*, 12 May 1985, p. 7.
56. These are particularly evident in Leicester, for reasons that are not readily apparent.
57. *The Brixton Disorders, supra* note 34, paras 4.37–4.41 and 4.75–4.80.
58. *Ibid.*, para. 4.75.
59. J. Rollo, 'The Special Patrol Group', in Peter Hain (ed.), *Policing the Police Volume 2*, London: Calder, 1980.
60. Jefferson and Grimshaw, *Controlling the Constable, supra* note 32, p. 14.
61. 'The police of London', *London Quarterly Review*, July 1870, p. 48: cited by Silver, 'The demand for order in civil society', *supra* note 7, p. 14.
62. Sarah Manwaring-White, *The Policing Revolution: Police Technology, Democracy and Liberty in Britain*, Brighton: Harvester, 1983, p. 213.
63. David Lancashire, Associated Press, February 1969.
64. The PSI survey found 83 per cent of the sample thought policemen should not normally carry guns: *Police and People in London*, Vol. 1: David J. Smith, *A Survey of Londoners*, London: Policy Studies Institute, 1983 (PSI No. 618), p. 268.
65. *Police Review*, 28 October 1983.
66. See for example, B. Cox, J. Shirley and M. Short, *The Fall of Scotland Yard*, Harmondsworth: Penguin, 1977; Sir David McNee, *McNee's Law*, London: Collins, 1983; Sir Robert Mark, *In the Office of Constable*, London: Collins, 1978, chs. 7–10; M. Punch, *Conduct Unbecoming: The Social Construction of Police Deviance and Control*, London: Tavistock, 1985.
67. *Police and People in London*, Vol. 1: Smith, *A Survey of Londoners, supra* note 64, pp. 248–261; Vol. 3: Smith, *A Survey of Police Officers, supra* note 50, pp. 150–155.
68. *Police and People in London*, Vol. 3: Smith, *A Survey of Police Officers, supra* note 50, pp. 148–151; Vol. 1: Smith, *A Survey of Londoners, supra* note 64, Ch. 9, and pp. 324–327.
69. Mike Hough and Pat Mayhew, *The British Crime Survey: First Report*, London: HMSO, 1983 (Home Office Research Study No. 76) pp. 28–31; Peter Southgate and Paul Ekdom, *Contrasts between Police and Public: Findings from the British Crime Survey*, London: HMSO, 1984 (Home Office Research Study No. 77); David Moxon and Peter Jones, 'Public reactions to police behaviour: some findings from the British Crime Survey', *Policing* Vol. 1, 1984, pp. 49–56; see also Mike Hough and Pat Mayhew, *Taking Account of Crime: Key Findings from the Second British Crime Survey*, London: HMSO, 1985 (Home Office Research Study No. 85).
70. Quoted by Martin Kettle and Lucy Hodges, *Uprising! The Police, the People and the Riots in Britain's Cities*, London: Pan, 1982, p. 241.

71. See for example *Police and People in London*, Vol. 4: Smith and Gray, *The Police in Action, supra* note 17, pp. 97–108; Robert Reiner, *The Blue-Coated Worker*, Cambridge: Cambridge University Press, 1978, pp. 213–217;
72. Richard Clutterbuck, *Britain in Agony*, Harmondsworth: Penguin, 1980, p. 75.
73. For differing, and perhaps rather partial, accounts see Cathie Lloyd, 'A national riot police: Britain's "third force"?' in Bob Fine and Robert Millar, (eds.), *Policing the Miners' Strike*, London: Lawrence and Wishart, 1985, pp. 65–78; Tony Judge, 'Orgreave: "the beginning or the end?" ' *Police*, Vol. 16, July 1984, pp. 8–12.
74. 'The day the police stormed Armthorpe', *The Guardian*, 3 December 1984, p. 15.
75. *The Brixton Disorders, supra* note 34, paras. 4.62–4.68 and 4.1–4.4.
76. Clare Demuth, *'Sus': a Report on the Vagrancy Act*, London: Runnymede Trust, 1978; Philip Stevens and Carole Willis, *Race, Crime and Arrests*, London: HMSO, 1979 (Home Office Research Study No. 58), pp. 31–33.
77. The literature is huge; for a general review and appraisal see John Benyon, 'Spiral of decline: race and policing' in Zig Layton-Henry and Paul Rich (eds.), *Government and Race in Britain*, London: Macmillan, 1986; and John Benyon, *A Tale of Failure: Race and Policing*, Coventry: University of Warwick Centre for Research in Ethnic Relations, 1986; see also Institute of Race Relations, *Police Against Black People*, London: IRR, 1979; Derek Humphry, *Police Power and Black People*, London: Panther, 1972; Paul Gordon, *White Law*, London: Pluto, 1983; John Lambert, *Crime, Police and Race Relations*, London: Oxford University Press, 1970; Stuart Hall, *et al.*, *Policing the Crisis: Mugging, the State and Law and Order*, London: Macmillan, 1978; John Lea and Jock Young, *What is to be done about Law and Order?* Harmondsworth: Penguin 1984.
78. Select Committee on Race Relations and Immigration, Session 1976–77, *The West Indian Community*, Vol. 1, *Report*, Vols. 2 and 3, *Evidence*, HC 180, London: HMSO, February 1977; comments made by Dudley Smith, MP, in Vol. 3, pp. 432–433, para. 1103.
79. Select Committee on Race Relations and Immigration, Session 1971–72, *Police/Immigrant Relations*, Vol. 1, *Report*, Vol. 2, *Evidence*, Vol. 3, *Evidence, Documents and Index*, HC 471, London: HMSO, August 1972; comments made by William Deedes, MP, in Vol. 2, p. 72, para. 221.
80. *Police and People in London*, Vol. 1: Smith, *A Survey of Londoners, supra* note 64, pp. 89–154; quotation is from p. 117.
81. Anne Brogden, '"Sus" is dead but what about "Sas"?' *New Community*, Vol. 9, 1981; Peter Southgate, 'The disturbances of July 1981, in Handsworth, Birmingham', in Simon Field and Peter Southgate, *Public Disorder*, London: HMSO, 1982 (Home Office Research Study No. 72), pp. 50–51; Mary Tuck and Peter Southgate, *Ethnic Minorities, Crime and Policing*, London: HMSO, 1981 (Home Office Research Study No. 70); Carole Willis, *The Use, Effectiveness and Impact of Police Stop and Search Powers*, London: Home Office, 1983 (Research and Planning Unit Paper 15).
82. For a discussion of race, crime and arrests see Benyon 'Spiral of decline: race and policing', and Benyon, *A Tale of Failure, supra* note 77; Stevens and Willis, *Race, Crime and Arrests, supra* note 76; Lea and Young, *What is to be done about Law and Order?*, *supra* note 77; Hall *et al.*, *Policing the Crisis, supra* note 77.
83. *Police and People in London*, Vol. 4: Smith and Gray, *The Police in Action, supra* note 17, pp. 109–131; see also Peter Southgate, *Racism Awareness Training for the Police*, London: Home Office, 1984 (Research and Planning Unit Paper 29) and Peter Southgate, *Police Probationer Training in Race Relations*, London: Home Office, 1982 (Research and Planning Unit Paper 8).
84. Bethnal Green and Stepney Trades Council, *Blood on the Streets: A Report on Racial Attacks in East London*, London: The Trades Council, 1978; Commission for Racial Equality, *Brick Lane and Beyond: An Inquiry into Racial Strife and Violence in Tower Hamlets*, London: CRE, 1979; Home Office, *Racial Attacks: Report of a Home Office Study*, London HMSO, November 1981; Francesca Klug, *Racist Attacks*, London: Runnymede Trust, 1982; Greater London Council, *Racial Harassment in London*, London: GLC, 1984; Benyon, *A Tale of Failure. supra* note 77.
85. Colin Brown, *Black and White Britain: The Third PSI Survey*, London: Heinemann, 1984, table 138, p. 276; see also pp. 256–263; see further, *Police and People in London*, Vol. 1: Smith, *A Survey of Londoners*, pp. 242–247.

86. *Police and People in London*, Vol. 4: Smith and Gray, *The Police in Action, supra* note 17, p. 332.
87. Humphry, *Police Power and Black People, supra* note 77, pp. 11–12.
88. Reiner, *The Politics of the Police, supra* note 6; R. Reiner, 'A watershed in policing', *The Political Quarterly*, Vol. 56, April–June 1985, pp. 122–131; R. Reiner 'From "plods" to "pigs"', *Police*, Vol. 17, March 1985, pp. 26–32; Baldwin and Kinsey, *Police Powers and Politics, supra* note 45; Martin Kettle, 'The politics of policing and the policing of politics' in Hain (ed.) *Policing the Police Volume 2, supra* note 59; Stuart Hall, *Drifting Into a Law and Order Society*, London: Cobden Trust, 1979; E. P. Thompson, *Writing by Candlelight*, London: Merlin, 1980.
89. Sir Robert Mark, 'A sufficiency of seed on fertile ground', in *Policing a Perplexed Society, supra* note 43, pp. 117–122; the 1973 Dimbleby Lecture is printed under the title 'Minority verdict' on pages 55–73.
90. Reiner, *The Politics of the Police, supra* note 6, pp. 73–76.
91. *Ibid.*, p. 74
92. 'Police chief's speech is nonsense, says Hattersley', *The Times*, 17 March 1982, p. 1; 'Tory turmoil on crime condemned by minister', *The Times*, 18 March 1982, p. 1, 'Anderton: evangelist with an accordion', *The Times*, 18 March 1982, p. 12.
93. *Ibid.*, and *The Guardian*, 17 March 1982.
94. Reiner, *The Politics of the Police, supra* note 6, p. 75.
95. 'Curtis stands by his speech', *Police*, Vol. 17, November 1984, pp. 10–12.
96. Sir Harold Scott, *Scotland Yard*, London: Andre Deutsch, 1954, p. 21.
97. *The Confait Case: Report by the Hon. Sir Henry Fisher*, HC 90, London: HMSO, December 1977; C. Price and J. Caplan, *The Confait Confessions*, London: Marion Boyars, 1977; Patricia Hewitt, *The Abuse of Power*, Oxford: Martin Robertson, 1982, ch. 1; in 1981, the Home Office offered the three boys a total of £65,000 compensation for the three years they had each wrongfully spent in detention.
98. Royal Commission on Criminal Procedure (Chairman: Sir Cyril Philips), *Report*, London: HMSO, January 1981 (Cmnd. 8092); see also *The Investigation and Prosecution of Criminal Offences in England and Wales: The Law and Procedure*, London: HMSO, 1981 (Cmnd. 8092–1).
99. See for example Leon Brittan's speech introducing the second reading of the Police and Criminal Evidence Bill: House of Commons Official Report, Parliamentary Debates (*Hansard*) Session 1983–84, Sixth Series, Vol. 48, 7 November 1983, cols. 25–26; see also, Home Office, *Criminal Justice: A Working Paper, supra* note 38.
100. Reiner, *The Politics of the Police, supra* note 6, pp. 171–172.
101. *The Brixton Disorders, supra* note 34, para 4.57.
102. P. A. J. Waddington, '"Community policing": a sceptical appraisal', in Philip Norton (ed.), *Law and Order and British Politics*, Aldershot: Gower, 1984, p. 95.
103. Paul Harrison, *Inside the Inner City*, Harmondsworth: Penguin, 1983, p. 362.
104. Hough and Mayhew, *The British Crime Survey, supra* note 69, pp. 15–24; see also Michael Gottfredson, *Victims of Crime: The Dimensions of Risk*, London: HMSO, 1984 (Home Office Research Study No. 81); Hough and Mayhew, *Taking Account of Crime: Key Findings from the Second British Crime Survey, supra* note 69.
105. Harrison, *Inside the Inner City, supra* note 103, pp. 368–369.
106. 'Police dissatisfied with methods and liaison, Merseyside survey says', *The Times*, 2 July 1985, p. 2; 'Chief constable advised to double police on beat', *The Guardian*, 3 July 1985, p. 2.

PART 2

On the Streets: Stop, Search and Arrest

CHAPTER 2

Policing the community: powers, procedures and participation

JOHN BENYON

During the 1970s the mass media, politicians, opinion leaders and the police themselves expressed growing concern about crime, violence and disorder. However, anxiety about increased lawlessness is not in itself new: in 1941 Mannheim recorded the prevalence of newspaper stories detailing 'thieving from the docks, bag-snatching, assaults on police or on women, and other forms of hooliganism'.[1] Most people seem to recall the war years as a period when a united country faced a common enemy and internal social order was assured, and yet it appears that crime was a continuing concern.

Indeed it is difficult to find a period when rising crime was not a central feature of public debate. Some have claimed that the 1930s were a decade of relative tranquillity, but a cursory glance at newspapers of the period shows that crime and disorder were much in evidence and a more detailed examination reveals that at least in some areas violence was a frequent occurrence.[2] During the 1950s, which the previous chapter suggested was the 'Golden Age' of policing, crime was daily in the news. At Blackpool in 1958 the Conservative Party debated 'the disturbing increase in criminal offences' and it was stated that 'our wives and mothers, if they are left alone in the house at night, are frightened to open their doors'.[3] *Criminal Statistics* for 1957 reveals that 'this sudden increase in crime and brutality', as a Conservative delegate called it, amounted to a *total number* of indictable offences of *545,000*; oh halcyon days!

Twenty years later, when the Royal Commission on Criminal Procedure was announced in 1977, the annual crime figure had quadrupled, there had been a 'moral panic' over 'mugging' and Sir Robert Mark had entered the fray with calls for all manner of changes in the criminal justice system to enable the police to wage war effectively on the criminals. Looking back over the decade, in 1979 Clutterbuck stated they were

> agonising years for the British people, who felt frustrated, humiliated and insecure . . . Throughout the nine years there was a ground swell of

45

fear . . . Is our tradition of minimum force and non-violence in resolving our social and political problems breaking down? Is respect for the rule of law declining? Or is the community losing the will to enforce its laws?[4]

'Powers and procedures suited to the circumstances'

In his stimulating essay in this book Kenneth Oxford considers some of the changes which have affected society and the police. Although some might consider that his description of the era in which he was brought up is a little nostalgic, he is surely right to highlight the increased mobility in society, and the impact of factors such as television. The latter seems to have an infatuation with 'cops and robbers', and projects unreal images and expectations into millions of homes. There can be little doubt that television fictional presentations of crime and policing have had a considerable impact on popular culture. TV policemen invariably solve the crimes, often employ violence and, particularly in American imports, seem to spend a lot of their time rushing around in fast cars. The *Starsky and Hutch* syndrome affects public expectations of how police will behave, and what they can achieve, and may also explain the 'action and crime-fighting perspective' which studies of the police have found. Reiner, for example, stated that increasingly young police officers are attracted by

> the glamour, excitement and challenge of the crime-fighting aspects of the work, the 'machismo syndrome', the pull of 'big white cars and flashing blue lights' . . .[5]

This is a far cry from P.C. Dixon and the image of the calm, helpful, local police officer walking his beat. But as Kenneth Oxford argues society has changed and the police must respond and this was a point made by the Philips' Commission: 'Our society has changed dramatically . . . we need powers and procedures suited to the circumstances of the present day and the foreseeable future'.[6] However, if the arguments in the first chapter are right there is a danger of responding to the changes in the wrong way. If, for example, the public in a particular area are tending to offer less cooperation it will become more difficult for the police to combat crime, but if the response by the service is the wrong one local people may become even less cooperative with the result it is even more difficult to clear up offences. The point is an obvious one, but there is plentiful evidence to suggest that in a number of areas a downward spiral of this kind has occurred. Lord Scarman's account of policing trials and tribulations in Brixton shows how such a downward spiral can occur: he called the recent history of police–community relations in Brixton 'a tale of failure'.

In Lambeth, as in a number of the other London boroughs, a major complaint has been the way in which police officers have exercised their

Is your picture of police work coming through the right channels?

Television cops aren't exactly in the same line of business as ourselves.

They're not trained policemen. They're trained actors. And their job is to keep you entertained for fifty minutes or so, one night a week.

Admittedly, some programmes try to be as authentic as possible. But showing you what real police officers do all day, every day on the streets of London, isn't high on their list of priorities.

Unless it happens to be something that would make good viewing.

Our point of view.

For everyone who's thinking of joining the Met, we'd like to give you a more complete picture.

Despite what you see on the box, most crime is not solved by a car chase and a bit of a scuffle.

We prefer, whenever possible, to be one step ahead of criminals.

Not behind them.

Your back-up team isn't, as you might think from some programmes, just another car-load of TV coppers.

Naturally you can rely on your colleagues to give you all the help you need, whenever you need it.

But you can also rely on a very sophisticated computer-based information network which copes with much of the hard work behind the scenes.

Things like checking fingerprints, cross referencing details on a murder inquiry or establishing a pattern in a spate of burglaries.

Much of this wouldn't make for very good viewing, we admit. Although our work is in the public eye, we don't play to an audience.

Real life dramas.

Nevertheless, we do have our share of real-life dramas, of every type from the comic to the tragic.

Most police officers could tell you quite a few fascinating 'tales from the beat.'

And they'd be talking about dramas in which they'd

THE SWEENEY.

STARSKY AND HUTCH.

THE BILL.

played a leading part. Not watched from the comfort of their favourite armchair.

In fact, the average constable probably plays more roles in a week than most actors play in a year.

Criminologist, social worker, self-defence expert, marriage guidance counsellor, first aid specialist, tourist guide and speaking clock are just a few of them.

You can't get by on memorised lines, either.

You have to learn to think on your feet and react positively to the demands of each situation as it develops.

Are you right for the part?

Don't worry that you might not be able to cope.

If you pass our two day selection process, you'll spend five months at our training centre at Hendon.

Then you'll have 19 more months of theoretical and practical training at a police station.

After all that, you'll be able to cope all right.

To be considered, you'll need to be at least 172cms tall for a man, 168cms tall for a woman and physically fit. Some work experience wouldn't go amiss either.

Ideally, you should have at least five good 'O' levels.

But qualifications above or below the norm don't make the difference between a good officer and a bad one.

Just as important is a sense of fair play; a sense of duty; a sense of humour; and last but not least, plenty of common sense.

If you think you fit the bill, why not get in touch?

For further information, phone (01) 725 4575. Write to the Appointments Officer, Careers Information Centre, Dept. MD 963, New Scotland Yard, London SW1H 0BG. Or visit us at our Careers Information Office in Victoria Street.

A far cry from George Dixon: television portrays policing as glamorous, exciting and violent crime-fighting — but what impact does this have on the expectations and behaviour of the police themselves?

statutory powers to stop and search. The chapters by George Greaves, Ole Hansen and David Smith each draw attention to the adverse impact which these powers have had. And yet in his study of the Metropolitan Police David Smith found that it is the most widely used active police resource. The Policy Studies Institute research led inexorably to the conclusion that

the cost of the present policy, in terms of the relationship between the police and certain sections of the public, is shown to be substantial, and most stops are wasted effort, if they are seen as purely an attempt to detect crime.[7]

It appears that in London about one and a half million stops are made annually which result in 45,000 people being arrested and charged with an offence and 75,000 being reported for one. The imponderable aspect of the stop and search policy is the effect on the clear up rate in general. How does the resentment, which Lord Scarman and the PSI researchers discovered, affect police success in solving burglaries, for instance? Research highlights the importance of the public in providing information and cooperation if a crime is to be solved, but if, as Lord Scarman reported, 'significant sections' of local people have lost faith in the police and are hostile to them, will the information be forthcoming?

A central problem with stop and search powers is that they are difficult to govern by rules or to supervise. Both Ole Hansen and David Smith argue that they are permissive and discretionary, and so the frequency and the manner of their application largely depends upon the views and behaviour of individual officers. Leslie Curtis and Kenneth Oxford stress the need for the powers to curb crime and to deal with circumstances such as those in which a person may have an offensive weapon. They both consider that the safeguards in the new legislation should allay any fears of improprieties, and the Police Federation Chairman is particularly concerned that the procedures for informing a suspect, and for recording the details of the search, may prove to be unworkable.

George Greaves welcomes the new procedures for recording stops and searches, the details of which are spelled out in Richard Stone's chapter. He makes the point, echoed by Leslie Curtis, that the Police and Criminal Evidence Act does not, in fact, codify police powers. It does, though, define a constable's powers of arrest and section 25 causes concern to Richard Stone and Ole Hansen as it could lead to an increase in the use of arrest rather than summons. As Ole Hansen points out being arrested is a frightening experience, and is often far worse than any punishment subsequently visited upon the person by the courts. About 1.4 million people are arrested annually.

Other changes in the Act which affect policing in the community are the powers and procedures for setting up road checks — an issue which came to some prominence during the coal dispute of 1984–85 — and the provisions for entry, search and seizure. Kenneth Oxford considers the need for these, and Ole Hansen draws attention to the implications of section 18 which permits a constable to enter and search premises occupied or controlled by a person who is under arrest for an arrestable offence. This section clarifies some of the questions raised in *Jeffrey v. Black* [1978] QB 490 and *McLorie v. Oxford* [1982] 3 All ER 480, but Hansen considers that there is little doubt that sections 18 and 32(2) will be employed as a means to avoid the necessity of a search warrant. George Greaves draws attention to the annoyance and upset which is caused by the manner in which some police officers conduct searches of people's homes in Lambeth. He welcomes the stipulations in section 16, and hopes they will be followed in practice.

Public participation and policing policies

The difficulty of ensuring that the safeguards in the legislation are faithfully applied is considered by David Smith. In his perceptive analysis he identifies three kinds of rules — working, inhibitory and presentational — and he concludes that stop and search powers cannot be effectively regulated through the law: it is merely a source of presentational rules 'which exist to put an acceptable face on practices we prefer not to look at squarely'. He suggests that one way of shaping police practice would be to establish a structure for police and local representatives to consider the proper level and nature of the policy to be applied by police officers.

The Act does include a provision for arrangements to be made by each police authority for obtaining the views of local people and 'for obtaining their cooperation with the police' (section 106). George Greaves, who is a member of the Lambeth Community — Police Consultative Group, considers the implications of section 106 in his chapter. He concludes that there is no excuse for any authority or chief constable not to take proper advantage of the provision, and to involve local people *fully* in the policing of their areas.

George Greaves contends that proper consultation entails information on and a dialogue about various *operations*, and in support he cites Lord Scarman's view:

> Community involvement in the policy and operations of policing is perfectly feasible without undermining the independence of the police or destroying the secrecy of those operations against crime which have to be kept secret . . . the boundary between what may, and what must not, be disclosed has not been subjected to a close enough scrutiny.[8]

However, it is by no means certain that the 'arrangements . . . for obtaining the views of people' will operate in practice in the way hoped for by Lord Scarman. Many people, within the police service and outside it, have argued that a dialogue of the sort envisaged would interfere with police operations and jeopardise the jealously-guarded independence of chief constables.[9]

Much of the discussion of police independence has appeared to rest on a fallacy of police *autonomy*. They do not have the right of self-government for they are servants of the community, and so two important mechanisms are required — consultation and accountability. Section 106 is poorly framed — presumably the 'arrangements' could merely entail sending out questionnaires and a leaflet on crime prevention — but it provides the opportunity to establish meaningful structures for public participation, which would enable *both* consultation and accountability. The latter is important

> for it renders the police answerable for what they do. Thereby it prevents them from slipping into an enclosed fortress of inward thinking and social isolation which would in the long term result in a siege mentality — the police in their fortress (happy as long as it is secure) and the rest of us outside, unhappy, uncertain and insecure (for we do not know what they will do, or how they will do it).[10]

Meaningful participation would enhance the policing factors specified in chapter one. Identity, legitimacy, consent and effectiveness would each be strengthened, with consequent benefits for police and public alike. However, a number of the eight trends in policing which were outlined in the first chapter — particularly professionalisation — militate against proper consultation and accountability, and against 'outside interference' in policing. It will be interesting to see whether police forces and authorities are prepared to grasp the opportunity afforded by section 106.

Treating citizens 'with unfailing patience and courtesy'

Even if structures for proper police participation were established, a difficulty would remain over how to ensure that individual police officers apply general policies and behave with propriety. Ultimately it seems it is up to the discretion and inclination of particular constables whether their powers are applied fairly and correctly. The Act seeks to influence this behaviour through the stipulations on giving information on, and records of, stops and searches, and seizures, and also through the complaints and disciplinary procedures (sections 83–105). It remains to be seen how the amended complaints arrangements work in practice, and although many appear sceptical as to whether any real improvements will result, a generally welcome innovation, based on a suggestion by Lord Scarman, is the provision for informal resolution of complaints (section 85). However, the central problem remains that for a large number of complaints it boils down to the complainant's word against the officer's, and it is difficult to see how this can ever be satisfactorily resolved. An independent complaints system, though, would give the procedure more legitimacy.

A key question which is raised by policing on the streets in general, and by stop, search and arrest powers in particular, is how constables can be properly supervised and monitored. Rules and disciplinary procedures are of little consequence if they cannot be adequately supervised and enforced.

Lord Scarman drew attention to the need for improved management techniques and better supervision by inspectors and sergeants, and the Policy Studies Institute investigation revealed how little direct supervision occurs, and most of that which does take place is negative and critical rather than encouraging and rewarding of good practice.

The difficulties of proper supervision are partly inherent in the job and they are also affected by the intimate relations between the supervisory levels of inspector and sergeant, and those who are in their charge — the constables. The difficulties though have been exacerbated by the trend to centralisation and larger forces, with the resultant lengthening in lines of communication between senior officers and the officers on the beat. An interesting, and apparently successful, attempt to reverse the trend towards centralisation was launched in 1982 by the newly-appointed Chief Constable of Northamptonshire, Maurice Buck. The innovations are primarily based on a strategy of *devolution* of responsibility and management and the strategy has attracted considerable interest within the police service.[11]

This may be an important means to increase effective supervision of constables *and* to involve local communities. However, the discretionary powers ultimately remain with individual officers who often have to act in a split second under pressure, or who maybe have to deal with truculent young men behaving provocatively on the streets. In such circumstances much will depend upon the character and conduct of the particular officer concerned. In this regard it is interesting to note that in 1985 Sir Kenneth Newman issued to all Metropolitan officers a *Handbook for Guidance for Personal Behaviour* which sets out a nine-point 'code of professional principles'.[12] These do not depart from the approach adopted by the first Metropolitan Police Commissioners, Charles Rowan and Richard Mayne, who stressed the importance of civility and policing proprieties. They enforced their code strictly, as the very high turnover of officers showed, and perhaps the time has again come for a rigid application of the spirit and letter of the General Instructions:

> Every member of the force must remember that his duty is to protect and help members of the public *no less than to apprehend guilty persons*. Consequently, while prompt to prevent crime and to arrest criminals, he must look upon himself as *a servant and guardian* of the general public and *treat all law-abiding citizens, irrespective of their social position, with unfailing patience and courtesy*.[13]

Notes

1. Herman Mannheim, *War and Crime*, London: Watts, 1941, p. 133; cited by Geoffrey Pearson, *Hooligan: A History of Respectable Fears*, London: Macmillan, 1983, p. 241.
2. See for Example, S. Bowes, *The Police and Civil Liberties*, London: Lawrence and

Wishart, 1966; C. Cockburn, *The Devil's Decade*, London: Sidgwick and Jackson, 1973; P. Kingsford, *The Hunger Marchers in Britain 1920–1939*, London: Lawrence and Wishart, 1982. See also *Criminal Statistics for England and Wales*, London: HMSO (published annually by Command) for the 1920s and 1930s.

3. *78th Annual Conference*, London: Conservative Party, 1958, pp. 95–102, cited by Pearson, *Hooligan, supra* note 1, pp. 12–13.
4. Richard Clutterbuck, *Britain in Agony*, Harmondsworth: Penguin, 1980, pp. 19–22.
5. Robert Reiner, 'Who are the police?', *The Political Quarterly*, Vol. 53, April–June 1982, p. 178; see also *Police and People in London*, Vol. 4: David J. Smith and Jeremy Gray, *The Police in Action*, London: Policy Studies Institute, 1983 (PSI No. 621), pp. 49–108.
6. Royal Commission on Criminal Procedure (Chairman: Sir Cyril Philips), *Report*, London: HMSO, 1981 (Cmnd. 8092), para 2.2, p. 14.
7. Police and People in London, Vol. 1: David J. Smith, *A Survey of Londoners*, London: Policy Studies Institute, 1983 (PSI No. 618), p. 117.
8. *The Brixton Disorders 10–12 April 1981: Report of an Inquiry by the Rt. Hon. The Lord Scarman, OBE*, London: HMSO, 1981 (Cmnd. 8427), para. 5.56.
9. See for example, Tony Jefferson and Roger Grimshaw, *Controlling the Constable*, London: Muller, 1984.
10. *The Brixton Disorders, supra* note 8, para. 5.58; See Stephen Savage, 'Political control or community liaison?', *The Political Quarterly*, Vol. 55, Jan–March 1984, pp. 48–59 for a discussion of possible strategies for accountability.
11. See Simon Caulkin, 'Revolution starts in Northampton', *Police*, Vol. 17, April 1985, pp. 8–14 and 44–46.
12. See 'Nine points for the law', *Police*, Vol. 17, January 1985, pp. 22–23.
13. Cited by Ben Whitaker, *The Police in Society*, London: Sinclair Browne, 1982, pp. 40–41 (italics added.)

CHAPTER 3

Police powers after the Act

RICHARD STONE

The Police and Criminal Evidence Act 1984 has been widely perceived as greatly extending police powers. What I have tried to do in this chapter, is to provide, as far as possible, an objective account of the powers of the police 'on the streets' which exist after the Police and Criminal Evidence Act came into force on 1 January 1986. I shall concentrate on the powers of 'stop and search' in Part 1 of the Act, but I shall briefly consider road blocks, and powers of arrest.

Before starting to look at the detailed provisions, two general points about the Act should be made. *First*, it is important to remember that the Act does not codify police powers entirely. One will not by looking at the Police and Criminal Evidence Act find all the powers of the police, and that is a point to which I will return at the end of the chapter.

Second, the text of the Act itself is, of course, explained and supplemented by the codes of practice approved by Parliament, which provide guidance to the police in the operation of the Act. These codes are provided for by Section 66 of the Act, and their status is governed by Section 67. Essentially Section 67 provides that non-compliance with a provision of the codes of practice by a police officer will not in itself render that officer liable to any civil or criminal proceedings. But breach of the code will in itself constitute a disciplinary offence. The codes should, therefore, be very important in practice, and I shall be looking at some aspects of them in detail particularly the Code on 'stop and search'.

The 'stop and search' powers

Of course the police have long had powers to search people under both local and general legislation. A number of the powers under general acts survive the Police and Criminal Evidence Act, perhaps most noticeably the powers under the Misuse of Drugs Act 1971, Section 23. The local powers are repealed. The Act itself provides for certain powers of 'stop and search', but it also contains a number of protective provisions which are applicable to virtually all powers of 'stop and search'.[1] In addition, the provisions of the Code of Practice on 'stop and search' are applicable to virtually all 'stop and search' powers.[2]

The powers under the 1984 Act

Turning first to the new powers contained in the Act itself, section 1 provides a power for any constable to search a person or vehicle if he has reasonable grounds for suspecting that he will find stolen or prohibited articles (Sections 1(2) and 1(3)). The Act does not specifically grant a power to 'stop' people, but this must surely be inferred from the section. As regards vehicles which are in motion, only a constable in uniform may exercise the power to stop such a vehicle (s.2(9)).

The definition of 'stolen articles' will presumably be based on the definition of 'theft' under section 1 of the Theft Act 1968, and there do not seem to be any particular problems which need to be dealt with here.[3]

Moving to the category of prohibited articles, there are two main types of prohibited article recognised by section 1: first, articles made, adapted or intended for use for various Theft Act offences, such as burglary, taking a motor vehicle without permission, and so on (s.1(8)), and secondly, 'offensive weapons'. An offensive weapon is defined in much the same way as in the Prevention of Crime Act 1953. That is, it means an article made, adapted or intended for use for causing personal injury (s.1(9)).[4] Where is this power of search exercisable? First, it may be used in a public place. Here the definition corresponds largely to the definition of a public place under section 9 of the Public Order Act 1936, that is a place which the public or a section of the public has a right or licence to enter at the material time (s.1(1)(a)). It will cover not only the streets themselves, but also the inside of buildings such as football stadiums at a time when the public are admitted to such places.[5]

Additionally, however, the power may be exercised in any place other than a dwelling to which people have 'ready access' at the material time (s.1(1)(b)). The intention here is to catch the suspect who on being approached by a police officer in the street slips through a nearby garden gate, stands on the other side of the fence, and says, 'you can't touch me here'. By becoming a trespasser he tries to put himself out of reach of the 'stop and search' powers. This additional provision in section 1 relating to where the power can be exercised — covering this area, other than dwellings, to which people have ready access, though they have no right to enter onto the land — seems to be intended to cover that type of situation.

If this is intended to give the police a power of entry onto an innocent third party's land, it is a pity that that is not spelt out a little more clearly. There is no reference to it in the provisions of the Act dealing specifically with entry powers. It seems, however, that the Home Office view is that the police would only be entering under a licence, which could be terminated by the occupier.[6]

The exercise of 'stop and search' powers under the Act on land to which people have ready access, is not exercisable in relation to land attached to a dwelling, unless the constable has reasonable grounds to believe that the suspected person or vehicle is on the land without authorisation (s.1(4), (5)).

The general provisions on 'stop and search'

Certain provisions of the Act and the Code affect all 'stop and search' powers including those just mentioned. Crucial to the exercise of these powers is the concept of 'reasonable grounds for suspicion'. In the past, while claiming to apply an objective test, the courts have never required very much of the police in this respect. As long as the police officer could show *some* grounds for this suspicion, then that was enough.[7] Nor does the Police and Criminal Evidence Act itself elaborate on this. But the Code of Practice, rising to the challenge put forward by the Royal Commission (which stated that in its view the task was impossible) does attempt to give some guidelines as to what constitutes reasonable grounds for suspicion. These are contained primarily in Annex B to the Code of Practice.

The Annex makes it clear, first of all, that the level of suspicion required is the same as the level of suspicion which would justify an arrest (para. 4). In other words there are not two levels of suspicion, one justifying 'stop and search', one justifying arrest, it is the same thing in both cases. The use of 'stop and search' powers may simply obviate the need for an arrest.

Secondly, the Annex states that reasonable suspicion must be more than an individual officer's hunch or instinct. It must be based on something capable of objective evaluation, for example, a specific observation by the officer, or some information which he has received (paras. 1 and 2). Thirdly, membership of a particular group, even if the group is statistically likely to commit certain offences, can never in itself be enough to justify reasonable grounds for suspicion. Nor can a particular mode of dress or hairstyle, or perhaps most importantly, colour of skin. Similarly, the fact that a person has previous convictions, for example, for carrying offensive weapons, is not in itself reasonable grounds for suspicion for a 'stop and search' for such weapons on a later occasion (para. 3).

So what can constitute grounds for reasonable suspicion? Here the Code becomes rather more vague. It says that reasonable suspicion may arise from the nature of property being carried, or suspected of being carried, coupled with other factors, including the time, the place and suspicious behaviour of the person concerned or those with him (para. 2). This does not seem very helpful to a constable required to make an 'on the spot' decision.

Slightly more specifically, the Code does provide that information received, such as the description of a suspect, may give rise to reasonable suspicion in respect of a person who matches the description, as may prior knowledge of a person's behaviour. So, I would suggest for example, that if a person is seen talking to an individual whom a constable knows to be a pusher of drugs, and something changes hands between them, there would be reasonable grounds for a search, under the Misuse of Drugs Act, of the person talking to the pusher.

But what of a more difficult case, perhaps a person simply seen walking through the streets at 2 a.m. carrying a suitcase? Is that enough to give rise to a suspicion that he is carrying stolen goods or prohibited articles? Presumably not, without some further information, such as that a burglary has recently been committed in the area, or that someone of that description has been seen leaving premises in suspicious circumstances.

But the Code of Practice makes it clear that the further information which might lead to that circumstance giving rise to reasonable grounds of suspicion, cannot be obtained by stopping the person and asking him questions. The suspicion must arise *before* the stop takes place, and thus a refusal by our night walker to open his suitcase could not be used as reasonable grounds for suspicion justifying a forcible search. Questioning may confirm or dispel an existing suspicion, but it cannot be used to justify a stop made without reasonable grounds (paras. 2.1. and 2.3).

What about the other general provisions contained in the Act and the Code of Practice? Taking up the Royal Commission's suggestion that one protective provision which was needed was that people stopped and searched should be given the fullest information, the Act makes provision for this in section 2. Of course, a person stopped under the 'stop and search' powers does not necessarily have to be searched (s.2(1)).[8] But if the constable decides that, having stopped the person, a search should be carried out, he must give certain information. If he is not in uniform he should show his warrant card.[9] In any case he must tell the suspect his name and the station to which he is attached, and explain the object of the search, and the grounds for undertaking it (s.2(3)). Neither the Act nor the Code of Practice specifies a means for doing this; it could be done by word of mouth, or possibly by handing over a piece of paper containing the required information.

The conduct of a search

As to the conduct of the search itself, the Code encourages the police to be courteous and considerate in exercising these powers (para. 1A). Reasonable force, as permitted by section 117 of the Act, should only be used as a last resort (para. 3.2). The Act provides that for a search in public, only 'outer clothing' may be removed, meaning an outer coat, jacket and gloves but excluding headgear and footwear (s.2(9)). A more extensive search should take place, for example, in a police van or nearby station. The time for which a person or vehicle may be detained for a search is limited to what is reasonable to permit such a search to be carried out on the spot or nearby (s.2(8)).

The Code of Practice expands on this to some extent by relating the extent of the search to the grounds for suspicion. For example, if the suspicion relates to an offensive weapon or something which is thought to be an offensive weapon being slipped into a pocket, only that pocket should be searched (para. 3.3). The Code concludes by saying it is an unusual search that cannot be completed within a minute or so. So searches should in general be fairly brief affairs.

Recording of searches

After the search, following the Royal Commission's recommendation, the Act provides for the recording of information about each search (s.3). The suspect should normally be informed before the search is carried out that this information will be recorded and that he is entitled to receive a copy of this information on request within the twelve months following the search (s.2(3)). The record should be made on a special form ('the national search record'), and will record the general details of the search, the name or a description of the person searched, the object of the search, and the ground for making it, as well as things like the date, time, place, and result of the search (s.3(5)). The record should be made on the spot or as soon as practicable thereafter.

This record must always be made unless it is not practicable to do so. The Act does not give any examples of when it may be impracticable to do so. The Code of Practice suggests situations involving public disorder occurring in seaside areas during Bank Holiday weekends, or the search of football supporters entering or leaving a ground where a considerable number of searches are quickly required (para. 4.1). But how does this relate to the requirement of reasonable suspicion? Can you ever have reasonable grounds for suspecting a large number of people? If a constable has seen an offensive weapon in the hands of one of a small group of people, there may be reasonable grounds for suspicion for searching each of the members of the group in turn until the offensive weapon is found. But this would not justify large scale searches of the kind suggested here. There does seem to be some conflict between the statements as to what constitutes reasonable grounds for suspicion, and this recognition of the possibility of searches of large numbers of people.

Road checks

Section 4 provides a statutory framework for the exercise of the previously rather uncertain power of the police to conduct 'road checks' or 'road blocks'. The section applies where the police wish to use their general power to stop vehicles under section 159 of the Road Traffic Act 1972 in such a way as to stop all vehicles passing along a road, or all vehicles selected by some criterion — for example type, colour, age, occupants (s.4(2)). It is fairly restricted in that it can only be used to search for *people*, not evidence, and only as regards a person 'unlawfully at large' or reasonably suspected of being involved in, or a witness to, the commission of a 'serious arrestable offence'. Section 116 defines 'serious arrestable offence', and although the definition does contain some uncertainties, it mainly covers offences such as explosives offences, serious crimes of violence, and serious sex offences.

The exercise of the Section 4 power will be under the general supervision of an officer of at least the rank of superintendent. Once again the Act provides safeguards in the form of record-keeping, and any person stopped is entitled to a written statement of the reasons for the road check, on application within twelve months (s.4(15)). It should be noted that Section 4 recognises no power other than that of stopping vehicles. If the police wish to search a stopped vehicle, or people in it, they will have to rely on some other power, e.g. under Section 1.[10]

Arrest

Moving on to arrest, the basic definition of an arrestable offence is little changed by the Act. The definition based on the possibility of a five year sentence of imprisonment remains. A number of specific offences, however, are added to the definition of arrestable offence, such as offences under the Customs and Excise Acts, and the Official Secrets Acts (s.24(2)). The conditions for exercise are substantially repeated from Section 2 of the Criminal Law Act 1967 (s.24(4)–(7)).

Perhaps more importantly, Section 26 of the Act repeals most specific statutory powers of arrest.[11] Section 25, however, gives a new power of arrest. This arises where the constable has reasonable grounds for suspecting that a non-arrestable offence has been, or is being committed or attempted, and it appears to the constable that service of a summons is impracticable or inappropriate because one of what are called the 'general arrest conditions' is satisfied.

So this power is available wherever a constable suspects any offence, no matter how minor, of having been committed or being in the process of being committed. The constable may arrest any person whom he has reasonable grounds to suspect of having committed or attempted to commit the offence or of being in the course of committing or attempting to commit it.

The general arrest conditions which will justify the arrest fall into two groups (s.25(3)). The first covers the situation where the constable cannot get relevant information needed for the service of a summons, for example the name of the suspect or the suspect's address, or where the constable has reasonable grounds to suspect the name and address which are given are not the suspect's real name and address.

Secondly, there is a group of arrest conditions which relate to actions which the suspect may take. If the constable has reasonable grounds to believe that the suspect may cause physical injury, suffer physical injury, cause damage to property, commit an offence against public decency, cause an unlawful obstruction of the highway, or that the arrest is necessary to protect a child or other vulnerable person, then the arrest will be justifiable under the Section 25 power.

This is a wide power, and could lead to the police arresting people more frequently than at present. In relation to arrest of course, there is no provision for a code of practice, and so we will have to wait until the Act has been in force for a time before we see how exactly the police make use of that arrest power and how the general arrest conditions are operated.

After an arrest has taken place, the person arrested must, as soon as practicable, be informed that he is under arrest, and the grounds for it, even if those grounds are obvious (s.28(1) & (2)). So the person found in front of the empty safe with the used fivers sticking out of his pocket must still be informed of the grounds on which he is being arrested.

An arrested person may be searched, for example if the constable has reasonable grounds to believe that he may present a danger to himself or others, or that he may have items on him which he might use to assist his escape or which might be evidence of an offence (s.32(1), (2)).

The Act provides for two powers of entry following arrest. The premises on which the arrest took place or which the arrested person was on immediately prior to the arrest, may be searched for evidence (s.32(2)). If the arrest is for an arrestable offence then, in addition, premises which are occupied or under the control of the person arrested may be entered and searched for evidence (s.18(1)).

Conclusion

The Act contains important new powers, and a framework of safeguards. The new powers should not, however, be seen as constituting a radical shift in the balance of power between the police and the public 'on the streets'. There is still no general power to stop, in the absence of 'reasonable suspicion', nor is there any general obligation to answer questions.[12] As to the safeguards, some may feel that they will simply end up being an administrative nuisance for the police without having any very beneficial effects for the suspect. And, of course, any police action taken with the *consent* of the member of the public, will not be subject to the notification and recording provisions.

I should like to conclude, however, by returning to the point that the Act does *not* codify police powers. If we are looking at the powers of the police on the streets, it is very important to note one particular area which is left untouched, and that is the common law power to deal with actual or reasonably apprehended breaches of the peace. That power is totally unaffected by the Act. Its usefulness has been emphasised recently in the case of *Moss v McLachlan* arising out of the miners' strike.[13] And of course it is not subject to any statutory recording provisions or any Code of Practice. I think it is very important in looking at the powers of the police on the streets from 1986 onwards that we give these common law powers their due recognition as a flexible supplement to the more rigidly defined powers under the Act.

In day to day policing they may be just as important.

Notes

1. See ss.2(2) and 3(1). The Royal Commission on Criminal Procedure recommended the codification of all stop and search powers — *Report*, Cmnd. 8092, paras. 3.20, 5.5.
2. Annex A to the Code.
3. But note the wider definition of 'stolen goods' in Section 24 of the Theft Act 1968. It is possible, though unlikely, that this definition could be adopted in relation to the 1984 Act.
4. Sections 1(8) and 1(9) make it clear that articles in the possession of one person, but intended for use by another, may still be 'prohibited articles'. This would presumably allow the police to search for an article 'dumped' on an innocent bystander.
5. *Cawley* v. *Frost* (1976) 64 Cr App Rep 20.
6. See H. C. Deb., Standing Committee E. 29 November 1983, col. 123.
7. See e.g., *Nakkuda Ali v Jayaratne* [1951] AC 66; *Dumbell v Roberts* [1944] 1 All ER 326; *Dallison v Caffery* [1965] 1 QB 348, and cases discussed by Bailey and Birch in [1982] *Crim LR* 475.
8. It seems that there is no recording of information required in relation to stops which do not lead to a search.
9. Section 2(2), and Code of Practice, para. 2.5.
10. Note also the way in which the powers of the police to prevent breaches of the peace may apparently be used to create a *de facto* road block — *Moss* v. *McLachlan, The Times*, 29 November, 1984.
11. Certain powers, listed in Schedule 2 to the Act, are preserved.
12. Though, of course, failure to answer questions may lead to one of the 'arrest conditions' being fulfilled.
13. *The Times*, 29 November, 1984.

CHAPTER 4

The power to police effectively

KENNETH OXFORD

When the historians of the future look back over the period of the past ten or fifteen years they are likely to identify it as a revolution, rather like the industrial revolution of the last century, but on this occasion it will be seen as a social or technological revolution born in the middle and late sixties and reaching maturity in the mid-nineteen eighties.

In truth, we have reached a rather critical point in our history, a time for re-appraisal of our past actions, and a time to consider with great skill and care our decisions for the future if we are to ensure a successful economic and social climate for our descendants. In order to decide our actions we must be able to understand the problems facing us because I feel that understanding is the cornerstone upon which the foundation of solutions can be built.

Order in an unsettled society

I was brought up in a rather different era and many would say, despite the problems facing our generation, we had a sense of discipline and purpose, and a community spirit, which is often lacking today, but which gave us the foundations upon which we could build our future. It may well be true, but today our society has changed considerably and we are faced with different problems, and it is still our responsibility to help resolve our difficulties.

I would like to consider a number of fundamental changes which have influenced our society, and although I relate their effect to the police service, they have an influence on almost all forms of human behaviour and organisations.

Nowadays we live and work in a rapidly changing society, sometimes in a situation of tension, and all too often it seems that society does not know its own mind or what its aims and objectives are. This confusion is a result of continuing change. We can make up our own list of the major manifestations which have affected the lives of all of us, and if we relate

61

them to the living and working conditions of specific groups some of real significance can be identified.

The flooding of people into the cities is a global phenomenon. The increased mobility of people is worldwide, wherever the jet plane flies and the roads run. Instant reportage of what goes on is possible wherever radio and television can transmit. Meanwhile, partly as a product of the technologies, changes take place at the heart of human society: beliefs change or wither and family life often does the same; class structures crumble or are replaced; wealth increases for some, decreases for others, and is venerated by all, thus helping to create the materialist tempo of these times.

Let us look at increasing mobility, for instance. In the police service it means that much of our time and resources are utilised in dealing with the problems of public disorder, industrial disputes, terrorism, the motor vehicle, domestic strife, drug abuse in all its current manifestations, and other criminal offences. Detectives are increasingly concerned with the mobile criminal moving from place to place, from country to country, from force area to force area, and committing crimes miles away from where he may live.

But there is also a more basic problem. Increased mobility means that the majority of people do not stay in the same place for long: they can live in one area and work in another miles away, and they can travel all over the world if they have a mind to. In effect they have no roots. There is an inscription on a tomb in one of our English cathedrals which reads: 'He was born here, lived here, died here'. These words were regarded as high praise by those who caused them to be inscribed, because it meant the person to whom it was dedicated had roots. He had a place to which he belonged. He knew everybody in his area, and they knew him. How many people can say the same today, or how many would wish to? To keep moving is a necessity for many, and is even seen as a virtue for some.

The implications for the police service of an unsettled community are great. One important element of police work has always been a knowledge of people, who they are, what they are, and what makes them tick. It helps create a climate of understanding between the police and the community, but such a climate is more difficult to achieve if the members of the community, or even the police officers, do not stay in the area long enough to become known.

Connected with increased mobility, but with even greater implications, is the increasing urbanisation of society. In Great Britain, like most other countries, the great majority of the population now live in the large cities and urban conurbations. The increase in crime is more associated with such communities and city life can be a great destroyer of community loyalties and community self-knowledge. The anonymity of mass living produces crimes and violence as certainly as it produces loneliness. Police officers see examples every day and we are all aware of them through the reports in newspapers, on radio or television. How often have we read of old people being attacked in the street or even worse, being found dead in their homes, and they have not been missed by their *neighbours* for days, weeks or even months?

Responding to changing times

The increasing ease of communications is another facet which has far-reaching implications upon the human scene. The rapid transmission of ideas and reportage of events, made possible by the new technologies of communication, have important connotations in social change. They cause confusion in the minds of many people about standards of behaviour. When so many can be seen and heard doing and saying so many different things, pursuing so many different ends, in so many different ways, it is easy to see how an individual can be driven back in confusion as to how he should behave.

The old liberal idea that ease of communication would bring greater harmony and understanding among people, an idea enshrined in the old motto of the B.B.C. 'Nation shall speak peace unto nation', has turned out to be mistaken.

Two other changes in the social scene which have discernible consequences for the police service and society as a whole should be maintained. The decline of religious belief as a sanction of personal conduct and the erosion of the idea of parental authority and control, is something which my generation finds difficult to understand, but it is true that these disciplines have been eroded since our formative years. The latter aspect is often highlighted by people working in contact with our young people: social workers, teachers and police officers. Whatever the reasons are, and there are many suggestions, it does seem surprising that parental involvement in the guidance of their own children has declined to such a marked extent.

Not too long ago one of my chief constable colleagues said of the police service, 'twenty-five years ago policing was 90% boredom and 10% bloody terror. Today it is 90% bloody terror and 10% boredom'. Perhaps this is a slightly cynical over-statement of the truth, but it does make the point of the changes in society and the changes in policing.

The police response to these changing times for some time now has been the subject of great debate both inside and outside the service. We are faced with an apparent paradox. On the one hand public opinion polls continue to place the police service at the top of the list of organisations in which they have most confidence, whilst on the other hand the service is being subjected to an increasing barrage of criticism on all manner of subjects, from complaints against the police, democratic accountability, the use of technology, to the policing of inner cities and racially-sensitive areas. The role of the police everywhere is being scrutinised more critically than ever before by politicians, the press, pressure groups, the general public, and by the police themselves, and although it would be true to say that those who complain the loudest on behalf of the public are not necessarily those most concerned for its welfare, it would be foolish for the police to brush aside every criticism as ill-motivated.

There is a well-established principle of policing in this country which has been unchanged over the past 150 years, and that is policing should be by consent of the community it serves rather than by coercion.

The first Commissioners of the Metropolitan Police decided that the prime functions of the police were the protection of life and property, the prevention and detection of crime, and the preservation of the peace. This tradition is still quoted to, and learned by all new recruits to the police service, having been re-enforced by the Royal Commission on the Police in 1960[1] — and re-stated by the Royal Commission on Criminal Procedure in 1981[2].

The balance between consent and enforcement

In the past the balance between consent of the community and the enforcement of law was accepted by the public because the law and public opinion were in general agreement. That did not mean that people did not break the law, but rather that those who did were likely to be condemned by a majority of the general public. It was certainly a period when the idea of authority commanded general acceptance. In the more recent past it has been suggested that the police service has been too much concerned with enforcing the law and have alienated the support of certain sections of the community.

This question and concept of policing was considered by Lord Scarman in his Inquiry into the disorders in Brixton[3] and it is interesting to note that in his report he suggested that there should be a change of emphasis in our traditional policing principles, in an attempt to create a more acceptable balance between consent and law enforcement. In effect, he said the primary function of the police should be the maintenance of public tranquillity, and if law enforcement puts public tranquillity at risk, then the police should test the wisdom of law enforcement by its likely effect upon public order. He reasoned that law enforcement, involving as it must the possibility of force, can create acute friction in a community, particularly if that community is tense and the cause of the law breaker is not without support.

I wonder if Lord Scarman's suggestions are not too simplistic. There are undoubtedly circumstances when this philosophy will highlight the most appropriate course of action, but I have some doubts about its general application in all circumstances. There is a danger that members of the public will not accept the idea, particularly if they happen to be victims of a crime or to live in an area which suffers from a high rate of criminal acts. Discretion is one of the most valuable assets in any police officer's armoury, but it must be exercised with great care. It is undeniable that there is only one law for all, and the police service would soon come under attack if they were to apply any unfair standards in their law enforcement. There is no reason why positive law enforcement should not be harmonious with so-called community policing.

To meet the changes in society my colleagues and I have accepted the need for a constant re-appraisal of police tactics and procedures. This is nothing new, and neither is the fact that we continually consider suggestions from bodies outside the police service. If we are to continue to police with the consent of the public, we must be aware of public opinion, or else the alternative would be rather unpalatable to both police and public. There is one point I must make, and that is the police service will not succeed without the help of the community. In fact it is high time that society stopped running away from its responsibilities, and the problems it faces, and began to tackle them intelligently and courageously.

Section 106 of The Police and Criminal Evidence Act 1984 reflects this need for a 'social contract' by way of legislation. It will be interesting to see how this Section of the Act is pursued by the various 'interested' parties and the real community.

The prolonged debate on the Bill

It is difficult to reconcile an effective system of police, with that perfect freedom of action and exemption from interference, which are the great privileges and blessings of society in this country; and Your Committee think that the forfeiture or curtailment of such advantages would be too great a sacrifice for improvements in police, or facilities in detection of crime, however desirable in themselves if abstractedly considered.[4]

The foregoing is not an extract from the committee stages of the Police and Criminal Evidence Bill 1984, but from a parliamentary committee of 1822, chaired by the newly appointed Home Secretary Robert Peel, which regarded any formation of a police force as incompatible with British liberty. When one considers much of the contribution to the prolonged debate, both in committee and subsequently in debates in the Lords and Commons, it might well have been said in 1984. One had the distinct impression that the opponents of the Bill were the reincarnation of the parliamentarians of the 18th and 19th century who vociferously opposed the police idea and viewed its formation with disfavour. I wonder whether we are to be prisoners of our own history.

It is not too often that we hear of solicitors in this country picketing courts in our major cities. It is unusual that politicians, journalists, doctors, clergymen and civil libertarians join together to demonstrate outside Scotland Yard. It is rare indeed for one of our more well known women's magazines[5] to publish a major article of critical comment on proposed legislation. It may be unique that chief officers of police, police superintendents and members of the Police Federation all made rather scathing attacks on a Bill designed to codify police practice as well as protect civil liberties.

The birth and passage of the Police and Criminal Evidence Bill through Parliament forged some rather unusual alliances with the common objective of attacking, criticising or preventing the Bill reaching the statute books. Even distinguished members of the House of Lords expressed apprehension at the possibility of being stopped, searched and arrested outside Harrods in Knightsbridge whilst on a perfectly innocent shopping expedition![6]

It remains to be seen how much of the well publicised criticism will be justified, how many of the fears will be realised and how useful this legislation will be to the police and public alike. What is undoubtedly true is that the Police and Criminal Evidence Act is the most controversial and I believe the most misunderstood piece of legislation ever to be considered during my professional career. Hundreds of amendments were made to the Bill and it is said to have taken the largest period of parliamentary time in history to pass from the Commons to the Lords.

We might ask ourselves, why on earth, in view of all the controversy, was this piece of legislation ever considered necessary at this particular time? To answer this it is important to look back to 1977 when the idea was mooted.

It was on 24 June 1977, that the then Labour Prime Minister, James Callaghan, told the House of Commons in a written answer[7] that the time had come for the whole criminal process, from the start of the investigation to the point of trial, to be reviewed. He stated that in recent years some reforms had been introduced into the criminal justice system, and many more were proposed, but the approach had been piecemeal and no complete review had been mounted at any time during this century.

There had been for a number of years a growing anxiety about the continuing rise in the level of crime, particularly robbery, drug trafficking, and so-called 'street crime' as well as fraud and the criminal use of firearms. Nothing much has changed in the last nine years except that the levels of all these crimes have continued to rise at a fairly steady rate.

The Prime Minister in his written answer in the Commons[8] outlined other aspects which influenced him to seek to review the criminal justice system. He said there was public ignorance and confusion about the ways in which crime was investigated and prosecuted and about whether, if these were improved, they would bring the growth of crime under control. On one hand it was asserted that the police job of fighting crime was being made unwarrantedly difficult by the restraints of criminal procedure; and on the other hand the use of police powers of investigation was often open to grave question.

The consideration of these aspects, as well as disquiet over cases involving juveniles and the mentally handicapped and changes in public awareness and opinion, lay behind the birth of the Royal Commission on Criminal Procedure which was to be the foundation of the Police and Criminal Evidence Act. So it was the Labour Government which in 1978 established the Royal Commission on Criminal Procedure under the Chairmanship of Sir Cyril Philips.

The quest for a fundamental balance

The terms of reference of the Royal Commission[9] contained the most important concept of 'fundamental balance' and members of the Commission had to take regard of the interests of the community in bringing offenders to justice and to the rights and liberties of persons suspected or accused of crime. The Prime Minister expressed the view that there was 'a balance to be struck here between the interests of the whole community and the rights and liberties of the individual citizen . . . the Government consider the time has come for the whole criminal process . . . to be reviewed with the fundamental balance in mind'.[10]

The whole concept of 'fundamental balance' was the central challenge to The Royal Commission and indeed successive Home Secretaries have constantly reinforced this principle in their public pronouncements.

The Police and Criminal Evidence Bill was drafted with this delicate balance in mind and many of the clauses reflected the recommendations made by the Royal Commission. The then Home Secretary, Leon Brittan, when moving the second reading of the Bill in the House of Commons, reinforced the assertions made by his predecessors when he said it was needed for three reasons: because the present state of the law was unclear and contained many indefensible anomalies; because the police needed adequate and clear powers to conduct the fight against crime, and the public needed to have proper safeguards against any abuse of such powers; and because the measures played an essential part in an overall strategy designed to create more effective policing.[11]

I cannot disagree with this broad statement of intent and it is possible in the longer term that the Act will assist the police. However, I would question whether in fact the 'fundamental balance' has been achieved. I would venture to suggest that few people would agree that the correct balance has been struck; certainly I and my fellow chief constables feel the balance has been tipped too far in favour of the wrongdoers against the interests of the law-abiding citizen and an effective police service.

The Bill was the subject of intense public debate, much of which was ill-informed and at times totally misleading. Probably the most quoted piece of misinformation is that the Act gives to the police 'draconian new powers'. This simply is not true. The Act merely codifies and, in some cases, *curtails* actions which the police have always carried out either by consent or because they were never challenged.

Increasingly since 1984 my colleagues have entered the public debate in an attempt to challenge and to clarify some of the misconceptions which have continued to gain credibility,[12] although some of the views of chief constables would, in media terms, appear to have gone by default.

It has always been my hope that the Police and Criminal Evidence Act would provide a comprehensive framework of the powers and duties of the police and give the service an opportunity upon which it can construct a strategy for combatting crime. The 120,000 officers who comprise the police service in England and Wales are extremely anxious to combat all forms of crime and given the right tools and the right lead, in the form of clear and comprehensive police powers, there is much that we can do to reduce crime and improve our effectiveness.

It is, of course, unreasonable to think that one piece of legislation can overcome the many factors which have led to the tremendous growth of crime over the past two or three decades, particularly in some of our decaying inner city areas. But a clear statement of police powers and police conduct for the investigation of crime, which is understood and supported by the general public, can only lead to an improved appreciation of the role of the police in our society, and thereby, hopefully, to an enhancement of police–public relations. In this regard I feel the Act should not be looked upon merely as updating police powers, but rather as a statement of civil liberties combined with a realistic desire for tackling crime. The more the public are properly informed about the true purpose and effects of the Act, the more they will come to recognise the false fears that have been aroused.

I have always accepted the guiding principles articulated by its founding fathers that the Act should maintain the delicate balance between providing powers for the police, to enable them to be effective, while at the same time ensuring the rights and liberties of individual citizens are properly safeguarded. There were occasions when I and my colleagues sought to expand certain police powers because we felt they would assist police effectiveness and we made our specific views known in this regard. We also accepted that where our recommendations were rejected, good reason applied. Unfortunately, opponents of the Act seemed to refuse to accept this same good faith and increasingly the police service became more alarmed by many of the statements condemning the Act and making assertions which, even with the most generous interpretations, can only be described as misleading and in some cases depressingly naïve.

Powers to stop and search

I would like to highlight a number of issues which have wrongly been described as 'draconian police powers' and which if compromised any further would give marked advantages to the criminal to the detriment of the general public.

It has been suggested that the Act incorporates a wide extension of police powers to stop and search (Sections 1–3) and to carry out road checks (Sections 4 and 5). These powers already exist in many areas of the country, particularly in the major conurbations and where they have existed they provided a significant means available to the police officer to prevent and detect crime. There is little doubt that without such powers being available in areas such as Merseyside and the large urban areas many more offences would go undetected or could not be prevented.

In their deliberations on this particular issue the House of Lords carried an amendment which precluded plain clothes officers from using the powers to stop and search, the powers only being given to uniformed officers.[13] The noble Lords felt that identification of the person stopping a citizen on his lawful passage was of vital importance. They believed that an officer in plain clothes would create the possibility of conflict or at the least a state of apprehension. In order to avoid confrontation between the police and the public it was argued that in the interests of the police and the public the powers of stop and search should not be granted to a plain clothes police officer. Had this amendment reached the statute book the whole detective force would have been virtually immobilised. The number of unnecessary arrests and subsequently damaged police–public relations would have been disastrous.

The law on this subject was a mess with many illogical features about the extent of police powers to stop and search. There were powers to stop and search a person carrying, for example, wild birds' eggs or protected plants, but until now we have lacked clear powers to guide an officer to stop and search for property suspected of having been stolen, offensive weapons or the tools of a burglar's trade.

I and my colleagues are very conscious of the damage that can be caused to relations between the police and the public where such powers are used injudiciously and I accept the need for the conduct of stop and search procedures to be a matter of regulation with clear parameters for police and public alike.

It is also worth briefly looking at the powers to hold road checks which the police have used very successfully for many years. Under the new Act, such checks will usually only be conducted with the authority of a superintendent and then only in a few exceptional circumstances (Section 4). This can hardly be described as an extension of police powers!

Detention of suspects

Perhaps the most critical and vociferous comments levelled at the Act have concerned the detention of a suspect (Part IV, especially Sections 41–44). Much has been said and written about the proposed power to detain a suspect without charge for 36 hours, subject to the authority and arrival of a superintendent, before the suspect must appear before a court (Sections 42 and 43). As the law has stood, detention in police custody before charge has been open-ended and all the critics must surely concede that the measures in the Act represent some improvement on what has previously applied. Many figures have been suggested as the maximum time period: 4 hours, 6 hours, 24 hours, 48 hours, even 72 hours but there is no rational basis for any of these figures other than to keep the period of time a person is detained without charge to a fixed minimum.

In contrast, the provisions of the Police and Criminal Evidence Act dealing with detention without charge have been drafted in the full knowledge of the small number of exceptional cases involving the most grave crimes where fairly prolonged detention is vital, subject to strict and proper safeguards. To set an earlier time limit would oblige the police to bring charges which may not stand up in court, or break off prematurely the investigations of a serious crime. The prosecution of grave crimes is essential to the protection of the public, and the question I would pose is whether it is right, in a small number of cases, to abandon the search for evidence in order to avoid detention for more than 36 hours.

Our researches have shown that detention beyond six hours occurs in only a quarter of cases and beyond 24 hours in as few as 2 per cent of cases. Quite clearly, the vast majority of offenders will be properly dealt with and either released or charged within the 24 hour time limit. The professional criminal, however, when detained for a serious arrestable offence, will be aware of:

— the reviews of detention which must take place after six hours by an inspector, and thereafter at nine-hourly intervals (Section 40)
— his entitlement to eight hours rest free from interview (Code of Practice, paragraph 12.2)
— his entitlement to a break from interviews every two hours and for meals at reasonable times (Code of Practice, paragraph 12.7)
— the requirement after 36 hours, if he has not been charged, for an *inter partes* hearing when the police will have to disclose the evidence against him to justify further detention (Section 42)

There is, in my view, a strong possibility that such a person will use these safeguards, not only to discover the strength of the police case at an early stage, but also during any subsequent proceedings to make fallacious attacks upon the officers responsible for the investigation in an effort to escape conviction. Thus it could be argued that it is the very element from whom society needs the greatest protection, who will reap most benefit from the limits being placed upon detention.

Searches for evidence

There is one other area which has excited great public criticism, particularly from doctors, clergymen and journalists and which is worthy of some explanation and clarification. The concern this time is levelled at the powers to search for evidence in Part II of the Act.

Sections 8 and 9 outline powers for a Justice of the Peace or, in certain circumstances (see schedule 1), a circuit judge to issue orders or warrants to allow police to obtain or have access to evidence of a serious arrestable offence. The original proposals were designed to provide a power for police to search for, and obtain, evidence such as a murder weapon, blood-stained clothing, or even a dead body which is concealed in premises or held by some third party, whether innocent or not, and included such matters held on an undertaking of confidence.

There has never been any suggestion that police should have a power to examine confidential records such as those held by doctors or priests, nor has it been proposed that police should have a power to seize such items. The proposals were not intended to replace existing methods of voluntarily obtaining evidence from doctors and such, by way of written statement, or where necessary by subpoena or witness summons, nor were they intended for the gathering of information or intelligence.

The criticism levelled by the British Medical Association and other groups was made on the basis that the powers to search for evidence extended to such items as records kept by doctors, priests and journalists. It has become clearly apparent that these critics and many parliamentarians did not understand the meaning of the word 'evidence'. They did not appreciate the distinctions between evidence and information or between evidence adducible by a police officer and that which requires the attendance of a private witness.

Let me explain my last statement a little further with this example. A note made by a doctor on a patient's record is in effect the doctor's 'pocket book' and any evidence relating to a prosecution would have to be adduced to a court verbally by the doctor using the note as an *aide memoire* if necessary. It is not possible for a police officer to seize the doctor's note and adduce it in evidence and therefore such matters should not be attracted to the power to search for evidence.

The call to provide exclusionary areas is very dangerous and would lead to a reduction in the efficiency of many criminal investigations. It is likely that the professional criminal will exploit such provisions to hide or protect any evidence and doctors, bankers and other professionals who hitherto might willingly have given information or evidence may be prevented from doing so in fear of the possibility of civil action for breach of confidence.

What is certainly true is that these provisions are most complicated in the way they have been drafted and some further attempt at clarification or simplification would go a long way to reducing the often inaccurate criticism.

The Act in practice

There are many other areas which have attracted adverse publicity and I don't have space to go through them all but when they are fully explained many of the fears prove groundless. For example, the powers to arrest for any offence (Sections 24 and 25) are in essence a rationalisation of powers of arrest and will provide the police with the ability effectively to enforce law by arresting, when to proceed by summons is inappropriate or impossible. It must be stressed, however, that this power will only be available when the actions of the suspect render it necessary and the subject's co-operation will negate completely this power of arrest. It should also be noted these provisions will repeal over 70 existing powers of arrest without warrant (Section 26).

Similarly, if explanations are given on the powers to search a detained person, inherent in the duties of police officers to protect life and property, it is shown that the Act places many limitations upon the extent of the search which do not apply at present (Sections 53 and 54).

Finally, on the subject of specific police powers I should stress that many of the new powers exercised by the police under the Act depend upon the definition of 'serious arrestable offence' and there is lobby which considers that the present definition is drawn too wide (Section 116 and Schedule 5). It is my view, fully supported by my colleagues, that far from being too wide, it is only just sufficient to attach those powers in the Act to the very serious offences for which they are most needed.

There are some further implications of the Police and Criminal Evidence Act which merit attention. The additional financial burdens which will be imposed on the police service will be considerable. There is a need to train all officers in the content and effects of the new legislation and this has to be implemented at the same time as the other additional training commitments with which we are now faced, such as longer probation training for constables, public order training and firearms training. It is almost impossible to quantify the cost of this but even if we only take account of the salaries of officers, the cost of their replacements on operational duties will run into many hundreds of thousands of pounds. Taken nationally the ultimate cost will be many millions of pounds.

The implementation of safeguards and the need for high ranking officers to make many of the necessary day-to-day decisions will create, in my opinion, an unnecessarily excessive administrative burden on the service, and will again require additional finance. For example, the new custody record sheet could necessitate as many as fifty separate entries and every police station which receives prisoners will require constant 24 hour cover by a sergeant solely designated as a custody officer. We have yet to discover what implications in manpower terms these provisions will have in the staffing of one police station, but it is certain there will be no reductions at this level.

The Police and Criminal Evidence Act is now a reality and we must apply it as effectively and efficiently as possible. Let me conclude with an extract from a previous paper which I presented on 'Policing by consent' and which was published in the book entitled *Scarman and After*. In my view the choice presented in the quotation is particularly pertinent to the current debate on police powers:

> In the end it is the public who will decide what kind of police force it wants because its police force will reflect the nature of the society in which it operates. The public must decide whether there should be unrestricted freedom for the individual with all that this implies, or whether liberty should be exercised with a responsibility to the whole community where people can live in their houses in safety or walk the streets of our inner cities without fear of personal attack.[14]

Notes

1. Royal Commission on the Police, *Interim Report*, London: HMSO, 1960 (Cmnd. 1222); *Final Report*, London: HMSO, 1962 (Cmnd. 1728).
2. Royal Commission on Criminal Procedure (Chairman: Sir Cyril Philips), *Report*, London: HMSO, 1981 (Cmnd. 8092).
3. *The Brixton Disorders, 10–12 April 1981: A Report by The Rt. Hon. The Lord Scarman, OBE*, London: HMSO, 1981 (Cmnd. 8427); see especially paragraphs 4.55–4.60. See also discussions in John Benyon (ed.), *Scarman and After*, Oxford: Pergamon, 1984, particularly part 3.
4. Quoted in Thomas A. Critchley, *A History of Police in England and Wales*, London: Constable, 1978, p. 47.
5. *Woman's Own*, 13 March 1984.
6. House of Lords Official Report, Parliamentary Debates (*Hansard*), Session 1983–84, Vol. 453, 26 June 1984, cols. 793–801.
7. House of Commons Official Report, Parliamentary Debates (*Hansard*), Session 1976–77, Vol. 933, Written answers, 24 June 1977, cols. 603–605.
8. *Ibid.*, col. 604.
9. See Royal Commission on Criminal Procedure, *Report*, paragraphs 1.11–1.31.
10. House of Commons Official Report, Parliamentary Debates (*Hansard*) Session 1976–77, Vol. 933, Written answers, 24 June 1977, col. 604.

11. House of Commons Official Report, Parliamentary Debates (*Hansard*), Session 1983–84, Vol. 48, 7 November 1983, cols. 25–26.
12. See for example *The Times*, 15 June 1984; *The Daily Telegraph* 3 July 1984.
13. House of Lords Official Report, Parliamentary Debates (*Hansard*), Session 1983–84, Vol. 453, 26 June 1984, cols. 787–803.
14. Kenneth Oxford, 'Policing by consent' in John Benyon (ed.), *Scarman and After: Essays reflecting on Lord Scarman's Report, the riots and their aftermath*, Oxford: Pergamon Press, 1984, p. 121.

CHAPTER 5

The police and their public

GEORGE GREAVES

It should be stressed at the outset that whereas the police deal with a variety of publics, I will consider the relationship between the police and just one of these. The public I have in mind is that in the London Borough of Lambeth or maybe more specifically the public of Brixton. Lambeth is an area in which the population consists of about twenty-five per cent of people who were born in what is politely termed the New Commonwealth. The Police and Criminal Evidence Act has general implications for policing the streets of the Borough but seems likely particularly to affect the black people of Lambeth.

Minimum necessary safeguards

Many police officers argue that the rules and procedures with which they are obliged to comply enable professional criminals to manipulate the system — see for example Kenneth Oxford's preceding chapter. The police claim that even the new powers which the Act gives them will not prevent these criminals from circumventing the process of justice. This may unfortunately be so, but the other side of the argument must be put as well. My firm impression now, as it was at the height of the disturbances in Brixton in 1981 and 1985, is that insufficient attention is paid to the impact of policing powers on ordinary members of the public. While professional criminals may avoid the long arm of the law, local residents going about their business may be seriously affected by it, and experience in London shows that young black people are the most likely to be stopped by police officers. The dilemma inherent in the Act is how to strike the balance between protecting the rights and liberties of law-abiding citizens and apprehending criminals.

My own impressions are based on the cases which I have witnessed, and on accounts which I have heard. Usually these involve individuals who are themselves innocent of any crime but come into contact with the police because of some misdemeanour of a friend or relative, or who are stopped and searched in the streets.

The Police and Criminal Evidence Act has attempted to create a position whereby the police will have to act and behave according to certain guidelines which are there for everybody to see. This is important because even though discretion is a significant consideration in police work, the rules of behaviour ought to be understood by, and ought to be the same for, all police officers. The safeguards which the Act and the Code of Practice specify seems to be the minimum necessary to achieve a proper balance between the rights of the public and effective policing. How these safeguards work in practice remains to be seen, but I feel that people in Brixton will be pleased to see that they exist.

Some police officers argued fiercely against the amendment moved in the House of Lords which tried unsuccessfully to limit the powers of stop and search to officers in uniform.[1] The view that plain clothes detectives need this power to apprehend criminals may seem fair and reasonable, but it can be looked at in a rather different way.

It is common knowledge that racial attacks on members of the ethnic minorities are a serious problem and are increasing. The Home Office report published in 1981 found considerable evidence of this, and in his foreword to the report, the Home Secretary stated:

> The study has shown quite clearly that the anxieties expressed about racial harassment are justified. Racially motivated attacks, particularly on Asians, are more common than we had supposed; and there are indications that they may be on the increase.[2]

Further evidence is provided in the Greater London Council report on racial harassment published in 1984, and elsewhere.[3]

With this in mind it does not seem unreasonable for a black person in certain parts of London to be apprehensive if he sees one or more white men with short hair, and wearing jeans, approaching him in a very purposeful and determined manner. In these circumstances the black person may have good reason to believe that he is about to be the victim of a racial attack, as unfortunately so many people are on the streets of London and other cities. How is he to know that the men approaching are plain clothes police officers about to exercise their powers to stop and search? The person who is approached may turn and run, which may then be regarded as highly suspicious, or in a state of fear he may seek to defend himself, and end up being charged with obstructing a police officer — or worse. Thus a perfectly innocent man may be adversely affected by the powers of the plain clothes officers.

A case which comes to mind is that of the Newham Eight whose trial at the Old Bailey began on 17 November 1983 and lasted for five weeks. It was alleged that on 24 September 1982 the eight young Asian men had attacked and injured three plain clothes officers, but they were all acquitted of assault and offensive weapons charges, with the exception of one who was convicted of common assault. The jury acquitted four of affray, finding the other four guilty. During the trial it transpired that the Asian men were protecting schoolchildren who had repeatedly been victims of racist threats and assaults about which the police had taken no action. The three plain clothes officers had suddenly arrived in an unmarked District Support Unit car and became embroiled with the men who were protecting the schoolchildren.

Cases like this demonstrate the dangers of plain clothes officers having powers to stop people in the street. It would certainly seem reasonable that only uniformed officers should stop *cars* for a plain clothes officer trying to stop a vehicle is at greater risk than one trying to stop a person! Section 2(9) (b) stipulates that a constable not in uniform is not authorised to stop a vehicle.

'Stop rates for blacks are markedly higher'

It should be stressed that in an area like Brixton the police use of stop and search powers is one of the most annoying actions, and needs to be exercised with great care and discretion. Unfortunately these powers have too often been applied in a heavy-handed fashion, as was Section 4 of the Vagrancy Act of 1824 — popularly known as the 'sus' law — before its repeal in 1981.[4] The prelude to the disturbances in Brixton in April 1981 was a massive stop and search operation, in which 943 people were stopped. The operation, known as 'Swamp 81' was described by Lord Scarman as 'a serious mistake'.[5]

All the evidence shows that the police powers of stop and search are applied disproportionately to black people. Carole Willis in her Home Office Research Unit study carried out in 1982 reported 'that at all four police stations studied annual recorded stop rates for blacks were markedly higher than those for the population as a whole'.[6] She found that young black males were stopped particularly frequently and this finding was confirmed by the detailed Policy Studies Institute investigation which reported a 'radically higher' likelihood. 63 per cent of black men aged between 15 and 24 had been stopped on foot (45 per cent) or in a vehicle (34 per cent) in the past twelve months.[7] Many of these young men had been stopped frequently, and so perhaps it is not surprising that a degree of friction occurs between them and the police.

A welcome inclusion in the Act is the statement that a constable who detains a person or a vehicle need not then conduct a search if it appears to him that it is not required or that the search would be impracticable (Section 2(1)). One is reminded of the incident which sparked off the disturbances in Brixton on Saturday 11 April 1981. On this occasion two officers in plain clothes, involved in the infamous 'Swamp '81' operation, stopped and searched a minicab driver and his vehicle ouside the S & M Car Hire offices in Atlantic Road.[8]

The two young policemen said in evidence to the Scarman Inquiry that it was routine for them to search a person's vehicle, once they had stopped and searched him. They did this outside the S & M Car Hire office even though the hostility of the growing crowd was plain. At Lord Scarman's investigation the following exchange took place:

'If you are getting unfriendly reactions from a crowd is this not something that you might take into account in evaluating whether you are serving the cause of public peace better by continuing or not continuing the search of this kind?'

'I think I would be failing in my duty if I was ever intimidated by a crowd in exercising my authority.'

I believe that a similar attitude was evident among senior ranks in the Metropolitan Police, for when on that evening of 11 April 1981 some people managed to penetrate the lines of rioters an offer was made to Commander Fairbairn which broadly said 'withdraw your men and the rioters will disperse'.[9] The Commander's response was to stand firm, but maybe had he pulled his men back the disorder would have abated. In my view, at this stage, what the people were asking for was some space and an escape route through which to leave the scene.

Powers of entry and search

Another feature of police behaviour which has caused annoyance and upset is the way in which the powers of entry and search have been practised. There seem to be three aspects of these powers which have concerned people. *First*, it appears that very frequently police officers enter a house without showing the occupants any proper authority for doing so. A quick flash of a document as the police barge their way in does not enable the residents to see the authority for the search — if indeed it exists. The Act is quite explicit not only on the requirement for officers to identify themselves but also on the need to produce the search warrant and supply the occupier with a copy of it (Section 16). If the occupier is not present, the copy of the warrant must be left in a prominent place (Section 16(7)).

This stipulation is a welcome improvement and we must hope that it is faithfully followed in practice. However, there is a *second* and even more annoying problem which arises. On many occasions people have complained that policemen have looked in places where the articles identified on the warrant could not possibly be, and have used unnecessary force in conducting the search. For example, cases have arisen where police officers, with a warrant to search for a 26-inch television, emptied drawers, cupboards and other places where a modicum of common sense reveals a large television could not possibly be located. Whether these were what policemen call 'fishing trips', or whether the damage and inconvenience was deliberately being caused, is a matter of speculation. The Code of Practice for the Searching of Premises states that due consideration must be paid to the property and privacy of the occupier with no more disturbance than necessary (paras. 5.8 and 5.9). Those people who have suffered damage as a result of police searches will be interested to see what improvements occur.

The *third* point about the powers of entry concerns those occasions when the occupier is absent from the property and the police arrive to carry out a search. Who is to check the warrant and keep an eye on the officers' conduct? The Act specifies (Section 16) that where some other person appears to be in charge he or she shall be afforded the rights spelled out but the position of juveniles may need clarification. One of the complaints often made is that police officers frequently wait until adults are out of the house before executing a search warrant. For example, the husband may have gone to work and his wife has left home early to do a cleaning stint, leaving the children ready to go off to school and it is then that the police choose to serve their warrant. Consequently there is no adult to witness the manner in which the police carry out the search, and this is a factor which worries many people in Brixton.

Part III of the Act deals with the powers of arrest and it is worth drawing attention to the general arrest conditions outlined in Section 25. One aspect of these which concerns me is that a police officer is given the power to arrest someone if he has 'reasonable grounds for doubting whether an address furnished by the relevant person is a satisfactory address' for subsequent service of a summons (Subsection 3(c)). This does seem likely to place certain people at risk of almost certain arrest for relatively minor matters, if they happen to lead certain lifestyles. For example, police officers may consider that people living in squats fall into this category. I hope the police will interpret these arrest conditions liberally and fairly.

Community involvement in policing policy

Although it is welcome to see Section 106 in the Act one wishes it had perhaps been a more comprehensive attempt to introduce meaningful consultation. This section stipulates that 'arrangements shall be made in each police area for obtaining the views of people in that area about matters concerning the policing of the area and for obtaining their co-operation with the police in preventing crime'. A cynic might be forgiven for believing that this last objective is the real motivation. Perhaps it is worth quoting Lord Scarman's views on this subject:

Community involvement in the policy *and operations* of policing is perfectly feasible without undermining the independence of the police or destroying the secrecy of those operations against crime which have to be kept secret . . . the evidence which I have received convinces me that the boundary between what may, and what must not, be disclosed has not been subjected to a close enough scrutiny.[10]

I do not wish to be drawn into an argument about consultative groups versus police authorities, and in many repects I feel it is a pretty futile debate. In London this is a continuing argument and my own view is that *both* a police authority and consultative groups are necessary, just as proper accountability and consultation are similarly desirable. They are not alternatives and it might be worth pointing out that the proponents of a London police authority may be deluding themselves about the power which such a body would have. I stress this having observed the conduct of the policing of the 1984–1985 miners' strike and the apparent lack of power of the various police authorities to do anything about it.

During the disturbances in Brixton in 1981 and in 1985 I was struck by two things which concern this topic of police–public consultation. First it was clear that the disorders were the culmination of years of growing distress and resentment at police methods and behaviour.[11] Had there been the opportunity for members of the Brixton community to influence and comment on policing practice the downward spiral of relations might have been halted. Second, I also felt that had there been some forum to which people could have gone over that weekend in 1981 it might have been possible to have shortened the duration of the riots.

Recently I read a review of *Scarman and After*[12] in which the Lambeth Community-Police Consultative Group was described as a sort of Hyde Park Corner where people can go and shout at the police and let off steam. To me, anyone who takes this view is being unduly simplistic, for it is like saying that broadcast selections on *Yesterday in Parliament* (BBC Radio 4) is all that Parliament is about. It may be true that the Lambeth Consultative Group does provide an opportunity for people to articulate their concerns, angers and anxieties and to communicate them to the police. But it is also true that it has performed many important functions, not only as a full council but also in its *ad hoc* groups and committees. For example the Consultative Group made several recommendations for amendments to the Police and Criminal Evidence Bill when it was going through the Commons and the Lords. It was also one of the first groups to establish a lay visiting system to police stations, and to check on prisoners in police custody, along the lines suggested by Lord Scarman.[13] It has recently been studying a particular housing estate in the area in order to improve the quality of life for those living there, in terms of creating better community–police relations and combatting crime. So despite the rather dismissive attitude of some, the Consultative Group has an important job to do, and is trying to do it.

Enabling a genuine dialogue

My primary concern about the approach to consultation in the Act is that it is left up to the respective police authorities in consultation with their chief constables to decide upon the appropriate arrangements. In practice in many areas of the country this means the chief constable himself will decide which arrangements best suit him, and that may not necessarily be what is best for the local communities. Clearly different areas may benefit from different methods of consultation, but one hopes that the Home Office will ensure that whatever arrangements are adopted do in fact enable a meaningful dialogue to occur and are not mere 'window dressing'. To achieve this there are two minimal requirements. First, the police themselves must be part of the consultative group and able freely to answer, and to ask, questions and to make comments. Secondly, the committee's meetings and deliberations must take place in public and furthermore members of the public who are not formally on the committee must be allowed to have their say when necessary.

I feel this last point is particularly important, as some people have criticised existing consultative groups on the grounds that they are unrepresentative of some members of the community or are not sufficiently accountable. My experience is that frequently when the Lambeth Consultative Group is in session people in the public gallery ask questions and make comments. This is one of the highest forms of accountability, for when members of the group including the Commander, who always attends, are forced to answer directly the fears, qualms and questions of local people this is the community speaking to their police without the intervention or mediation of anyone. In this way a genuine dialogue can occur.

For example I remember sitting in a meeting of the Consultative Group one evening when three young men walked in and sat quietly in the public area. One could sense that something was agitating them and when the appropriate time arrived they asked for permission to speak. One young man asked one question of the Commander: 'Is it your policy that young men should be asked to drop their trousers and underpants in the streets while they are being stopped and searched?' The Commander said it certainly wasn't his policy, that it shouldn't happen and if it had occurred he apologised. But the matter went further than this, for a formal inquiry was established. Without the local forum, this unsatisfactory police behaviour would probably have gone unreported.

In this way the police force can be confronted with the people they claim to be serving and thus gain a first-hand assessment of public reaction to policing policies and methods. And if we go back again to the Scarman Inquiry it came out quite plainly that the police officer who was supposed to keep the Commander informed about feelings in the community had palpably failed to do so. Community leader after community leader went before Lord Scarman to testify to the heightened level of tension even *prior* to the infamous Operation Swamp yet the man whose responsibility it was to inform Commander Fairbairn advised him to proceed with it. Lord Scarman's view on Operation Swamp provides strong support for the desirability of consultation:

> I do not believe that, consistently with the principles of policing acknowledged as sound by the Metropolitan Police, it could have been authorised in April, *had there been consultation with local leaders* as to the wisdom of mounting it.[14]

It was he said 'a serious mistake'. And my opinion of this episode was strengthened quite recently when I was speaking to newly-promoted sergeants at the Metropolitan Police College at Hendon. One of them said, 'I was stationed at Brixton, and the month before the riots we knew something was happening. People in Railton Road were relating to me differently and I could feel the tension'. So one is left wondering why this information wasn't available to the senior officers who were planning Operation Swamp. If they had consulted their public, as Lord Scarman said, the outcome might have been rather happier.

The police and their public

So there is no excuse for any police authority or chief constable not to take full advantage of Section 106 of the Act and to institute full and effective public–police consultation. This means involving the consultative committee in discussions about all aspects of policing their area, including a dialogue about, and information on, various operations. In support of this contention let me again quote Lord Scarman:

> If a rift is not to develop between the police and the public as a whole (not just the members of the ethnic minority communities), it is in my view *essential* that a means be devised of enabling the community to be heard not only in the development of policing policy but *in the planning of many*, though not all, *operations* against crime.[15]

Let us hope that Section 106 is interpreted sufficiently wisely to fulfill Lord Scarman's prescription.

Whether the hopes and fears which have been expressed about this Act come to be realised remains to be seen. Certainly, from my point of view, there have been some real improvements introduced since the Bill first saw the light of day and if things work out the amendments in the Act should give greater protection to people's rights and civil liberties. I have been concerned to explore some aspects of the Act as it affects policing on the streets, although of course it will have considerable impact in the police station and in the courts and others in this book examine these areas.

With the best will in the world, legislators cannot determine how their laws will be applied in practice and we must hope that police officers will use their powers sensibly having learned from past mistakes. Hopefully, too, the new safeguards and effective consultative machinery will lead to better police practice in areas such as stop and search, which have led to so much friction in the past.

Ordinary people need to be informed about their new rights, new powers of the police and the safeguards against abuse, and it is up to community organisations, such as my own Council for Community Relations in Lambeth, to do this. Police officers are of course left with tremendous discretion about how to enforce the law and about which individuals to detain and charge and which to caution and release. Much will depend on how police officers interpret the new Act, whether they comply with the letter and the spirit of the legislation or whether they choose to bend the rules and circumvent the safeguards. Consequently, we must look to senior officers to be vigilant and determined in their supervision and internal management. So although certain parts of the Police and Criminal Evidence Act 1984 can be welcomed, and other parts can be viewed at best with some suspicion, final judgement must be reserved until 1987 or 1988 after it has been in operation for a year or two.

Notes

1. House of Lords Official Report. Parliamentary Debates (*Hansard*) Session 1983–84, Vol. 453, 26 June 1984, cols. 787–803; the amendment was passed by the Lords but subsequently removed by the Government in the Commons after strong police lobbying.
2. Home Office, *Racial Attacks: Report of a Home Office Study*, London: HMSO, 1981: foreword by the Home Secretary.
3. *Racial Harassment in London*, London: the Greater London Council, 1984; see also: Bethnal Green and Stepney Trades Council, *Blood on the Streets: A Report on Racial Attacks in East London*, London: the Trades Council, 1978; Commission for Racial Equality, *Racial Harassment on Local Authority Housing Estates*, London: CRE, 1981; House of Commons, *Racial Disadvantage: Fifth Report from the Home Affairs Committee, Session 1980–81*, HC 424, London: HMSO, 1981; Colin Brown, *Black and White Britain: the Third PSI Survey*, London: Heinemann, 1984, chapter IX, p. 259–263.
4. For further discussion see George Greaves 'The Brixton disorders' in John Benyon (ed.), *Scarman and After*, Oxford: Pergamon Press, 1984, p. 64–67.
5. *The Brixton Disorders, 10–12 April 1981: A Report by The Rt. Hon. The Lord Scarman, OBE*, London: HMSO, 1981 (Cmnd. 8427), paragraph 4.76.
6. Carol Willis, *The Use, Effectiveness and Impact of Police Stop and Search Powers*, Research and Planning Unit Paper 15, London: Home Office, 1983, p. 14.
7. *Police and People in London*: Volume I: David J. Smith *A Survey of Londoners*, London: Policy Studies Institute, 1983 (PSI No. 618), 95–101. Of course many people were stopped both in a car *and* on foot, which explains why the figures for those stopped in a car and on foot add up to more than the total of 63 per cent who had been stopped.
8. For a full account see *The Brixton Disorders 10–12 April 1981*, *supra* note 5, paragraphs 3.30–3.38.

9. For a verbatim account of this incident see John Clare 'Eyewitness in Brixton' in John Benyon (ed.), *Scarman and After*, Oxford: Pergamon Press, 1984, 48–50; see also *The Brixton Disorders, supra*, note 5, paragraphs 3.57–3.59.

10. *The Brixton Disorders, supra* note 5, paragraph 5.56 (emphasis added).

11. See Lord Scarman's account, *ibid.*, paragraphs 4.1–4.4 and 4.16–4.50.

12. John Benyon (ed.), *Scarman and After; Essays reflecting on Lord Scarman's Report, the riots and their aftermath*, Oxford; Pergamon Press, 1984; see review by Martin Ennals in *Rights*, Vol. 8, No. 2 (Winter 1984) p. 10

13. *The Brixton Disorders, supra* note 5, paragraphs 7.7–7.10.

14. *Ibid.*, paragraph 4.76 (italics added).

15. *Ibid.*, paragraph 5.56 (italics added).

CHAPTER 6

The framework of law and policing practice

DAVID J. SMITH

Administrative agencies are regulatory bodies created to supervise relationships within their jurisdictions. The police on the other hand are not instructed to regulate; their purpose is to enforce prohibitions articulated by the legislature. We do not say to the police: 'Here is the problem. Deal with it.' We say: 'Here is a detailed code. Enforce it.' In short, the police perform a very different function from that of a regulatory agency.[1]

This is the nutshell into which Ronald J. Allen, writing in 1976, put his view about the proper relation between the law and policing practice. Allen was writing of the United States, and he was specifically arguing against the idea that the police properly have the power to make or act on 'substantive rules' which have the effect of changing the laws: for example, by not enforcing some of them. But if we liberate Allen's nutshell from its specific context, it amounts to a neat statement of what might be called the simple theory of the relation between the law and the pattern of policing. The legislature enacts the laws, the police have the duty to enforce them and all of them equally. Does the legislature wish to control the manner in which the police go about their duty of enforcing all of the laws? Very well, it passes further laws that define limits of conduct and effectively set out a code of behaviour for the police, who of course have a duty to obey. On this view policing is essentially a matter of following rules that derive from the law. If the police do not, in practice, follow these rules, the remedy, as in the case of drivers who park on yellow lines, is the consistent application of suitable sanctions.

Legal opportunities and constraints

The purpose of this chapter is to show that this simple view is fundamentally mistaken. Very little of the shape of policing or of its detailed texture can be understood as deriving directly from rules enshrined in law. We *do* say to the police: 'Here is a problem. Deal with it.' We *also* say to them: 'Here is a code. Be limited and guided by it.' But we are mistaken if we think that the pattern of policing can be simply a function of the code, or if we think that by producing a code, which is bound to lack detail in many important respects, we have done all that is necessary or all that we can to shape and control policing behaviour.

Following on from this general argument, a secondary purpose of this essay is to show that the detailed changes in the code that are contained in the Police and Criminal Evidence Act, particularly those concerned with police activity on the streets, *will have only a marginal influence on practice*. The Act is *not* an attempt to reshape British policing in the light of the conditions obtaining in the last part of the twentieth century. It is neither a great extension of policing powers at the expense of the individual nor an issue to the police of the armaments they need in the fight against crime, nor a set of liberal measures that will effectively control and circumscribe police discretion. Mostly it is just a combing out of snags and a tying up of loose ends that leaves unaltered the basic conditions and constraints within which the police operate and which shape their behaviour.

Of course, the broad structure of the system of which the police are part — the system of law and administration of justice — has an enormous influence, and in some respects the decisive influence, in shaping policing practice in general and police behaviour at the individual level. However, this influence is not exerted in a direct, simple or straightforward manner. It is not possible to understand the influence by picturing the police as obeying instructions contained in the law or responding directly to imperatives that are otherwise made explicit by the criminal justice system. For example, the police tend to arrest suspects in preference to acting by means of a summons, hold them for a while before charging them and encourage them in various ways to make a confession. There is no law that imposes this policy on them — in fact some argued that before the Police and Evidence Act that various aspects of this policy were unlawful.

Furthermore, this policy does not seem to flow from an explicit imperative of the system in that confession evidence, though usually present, is crucial in only about 20 per cent of Crown Court cases, according to research carried out by John Baldwin and Michael McConville.[2] But research also shows that suspects who have made a confession strongly tend to plead guilty so that their cases are usually dealt with by summary trial.[3] This saves an enormous amount of time and trouble for the police and incidentally for the courts.

Thus, the properties of the system — the huge difference between summary and full trial, the fact that the plea often determines the form of trial — induce the police to place a high value on confessions, to proceed by arrest rather than summons, and to hold suspects before charging them. It is significant that the Police and Criminal Evidence Act seeks to regulate the resulting police practices affecting suspects at police stations by means of detailed rules, but does not seek to change the basic conditions that lead to the reliance on confessions as evidence.

The law and the criminal justice system do not primarily influence the police by means of direct and explicit instructions, and especially not by detailed ones. It is more helpful to say that they define a set of opportunities and constraints. Powers conferred by the law are resources that the police may use in pursuing any of their objectives. The boundaries of these powers, if there are any penalties for over-stepping them, are constraints on the freedom of the police in choosing the means to pursue objectives. Thus policing is shaped around the framework of opportunities and constraints defined by the law and criminal procedure, but as the constraints are not absolute the skeleton is flexible. Another way in which the law has an influence is as one source of the inward principles that guide the conduct of police officers. But these inward principles also come from other sources and may contradict the law: for example, our research in London suggests that a considerable number of police officers sincerely believe that some offenders (such as child molesters) ought to be beaten up at police stations.[4]

The idea that police powers are police resources is not a cynical interpretation, and it does not arise solely from adopting a police perspective: on the contrary, it is built into the law itself. Much of the vocabulary of the law, especially in the civil field, is about 'remedies that are available', or in other words resources that the citizen may use to try to get what he wants. In the criminal field, a number of offences are intentionally defined vaguely to give the police discretionary powers or the citizen a recourse to the law in extreme cases. The most obvious examples are 'threatening, abusive or insulting words or behaviour with intent to provoke a breach of the peace, or whereby a breach of the peace may be occasioned'; 'resisting or obstructing a constable in the execution of his duty'; 'obstructing the free passage along a highway'.

Offences such as these are only intelligible as charges which the police may use to help them control a situation they judge needs controlling; they simply cannot be understood as definitions of acts or cirumstances against which the police are instructed to proceed.

At the same time the existence of such offences is among the most fundamental and important of police powers. The power to stop and search, which will be discussed in more detail later, is a prime example of a power that has intentionally been defined vaguely so as to give the police a flexible resource.

Three kinds of policing rules

It is important to emphasise that the law and the criminal justice system are a source of opportunities and constraints for police officers, but the traditional view that they are a source of rules also has some truth in it. Here two qualifications are important. The first is the one already made: that rules may also come from other sources, for example from the occupational culture. The second qualification is that rules may be of different kinds, and depending on their kind they will have a more or less consistent influence.

Because a rule exists, it does not follow that it rigidly governs day-to-day policing behaviour. At the extreme, a rule may be universally ignored and never invoked to discipline anyone. More important are the intermediate cases where a rule is invoked only in certain circumstances, and where it has some effect but not the simple and direct influence that might be imagined. There are many reasons why this should happen. There is usually considerable scope for different interpretations, for example of the rule that officers should only use what force is necessary to make an arrest. Information about what the officer actually did is usually very limited because of a lack of independent witnesses, the strong tendency for officers to back each other up and the small amount of direct supervision. Also, there may be a sharp conflict between 'doing the job well' — that is, achieving objectives that are widely recognised inside or outside the force as being desirable — and sticking to the rules. For all of these reasons, a gap opens up between the formal rules and procedures and the kind of behaviour that police officers generally recognise as being acceptable.

One way of putting this is to say that while police officers know what the rules are and bear in mind the consequences of being found to have broken them, not all the rules become internalised into guiding principles of their behaviour. To take a minor example, an area car is formally forbidden to drive at high speed, with siren going and light flashing, to a call to which it has not been assigned. The driver may not think it is wrong to do this, he may not blame himself for doing it, but he knows that if he crashes the car on the way he is liable to be disciplined. In that case, the rule has an influence as an external hazard with which the driver has to contend and not as a personal rule of conduct. The driver has to weigh up the chances of coming unstuck if he goes to the call, but may well decide to risk it, especially if he feels (according to a different code) that he is expected to go because another police officer is in danger.

Where the rules *are* internalised, they are likely to have a far more consistent controlling influence. For example, if officers believe that it is wrong to behave oppressively towards suspects in order to get confessions, they will never, or almost never, do so; if they do not believe it is wrong, at any rate in certain circumstances, but regard the rule as a hazard to be taken into account in deciding how to behave, they will still be restrained to some extent by the rule, but may behave oppressively if they personally feel it is justified and they think they can get away with it.

A third kind of function of rules is to put a gloss on policing behaviour so as to make it acceptable to the wider public. I would argue, for example, that the limitation by law of police powers to stop and search people on foot amounts to a set of rules with a largely cosmetic function. *In theory*, police officers may only stop and search people who they 'reasonably suspect' to be in possession of stolen goods or controlled drugs; *in practice* they can stop and search virtually anyone, and a police officer will rarely be disciplined or reprimanded for making a stop where he was not entitled by law to do so, though he may be criticised for making a stop that is most unlikely to produce a 'result'.

A convenient way of summarising this analysis is to distinguish three kinds of rules. *Working rules* are those that are internalised by police officers to become guiding principles of their conduct. *Inhibitory rules* are those which are not internalised, but which police officers take into account when deciding how to act and which tend to discourage them from behaving in certain ways in case they should be caught and the rule invoked against them. *Presentational rules* are ones that exist to give an acceptable appearance to the way that police work is carried out.

It is important to realise that it is not only or even mainly the police who seek to put this gloss on the reality of policing behaviour. Most of the presentational rules derive from the law and are part of a successful attempt by the wider society to deceive itself about the realities of policing. In addition to this complexity of rules, only some of which come from the law, there are policing *goals* to be considered. Admittedly, it is one of the most striking features of police forces that they do not have, at the level of organisation, a clear idea of what they are trying to achieve. But constables do have goals of their own, which shape their behaviour. Yet the law does not define goals for the police except at the most general level ('keeping the peace' or 'enforcing the law'), so specific policing objectives have to come from somewhere else.

The unchanged basic structure

Here is a summary of the argument so far. Discussion of the Police and Criminal Evidence Act tends to be based on a false picture of the relation between the law and policing practice. This picture is that the law specifies what the police should and should not do by enunciating a set of detailed instructions, and the obedience of the police to these instructions is enforced by the criminal justice system. It is true that the broad structure of the law and of the system for administering justice do play a crucial part in shaping the pattern of policing, but detailed provisions of the law do not influence the police in a direct and simple way.

One reason for this is that some of the most important police powers are intentionally defined very vaguely, so that the law provides a set of flexible resources and constraints rather than a set of instructions to the police. Secondly, while the law is a source of rules for the police, there are other equally important sources and there is a complexity of different kinds of rule which do not all have consistent or rigid effects (especially those deriving from the law). Thirdly, small groups of police officers and individuals have policing goals which are not given by the law at all.

A further weakness in the simple model lies in the assumption that the criminal justice system can enforce obedience by the police to the specific instructions that are supposed to be contained in the law. The particular problem that arises here is one of *self-reference*. The police themselves are a central part of the criminal justice system which is supposed to enforce their obedience. The familiar complaint about the police complaints system — than it involves the police investigating the police — is only a particular case of the difficulty that arises when the principal method of controlling the enforcement agency is for it to enforce the law on itself. Of course, there may be an attempt to install jaws, equipped with enforcement teeth, in parts of the criminal justice system that are as distinct from the police as possible, but even then some co-operation from the police is usually required if the jaws are to bite them.

The difficulty is increased by the tendency, over the past hundred years, for the police to spread into areas not originally set aside for them — for example, to take on an inquisitorial role — so that finding places to install the teeth that they do not influence is difficult. At the simplest level, police evidence is usually crucial in any case in which the police are alleged to have exceeded their powers. This does not mean that all enforcement is impossible or that the law cannot be a constraint on serious police misconduct. It does mean that enforcement is intrinsically difficult and that we had better look also to other methods of shaping police behaviour.

In all of these circumstances, detailed changes in the law are not likely in themselves to have an important effect on police practice. For the most part, the Police and Criminal Evidence Act does not alter the broad structure of law and procedure that surrounds the police. Arguments about whether the provisions for holding suspects at police stations are an attack on ancient rights or an attempt to safeguard the individual are largely arguments about nothing. These provisions may reasonably be expected to lead to an improvement, from the suspect's point of view, on recent practice. They may, at the same time, be held to be a statutory concession of what the courts had already conceded, at least by default, and hence an attack on rights still theoretically existing if not, at least in recent times, exercisable in practice. In any case, these are not important structural changes in that suspects have in recent times been arrested and held at police stations prior to charging, sometimes for several days, and this will continue to happen, subject to slightly improved safeguards (the Act, Sections 34–52). The decision to legitimise this practice is not, of course, based on any proper analysis of the contribution that it makes to the detection or prevention of crime.

Similar comments could be made about the codification of the arrest and search powers (Sections 1–33). The most basic aspects of the structure, which profoundly influence police behaviour, remain unchanged by that Act: the clearest examples are the relation between guilty plea and summary trial, and the influence of the police over whether or not a suspect is granted bail. The one provision of the Act that does affect 'deep structure' is the facilitating of tape-recording of interviews of suspects in police custody (Section 60). Depending on just how this is implemented, it could be a way out of the problem of the police being responsible for imposing standards on themselves. Another proposal that will affect the 'deep structure', is the creation of a Crown Prosecution Service by the Prosecution of Offences Act 1985. It should be noticed that these changes, which will influence policing, are not detailed codes of instructions to the police, but changes in the *basic conditions* within which they work.

The operation of stop and search

Stop and search is the clearest example of a pattern of policing policy, which cannot effectively be controlled by instructions contained in the law. The study of *Police and People in London* that we carried out at the Policy Studies Institute provided the clearest possible evidence of the impotence of the legal constraints in limiting stop and search. Evidence was provided by three complementary studies: a survey of 2,420 Londoners in which they described the particular occasions on which they had been stopped by the police in the previous twelve months; a survey of 1,800 police officers who described the stops they had made on the last day within the previous two weeks when they had done any work of this kind; and observation of police work (including stops) by two researchers over a two-year period.[5]

Our findings from all three sources agree in showing that the criterion of 'reasonable suspicion' did *not* act as an effective constraint on police officers in deciding whether to make a stop. In a substantial proportion of cases where stops were reported in the survey of police officers, the officer did not give what we judged to be a 'good' reason for making the stop.[6] We could see no good reason for the stop in one-third of the cases recorded in the course of our observational work[7]; closely in accord with this, the survey of Londoners showed that for 38 per cent of stops the person involved thought the police had no good reason for making the stop.[8]

Further, it was clear from the way that police officers talked about stops that the question of what their legal powers might be did not enter into their decision-making except in the case of rare individuals. They did, of course, consider the chance of getting a 'result', but factors that they associated with the chance of getting a 'result' were often unconnected with the concept of 'reasonable suspicion' on which the legal rules are based. One reason why the legal powers have little relevance is that most people do not know what they are. We never saw anyone openly challenge the right of the police to stop, search and question them, nor did anyone ever refuse to answer questions.

Our studies clearly show that stop and search was easily the most widely used active policing policy in London in 1981–1982, in spite of the fact that a substantial proportion of stops was not justifiable within the terms of the law. We estimate that stops were being carried out at a rate of about 1.5 million a year, or a higher rate if the accounts of police officers in the survey are taken as the basis for the estimate.[9] A substantial minority of the population (16 per cent) had been stopped by the police once or more often in the previous 12 months, but certain population groups were far more likely to be stopped than others: within certain groups, the chance of being stopped in a twelve-month period was well over 50 per cent, and a high proportion of these groups had been stopped several times in that period. The groups most likely to be stopped were young people, men and people of West Indian origin; and young men of West Indian origin had the highest chance of being stopped.[10]

Stops therefore bring the police into frequent contact with members of certain highly specific groups, but very rarely with the majority of the public who do not belong to these groups. The policy is, therefore, in a sense, divisive; if there is a price to be paid in terms of police–public relations, it will be in relations with specific groups and in a sharp division of experience and opinion between the minority who are stopped and the majority who are not. Our studies confirm that there is such a price to be paid, and that it is substantial. People who have been stopped by the police, and especially those who have been stopped repeatedly, tend to be far more critical of the police than others.[11] This is an important part of the explanation for the strong hostility to the police that is expressed by half or more of young black Londoners.[12] The policy of carrying out stop and search on a large scale has this effect, paradoxically, in spite of the fact that four-fifths of stops are reasonably amiable encounters, as we know from the concordant accounts of people stopped, of police officers and of independent observers.[13] It is, however, interesting and important that the minority of cases where people complain about police behaviour in making a stop are most likely to occur where the police officer failed to convey an explanation or reason. Still, our findings make it clear that the fact of being stopped, especially if it happens repeatedly, causes people to be hostile to the police even where there are no specific criticisms to be made of police behaviour on these occasions.

Effective regulation of police policy

This discussion has shown that the policy of stop and search on a large scale that was in operation in London in 1981–1982 did not flow from the law as from an instruction; indeed, many of the stops were contrary to the law, but the boundaries set by the legislation were largely irrelevant and ineffective as a constraint on police behaviour. Secondly, it has shown that the policy carried substantial costs in terms of relations with certain population groups. Our studies are also able to provide some assessment of the benefits. The two surveys are in agreement in showing that only a small proportion of the individuals who were stopped (between 3 and 5 per cent) were arrested as a result, and the survey of Londoners shows that a further 5 per cent were reported for an offence (generally a traffic offence).[14]

Overall about one in twelve stops lead to a 'result' that is an arrest or report. From one perspective, this strike rate seems low. It means that the great majority of people stopped must be presumed to be 'innocent persons', and this of course re-emphasises the point that in many cases the criterion of reasonable suspicion was not met. From a different perspective, our findings show that the stops made in London at the time resulted in the detection of a very substantial number of offences — perhaps more than 100,000 a year. Also the survey of police officers shows that about one-quarter of arrests arise directly from a stop.

Perhaps the most important implication of these findings is that a policy like stop and search *cannot be effectively regulated through the law* and its embodiment in the criminal justice system. A law on stop and search is essentially permissive; like the law against obstructing a police officer it represents a resource that the police may use. We can argue about whether the police exceed their statutory power — I say they do — but this is ultimately irrelevant since there is no conceivable way in which such a vague (and necessarily vague) criterion as 'reasonable suspicion' can be made to constitute an effective constraint. In this field, the law is just a source of *presentational rules* which exist to put an acceptable face on practices we prefer not to look at squarely.

In my view, the changes in the Police and Criminal Evidence Act to stop and search powers — in relation to the extension to offensive weapons (Section 1) and the recording provisions (Section 3) — do not make any substantive difference. Parliament did have the serious option of withdrawing the powers altogether. Given that is was not going to do that, we are left with a permissive power, and the second implication of our findings is that this power could and can be exercised in many different ways — the scale of stopping practice and the way it is done can vary infinitely within the provisions of this law. I do not complain about this. But the conclusion that emerges particularly clearly from this example, as also from others, is that we must consider the many factors other than the law which contribute towards shaping policing practice, and we must find ways of influencing policing policy other than through the law.

There should be a structure within which police and elected representatives can consider not the *legality* of stop and search, but *what level and nature* of stop and search *policy* is most productive in terms of the objectives it is thought are proper to policing. Here one of the first questions to be considered is whether the 100,000 offences detected per annum by stop and search in London could be detected or prevented by alternative policing policies that are no more expensive in police time but less costly in relations with the public. The tidying up exercise that the Police and Criminal Evidence Act represents should not divert us from these other, more important, issues.

Notes

1. Ronald J. Allen, 'The police and substantive rulemaking: reconciling principle and expediency', *University of Pennsylvania Law Review*, November 1976, p. 97.
2. John Baldwin and Michael McConville, *Confessions in Crown Court Trials*, London: HMSO, 1980 (Royal Commission on Criminal Procedure Research Study No. 5).
3. Michael McConville and John Baldwin, *Courts, Prosecution and Conviction*, London: Oxford University Press, 1981.
4. *Police and People in London*, Vol. 4: David J. Smith and Jeremy Gray, *The Police in Action*, London: Policy Studies Institute, 1983 (PSI No. 621), see Ch. 3, pp. 49–108, and pp. 181–2.
5. The findings of this study were published by the Policy Studies Institute in 1983 in four volumes under the title: *Police and People in London*. Vol. 1: David J. Smith, *A Survey of Londoners*, London: Policy Studies Institute, 1983 (PSI No. 618); Vol. 2: Stephen Small, *A Group of Young Black People*, London: Policy Studies Institute, 1983 (PSI No. 619); Vol. 3: David J. Smith, *A Survey of Police Officers*, London: Policy Studies Institute, 1983 (PSI No. 620); David J. Smith and Jeremy Gray, *The Police in Action*, London: Policy Studies Institute, 1983 (PSI No. 621). Volumes 1 and 2 are also available as a book published by Gower in 1985; page references are given to the original edition.
6. Smith, *A Survey of Police Officers*, *supra* note 5, pp. 97–103, and p. 185.
7. Smith and Gray, *The Police in Action*, *supra* note 5, pp. 230–239.
8. Smith, *A Survey of Londoners*, *supra* note 5, pp. 89–118; see table IV. 12, p. 110 for data on assessment of police behaviour.
9. The derivation of the estimate from the survey of Londoners is given in Smith, *A Survey of Londoners*, *supra* note 5, p. 92.
10. *Ibid.*, pp. 90–102.
11. *Ibid.*, pp. 276–285.
12. *Ibid.*, pp. 187–201, 317–319.
13. *Ibid.*, pp. 111–113; Smith, *A Survey of Police Officers*, *supra* note 5, pp. 99–103; Smith and Gray, *The Police in Action*, *supra* note 5, p. 234.
14. Smith, *A Survey of Londoners*, *supra* note 5, pp. 113–118; Smith, *A Survey of Police Officers*, *supra* note 5, p. 103.

CHAPTER 7

Policing the streets

LESLIE CURTIS

It will come as no surprise to most people to learn that the Police Federation's view[1] of the Police and Criminal Evidence Act is the complete opposite of that of its critics. However, the Act is on the statute book and there is nothing to be gained by a re-run of all the bitter arguments — often wild flights of fancy — that surrounded the long passage of the Bill through Parliament.

The need to rectify an illogical position

I want to look at this subject — the way in which the Act is likely to operate on the streets — through the eyes and minds of the people for whom we in the Police Federation speak — the thousands of ordinary, and in the main very young, police constables. Day after day and night after night, these officers are carrying out their duties in a society where, in many areas, *the fear of crime*, which I accept is different from the *reality of crime*, has never been greater.[2]

Let me start by going back, briefly, to what the Police Federation said to the Royal Commission on Criminal Procedure.[3] We pointed out then that although the police service had doubled in size since the end of the war the crime rate had increased fivefold. We said, 'The chances of arresting, and still less of *convicting* the more dangerous, cunning and resourceful of criminals, appear to be diminishing year by year'.

Of course we fully accept that in the vast majority of cases which first come to the notice of police officers doing duty on the streets, and the type of suspect they come across, do not fit into the 'dangerous', 'cunning' or 'resourceful' category. However, the crime statistics certainly look daunting especially since they passed the three million mark.[4] The vast majority of offences, thank goodness, are relatively trivial, non-violent, and not attributable to professional, organised crime. Yet it has to be the same Act which governs police powers when dealing with the sneak-thief, the shop lifter and all the other petty offenders, up the scale to the armed robber, and the murderer.

This is why I believe that there was an air of unreality about so much of the criticism of the so-called extensions of the police powers in the Act. It really was stretching the imagination too far to suggest, as some opponents of the legislation have done, that powers to detain without charge are going to be used as the rule, rather than the exception. After all, more than a million arrests for crime are made every year with the overwhelming majority of those arrested being given bail within a matter of a few hours of their arrest.

The same point applies to the arguments about stop and search powers, which are of immediate concern to ordinary police officers, and the Police Federation welcomes the general power of stop and search, which the Act gives to the police throughout England and Wales. As we told the Royal Commission, it has been a totally illogical position that some forces, notably the Metropolitan Police, have had a specific power to stop and search, while the rest have not.

Confusion still reigns

The question of the use of police powers on the streets has been at the core of local tensions between the police and some sections of the community for many years. Independently of the Royal Commission, and of this Act, the present Government repealed the Vagrancy Act section dealing with suspected persons, and replaced it with the Criminal Attempts Law.[5] But there is no doubt that a great deal of confusion still reigns about this question of 'sus', and it has become a kind of general term to apply to stop and search powers by the police in general.[6]

Our anxiety about the abolition of the power of arrest of suspected persons was that it would be interpreted as a general prohibition on the existing powers of stop and search in the Metropolitan Police area. As we told the Royal Commission:

> Over the last few years more and more members of the public, particularly young people, have become aware of the limitations of the powers of the police in stopping someone on the street. Often their reaction is simply to abuse the police officer and to tell him to leave in no uncertain colloquial fashion. The young policemen finds this situation far from humorous. It can give rise to bitterness on both sides.

Therefore, the Police Federation is obviously pleased that there is to be a general power of stop and search. But what needs to be emphasised is that this power is now far more clearly defined, and far more *restricted* than ever it was in the past (the Act: Sections 1–3).

The *Code of Practice for the Exercise by Police Officers of Statutory Powers of Stop and Search* spells this out. For example, the Code says that before any search of a detained person or vehicle takes place the officer is obliged to give the person to be searched, or in charge of the vehicle, his name and the name of the police station to which he is attached, the object of the search, and his grounds for undertaking it (Section 2, subsections (2) and (3) of the Act; paragraphs 2.1–2.4 of the Code). *And* if the officer is not in uniform, he has to produce his warrant card (Section 2, subsection (2); paragraph 2.5 of the Code). I must stress in passing that the Police Federation welcomed the rejection of the wholly absurd amendment, passed in the House of Lords, which would have restricted stop and search powers to police officers in uniform.[7]

Furthermore, having established his own identity as a police officer, and having explained the object of the search and the grounds for making it, the officer has to tell the person concerned that he is entitled to a copy of the record of the search if he asks for it *within a year*. If a person asks for it *there and then* the officer is obliged to make out the record of the search at that time, unless there are circumstances which make it impractical. In which case the person must be told that he can have it if he asks for the copy at the officer's police station (the Act: Section 3; the Code: paragraphs 2.6–2.7). Bearing in mind the practical application of stop and search powers to some incidents on the streets, the imagination boggles as to how young police officers are going to fulfill all of the obligations placed upon them.

Practical problems with the stop and search procedures

We are probably all familiar with the Hollywood crime series, in which the detective spells out the *Miranda* warning to people he has arrested, or he says to a subordinate, 'read him his rights, Al'. I have a picture in my mind of a young police officer attempting to detain a struggling suspect, who is anxious to escape, and trying to hold him still long enough to say:

> My name is Police Constable 455 Algernon Nigel Arbuthnot. I am attached to Paddington Green Police Station. I am trying to detain you in order that I can search you because I suspect that you have just mugged an old lady around the corner, and I am looking for her purse. The reason I suspect you, is that you answer the description of the young man seen running away, and you were running when I stopped you. I also have to inform you that you are entitled to a copy of the record of this search which I am obliged to make straight away, but as it is raining. . . .

The Code even states that it is required, in accordance with the Act, that if the person to be searched cannot understand what is being said, then 'the officer must take reasonable steps' to ensure that the person does understand that he is being stopped and searched by a police officer and the reasons why, and that he is entitled to a record of the search (the Code:

paragraph 2.7). So the extent to which the police powers have been *restricted*, rather than massively extended, by this Act becomes very clear the more we delve into the question of stop and search.

For example, to quote again from the Code of Practice:

> The thoroughness and extent of a search must depend on what is suspected of being carried and by whom. If the suspicion relates to a particular article, for example an offensive weapon, which is seen to be slipped into a person's pocket then, in the absence of other grounds for suspicion or an opportunity for the article to be moved elsewhere, *the search must be confined to that pocket* (the Code: paragraph 3.3, emphasis added).

Must it indeed?

The codes are statutory so they have the force of law. What happens, then, if having searched the pocket on reasonable suspicion and having drawn a blank, the officer becomes aware of a bulky package in *another* pocket, which turns out to be a parcel of drugs, or an offensive weapon, or stolen property? As the Code specifically restricts his right of search to the pocket which he believed when he made the search contained an offensive weapon or stolen property, and there has been no opportunity for the article to be moved elsewhere, then the officer's action in searching that other pocket would appear to be illegal.

I suppose the correct course of action will be for the officer to say, 'Well, I am now satisfied that your left hand pocket does not contain, as I suspected, a flick-knife but my reasonable suspicions have now been aroused about the contents of your right hand pocket.' Then he must begin all over again:

> I am Police Constable 455 Algernon Nigel Arbuthnot. I am attached to Paddington Green Police Station. I am trying to detain you in order that I can search you because I suspect. . . .

For the benefit of both the public and our members, the Police Federation asked the Royal Commission for a statutory code which would cover police powers of stopping and searching, arrest, detention and questioning. However, I am bound to comment that what has emerged from the Home Office bedevils description.

Further problems with the Code

We were forced to write to the Home Secretary to protest that the section in the Code of Practice on searching was drafted by somebody who has never made a search in his life, and has never seen the kind of problems that the policeman faces on the street. The Code, for example, goes into great detail about how far an officer can go in making a search in the street.

Paragraph 3.5 draws attention to Section 2(9) of the Act which states that there is no power to require a person to remove any clothing, other than an outer coat, jacket or gloves. Parliament specifically rejected a Police Federation amendment which would have enabled an officer to require a person to remove his *hat*.

This may sound amusing or even trivial but we had good reason to propose this amendment. A couple of years ago, a young officer in a county force put a prisoner in the back of his panda car after a superficial search. He didn't ask his prisoner to take off his woolly hat. On the way to the police station, the prisoner in the back seat removed a razor blade from that hat and cut the policeman's throat. Fortunately the officer survived after an emergency operation.

The Code says that if a police officer wants somebody to remove his headgear, then he must take him to a police van or a nearby police station if there is one, or to somewhere else out of the public view (the Code: paragraph 3.5). It never seemed to occur to the legislators, or to the civil service minds which drew up this Code of Practice, that the very action of taking a suspect out of the public view, in some circumstances, will lead to the kind of incident that this Code of Practice is at such pains to avoid. Moreover, what are police officers to make of a Code which says in the notes for guidance, 'a search in the street itself should be regarded as being in public . . . even though it may be empty at the time a search begins' (paragraph 3A). The novel idea that a highway ceases to be a public place because the only people present are the police officer and a suspect, had never occurred to the Police Federation.

The same paragraph states: 'Although there is no power to require a person to do so, there is nothing to prevent an officer from asking a person voluntarily to remove more than an outer coat, jacket or gloves in public.' What it really means is that the police constable says to the suspect. 'And would you mind removing your hat?' and the suspect says, 'Actually officer, I'd rather not', or words to that effect. I suppose it is permissible to have a little bit of fun with these, no doubt, well-meaning efforts to spell out the extent of police powers for the benefit of the police and the public alike. The serious side of the coin is that the Code and the wording of the Act make nonsense of the hysterical onslaught which was mounted upon the Police and Criminal Evidence Bill in general.

It is necessary to stress again and again that the statutory codes of practice[8] are going to govern the actions of police officers going about their normal duties of crime prevention and investigation on the streets of this country and that any breach of those codes of practice may in itself constitute a police disciplinary offence. Further I should point out that Parliament, not in its wisdom but as part of a shabby procedural deal between the Government and the Opposition, has added the racial discrimination clause to the Police Discipline Code (the Act: Section

Policing the streets has become more and more difficult as the years have passed — but will the Police and Criminal Evidence Act make a real impact in the fight against crime?

101(6)). This, in our view, has added immeasurably to the difficulties facing young officers in multi-racial areas where tensions exist.

The Act which fails to measure up

It is not the view of the police service that the Police and Criminal Evidence Act measures up to what was required: that is a comprehensive statute embodying all police powers in the criminal investigation process which could be clearly understood by all concerned. The Police Federation wanted legislation which maintained the balance between the interests of society in fighting crime and the rights of the suspects and this fundamental balance was after all the basis of the Royal Commission's terms of reference.[9] Police officers will still be faced with a multitude of conflicting powers arising from different pieces of legislation.

There will have to be a massive programme of training for the police before the Act becomes fully operative, and what disturbs me is that there is not going to be a corresponding programme of *public* education. On the contrary, in the case of that part of the population which is most likely to find itself in conflict with the police there has been a massive campaign of disinformation and downright lies which have produced an atmosphere of greater hostility, greater suspicion and greater misunderstanding from the outset.

The part of the Act with which I am particularly concerned in this chapter — the Act on the streets — is likely to be the testing ground for case after case in which the actions of individual, and largely inexperienced, officers are going to be subjected to detailed scrutiny in the criminal courts. The test of the Act will be whether it can be sustained in the courts or whether it will become another of those pieces of legislation which turn out to be shot through with legal loopholes. Meanwhile, for officers themselves policing the streets, the result of the Act is likely to be less positive than we had hoped in 1978 and 1979 when the Royal Commission got down to work. The fact is that policing the streets has become more and more difficult as the years have passed and it requires a degree of understanding and political and social awareness that used not to figure in police training or indeed in police experience.[10]

In the long run the police service will probably be well advised to pin its faith on more sophisticated, and more practically-based, training of officers in street duties and human awareness than in the ability of this Act to make a real impact in the fight against crime.

The police service has shown in recent years a measure of adaptability and a readiness to submit itself to self analysis, as well as to outside examination, and a willingness to accept change where change is needed. The pity is that the most conservative elements are those who have spent the last ten or fifteen years in constant criticism of the police and will not themselves face up to what is so obvious: that police efforts to improve the level of understanding and co-operation on the streets of our inner cities will not succeed unless there is a corresponding movement to raise the level of *public* support and understanding of police objectives.

The campaign against the Police and Criminal Evidence Act set out to do real damage to those objectives. I hope that the Act in practice will lead to better things, but unfortunately I have my doubts.

Notes

1. The Police Federation of England and Wales is the statutory body which represents the ranks of the police service up to and including chief inspectors. The Federation is charged with making representations on all matters affecting the welfare and efficiency of the police service. Full details on its work can be obtained from the Secretary, Police Federation of England and Wales, 15–17 Langley Road, Surbiton, Surrey. KT6 6LP.
2. See, for example, Mike Hough and Pat Mayhew, *The British Crime Survey: First Report*, Home Office Research Study No. 76, London: HMSO, 1983; Michael Maxfield, *Fear of Crime in England and Wales*, Home Office Research Study No. 78, London: HMSO, 1984; Michael Gottfredson, *Victims of Crime: the Dimensions of Risk*, Home Office Research Study No. 81, London: HMSO, 1984.
3. Royal Commission on Criminal Procedure, *The Investigation and Prosecution of Offences in England and Wales: The Law and Procedure*, London: HMSO, 1981 (Cmnd. 8092–1).
4. See Home Office, *Criminal Statistics: England and Wales*, London: HMSO, published annually by Command. The number of notifiable offences passed three million in 1982 but in the following year actually showed a small drop: Home Office, *Criminal Statistics: England and Wales, 1983*, London: HMSO, September 1984 (Cmnd. 9349), pp. 18–19. See also *The British Crime Survey*, *supra*, note 2.
5. 'Sus' was the popular shorthand for the charge of being a suspected person under Section 4 of the Vagrancy Act 1824, the relevant parts of which were repealed by Section 8 of the Criminal Attempts Act 1981. The subject was examined in detail by the Home Affairs Sub-Committee of the House of Commons on Race Relations and Immigration: see, House of Commons, *Race Relations and the 'Sus' Law: Second Report from the Home Affairs Committee, Session 1979–80*, HC 559, London: HMSO, 1980.
6. See for example A. Brogden, '"Sus" is dead but what about "Sas"?', *New Community*, 9, 1 (Summer 1981).
7. House of Lords Official Report, Parliamentary Debates (*Hansard*), Session 1983–84, Vol. 453, 26 June 1984, cols. 78–303.
8. Section 66 of the Police and Criminal Evidence Act 1984 requires the Home Secretary to issue codes of practice in connection with:
    (a) The exercise by police officers of statutory powers —
        (i) to search a person without first arresting him; or
        (ii) to search a vehicle without making an arrest.
    (b) The detention, treatment, questioning and identification of persons by police officers.
    (c) Searches of premises by police officers.
    (d) The seizure of property found by police officers on persons or premises.
    Two codes have been issued in respect of (b) above, a further code covers (c) and (d) and the fourth code covers (a); it is this code which is considered in this chapter.
9. Royal Commission on Criminal Procedure (Chairman: Sir Cyril Philips), *Report*, London: HMSO, 1981 (Cmnd. 8092), paragraphs 1.11–1.12.
10. For a discussion of this point see Basil Griffiths, 'One-tier policing' in John Benyon (ed.), *Scarman and After*, Oxford: Pergamon Press, 1984, pages 125–134.

CHAPTER 8

A balanced approa

OLE HANSEN

The Police and Criminal Evidence Act is a significant addition to the body of law, and it must be interpreted as such by those who implement it. However, as David Smith argues in his chapter, the legal framework is just one of the influences on police behaviour and, particularly for police activity on the streets, provides only a loose framework which has an indirect effect on what actually happens. The views of many police officers, including some in this book, provide ample confirmation of this. These boil down to the position that police officers out on the streets must be permitted to act as they see fit and the new Act, while stipulating constraints and procedures, remains just one determinant of police behaviour.

It is nonetheless important to examine the Act, if only because it is the product of a long process of consultation, debate, investigation and compromise. The resultant Act of Parliament can thus be seen as the considered view of what powers the police should have and what safeguards these require. Therefore, to put it no higher, the legislation does represent a clear signal to the police, and to the public, of how they are expected to act in the future. To this extent one might expect the Act to influence indirectly the working practices of the police, as well as specifying inhibitory rules and presentational rules, as David Smith describes in his essay.

The use and misuse of stop and search powers

Whether we like it or not, the context within which policing is carried out in many areas is one of deteriorating relations between the police and some members of the public. For example, in his report into the 1981 riots, Lord Scarman found there was a 'loss of confidence by significant sections . . . of the Lambeth public in the police'. He stated:

The loss of confidence and the attitudes and beliefs to which it gave rise ted a serious break-down in relations between the police and community they were serving.[1]

He found that the use of stop and search powers was a contributory factor, and in particular he criticised Operation Swamp which was 'a serious mistake'.[2]

Friction seems to be especially evident between police officers and young people. The Policy Studies Institute Report on the Metropolitan Police found that among the 15–24 years-old age group 32 per cent said that the police had not been polite during a stop incident, and 26 per cent of this group said the police did not behave in a fair and reasonable manner.[3] The first British Crime Survey reported a worse figure amongst young men: 52 per cent said they had received impolite treatment and 20 per cent reported improper police behaviour.[4] These figures clearly reveal that the interaction between police officers and some groups in society is in need of improvement.

One of the features of stop and search powers is that they are difficult to supervise and to monitor. They are examples of what have been referred to as *powers of low visibility* as it is difficult in practice for them to be checked by senior police officers, lawyers or the courts. Their low visibility means that the powers lend themselves to differential law enforcement, and some sections of the community may have stop and search powers applied to them in a different fashion, or more frequently, than others. Thus young people in general, and young black people in particular, are stopped more frequently by the police than are other sorts of people.[5]

The Policy Studies Institute report found that about 1.5 million stops are made by the police each year, although the number recorded by the police themselves was less than half this total.[6] The survey also found that the total 'strike rate' — the proportion of stops that lead to the detection of an offence — is about one out of 12, or put another way 91 per cent of stops do not lead to the person being reported, summonsed or arrested. Very large numbers of people are stopped and searched by police officers on the streets of London every day who are in fact entirely innocent and there are clear implications for relations between police and ordinary citizens.

There are I would suggest strong reasons for considering whether the police should have stop and search powers at all. It can be argued that police resources could be employed more effectively, and less counter-productively, in other ways and this point was put to the Philips Commission[7] and subsequently it was ventilated in the House of Commons. The very fact that it was rejected may turn out to be influential in determining how police officers exercise their powers. The debate may have sent indirect signals that the way in which stops and searches have been carried out in London and other areas is acceptable and can be applied across the country in line with section 1 of the Act.

This is the section which also extends stop and search powers to include 'prohibited articles' such as offensive weapons. Of course it sounds perfectly reasonable that police officers should have powers to search people suspected of possessing offensive weapons, but virtually anything can be so regarded. A bunch of keys, or a ruler, or coins of the realm can be used in an offensive manner and so if a police officer wishes to stop and search someone it does not take much imagination to find *something* in their possession which might be construed as an offensive weapon and which therefore justifies the search.

An increasing estrangement of whole communities

An offensive weapon need not be something which has been specifically adapted for use as such, it can simply depend upon the intention of the person who has it, and this intention may be only to use the article as a defensive weapon if attacked. Police officers may argue that they are in the best position to judge whether a certain person has a particular article for use in an offensive manner and hence that they need powers to stop and search people to discover these weapons. They claim that they are the 'hard-headed practical officers' who are out on the street enforcing the law while the well-meaning do-gooders are frustrating their efforts. However, although police officers have a particular kind of experience — of law enforcement on the streets — they are not the only people who have expertise in this area. Others who are involved have noticed the increasing estrangement of whole communities as a result of police behaviour on the streets and, as George Greaves observes in his chapter in this book, much of this gulf has come about because of the way in which police powers of stop and search have been exercised.

In the nineteen seventies I spent seven years in legal practice in Hackney, in the East End of London, and during that period I noticed a clearly discernible change of attitude on the part of what I might call our client community. We had a large West Indian community there, and the change in attitude towards the police, especially among older black people, was very noticeable. In the early nineteen seventies the community was very supportive of the police and accepted almost without question whatever they did. If one of their children got into trouble the parents, especially black parents, tended to be more punitive towards them than were the police or the courts or probation officers. The idea that their children could break the law was quite abhorrent.

But during the nineteen seventies one saw a complete change of attitude. This was partly a result of 'sus'[8], partly a result of stop and search and partly a result of searches of homes so that now one finds a widespread antipathy towards the police. If, for example, a black youth criticises the way in which he or she has been treated by the police the parents of the youth will almost certainly back them up and this is because of the experiences which the Afro-Caribbean community as a whole has had at the hands of the police. Of course not all the stories about police harassment are true, but there has been a sufficiently large number of instances of malpractice for there to be a widespread mistrust of the police. Lord Scarman found this, as the quotation given earlier shows, and he reported that:

> The riots were essentially an outburst of anger and resentment by young black people against the police.[9]

The riots, and the widespread suspicion of the police in these communities, did not occur as a result of agitators but as a consequence of people's experiences of police behaviour. And a central factor has been, and continues to be, the manner in which many police officers exercise their powers to stop and search people.

Safeguards or presentational rules: the stop and search stipulations

A central argument by those who support the provisions of the Police and Criminal Evidence Act is that it stipulates a number of safeguards which will prevent misuse of the stop and search powers. The first of these is that a search of a person may only occur if the constable has 'reasonable grounds for suspecting that he will find stolen or prohibited articles' (section 1(3)). However, this has supposedly been a criterion in the past for the exercise of stop and search but it has, to put it kindly, been interpreted rather loosely. Indeed the draft Code of Practice on this part of the Act found it necessary to include a guidance note stating:

> Statistics on the use to date of powers of stop and search indicate that in most cases no such article was found, and there is strong evidence that on many occasions these powers have been used where reasonable grounds to suspect the individual concerned of having the article in question on him did not in fact exist *(The draft Code of Practice for the exercise of powers of stop and search, issued 2 January 1985, paragraph 1B; the statement is excluded from the final Code of Practice, which came into effect on 1 January 1986).*

It is difficult to see how the 'reasonable grounds' criterion can be properly supervised to ensure that police officers do not misuse their powers, for example by picking on certain people. Similarly, the various provisions about what a constable must say and do (the Act, sections 2 and 3) have a rather hollow ring to them. What happens if the officer does not follow the proper procedure and after stopping and searching someone, and finding nothing sends that person on their way? Who is to know whether anything has ever happened at all, except the two participants? It is clear from the Policy Studies Institute research that many searches are never recorded and my experience in practice is that many people claim that the police had scant regard for any of the formalities. Quite honestly I believe that these provisions are likely to become, as the caution has in some areas, a mere formality. They are really *presentational* rules, as David Smith describes them in his chapter, which are there to give a good appearance and which it can be claimed were followed if the need arises. Of course if someone is stopped *without* reasonable suspicion, and if the proper procedures are *not* followed, but if a stolen or prohibited article *is* found then it probably will not matter greatly in court or anywhere else that the formalities were not observed.

Some people have argued that section 78 of the Act is likely to ensure that the proper procedures, for the exercise of powers such as stop and search, will be followed. This section (1) states:

> In any proceedings the court may refuse to allow evidence on which the prosecution proposes to rely to be given if it appears to the court that, having regard to all the circumstances, including the circumstances in which the evidence was obtained, the admission of the evidence would have *such an adverse effect on the fairness of the proceedings that the court ought not to admit it* (italics added).

However, it seems most unlikely that the prosecution will be penalised 'merely' because a police officer failed to observe the correct procedures and letter of the law in obtaining evidence through the use of stop and search powers. And so, in short, a clear signal goes out to police constables that the stop and search powers are good — go out and do it. The safeguards, on the other hand, seem to be rather ineffective and the consequence of this part of the Act seems likely to be a further deterioration in relations between police and their local communities.

The road check provisions

Another section of the Act which deserves attention is that which empowers police officers to carry out 'road checks'. One must first express relief that the initial proposals in clause 4 of the Bill were extensively modified during its passage through Parliament. The original proposal was to allow police to establish road checks in areas where they believed there was a pattern of crime that led them to suspect that serious arrestable offences would occur. This was removed during the progress of the Bill and the road check powers in the Act are consequently much less objectionable than they might have been.

However, problems still remain with section 4. Road checks can be authorised for the purpose of ascertaining whether a vehicle contains someone who is 'unlawfully at large' or who has committed or is intending to commit a serious arrestable offence or who is a witness to one. But what is meant by this criterion of a 'serious arrestable offence'? At least the ludicrous provision in the Bill was removed which defined such an offence as one which the police regarded as serious. However, in section 116 of the Act we still learn that any arrestable offence is serious if it has led to 'serious financial loss to any person' (subsection 6(f)) and

> Loss is serious for the purposes of this section if, having regard to all the circumstances, it is serious for the person who suffers it (section 116, subsection 7).

I am not suggesting that the loss of one pound, for example, is not serious to many people but this open definition of a serious arrestable offence, coupled with the provision in section 4(5) of the Act, which allows any officer to authorise a road check, does mean that this power may be open to abuse.

Late in 1984 I was stopped in Hackney while driving home. When I asked the officer why I had been stopped he told me it was just a 'routine stop'. When I pointed out to him that he did not actually have the powers to carry out a routine stop he said, 'Have you been drinking sir?' I could not quite see the connection, but I had indeed had one pint and so felt at something of a disadvantage. The policeman was perfectly courteous, he asked to look in my bag, which he had no reason or right to do, and when he saw it was full of law books he looked no further. When he asked me for identification I showed him my press card whereupon he wished me a cordial good night. But I wonder whether everyone would have been treated in this way, and as my own experience shows the proper rules were not being followed.

A further consideration arises as a result of the road checks — most people would regard them as road *blocks* — which were set up by police forces during the 1984–1985 coal dispute. These were apparently established under common law powers not under section 159 of the Road Traffic Act 1972. It is doubtful whether these road checks would come under section 4 of the Police and Criminal Evidence Act 1984 and so the safeguards would not apply. For example, apart from the information to which the person in charge of the vehicle is entitled (section 4 subsection 15) the Act requires each chief constable to give details of the road checks in his area in his annual report (section 5). However, if the police can go around setting up road checks under the common law it is difficult to see the value of these so-called safeguards.

Powers of arrest: the general conditions

Another main area of concern is the new provisions about arrest contained in the Act. I should stress that I have no quarrel with the general intention which is to try to codify the confused powers of arrest which have previously existed. It is important to rationalise these powers, not only from the point of view of police officers who must have found it extremely difficult to operate all the varied and different enactments and powers, but it is even more vital from the point of view of the public. It is surely desirable that people should know what their rights are and that they should clearly understand the circumstances in which they are liable to arrest.

There seem to be few problems with section 24, which sets out the application of powers of summary arrest, and section 26 abolishes statutory powers of arrest other than those specified in the Act, particularly in schedule 2. The problem occurs with section 25 which appears to confer a power of arrest on the police for any offence however trivial.

Perhaps it might be argued that it is absurd to have offences in law for which the police cannot arrest the person if he or she refuses to give their name and address. But have we struck the right balance if someone is arrested for a minor offence simply because 'the constable has reasonable grounds for doubting whether a name furnished by the relevant person as his name is his real name' (section 25 subsection 3)? I think it is wrong and anti-social for someone to drop litter, but I do not want to live in a society where the police have the power to arrest that person merely for refusing to give their name and address.

It is clear that there is a disposition on the part of some police forces to proceed by way of arrest rather than summons. The Philips Commission, for example, reported that, whereas some forces such as Derbyshire, Thames Valley, West Yorkshire and North Wales brought over 40 per cent of adults accused of indictable offences to court by summons other constabularies such as Cambridgeshire, Greater Manchester and the Metropolitan Police used this means in *one* per cent or less of such cases.[10] The argument was strongly put to the Commission that the police should *usually* proceed by summons and only if that is clearly impractical should they use arrest powers.

The experience of being arrested and detained is in itself an horrendous event for the person who is subjected to it and indeed it is frequently far worse than anything that happens to that person in court or by way of punishment. It is often out of all proportion to what the person has actually done and the police should in all cases endeavour to avoid it. And yet in each year as many as 1.4 million people are arrested.[11] The effect of section 25 of the Police and Criminal Evidence Act may be to increase this total yet further, for the 'general arrest conditions' specified in this section are indeed wide-ranging.

The conditions listed in section 25 of the Act will considerably increase the discretionary powers of police constables. Henceforth a police officer can choose to arrest someone who has *not* committed an 'arrestable offence' but whom he suspects of being involved in a less serious offence, if that person's name is unknown to, and not readily ascertainable, by the constable. Similarly a person can be arrested if he or she fails to furnish a 'satisfactory' address for service of a summons or if the constable has 'reasonable grounds for doubting' that the address is a 'satisfactory' one or that the name given is that person's real one. If the constable has 'reasonable grounds for believing' that a person must be restrained from causing injury to himself or to others, or from causing an unlawful obstruction of the highway, or from causing loss of or damage to property then the officer may arrest that person. These conditions raise so many questions it is difficult to know how a police officer is supposed to act in particular circumstances. Another general arrest condition applies if the constable believes a person needs to be prevented from committing an offence against public decency. What does this mean? In practice it means that a police constable's own opinions on public decency will determine whether or not a person is arrested for a trivial offence which Parliament itself has decided is insufficiently serious to come within the category of an arrestable offence. The possibilities for abuse of the powers of arrest which section 25 contains should not be underestimated.

Search of an arrested person's premises

Outside the area covered by section 25 there are several reasons why the police might wish to arrest someone rather than proceed by summons and an important one of these is to be found in section 18 of the Act. This gives the police the power to search the premises of a person who is under arrest for an *arrestable* offence and it enables them to avoid the necessity of obtaining a search warrant under section 8 of the Act. This legislation contains the most ludicrously elaborate and complicated provisions for search and seizure (sections 8–16) but if someone is arrested the police can get round these by using section 18. The alleged safeguard here is that it must be authorised by an inspector or more senior officer, but there is even a way round this if the constable believes that the presence of the person who has been arrested is necessary at a place other than a police station in order to carry out the investigation.

One can imagine all sorts of ways in which these provisions may be applied. A police officer who carries out an arrest in a street can argue that he needs that person present to help him carry out an investigation, perhaps to identify someone, or to point out where an offence took place, or where stolen articles are to be found. Whatever the argument, the constable can use section 18 to get round the search warrant conditions and safeguards in the Act and can go directly to the arrested person's home and search it. It seems clear from this that there is a strong incentive to carry out an arrest.

This incentive is further increased by the provisions in section 32(2) which enable police officers to enter and search any premises, in which the arrested person was immediately before he was arrested, to look for relevant evidence.

There is little doubt that these powers will be employed often as a means to circumvent the need for a search warrant. Some recent research by Ken Lidstone, which was published in *The Criminal Law Review*,[12] showed that of 289 searches of premises by police officers 240 were carried out without a warrant. 44 per cent of these took place either with the 'consent' of the suspect (one might consider that 'consent' is being loosely employed) or in exercise of the common law power after arrest which has now been enshrined in the Police and Criminal Evidence Act.

One reason which Lidstone identified for the fact that police officers would rather use these other powers than apply for a warrant was

> the 'machismo' of the seasoned detective who sees the ability to 'front', or bluff one's way into premises, as a mark of the 'good' detective.[13]

In the article a senior detective is quoted as saying:

> There would be something wrong if local detectives working their own patch had to get a warrant to search the houses of local villains.[14]

This is the context within which one must examine the powers of arrest, and the consequent powers of search, which are provided in the new Act.

A move in the wrong direction

In conclusion it is difficult to see the Police and Criminal Evidence Act as legislation which has struck an appropriate balance between citizens' rights and police powers. In some cases the powers given by the Act are extensions, in other cases they are confirmation and codification of existing powers and in all cases they are statutory acknowledgement of existing police practice. But the Act does add a new element which is that it makes it easier for the police to carry out practices which were previously not enshrined in statute. The legislation gives the go ahead — the green light — to police practices and behaviour which are likely to prove counter-productive in terms of good policing and tackling crime.

The safeguards, which it has been claimed are in the Act, seem likely to prove largely illusory. They are mainly bureaucratic form-filling and will prove irksome to police officers but they are not real controls or real safeguards for the general public. Even more discretionary power has been vested in the hands of constables out on the streets and the net result is likely to be a further deterioration in relations between the police and many communities. The Act is thus not going to help the police any more than it will help the public. It is a move in the wrong direction and I am deeply pessimistic about its long term effects.

Notes

1. *The Brixton Disorders 10–12 April 1981, Report of an Inquiry by the Rt. Hon. The Lord Scarman, OBE*. London: HMSO, 1981 (Cmnd. 8427), paragraphs 4.1–4.2.
2. *Ibid*., paragraph 4.76, see also paragraphs 4.37–4.43 and 4.72–4.74.
3. *Police and People in London*, Volume I: David J. Smith, *A Survey of Londoners*, London: Policy Studies Institute, 1983, (PSI No. 618) p. 110.
4. Mike Hough and Pat Mayhew, *The British Crime Survey: First Report*, Home Office Research Study No. 76, London: HMSO, 1983, p. 30; see also Peter Southgate and Paul Ekblom, *Contacts between Police and Public: Findings from the British Crime Survey*, Home Office Research Study No. 77, London: HMSO, 1984.
5. See *Police and People in London*, Volume I, *supra* note 3, pp. 95–107; see also Carole F. Willis, *The Use, Effectiveness and Impact of Police Stop and Search Powers*, Research and Planning Unit Paper 15, London: Home Office, 1983, p. 14.
6. *Police and People in London*, Volume I, Appendix B, pp. 350–351.
7. Royal Commission on Criminal Procedure (Chairman: Sir Cyril Philips), *Report*, London: HMSO, 1981 (Cmnd. 8092), see chapter 3.
8. The offence under section 4 of the Vagrancy Act 1824 of being a suspected person, colloquially known as 'sus', was repealed by section 8 of the Criminal Attempts Act 1981.
9. *The Brixton Disorders, supra* note 1, para. 3.110(7).
10. Royal Commission on Criminal Procedure, *Report, supra* note 7, p. 43; see also R. Gemmill and R. F. Morgan-Giles, *Arrest, Charge and Summons: Current Practice and Resource Implications*, Royal Commission on Criminal Procedure Research Study No. 8, London: HMSO, 1980.
11. Royal Commission on Criminal Procedure, *Report*, p. 43.
12. K. W. Lidstone, 'Magistrates, the police and search warrants,' *The Criminal Law Review*, August 1984, pp. 449–458.
13. *Ibid*., p. 454.
14. *Ibid*., p. 454.

PART 3

In the Station: Detention and Interrogation

CHAPTER 9

Powers and proprieties in the police station

JOHN BENYON

In 1972 a considerable stir was caused by the *Eleventh Report* of the Criminal Law Revision Committee.[1] This asserted that since crime was rapidly increasing and the public felt that 'criminals were getting the better of the law' there was 'a good deal of feeling that the law of evidence should now be less tender to criminals generally'. It is unclear from the Report how the Committee was able to ascertain that the public 'generally' felt this, but a central proposal was 'to restrict greatly the so-called "right of silence" . . .'

> The subject will still have the 'right of silence' in the sense that it is no offence to refuse to answer questions or tell his story when inter-rogated; but if he chooses to exercise this right, he will risk having an adverse inference drawn against him at his trial.[2]

Understandably, the suggestion proved to be highly controversial and it provoked a sustained outcry within Parliament and the legal profession, and in newspapers and journals. Sir Robert Mark, the newly-appointed Metropolitan Police Commissioner, entered the debate arguing that the right to silence, and other aspects of the 'complicated framework of rules . . . were designed to give every advantage to the defence'.[3] Furthermore:

> Let there be no doubt that a minority of criminal lawyers do very well from the proceeds of crime. A reputation for success, achieved by persistent lack of scruple in the defence of the most disreputable, soon attracts other clients who see little hope of acquittal in any other way. Experienced and respected metropolitan detectives can identify lawyers in criminal practice who are more harmful to society than the clients they represent.[4]

The 'golden thread' of the criminal justice system

Not surprisingly Mark's comments were greeted with less than unanimous approval, especially amongst lawyers, but they did seem to be well received in some quarters, particularly within the police service. It is obviously understandable that police officers, who work hard to solve a serious crime and who are convinced that a particular suspect is the culprit, should feel frustrated and incensed if that person is found not guilty. However, the central tenet of the criminal justice system in England and Wales is that the prosecution must prove the guilt of the accused, and until that has been done to the satisfaction of the judge and jury, or, in the vast majority of cases, the magistrates, then the accused must be regarded as innocent.

The Royal Commission on Criminal Procedure quoted the words of Lord Devlin in the *Bodkin Adams* case, which underlined the principles of the right to silence and the requirement of the prosecution to prove its case:

> So great is and always has been our horror that a man might be questioned, forced to speak and perhaps to condemn himself out of his own mouth, that we grant to everyone suspected or accused of crime at the beginning, at every stage and until the very end, the right to say, 'Ask me no question. I shall answer none. Prove your case.'[5]

In short, in Lord Sankey's words, the 'golden thread' which runs through the system of criminal justice is 'the duty of the prosecution to prove the prisoner's guilt': *Woolmington v. DPP* [1935] AC 462. The Confait case was an example of the Devlin principle not being applied, for the three boys did indeed condemn themselves out of their own mouths, and, as was subsequently shown, their 'confessions' were false; yet each spent three years in detention for crimes they did not commit.

The Royal Commission came to the view that the right of silence should be retained. Indeed research for the Commission showed that few people make use of the right: only 4 per cent refused to answer all questions, and 8 per cent refused to answer some questions.[6] As Barrie Irving pointed out, 'to remain silent in a police interview room in the face of determined questioning by an officer with legitimate authority to carry on this activity requires an abnormal exercise of will'.[7] In his important chapter in this book, Irving stresses the need to appreciate the anxiety and fear that being arrested and detained in a police station can cause. This will vary from person to person, but many will become disoriented and some people may be prepared to admit whatever is asked of them in order to end the experience. A case in which this seems to have occurred was that of Errol Madden, who was arrested in October 1980 in South London on his way home from the cinema. After detention and questioning for some hours he 'confessed' to stealing two toy cars, but it was subsequently discovered that he had a receipt for their purchase and the case was dismissed by magistrates. Not only did Madden condemn himself out of his own mouth, but indeed he confessed to a crime which never took place.

Research for the Royal Commission found that in many cases, judged in evidentiary terms, confessions obtained by the police were not necessary. Softley reported that in only 8 per cent of cases did the police believe that questioning was essential to bring the matters to court, and both this study and that of Irving found that about 60 per cent of the suspects made a damaging admission or a full confession.[8] Baldwin and McConville's study of Crown Court cases found that 13 per cent required confessions to establish a *prima facie* standard and an additional 4 per cent would probably have been acquitted without this evidence.[9]

The Police and Criminal Evidence Act, in section 76, stresses that if it is suggested to a court that a confession may have been obtained by oppression or in circumstances which bring its reliability into question, then the prosecution must prove 'beyond reasonable doubt' that the confession was not obtained in this way. In chapter eleven in this book Barrie Irving welcomes this section, pointing out that this has to be the job of the court as there is no scientific way of gauging unreliability, but he also hopes that certain police tactics will invariably render confessions inadmissible. Michael Zander explains in chapter ten that section 76 merely encapsulates the common law position.

Section 77 of the Act provides that if the case against a mentally handicapped person depends on a confession made in the absence of an independent person the court shall warn the jury that there is special need for caution. The shadow of the Confait case lurks behind this convoluted section in that Lattimore, one of the three youths wrongly convicted, was mentally handicapped. However, it has been pointed out that section 77 would not have prevented the conviction on the basis of the 'confession' as there *was* an independent person present (an interpreter) as well as the three boys' parents.

Barrie Irving welcomes the inclusion in the legislation of the 'at risk' concept. The *Code of Practice for the Detention, Treatment and Questioning of Persons by Police Officers* (hereafter 'the Code') spells out the need to treat juveniles or people suffering from mental illness or mental handicap in a proper way. Paragraphs 13.1–13.3 and 13A–13D stress the problems of reliability and the dangers of self-incrimination.

The bible in the police station: the Code of Practice

The Code of Practice, which supersedes the Judges' Rules and Administrative Directions, stipulates the conditions for the interrogation of detained persons. In chapter twelve, Maurice Buck draws attention to the provisions, in paragraphs 12.2–12.7, for periods of rest, breaks from interviewing at meal times, and for questioning to take place in properly heated, lit and ventilated rooms. It is, says Tony Judge in his keenly-argued essay, 'a Code of Practice for prisoners and suspects against the abuse of police power which is without parallel in the rest of the world'. The Code alters the point at which a person must be cautioned, as Michael Zander explains in the next chapter. Under the new rules someone who is *suspected* of having committed an offence must be told:

> You do not have to say anything unless you wish to do so, but what you say may be given in evidence.

A key innovation is the introduction of tape-recording (section 60). This is welcomed by all the authors in this part of the book and, as Maurice Buck describes, the early signs from the experiments are encouraging. He sees tape-recording as a safeguard for the police as well as the suspect, and there may be gains in terms of more efficient questioning and less time spent in taking notes. Tony Judge hopes that tape-recording, and existence of custody records, will decrease the accusations by defence lawyers of improprieties. Sir Kenneth Newman, the Metropolitan Police Commissioner, gave a favourable verdict in his 1984 report on the tape-recording pilot schemes being run in London. He said that tape-recording has offered 'greater accuracy and credibility of record' and more economical questioning.[10] In chapter fifteen in this book, David Ashby MP, states that tape-recording should immediately be introduced across the country.

All the contributors agree on the significance of the Code of Practice. Michael Zander considers that it may come to be seen as even more important than the Act itself: 'it will become the bible for the officers in the police station'. He sees the Code being more important than the Judges' Rules and he anticipates that its prescriptions will become routinised and internalised — 'accepted as the ordinary way of doing daily business'. However, Gabrielle Cox, in chapter thirteen, is rather less convinced about the effect which the Code is likely to have. She detects considerable scepticism within the police, and she wonders whether there is a lack of commitment to the rules and procedures. Barrie Irving, too, stresses that the Code of Practice depends upon supervision, discipline and discretion and also on the police cultural norms and the integrity and character of individual officers.

Tony Judge and Maurice Buck stress the extensive safeguards which they see built into the legislation and the Code. Maurice Buck identifies 'a host of stringent safeguards', and in chapter twelve he incisively analyses how the Act will affect the detention, treatment and questioning of people detained in a police station. Buck, and Zander in chapter ten, both examine the procedures established by the legislation for the reviews of detention. David Ashby in chapter 15 agrees that the concept of time *limit* on the length of detention is an improvement, particularly in view of recent judgements on applications for *habeas corpus*, but he strongly disagrees on the actual *length* of detention which the Act permits.

The custody officers' 'bureaucratic nightmare'?

Michael Zander's succinct exposition on the legislation as it affects detained persons outlines the importance of the custody officer, custody records, the increase in information, the availability of duty solicitors and legal aid and the significance of the *inter partes* hearings in magistrates' courts if warrants of further detention are sought. The role of the custody officer is clearly crucial and both Maurice Buck and Tony Judge are concerned about the resource implications. Barrie Irving has a different concern, and that is whether the pressures on them will prove too great; in chapter eleven he writes:

> Custody officers are expected to stand up to everyone and be paragons of administrative and moral rectitude . . . obviously our legislators do not take too seriously the 'I will scratch your back' principle which oils the wheels of all our institutions.

Tony Judge, too, is anxious about whether the onerous tasks for the custody officer, particularly in a busy station, will turn out to be a 'nightmare'. Maurice Buck though is more sanguine, and he sees the enhanced status of the position facilitating the custody officer's role as quasi-independent guardian for the care of detainees and the protection of individual police officers.

It is clear that there is some considerable unease within the police service about the impact of the Police and Criminal Evidence Act. This was manifest at the Police Federation Conference in Blackpool, in May 1985, when the Home Secretary was barracked persistently as he spoke about 'the smooth implementation' of the legislation. Leslie Curtis told the Conference:

> Where police powers have been standardised they have been saddled with a bureaucratic nightmare of time-keeping and record-keeping. We are anticipating that criminal trials are going to be extended rather than shortened, as defending lawyers go step by step through the codes of practice in their desperate search for some slight error or omission on the part of the police.[11]

Leon Brittan tried to allay fears that the new procedures will prove time-consuming and impractical and he was jeered when he said, 'I do believe that the task will prove less difficult than it appears at first sight'. An emergency motion expressing grave concern at the effect of government policies and legislation on the police service was supported by the whole conference, with just one delegate against.

Both Barrie Irving and Gabrielle Cox, in their respective chapters, point out that police stations are closed institutions, and the new procedures to ensure proprieties appear essentially to depend upon *internal* review and enforcement. Gabrielle Cox describes the introduction in the Greater Manchester area of the scheme for lay visiting of police stations, and she highlights a number of improvements which have resulted. This kind of *external* review was recommended by the Home Affairs Select Committee, and the suggestion was endorsed by Lord Scarman who thought 'the effect would be salutary'.[12] However, lay visiting is not mentioned in the Police and Criminal Evidence Act and so the extension of these schemes to other areas depends upon the goodwill of senior police officers and the energy of police authorities.

Similar lay visiting schemes do exist in some other areas and they can be seen as a form of accountability by the police, and a willingness by the service in some areas to promote improved community relations and a policy of more open access. Michael Zander takes up the theme of accountability in his analysis of the legislation in chapter ten and he finds that it is enhanced by a number of the provisions and innovations. These forms of individual accountability are clearly important, and although they initially appear to depend upon internal reviews and procedures, Michael Zander highlights the *external* scrutiny, such as that by solicitors and the courts, which a number of the provisions entail.

Police powers and citizens' rights: finding the fulcrum

Gabrielle Cox, however, is more concerned with the consultation by, and accountability of, the police service at district, divisional and force levels. She finds that the provisions for consultative arrangements in section 106 of the act are 'pathetic and derisory' and also 'positively harmful'.

The desirability of proper means for public participation and involvement are discussed in chapters one and two of this book. If a real dialogue is established between police and citizens it will benefit the six policing criteria of effectiveness, identity, participation, legitimacy, consent and justice. Unfortunately, for various reasons such as the professionalism trend, senior police officers have shown a marked reluctance to consult or involve local people. Lord Scarman noted this in Lambeth, and even Evelyn Schaffer, in her sympathetic account of policing, recorded that the service was often guilty of 'excessive secrecy'. Incidentally her account of 'community involvement' in Strathclyde is interesting in that it appears to accept uncritically the view that it is a process of *police involvement in the community* rather than *community participation in policing*.[13]

Perhaps the educational service provides a model of accountability and consultation which might be adapted and improved for policing. The police authority could play a similar role to the educational authority, considering broad policies and the allocation of resources, while each district police station could, like every school, have a board of lay governors who would receive reports from the superintendent or chief inspector at the local level. The district, or divisional, police station governors could take initiatives suited to local circumstances and facilitate public participation and citizen involvement.

Many of the authors in this part of the book consider the notion of 'fundamental balance' which the Royal Commission discussed in its Report. As the Commission pointed out, an essential question is where the fulcrum should be located between police powers to fight crime and citizens' rights and liberties. The contributors in the chapters which follow do not agree on whether the Police and Criminal Evidence Act has struck the right balance. To take just two views, whereas Maurice Buck feels that the balance is too much in favour of the professional criminal, David Ashby, MP, believes that the legislation permits too great a loss of liberty and infringement of individuals' rights. Indeed, he states that 'it is an affront in a democratic society' that the police should be allowed to detain people for so long, and he also considers that 'we are poles apart from the Americans and many other common law countries in our concepts of human and civil rights and liberties'.

During its passage through Parliament the proposals provoked pro-longed debate and considerable opposition, and there seems little evidence that all the provisions of the Police and Criminal Evidence Act will now be quietly accepted. The debate will continue, but, as the questions posed in the first chapter suggested, are the assumptions valid? What do we as a society want from the police? Can they really 'fight crime on our behalf'? If the answer to the last question is 'no' or 'only to a very limited extent' perhaps it is now time to consider how to involve citizens actively in determining and implementing policing and crime control policies.

The 1964 Act, it was argued in chapter one, is a vague and unsatisfactory basis upon which to do this. The sensible course would be to establish a Royal Commission on the police and crime, to appraise where things have gone wrong in the last two decades, and to seek to reverse the undesirable trends. Such a commission should concentrate on policing but also examine crime and its causes. This would be the wise course, but it is unlikely to happen if only because the findings of such an inquiry would almost certainly prove rather embarrassing to the present Government.

Notes

1. Criminal Law Revision Committee, *Eleventh Report: Evidence (General)* London: HMSO, 1972 (Cmnd. 4991).
2. *Ibid.*, pp. 12 and 15–16.

3. *The Dimbleby Lecture*, BBC Television, November 1973, reprinted as 'Minority verdict' in Sir Robert Mark, *Policing a Perplexed Society*, London: Allen and Unwin, 1977, pp. 55–73; citation is from p. 63.

4. *Ibid.*, p. 65.

5. Cited in Royal Commission on Criminal Procedure (Chairman: Sir Cyril Philips), *Report*, London: HMSO, 1981 (Cmnd. 8092), para. 1.27, p. 9.

6. Paul Softley, *Police Interrogation: An Observational Study in Four Police Stations*, Royal Commission on Criminal Procedure Research Study No. 4, London: HMSO, 1980, pp. 75–86.

7. Barrie Irving, *Police Interrogation: A Case Study of Current Practice*, Royal Commission on Criminal Procedure Research Study No. 2, London: HMSO, 1980, p. 153.

8. Softley, *Police Interrogation: An Observational Study, supra*, note 6, chapter 6; Irving, *Police Interrogation: A Case Study, supra*, note 7, p. 150.

9. John Baldwin and Michael McConville, *Confessions in Crown Court Trials*, Royal Commission on Criminal Procedure Research Study No. 5, London: HMSO, 1980, p. 32.

10. *Report of the Commissioner of Police of the Metropolis for the Year 1984*, London: HMSO, June 1985 (Cmnd. 9541); see also Carole F. Willis, *The Tape-Recording of Police Interviews with Suspects: An Interim Report*, London: HMSO, 1984 (Home Office Research Study No. 82).

11. 'Police Federation barracks Brittan', *The Guardian*, 16 May 1985, p. 2.

12. House of Commons, *Deaths in Police Custody: Third Report from the Home Affairs Committee, Session 1979–80*, HC 632, London: HMSO, 1980, para. 13; *The Brixton Disorders 10–12 April 1981: Report of an Inquiry by the Rt. Hon. the Lord Scarman, OBE*, London, HMSO, 1981 (Cmnd. 8427), para. 7.9.

13. Evelyn B. Schaffer, *Community Policing*, London: Croom Helm, 1980; ch. 5, pp. 68–85 and p. 107.

CHAPTER 10

The Act in the station

MICHAEL ZANDER

The passage into law of the Police and Criminal Evidence Act 1984 marks a major change in the criminal justice system. Those of us who are involved in the training process find that even having worked with the two Bills, every time one opens the Act or the codes one still can learn something new. The training process involves not only the Act, but of course also the codes, which are an integral part of this whole new system, not something which is marginal or of slight importance, but absolutely central. I rather fancy that in the long run the codes will come to be seen to be even more important, certainly as important as the Act itself. They are intended to be rather more readable than the Act, as they are addressed to the concerns and the capacities of police officers, suspects, lawyers and anyone else likely to be directly affected by the Act.

The codes of practice

The Code on Detention, Treatment and Questioning[1] is a major development in terms of the way in which suspects are handled in the police station. It will become the bible for the officer in the police station, and will even perhaps be carried by some officers on the beat. But it is mainly a police station document.

Some have argued that the Code is not really of very great account because technically it is not law any more than the Judges' Rules were law. But I think that for various reasons, the Code will come to play a very much more important part in the whole scheme of things than the Judges' Rules ever did.

Firstly, the codes have been prepared after the most elaborate process of consultation. The Judges' Rules were laid down *ex cathedra* by the judges of the Queen's Bench Division with no consultation, not even any warning. They were, I think, resented by the police service as being something in which they had had no involvement, whereas the codes have been exhaustively considered and reconsidered. Before the final versions were agreed the codes were produced in various drafts and there was then a debate in Parliament prior to the promulgation of the final form of the codes. This elaborate process of consultation is likely to have given the police service more confidence in the final result than they ever were likely to have in the Judges' Rules, and indeed many of the police suggestions have been incorporated.

Secondly, although it is perfectly true that the Act clearly states that a breach of a code is not in itself a criminal offence, nor can it be made the subject of civil proceedings, the Act states in section 67(8) that a breach of a code is *ipso facto* a breach of police disciplinary rules. Although I do not anticipate there will be many occasions when a breach is visited with a disciplinary charge, the fact that it is technically a breach of police disciplinary rules will give officers some cause to think carefully about the codes. Also, thirdly, the codes have been debated in Parliament, are referred to in the Act, and were put into motion by a statutory instrument. They will therefore be of a technically higher status than the Judges' Rules.

But I think the crucial question will be the actual effect of the Code on the ordinary police officer, which will vary from area to area, dependent upon attitudes adopted by the more senior members of the service. I would foresee that the ordinary police officer will come to see the Code as setting out the routine method of dealing with suspects. What is routinised becomes internalised and accepted as the ordinary way of doing daily business: and therefore, the nice question as to whether a breach might lead to the exclusion of evidence is in my opinion somewhat beside the point. The real question is what happens on the ground. The Code is very detailed and comprehensive by comparison with the Judges' Rules and deals with the *substance* of the relationship between the suspect and the police officer. I believe it will come to be absolutely essential to the conduct of relations between suspects and police officers. So I take the codes as being a very major development and I think that is how they will come to be seen.

The Royal Commission was at great pains to establish accountability as one of the important principles that had to be adhered to. It is a problematic principle. It has all sorts of question marks attached to it and I want to look at some of the provisions that relate to the situation in the police station, from the point of view of accountability.

The custody record

One of the things which everyone knows is associated with this new scheme is the custody record, which I think will come to be an important document for two main reasons. First, it is intended that it should be extremely detailed; there are many instances where the Act, and more particularly the Code, requires that details of events be stated in the custody record form. It is a very long list indeed; and from the police officer's point of view it will prove to be an extremely tiresome list. Everything that happens to the suspect from start to finish has to be in the custody record. And that is in itself a very important fact.

Secondly, and equally important, the suspect must, if he asks for it, be given a copy of the record — which makes it that much more likely that the records which should be kept will in fact be kept. We know that human beings are fallible, they do not all do what they are supposed to do, and the custody record might be no exception to that general principle. Nevertheless, the fact that the police know that the suspect is entitled to ask for a copy, which he must be given, will help to focus attention on the custody record and make it probable that adequate records will be maintained. I think that is a step in the right direction in terms of the improved accountability of the system.

The custody officer

The Royal Commission proposed, and the Act incorporated the proposal, that there should be a custody officer responsible for the well-being of all the suspects in the police station. The Home Office accepted (at a very late stage) that there should be a difference between *ordinary* police stations, where there cannot really be expected to be the full apparatus of custody officers, trained and fully functioning at sergeant level, as the Act contemplates, and *'designated'* police stations where it would be normal to take suspects if there is any expectation that they are going to be held for more than six hours.

If a person is taken to a non-designated police station in the first instance, he must be transferred to a designated station within six hours, where there should be a fully qualified custody officer of sergeant level or above. In every police station, whether designated or not, there will always be someone who is acting as custody officer, but in the non-designated police station he may not be a fully qualified custody officer.

The concept of the custody officer is an important one. In every police station there is always somebody who is in charge. The desk sergeant is already a familiar concept, but what the Act contemplates goes beyond the present responsibility of whoever is in charge of the police station. Various responsibilities are specifically laid upon him, and he is made answerable and accountable for the proper treatment of suspects.

Furthermore, it is made clear in the Act (section 39(6)) that if there is any difference of opinion between himself and the investigating officers, who may indeed be of a more senior rank, then that difference of opinion will have to be referred up the line of authority. It is not the case that the custody officer can overrule a more senior investigating officer who is handling the case, but if there is any difference between them as to the conduct or handling of the suspect it has got to be referred up to a superintendent or above for resolution. That could be done by telephone if necessary, but it has to be done.

I think that this is an important principle in terms of establishing the duty of the custody officer to take an independent line in deciding how cases should be dealt with in the police station. Although that may be rather difficult for the custody officer to do, particularly in the initial period, once the system becomes established and custody officers begin to get the feel of the new arrangements, they will regard it as an important responsibility. Much of course will depend on leadership from the top. If the more senior officers give the more junior officers the sense that the custody officer is not really expected in practice to do much more than to rubber stamp what the investigating officer says, that attitude will very quickly be absorbed by the more junior ranks.

Informing the suspect

The third aspect of accountability that one might mention is the increase of information to the suspect. Suspects come into the station obviously in various states of shock and vary enormously as to their capacity to cope with the situation, but very few of them are particularly well able to cope. In the past the amount of information which had to be communicated to the suspect at an early stage was extremely limited: under the old system he had to be told why he had been arrested, and when he had been charged (which was frequently a long way on in the suspect's dealings with the police) he was usually given a piece of paper which informed him about various rights, including his right of silence. He may already have been told of that right when he was cautioned, but he was reminded of it and of his right to legal advice, although those items of information were not as useful at the point where he was charged as they might have been if they had been communicated earlier.

One of the important things that the Act and the Code do is to require that the suspect be given information at an early stage after his arrival at the police station. The custody officer must tell him the reasons for his arrest. That presumably confirms what he will have been told when he was arrested outside the police station. He must be told of his right to have somebody outside the police station informed of his whereabouts. That is the old section 62 of the 1977 Criminal Law Act, re-established in the new Act (section 56). He must be told about his right to have legal advice. This is an entirely new provision under which he must be informed that he has a right in the normal way to have a lawyer. He must also be told that he has a right to a copy of the custody record. The information to the suspect must be communicated not only orally, which may go in one ear and out the other ear, but also in writing. Presumably a pre-printed form will be handed to the suspect which will put him in possession of these items of information (the Code: paragraphs 3.1–3.2).

There is a slight problem about the person who comes *voluntarily* to the police station. Neither in the Act nor in the Code is there any requirement to inform somebody who has not been arrested or cautioned that he need not come down to the police station if he does not choose to. Attempts to get the Home Office to agree to such a change were not successful, so that there is no requirement to warn him that, if he wishes to refuse the invitation to come down to the police station he is entitled to do so. So he may come unaware of the fact that he is not technically under arrest; he comes under the pressure of being asked to come down to the police station to answer a few questions and his status is a little bit uncertain.

However, the Code in paragraph 3.9 goes quite far — not all the way, but quite far — in establishing the general principle that he should be treated, for the purposes of his rights and information, as if he were broadly speaking under arrest. The only trouble is that he need not be told about the fact that he is *not* under arrest until he is cautioned. At the point when he is cautioned, if he is not under arrest, he must be so informed and then told that he has a right to legal advice and that he has a right to leave if he wishes to do so. So the status of the 'volunteer' who is there helping the police with their enquiries in the proper sense of that term, is still a little bit ambiguous. But when he is cautioned he should be given information about his status which makes it reasonably clear to him that he is free to leave.

The review of detention

The fourth aspect of accountability which appears in the Act and the Code is the concept of the review of the propriety of further detention. *Necessity* is the lodestar by which one judges the need and propriety of further detention, and it is this concept which is central to the various reviews of the need for further detention which are required by the Act. At the first stage this has to be done by the custody officer himself (section 37(1)). He has to decide whether there is any ground for detaining the suspect on arrival at the police station, which he does by considering whether or not there is enough evidence to charge him.

If there is enough evidence to charge him at that stage, he must be charged. And then the basic rules which existed in the past apply, as these have continued in the Act. Broadly speaking the principle is, once charged questioning ceases though there is a possibility of continuing questioning on other charges as in the past. The subject then comes under the immediate or almost immediate supervision of the court and he must be brought to a court as soon as practicable.

That was the past formula, but it is given a little more concrete substance by a provision in the Act (section 46) that he must normally be brought to a court within 24 hours unless it is a weekend. A court must be found. If there is not one already sitting or about to sit within that period, the Justices' clerk must be informed and a court must be mobilised. So the idea of bringing the suspect before the court after he has been charged is strengthened. It should be noted that there do not have to be sittings on Sundays or on Christmas Day, but subject to that, it has got to be the next day.

If there is not enough evidence to charge the suspect then, the custody officer has to decide whether or not it is right in all the circumstances to detain him for the purpose of questioning and, if it is not right to detain him for the purpose of questioning, whether he should be released on bail (section 37(2)).

The test is a very broad one, but nevertheless it does have some limitations. The custody officer may authorise detention under the Act if it is necessary to secure or preserve evidence or to obtain evidence by questioning (section 37(2)). This has been the common law for some time, although it has adopted that position clearly only in recent years — see especially *Mohommed-Holgate v. Duke* [1982] Q.B. 209. But there is no doubt that that is the present common law and it is confirmed in the Act. So, if it is *necessary* — rather than *desirable* — to secure or preserve evidence or to obtain evidence by questioning him then he may be detained in the police station for the time being.

The further reviews that have to be carried out within the police station, are carried out not by the custody officer, but by a different person called the *'review officer'* (section 40(2)). He is supposed to be at the level of inspector or above, whereas the custody officer is normally at the rank of sergeant. The review officer must consider whether there is any continuing need to hold the suspect on the same grounds.

The reviews must take place at regular intervals, subject to some relaxation if the suspect is, say, asleep at the point when the review becomes due or is actually being questioned at that moment. But broadly speaking the time limits require a second review at the six-hour point and further reviews every nine hours thereafter. So the custody officer must undertake the review immediately on arrival at the police station, followed by the review officer at the six-hour point, and then after each passage of nine hours (section 40(3)).

When considering the need for further detention, the review officer must give the suspect and his lawyer, if he has one, the opportunity of making representations, either orally or in writing as he chooses (section 40(12)). The only exception is if he is not in a fit state. But again, the principle of accountability and the principle of dialogue are established because the suspect must be made aware of the fact that he has a right to make representations if he wishes to do so. I do not suppose the representations will be tremendously influential in most cases; but for what it is worth, it is in the procedure and that is important. In the majority of cases the review is likely to be somewhat perfunctory. It is obviously not going to be a full-scale hearing with contested arguments and so on; it is going to be a rather informal procedure.

The Act establishes the principle that at the 24-hour point there must be a proper review by a superintendent or above (section 42). Further detention of the suspect, if he is still there without having been charged after 24 hours, can only be lawful if it has been approved by a superintendent, and this is only possible if it is a serious arrestable offence as defined in section 116. Again representations can be made to him as to whether or not the suspect should be held yet further. He must be satisfied that the investigation is being conducted 'diligently and expeditiously'.

So far, subject to the availability of a solicitor, nobody from outside the police station has been involved, except possibly that somebody, a family member, relative or other person may have been informed, under the rules previously mentioned in section 56, which as has been seen simply continue the existing provisions of section 62 of the Criminal Law Act 1977.

Reviews by the magistrates

The next time limit at which further detention has to be authorised is the 36-hour point when further detention without charges has to be authorised by a magistrates' court. I emphasise the *court*, it is not by a magistrate; that is to say it is not permitted to approach a magistrate in his private home. It has to be a hearing in a magistrates' court and the clerk will have to be there with a properly constituted court.

The hearing is normally *inter partes*, a major concession by the Government during the passage of the Bill. The suspect not only has a right to be present, but he *must* be present. Not only that, but he has a right to have a lawyer present if he wishes. Moreover, there must be a written statement from the police as to the grounds on which they wish to detain the suspect further. There would therefore be a contested hearing, at which the police presumably would themselves often be represented by lawyers. Although there is no reason why the police cannot argue their own case, I dare say that if the defendant is represented, the police may want to be represented. There is then a hearing, in private, rather than in open court.

The grounds on which the magistrates can authorise further detention are exactly the same grounds as have already been applied by the custody officer and the review officer. The test remains the same, that is that it is necessary to detain the suspect either for the securing or preserving of evidence (whatever that means), or to obtain evidence by questioning. The scenario which I think is the most interesting and the most problematic is where the court is told by the suspect or his lawyer that he has not been cooperating with the police, he has not been helping them at all, he has not been answering questions, and he does not intend to do so.

In other words he has been exercising his right of silence. It is not a very common occurrence, in fact it is an *extremely rare occurrence*, but the suspect may say, 'Well they're holding me in order to break my intention not to say anything', and the police are in effect saying, 'Give us more time and we will in fact be able to crack him.' I do not think that would be a legitimate ground for holding him further. There is nothing in the Act or in the Code that spells this out, but the tenor of the debates in the House of Commons in particular make it clear that the Home Office ministers accepted that that would *not* be a legitimate ground for further detention.

I would certainly hope that the only proper grounds for permitting further detention by the magistrates would be that either he is presently helping the police and there is some expectation that he may help the police even more in the future, or that it is a complicated case where further inquiries are to be made in relation to him, or perhaps in relation to associates. But not where the magistrates have reason to believe that he is simply being held in order that through the passage of time his will should gradually be overcome — though we will probably have to wait for the Divisional Court or Court of Appeal to rule on this.

The hearing normally has to take place within 36 hours (section 42(2)), from the moment of arrival at the police station, not from the moment of arrest. That is an important detail. So if the police take the 'scenic route' to the police station, the timeclock has not started to run. There are provisions in the Act which I will not go through in detail here dealing with the problem of somebody being arrested in one area and taken for questioning to another area, but the basic rule is that the timeclock starts to run when he arrives at the place or the area where he is in fact wanted for questioning (section 41(5)). So if he is taken from Yorkshire to Sussex the rules specify he should not be questioned on the way and the timeclock does not start to run until he arrives in Sussex.

But the 36-hour limit, starting from the moment when the timeclock begins on arrival at the police station, may end at, say, three o'clock or four o'clock in the morning. Does there have to be a hearing at four o'clock in the morning? The answer to that is 'no'; obviously no one wants hearings in the middle of the night. The Code says that hearings should be between 10 a.m. and 9 p.m., and if possible during court hours. But the Act allows for an extra six hours' grace so that if it is possible for the court to sit within six hours of the ending of the 36-hour period, then that extension is permissible. So, if, let us say, the 36 hours was going to elapse at 4 a.m. and the court could sit at 10 a.m. then the hearing can be just before 10 a.m. even though that means the suspect has actually been held without charges for 42 hours.

The magistrates, if they authorise further detention, can do so for up to a further 36 hours at a time. If the police want more than a further 36 hours, they must go back to the magistrates' court. It would not necessarily be the same magistrates, although sometimes it might be. But they do not have to give 36 hours; they could give only six hours, or twelve hours, or whatever.

The aggregate time for which a suspect can be held from beginning to end, regardless of circumstances, is 96 hours. There is no possibility of extension beyond that time except for suspects held under the provisions of the Prevention of Terrorism Act. These have not been affected by the Act, although they have been improved slightly in terms of access to solicitors and in one or two other details. But terrorism suspects remain subject to the maximum of seven days with the authority of the Home Secretary.

There is one detail which may at first sight seem surprising. Let us say the police think it is a clear case, in which they are obviously going to need a lot more time than the 36 hours they can authorise, so they go to the magistrates, after, say, eighteen hours, to ask for permission to hold the suspect beyond the 36-hour point. If the magistrates refuse to authorise this, the police then can continue to hold that suspect for up to 36 hours. In other words the magistrates' permission only covers the stage from the 36-hour point onwards, regardless of the moment in time when the application to the magistrates is made.

The jurisdiction of the magistrates, therefore, relates only from the 36-hour point. Providing the police can justify detention according to the statutory principles, they are entitled to hold the suspect for up to 36 hours even though the magistrates have already said they may not hold him beyond 36 hours. They still have up to 36 hours providing, of course, that a superintendent, at the 24-hour point, is satisfied that according to the criteria there is a need to hold the suspect in order to secure or preserve evidence or to obtain evidence by questioning (section 42(1)).

So the time limits are the next point of accountability. They are in my view an enormous advance on the past position, which was fuzzy, open ended, unclear, in which nobody knew where they were. Suspects, the police, lawyers, and the judges, will now know what the position is in regard to these time limits.

I should perhaps say that there is provision in the Act that time limits are to be regarded as approximate (section 45(2)). That sounds like a rather peculiar provision. Having first laid down the time limits, is it not odd then to have almost a cancellation of the precision which the time limits give? I think the reason for it is clear. The Home Office was persuaded that it was not right for police officers to be walking around with stopwatches constantly worrying about the passage of every second. It is, however, certainly not intended that the police should regard that provision as being in effect a cancellation of the time limits. Not at all; the Home Office ministers made it clear that that was not the intention. It was just to give some flexibility so that if one runs over the time by a little, nobody is going to panic and worry about that. It is certainly intended that the time limits should give form and regularity to the proceedings so that everybody knows where they stand.

Access to solicitors

The next point of accountability which I think is worth mentioning, is access to lawyers. In the past, as is well known, the position was far from satisfactory in that very few suspects asked for lawyers and even those who did often did not get access to a lawyer, at least not at a point in time which was particularly helpful to them.

The Royal Commission hoped that there would be a dramatic change in this regard and if you read the Code it seems possible that there will in fact be a dramatic change. The Code provides (in para 3.1) that the suspect must be told of his right to have a lawyer. The Home Office has made arrangements that there should be generous provision of legal aid. Duty solicitor schemes have been set up by the Law Society. They are linked with the duty solicitor schemes in magistrates' courts and participation in the one is to be tied to participation in the other.

Hence if a solicitor wants to be on the 'gravy train' — if it is a gravy train — then he has got to be willing to turn out at unsocial hours to help suspects at the police station. That is the theory, though I fear that in practice it will not be very easy to persuade a lot of solicitors to turn out at unsocial hours. There is no means testing of the suspect; it is a free service regardless of means. The suspect will have to be told about the duty solicitor scheme, and I hope also told about this rather important detail, although it is not actually provided for as yet. This scheme also applies to the hearing before the magistrates, so that both in the police station and for the hearing before the magistrates it is a totally free non-means tested service.

The 'fly in the ointment', if there is one, comes in the qualifications. This is one of the compromises the Royal Commission struck which is reflected in the Act, so that the right to legal advice is not absolute. There is a saving clause to the effect that in serious arrestable offences, an officer of the rank of superintendent can authorise delay, on certain grounds (section 58). The grounds are that he believes that the exercise of the right of access to a solicitor would lead to interference with or harm to evidence, interference with or physical injury to persons, the alerting of others suspected but not yet arrested, or hindrance in the recovery of property obtained as a result of the offence. The delay cannot be for more than 36 hours because at the 36-hour point the suspect is entitled to have his lawyer to help him with the application to the magistrates. (There are similar provisions in section 56 in regard to informing somebody outside the police station of the suspect's whereabouts.)

There is a further qualification in the Code which was not discussed in the Royal Commission's Report, namely where the investigating officer believes that unreasonable delay would impede the investigation. This is a case where legal advice has been authorised and the solicitor has been called, but it now appears that there is going to be considerable delay, and that delay would unreasonably impede the investigation, then the questioning can start. It can also always start without waiting for the solicitor if it would involve a serious risk of harm to persons or serious loss of or damage to property. These are important qualifications which I think may come to be used quite frequently.

I am, however, more worried about a rather different aspect of the problem which is not one that has been much emphasised — namely that suspects will not very frequently ask for solicitors, even though the Act and the Code require that they be informed of their right to have a solicitor. Experience in the United States suggests that suspects often cannot be brought to understand the utility of having a lawyer at that point. You can tell them, you can advise them, you can caution them, you can give them written indications and suggestions that a solicitor is available and can be brought in without charge, but police officers may be somewhat surprised to know that suspects do not commonly avail themselves of this opportunity.

One might imagine by reading these provisions that solicitors will be swarming around police stations. I do not think so at all, I have already alluded to the difficulty of getting solicitors to turn out at unsocial hours. Even if they improve considerably in regard to that, the *real* problem will be to persuade suspects that it is a desirable thing to have a solicitor to hold their hand and help them.

Incidentally, the Code makes it clear that clerks to solicitors can be sent in lieu of solicitors themselves. But, and this is a very curious provision, a clerk, but not a solicitor, can be excluded from the police station if, in effect, the officer in charge thinks that he is not a proper person (the Code, para 6.9). On access to lawyers therefore, the scheme proposes a major change but the reality probably will turn out to be a more modest change. There will be more solicitors in police stations than in the past, but perhaps not quite as many as some have hoped, or as the case may be, have feared.

Cautions

Let me deal with two other matters. Firstly the caution: a small point but it may prove to be of some slight significance. The redraft of the caution provisions in section 10 of the Code is now very lengthy. It was very short and the Home Office even toyed with the idea of abandoning the time-honoured principle of having an actual set form of words. But they were eventually persuaded that a formula was desirable in that it helps people to know what they are supposed to say. There is provision for slight relaxation and indeed for a paraphrase of the caution, and some words of explanation if the person cannot understand the words as specified.

The more important point I think, is that the caution is supposed now to be administered when there are grounds to *suspect* an offence has been committed. This is a more liberal test of the time at which the caution is to be administered than existed under the Judges' Rules, which was where there was evidence, and indeed the courts held, admissible evidence. So under the law as it stood, the caution was supposed only to be administered when the officer had already amassed quite a good deal of evidence, whereas under the new rules, he has to administer the caution at a much earlier stage (paras. 10.1–10.6). The other point is that the Code (sections 11 and 12) does slightly tighten up the procedure as to the recording of the details of the exchange between the suspect and the police officer. It requires in paragraph 11.3, verbatim and contemporaneous record keeping, in so far as that is possible, or if that is not possible the record should be made as soon as it may be thereafter. It is supposed to be an accurate record of the exchange. There are of course experiments under way for tape-recording, and what is important is that the police have finally come round to the view that tape-recording is a very good thing.

For years they opposed it bitterly on the grounds that it would create all sorts of difficulties, but the experiment is apparently proving a very substantial success. It was intended to be a control on the police, and was accordingly seen by the police as a threat. It is now increasingly being understood by the police that tape-recording is a great advantage to them in that it first of all relieves them of much of the tiresome business of keeping a proper note, and secondly and much more importantly, it encapsulates the suspect's confession and admission, about which there can be little real room for argument thereafter. The tape-recording experiment is a major development which will come to be general practice in the very near future.

Confessions

A final point on confessions is worth making. The provisions of the Act on confessions look as if they are new. What is said in section 76 is that a confession is not admissible if it has been obtained as a result of oppressive conduct; that is already the common law. And secondly it is not admissible if it has been obtained by means which are likely to render it unreliable. Now that looks very different from the classic traditional/common law rule on this subject which is that a confession is inadmissible if it has been obtained by any threat or promise held out by a person in authority, which made a confession inadmissible because it was involuntary.

The courts have, in fact, substantially changed that rule in the last few years, particularly in two cases *DPP v. Ping Lin* [1975] 3 All E.R. 175 in the House of Lords and *R. v. Rennie* [1982] 1 All E.R. 385 in the Court of Appeal. The old principle of excluding statements made as a result of *any* threat or promise had in effect been abolished by the courts and what is now in the Act is not very different from what is already in the common law. The formula in the Act is what the Criminal Law Revision Committee in its ill-fated 1972 Report proposed should be the rule, which has in effect become the law in the meanwhile through common law decisions.

Notes

1. There are four separate codes of practice dealing with the exercise of stop and search powers, the searching of premises and the seizure of property, the identification of persons, and the treatment of suspects. The latter is entitled *Code of Practice for the Detention, Treatment and Questioning of Persons by Police Officers*, and it is this code which is considered in this chapter; it will usually be referred to as 'the Code'. The four codes were published late in 1985 in one booklet: Home Office, *Police and Criminal Evidence Act (s.66) Codes of Practice*, London: HMSO, 1985.

CHAPTER 11

The interrogation process

BARRIE IRVING

The discussion of the operation of the Police and Criminal Evidence Act in the police station presents certain problems. Police stations are closed institutions once you get beyond the front desk, and closed institutions have an unfortunate tendency to be titillating.

A police station's cell blocks, interview rooms, and charge rooms, are closed in two senses: access and egress are restricted. This applies to such other institutions as weapons establishments, prisons and mental hospitals. But police stations are closed also in the sense that brothels are closed; that is, you can get in and eventually you can get out, but you do not then talk freely to all and sundry about the intervening experience! And when you do, the listener, if he has not shared the experience, does not quite know what to make of it.

Such institutions are titillating and we need to beware of this when discussing what happens in police stations, what could happen, and how that might or might not be affected by an Act of Parliament.

Inside the police station

The time-honoured way for exploring closed institutions is either to refer to the carefully reported experience of those who have been in them, on business as it were, or to gain access by some kind of trickery, as Erving Goffman did in preparing his much acclaimed report on asylums.[1] Occasionally, however, such is the universal ignorance about a closed institution, and so significant is the need to know, that the breach in the institution's defences is actually arranged by an arm of government.

It is important to realise — because it demonstrates the true constitutional position of the police in this country — that when the Royal Commission on Criminal Procedure asked me to study interrogation at the police station[2] they could not *order* that research to take place and neither technically could the chief constable. Access to the chosen station had to be won by a slow process of negotiation and by building up trust at all levels in the force.

Times have changed. Police stations are now much more open places than they were, but I would ask the reader to keep in mind that for most people there is a wide gap between what they think they know about the inside of police stations and how they operate, and what they themselves would experience if they were a suspect detained during a criminal investigation.

The Police and Criminal Evidence Act, in common with most other pieces of legislation, is an attempt to control individual and organisational behaviour by a complex set of rules and, in places, by legislative exhortation. In this case the behaviour to be controlled is the way that certain policing tasks are carried out. If the Royal Commission's call for a balance between the needs of the police and the rights of the citizen has been struck[3], then the Act should give fairly evenly weighted packages — one controlling police work, the other enabling and facilitating it. I will try to describe what tasks and situations in the police station need controlling or enabling and whether the provisions of the Act seem up to the job. I leave the reader to judge whether the appropriate balance has been struck.

Making these subjective predictions about how legislation will work out in practice should not be an activity created to fill conference agendas. I would hope that some rational effort will be made to check on both whether the expected benefits of the Act eventuate and, perhaps more important, whether there are unforeseen negative consequences.

I want to start by listing the significant acts which take place behind the facade of police stations in the course of the investigation of criminal cases. I shall deal only with the treatment of suspects who know they are suspects and have been arrested either before they arrive at the station or shortly thereafter. I don't believe any serious problems exist for other classes of visitors to police stations. The first major event for such subjects is that the appropriate officer provides the arrested man or woman with information about his or her status, rights, responsibilities and about the process which he or she is about to go through.

Following the provision of information, officers have to deal with the property and possessions of the arrested person. A search may be necessary and articles of clothing and personal possessions may have to be taken from the suspect, sometimes against his will. Property will then be classified as either pertinent or not pertinent to the case under investigation and dealt with accordingly.

After this process of induction there are four aspects of what ensues which I think are of central importance. These are:

— the conditions of incarceration;
— the management of incarceration;
— the conditions of interrogation;
— the management of interrogation.

The provisions of the Act, whether they are aimed at enabling, facilitating or controlling police activities, make certain assumptions about aspects of police organisation and behaviour. The most important of these assumptions relate to discipline, supervision and discretion. It is also assumed that the police organisation is rational with a single set of goals. The legislation does not attempt to grapple with the informal police culture so vividly described in the recent study carried out by the Policy Studies Institute.[4]

The activities described above present problems for both the suspect and the police. Occasionally the interests of both parties coincide (for example it is in everyone's interest that no one dies in custody) but more often than not interests diverge. I'm not going to attempt to deal with the fine print of these matters and neither will I try to judge whether the provisions of the Act offer more or less by way of protection or facilitation than the previous hotch-potch of common law, precedent, legislation and established practice. I shall rely heavily on my own research, backed up by my more recent experience at the Police Foundation[5], to offer a critique of the Act. If I seem to concentrate on problems, it's because I see no point in focusing on the Act's many excellent qualities.

Let me at the outset admit a bias: I believe that the civilisation and the humanitarianism of a society is mirrored in how it treats those who are legitimately imprisoned by agents of the state. I also have a psychologist's view of what is and what is not acceptable treatment for prisoners, and some people may feel that I am over-sensitive about the psychological impact of incarceration and interrogation. Notice that I do not believe in euphemisms in this field: imprisonment is incarceration, and I do happen to take seriously the view that suspects are innocent until proved guilty in spite of the fact that over fifty per cent of suspects tend to be 'banged to rights', that is, self-evidently guilty.[6]

It is worth bearing in mind who we are talking about when we talk of suspects. The majority of course will be young men, although the proportion of women is increasing, and it is also the case that while many may have money to spend, the majority come from social classes D/E, have a less than brilliant academic record, and are likely to be unemployed, with all that such a sociological thumb-nail sketch suggests. Half of all suspects will have had previous experience of criminal investigation.

The rights of the prisoners

The first problem is the conflict which often arises for the police between the need to process suspects swiftly and efficiently, so that officers can get back to other duties, and the need to carry out important and difficult tasks such as imparting to the suspect vital information about rights and responsibilities. On Friday and Saturday nights for example this conflict can become acute. It can also be made acute by the suspect's behaviour or police assumptions about how the suspect might behave. Searching an aggressive or frightened suspect can and often does provoke a violent reaction — so does removing clothing and personal effects either for examination or to limit the chance of self-injury or injury to jailers.

When it comes to giving information, the suspect may be disoriented by the sudden change in his circumstances, frightened by the uncertainty of the immediate future or angry about his capture. All of these extreme emotions make it difficult for human beings to process information. I would ask the reader to imagine being ordered around and lectured by a rather strict travel courier on arrival at a foreign destination after a long night flight: the analogy is bizarre but it is a close parallel to the disorienting effects of sudden incarceration.

With all these things going on in a small office within the cell block, there is an obvious need to regulate how suspects are dealt with, and to ensure that regardless of the circumstances every suspect is given similar information about both his rights and responsibilities, and that arresting officers and others know what they are permitted to do in processing a new prisoner and what is not allowed. We now have in the Code of Practice a clear statement that rights must be issued to prisoners in writing, and they also have the right to see the Code of Practice itself (see paragraphs 3.1 and 3.2).

The stipulations follow pre-existing rules, that is the right to have someone informed, the right to legal advice, and of course the right to remain silent, contained in the caution. Note, however, that apart from the caution, these rights can be delayed where the offence concerned is a 'serious arrestable offence' (for definitions see Section 116 and Schedule 5 of the Act) and when the delay is authorised by an officer of the rank of superintendent or above. Such authorisation can be given where there is a chance that the right, if exercised, would harm the evidence, alert persons, or interfere in some other way with the investigation in hand (the Act: Sections 56 and 58).

This is a codification of previous practice with the additions that: (1) someone is now personally accountable for any decision to delay; and (2) a record of the request, the reasons for it and the result must now all be recorded. There is now also a time limit on withdrawing these basic rights. All of this codification is, I believe, an improvement on previous practice provided one assumes utmost good faith in the operation of the accounting and authorising procedures. It is also vital for the proper operation of this system that it is buttressed by an efficient complaints procedure. In my view the new system is likely to create a trail of records which must make outright abuse much more difficult, if not impossible. It would be extremely rare for one prisoner to be so important to the career of the superintendent that he would even consider abusing the system so as to deny these rights to that prisoner.

A much greater risk for the suspect is that delays, for whatever reason, will occur as the process of sanctioning drags on. If the authorisation process can reasonably be shown to take a certain length of time, then it would seem inevitable that this will become the error margin which suspects will have to accept between what the Act says should happen and what happens in practice. A crucial practical question is whether the sort of individuals who in the past habitually had access to solicitors delayed and who were usually held incommunicado will be treated differently now. I can't see that they will.

Some police commentators pessimistically believe that codification of accounting procedures will make an enormous difference to their work but I believe the main change will be in reducing the amount of variation in practice between forces, between stations and between individual officers. Officers who have always kept a meticulous record will have nothing to worry about, but those who were sometimes sloppy or even consciously manipulative in their past attitudes to prisoners' rights will find life rather difficult under the new regime.

What about understanding one's rights? Some suspects may not be able to read or may not fully be able to take in what is being said to them. The Code deals with persons at risk at paragraphs 1.4–1.7, 3.6–3.8 and 13.1–13.3. I and others who have worked to get recognition of the special needs of certain people at police stations are pleased to see the 'at risk concept' in the Code and the Act generally. There are obvious problems of diagnosis: police are not meant to be able to spot all forms of mental illness or mental handicap, but the Act and Code create a framework within which expertise in this area is likely to develop with help from other agencies. Also the provisions of the Act for third party attendance, and recognition of the need for the third party to be knowledgeable, should mean that eventually very few 'at risk' persons are interrogated without appropriate safeguards.

Some people have raised the case of the ordinary citizen who, once arrested, because of his emotional state or the behaviour of officers or both, does not fully appreciate his rights. I don't believe there can be any remedy for this situation in the police station itself. We should teach children and young people more about their civil rights and responsibilities so that they are better equipped to cope with the emergency of being a suspect and this must be even more important for those who statistically have a greater chance of experiencing arrest.

The role of the custody officer

Section 54 of the Act, on searches, codifies what can be taken from a prisoner and how. It can still leave the prisoner shuffling along, holding his trousers up with one hand, without a watch, pencil or pen, or indeed any other personal object. Given what at least one prisoner somewhere is known to have done with almost every object under the sun, this situation is perhaps inevitable. I argued to the Royal Commission that removal of all property was part of an important process of depersonalisation after an arrest, and that this process has important repercussions in interrogation.

At the same time I realise that suspects must be protected from themselves and jailers, and interviewers must be protected from suspects. The same goes for objects likely to have evidential value. Anything can have evidential value: but very few things actually do. Discretion to decide must of course be left with the investigating officers, and the custody officer is, through the Act (Section 54), given the job of deciding. This provision means that somebody not connected with the case has to be given a reason for taking an object or a piece of clothing from the suspect.

This is the first time I have referred to the role of the custody officer. Many cell blocks used to be run by jailers who kept copious records which, funnily enough, barristers and solicitors rarely seemed to consult. The best practice in this respect is now formalised in the role of the custody officer. It appears from Section 36 that anyone with the rank of sergeant or above can hold this role except those involved directly in the relevant investigation. It is worth pointing out that the custody officers will have to be prepared to stand their ground on many issues against their colleagues who may want to interpret the new rules to their advantage, particularly with important suspects and difficult cases. The custody officer may well be a young man with little experience, and he may have to control a detective chief inspector with perhaps twenty years' service: the possible difficulties and pressures are readily apparent.

The position on intimate searches is now at least clear. As I recall, the Royal Commission received no evidence on this issue so I don't think we know how many searches take place or the reasons for them. Controversy on this matter seems to have centred on:

— whether cross-sex searches should ever be allowed;
— whether police officers should search at all;
— where searches should be conducted.

The provisions in the Act (Section 55) are, to my mind, mostly unremarkable except possibly where discretion is given to a superintendent or above to authorise an intimate search by a police officer. One imagines that situations may arise when an immediate search is required for weapons or other evidence. There seems no other way of dealing with emergencies other than to give discretion to the police and to record carefully which orifices were searched and why. Recording provides the best available check on abuse. There remains the unlikely but possible danger that the threat of an intimate search for nebulous reasons might be used nefariously as a means of obtaining a confession or other evidence and this threat cannot be entirely eliminated.

It is up to the courts, solicitors and the complaints procedure to ensure that accountability is maintained and they can best achieve this by the outlawing of blanket or vague accounting on the record. 'Suspected concealed weapon', or 'information received', if accepted as proper accounts of decisions to allow an emergency search, could unleash intimate searches on anyone. Section 55 of the Act states there must be 'reasonable grounds to believe', but in the past there has been a tendency for 'reasonable grounds' to be whatever a police officer wants. If the recording system is to do the job it was designed to do, this cosy tradition will have to go.

The effects of incarceration

Let us now proceed to the stage where the suspect is locked in a cell, his property has been taken along with his belt, shoelaces, watch, etc. and he has either exercised his right to inform someone and contacted his brief, or those rights have been denied.

Those people who haven't tried it, should test the experience of being locked in a small bare room, not knowing what's going to happen, or when they are going to get out. It has rather startling effects on some people. I noted in my report to the Royal Commission that to a greater or lesser extent mental ill-health, alcohol and drug abuse, behaviour and personality problems were all over-represented in the suspect population compared with the population at large. Locking such people up will tend to exacerbate pre-existing difficulties and may indeed create new phobic reactions and consequently close supervision by jailers is essential. Best practice in the past by jailers has always involved careful monitoring of difficult prisoners and that practice is now enshrined in the Act. Defence lawyers who feel that custody has an untoward effect on their clients, or those suspects who wish to complain about their experiences, should now have a running record of their custody to which to refer. If that record is inaccurate, then the suspect can refuse to endorse it.

However, keeping such records in a full cell block is an onerous task and to be useful for the purposes for which they have been ordained, these records must be accurate and specific. Indeed, the Code of Practice insists that they must be (paragraphs 2.1–2.6) but I believe that this administrative burden may prove too great in some instances. It should also be stressed that it is not possible, given the standard layout of most cell blocks, to give prisoners supervision which is adequate for extreme circumstances. There will always therefore be events or behaviour which are not detected by custody officers.

Whatever the Act and Code say, in the nature of things every cell block will continue to run under the threat that some prisoner at some time will go berserk. Further, all the officers working on cell blocks will continue to be what they have always been in their interactions with prisoners — that is fallible human beings, and as such they may, under certain circumstances, abuse their power. The Act and Code do not tell the police how to deal with extreme circumstances and it would probably be inappropriate for legislation to take on that task.

It needs to be stressed, however, that the police will continue to need back-up in the station from doctors, psychiatrists, social workers and ambulance men. The 'at risk' category created by the Act should open up the station to other professions to a greater degree than has been the case in the past. Other professionals will now have a legitimate and codified role to play in helping to cope with difficult and extreme circumstances. In this context I think police officers working with prisoners need to understand that sudden unfocused and purposeless violent behaviour by those in custody is *prima facie* evidence of extreme mental distress, and should be treated as such, not as a planned assault or attempt to escape, unless there is clear evidence that that is the case.

Physical abuse of prisoners by police officers always remains a possibility. As far as I can see it always will, unless there is some form of constant independent supervision. What legislation there is can, in a closed 24-hours community, always be avoided; recording systems can be manipulated; there can be collusion between the custody officer and others. At bottom the safety and basic civil rights of a prisoner in custody depend on the moral character of the officers who deal with him and the power of the discipline system and accounting system to deter. So powerful are the emotions which are sometimes called to play in dealing with some suspects that only the strongest personal ethical sense and a balanced personality are likely to see police officers through.

I would therefore ask what provisions for monitoring the psychological health of police officers engaged in looking after prisoners are planned. It seems to me that the role of custody officer, which is so neatly waiting round every corner of this legislation, is a respectable cover for all that's most difficult and messy about cell block policing. Custody officers are expected to stand up to everyone and be paragons of administrative and moral rectitude, capable of diagnosing risk, predicting the unpredictable, and yet nothing is said about their training or vetting. Indeed, we learn they can be any police officers at all so long as they have attained the rank of sergeant and they do not have an interest in the case for which they are acting (Section 36 of the Act). Obviously our legislators do not take too seriously the 'I will scratch your back' principle which oils the wheels of all our institutions.

Conditions for interrogation

Before examining the central question of management of interrogation, I should mention the new guidelines on fitness to be interrogated. Those in the 'at risk' category (juveniles, mentally handicapped, and mentally ill) are now to have informed third parties present if possible and if they desire them in preference to relatives. The lessons of the Maxwell Confait case seem to have got through: however, the question of special training for those who will protect those 'at risk' is still unresolved. The Police Foundation's funding of the work by David Cahill and Bryan Tully on interviewing the mentally handicapped[7] has produced some hard data on what needs to be taught concerning this group, but there are no courses extant, and no effective teaching materials have as yet been produced. It must be firmly stressed that common sense is not enough in this area.

The restrictions on who may be interviewed, for how long, and where, are an enormous improvement on what was formerly the case. I have consistently argued for restrictions on interviewing persons under the influence of drugs or drink, or interviewing which denies people proper sleep and rest, or which takes place unreasonably late at night. The Code now lays down (paragraphs 12.2–12.7) reasonable conditions for interviews. They do not, however, carry the force of law or of any exclusionary rule, although of course Section 78 of the Act, based on Lord Scarman's amendment concerning evidence which has been unfairly obtained, and Section 76, may well be applied to any extreme cases. The preferred conditions of interrogation can be breached at the discretion of the officers concerned in the case, but here again reasons have to be given and those reasons are available for the defence to challenge in court. Again I would argue that this form of accountability provides reasonable safeguards as long as blanket reasons for changing the preferred conditions do not gain currency in the courts and the complaints procedure.

The Act provides an excellent chance for a new beginning in this regard which can all too easily be squandered. I hope that those people who have to deal with such issues within the criminal justice system will keep in mind what weight these accounting provisions are being asked to bear within this legislation. I am particularly worried about the way evidence of the conduct of interrogations will be handled in magistrates' courts which, after all, take the vast majority of cases.

So, if all goes well, we get to the interview room in a reasonable state at a reasonable hour, and reasonably rested; our relatives know where we are, and we have got legal advice if we want it. We know from having seen the Code that we can't be kept forever; that interviewing can only go on two hours at a time, and that we will get meal breaks. So far — with the caveats advanced — so good.

I have written enough about interrogation techniques and I don't want to detain the reader with that subject here.[8] One should be aware though that competent interviewers will be able to use their advantage in terms of information and authority to persuade most suspects of the wisdom of providing such relevant information as they possess. At its most impressive, the art of interrogation involves mere gestures, slight inflections to the voice, the smallest hints of underlying threat or inducement, usually of a psychological kind. At its crudest, tactics involve downright trickery and bargaining over overtly stated material threats and inducements. Now what have the Act and Code done to this can of worms? I shall deal with interviewing under three headings: tactics, recording and documentation, and tape-recording.

The tactics of interrogation

Those tactics are allowed which do not amount to oppression or are not of a kind that is likely to render admissions or other evidence obtained thereby unreliable. Oppression includes torture or inhuman or degrading treatment. I argued strongly to the Royal Commission that just as it was not possible to say what rendered a statement voluntary, so it was not possible to define what would or would not render a confession reliable or unreliable.

Of course it is a confession's reliability which matters: the tautological principle we now have, simply stated, is that confessions will only be admissible if they are good confessions, that is they are not false or likely to be false — not much help, one may think. Oppression as a legal concept has its own case law and on this I am in difficulties as well. What is oppressive, indeed degrading, to one person is water off the back of another. To distinguish what conditions have what effects with any reliability would require contemporaneous data which cannot possibly be obtained, or indeed processed, by the criminal justice system.

So there is no power in the concepts themselves. The sting comes in the onus of proof provision at Section 76, Subsections 2 and 3. If the tactics or circumstances of the interview look dodgy to the court, it's up to the prosecution to prove they did not oppress the suspect or render his admission unreliable. The weakness of the concepts is now smartly turned in favour of the defendant. If we cannot be sure what is oppressive, then *mutatis mutandis* the interview in all its respects must be completely above board if it is not to run the risk of rendering evidence obtained from it inadmissible.

I imagine that the judiciary will in fact work out their own view of where the line on what is acceptable should be drawn. Given that there is no scientific way of gauging unreliability, it seems that it is absolutely right to make it the job of the court, but I would hope that certain tactics will, if they come to light, always render admissions inadmissible. The ones I most object to are based on

— positive lying and trickery,
— threats or inducements relating directly to the role of the police.

It seems to me that these two sets of tactics call the criminal justice system itself into disrepute. There is also no need of them when other more defensible tactics are available. The onus of proof on the prosecution to show beyond reasonable doubt that confessions were properly obtained according to the Code throws the whole accounting system in the Act into sharp relief. If the prosecution is to demonstrate the propriety of a custodial interrogation, then they will have to produce written and oral evidence of a seamless process: gaps, vagueness as to what was done by whom, to whom and under what conditions, will provide significant ammunition for the defence.

I have always believed that if the courts were able to sit in judgement on accurate descriptions of what went on in cell blocks, then they would be well placed to make the necessary judgements about what kind of interrogation tactics should be permitted and which outlawed. I believe the Act sets up the precondition for this to happen. It is in police interests to describe exactly how they manage interrogation, passing responsibility for setting limits on what is fair to the courts. Once these limits have been set, we can leave behind the ludicrous situation in which detectives cannot be properly trained to interrogate because all the effective methods are technically against the law.

After much soul searching, I think it right that those who drafted this legislation did not try to ban particular classes of interrogation (although one attempt at this turned up in a draft of the Bill in 1983). There seem to be the right conditions now for a workable contract between police and courts. If the police provide accurate descriptions of interrogations, then they should expect the courts to work out some sensible rules about tactics.

Interview records and documentation

This leads me on to discuss recording of interview material. Accurate (but not verbatim) records can now be seen by suspects and/or third parties attending interviews to check reliability. There are specific instructions that written statements shall not be prompted or edited in any way. Gone, hopefully for ever, is the notion that a perfectly ordinary human being can talk to another for three hours and produce, two days later, a few pages which are purported to be a verbatim record of the interview.

It must, however, still be said that there can be many verbal interactions between suspect and investigating officers which will not be available to the court in the form of a statement. The courts must realise that statements, whether or not they are tape-recorded, will continue to be the final product of a process. There is nothing in this legislation which can eliminate informal negotiation between investigating officers and suspects, unless they are absolutely banned from all contact with each other except when formal interviews are taking place.

I used the word 'negotiation' above, and this usage needs defending. Efficient and effective interviewing depends largely on the suspect's own eagerness to see what he can win for himself. There is a strong gambling instinct in many suspects I have observed and they need little or no provocation to start looking for a bargain. Under these conditions, particularly where the suspect has a record, he will be as interested in having 'informal chats' with investigating officers as they are with him. Indeed, requests for meetings often come from prisoners. This means that with the best will in the world restricting contact to formal interviews is virtually impossible. The back-stop is again the custody record, which should contain details of all interactions between officers and prisoners. It would be well to assume that all such interactions are purposeful where detectives or investigating officers are concerned.

Tape-recording of interviews

Written statements which are not verbatim will not of course usually contain details of voice inflection, gesture, even of crucial bargaining moves by both sides. It is to attempt to plug this gap that tape-recording is being introduced (Section 60 of the Act). The Police Foundation is monitoring trials at Croydon and Leicester with the particular task of assessing the effect of tape-recording on the character of interviews. So far it seems that tape-recording has been readily accepted, and predicted major changes in interview technique and suspect behaviour have not occurred.

Tape-recording theoretically suffers from some of the drawbacks of written statements and records. It does not record gesture or expression and only formal interviews are recorded, but, if lawyers and the courts become expert in analysing taped interviews in difficult cases, the voice of the suspect and the interviewing officer will always betray more than written documents, even verbatim records.

Against this advantage must be set the time it takes to analyse tapes of interviews. Social scientists who have used this method will sympathise. If analysis is to be taken seriously, there is also the question of where the appropriate expertise will come from. Taped records present lawyers with a significant increase in the informational base from which to work and it may be some time before they learn how to exploit this change. Judging by American experience, one would expect cases built largely on taped confessions to polarise into a large number of uncontested cases and a relatively small number of complex heavily contested cases. But this polarisation may take some time.

A framework for police professionalism

I realise that there are many more issues which could be considered: finger-printing, intimate samples, bail, charging, but provisions in these areas, at least to the non-lawyer, look mainly cosmetic — tidying up regulations which have been around for some time and introducing the accounting procedure which is such an important thread running through the Act.

This piece of legislation is the culmination of a decade of rising concern about what goes on in police stations and elsewhere where the police interact with citizens. It was, as I have stressed, meant to strike a balance between ensuring the civil rights of the citizen and enabling the police to prevent and detect crime. The Bill had a rough passage and inevitably the signs of compromise are everywhere. In effect it codifies best practice rather than introducing new practices although time limits, tape-recording, and the whole concept of 'at risk' prisoners are welcome innovations in my field of interest.

The general compromise that seems to have been struck is: no interference with the general procedure of custodial interrogation, and no absolute exclusionary rule, granted in return for a comprehensive authorisation and accounting procedure. This is not a bad bargain, if the rest of the criminal justice system keeps firmly in mind how police organisations actually work. For those hard cases which do not come to court, then it is the complaints procedure which must take the strain. Although I have my doubts as to whether a wholly internal system can ever be trusted by some important sections of our society.

Having spent nine months working on a cell block, I personally know that the only real safeguard for the prisoner is the integrity of individual officers. In this regard the move by the Metropolitan Police to produce a code of ethics for police officers is the first step in what will undoubtedly be a long process, changing the meaning the police attribute to the term 'professional'. Professional status is acquired not by skill and dexterity alone, but by a consistent personal regard for an ethical code from every member of the profession, even under circumstances where breaking the code will go undetected.

It can be argued, if somewhat provocatively, that the police are the first occupational group in this country to have acquired the reward structure of a profession before demonstrating the full professional status which comes with a rigidly enforced ethical code. This anomaly is now being tackled and the Police and Criminal Evidence Act provides a reasonable framework within which police ethics can develop. Let us hope that police progress towards true professionalism will now be rapid.

Notes

1. Erving Goffman, *Asylums: Essays on the social situation of mental patients and other inmates*, Harmondsworth: Penguin, 1968.
2. Barrie Irving, *Police Interrogation: A Case Study of Current Practice*, Royal Commission on Criminal Procedure Research Study No. 2, London: HMSO, 1980; Barrie Irving and Linden Hilgendorf, *Police Interrogation: the Psychological Approach*, Royal Commission on Criminal Procedure Research Study No. 1, London: HMSO, 1980.
3. Royal Commission on Criminal Procedure (Chairman: Sir Cyril Philips), *Report*, London: HMSO, 1981 (Cmnd. 8092) see chapters 1 and 10.
4. *Police and People in London*, London: Policy Studies Institute, 1983; published in four volumes: (I) David J. Smith, *A Survey of Londoners*, PSI No. 618; (II) Stephen Small, *A Group of Young Black People*, PSI, No. 619; (III) David J. Smith, *A Survey of Police Officers*, PSI No. 620; (IV) David J. Smith and Jeremy Gray, *The Police in Action*, PSI No. 621.
5. See Irving, *op. cit.*, *supra* note 2; see also the Police Foundation projects, *Independent evaluation of an experiment in neighbourhood policing in Notting Hill and Camberley; Independent evaluation of the training of probationer constables (Metropolitan Police)*; see also other projects detailed in the Police Foundation newsletters available from 314–316, Vauxhall Bridge Road, London, SW1V 1AA.
6. See the Royal Commission on Criminal Procedure, *Report, supra* note 3, and *The Investigation and Prosecution of Criminal Offences in England and Wales: The Law and Procedure*, London: HMSO, 1980 (Cmnd. 8092–1); see also Irving, *op. cit, supra* note 2.
7. Bryan Tully and David Cahill, *Police Interviewing of the Mentally Handicapped: An Experimental Study*, London: The Police Foundation, 1984.
8. Irving, *Police Interrogation: A Case Study of Current Practice, supra* note 2, especially page 111, table 5.2; see also Paul Softley, *Police Interrogation: An Observational Study in Four Police Stations*, Royal Commission on Criminal Procedure Research Study No. 4, London: HMSO, 1980.

CHAPTER 12

Questioning the suspect

MAURICE BUCK

In his contribution to this book Kenneth Oxford outlines his perspective of modern day policing using the concept of a social contract between the police and the public. Within this framework he considers the Police and Criminal Evidence Act as it affects policing on the streets, whereas my contribution takes us inside the police station to the warm welcome that awaits us in the charge office cells!

Seeking the vital balance

The Police and Criminal Evidence Act, of course, had its origins in the Report of the Royal Commission on Criminal Procedure[1] and I feel it is important to highlight part of the terms of reference that Sir Cyril Philips and his colleagues were given. In the Royal Warrant dated 3 February 1978 the Commission was instructed to examine the prosecution process and

> the powers and duties of the police in respect of the investigation of criminal offences and the rights and duties of suspect and accused persons, including the means by which these are secured.[2]

The Commission was asked to strike a balance between bringing offenders to justice and protecting citizens' rights and liberties, and of course it is no easy task to achieve this. It took the Royal Commission over two and a half years of detailed investigations and deliberations before reaching its views on what changes were necessary.

When introducing the Bill at its second reading the Home Secretary stated that the legislation was needed for three reasons, which can be summarised as:

— the state of the law was unclear;
— the police needed adequate and clear powers to conduct the fight against crime; the public required proper safeguards against any abuse of such powers;
— the measures played an essential part in an overall strategy to create more effective policing.[3]

Only time will tell whether the Act meets Leon Brittan's objectives, but I feel bound to reinforce the reservations put forward by Kenneth Oxford in chapter four. Indeed it is the considered opinion of the Association of Chief Police Officers that the legislation falls short of providing the police with the clear powers they need to protect the public. It seems that during the lengthy debates in both Houses of Parliament which led to almost 1,000 amendments in total, the vital balance between police powers and the rights of the individual was radically changed from the Royal Commission's original intentions, and this was done in such a way that the *professional* criminal may be able to exploit the law to escape conviction.

This is clearly against the public interest. Nevertheless, I have no doubt that the new provisions will lead to a more professional approach by police officers and to this end I welcome the introduction of the codes of practice.[4] However, it would be a tragedy if the outcome of the legislation is that the police are so constrained that they are no longer able to protect society from those who are prepared to commit violent robbery, murder and other serious crimes.

I do not wish to give the impression that I take a totally pessimistic and gloomy view of the future. Already there are many encouraging signs and it is my sincere hope and belief that the whole package of changes, including tape-recording (section 60), the Crown Prosecution Service and other proposals for the streamlining of the criminal justice process will eventually provide society with a more open and workable system and so the balance I have referred to will not have been completely lost.

Nowhere in the Act and codes of practice is the need for that balance more clearly defined than in the detention, and questioning and treatment of suspects. In this chapter I would like to concentrate on some of the major changes and difficulties which are facing the police in these areas. I shall do so by looking in particular at custody officers, detention conditions, reviews of detention, extended detention and tape-recording.

Enter the custody officer

The idea of a custody officer who is responsible for all matters relating to the detention of prisoners is not new. Indeed, in London and the major cities the introduction of this post will not cause an unduly difficult problem for it will amount to little more than re-titling the officers who currently fulfil a similar role and some re-organisation of their duties. On a personal note, I do not expect too much difficulty in my own force in that in Northamptonshire effectively we already have six designated 'station sergeants' who will perform the new role. Certainly these officers will have greatly expanded responsibilities and I believe they will respond positively to the task.

During the course of the debates on the Act we were asked what the resource implications of custody officers would be and, as secretary of the Association of Chief Police Officers Crime Committee, I conducted a survey of all forces, with the exception of the Metropolitan Police, on the number of additional sergeants which would be needed. Without the 'saving provisions' — where the detention will not exceed six hours to which I will shortly refer — forces estimated that they would need several hundred more sergeants. We know, however, that it is most unlikely that resources on such a vast scale will be forthcoming and therefore there must be a penalty in that more sergeants will be removed from outside supervisory duties to occupy custody officer posts. This undermines much that the police service has been trying to achieve in the last few years in response to advice such as that from Lord Scarman[5] and others.

Because we are unlikely to obtain the extra resources, some police forces, particularly those with large rural areas, are faced with a dilemma. They either have to face the prospect of conveying prisoners over long distances to a police station where there is a custody officer, or designating some smaller stations with the consequent resource implications.

It was because of these difficulties that the 'saving clauses' in sections 30 and 36 were introduced. These provisions permit an arrested person to be taken to a non-designated police station if the detention is unlikely to exceed six hours. There is still, of course, the safeguard that an inspector must be informed (section 36(9)). Even so, the spirit of the Act demands that persons should normally be detained at police stations where there is a custody officer and suitable accommodation with full provision for the proper care of prisoners.

Over the years the status and role of the station sergeant has altered dramatically. With an increasing volume of work, more arrests and a whole host of ancillary duties such as the supervision of communications, the time available for the sergeant to devote solely to the care and treatment of detained persons has inevitably been reduced. In future, the status of the custody officer will be considerably enhanced for it is quite clear that although he may well have some other duties to perform in the police station his paramount role is that of a quasi-independent guardian for the care and treatment of all detained persons, and indeed the protection of individual police officers.

It is spelled out in the Act that the first decision when an arrested person arrives at the police station will be taken by the custody officer — this is a decision to 'accept' the prisoner because the detention conditions are fulfilled (sections 34 and 37). If the custody officer does not consider there is sufficient evidence to charge the person he can authorise the person's continued detention either to secure and preserve evidence relating to an offence for which the person has been arrested or to obtain such evidence by questioning (section 37(2 and 3)). The authority of the custody officer is further reinforced by requiring any disagreements with his decisions to be referred to the superintendent who is responsible for the police station (section 39(6)).

In short, after someone is admitted to the police station, the custody officer will be responsible for all aspects of the treatment of the arrested person whilst he is detained — except when he has handed the person over to another officer for interviewing. Even then he must ensure, when receiving the detainee back into his custody, that the provisions of the codes of practice have been implemented and he must report any breaches to a senior officer (section 39). So the custody officer will occupy a vital position inside every designated police station.

Detention: reviews and extensions

Superimposed on the custody officer's duty to safeguard the rights of the detained person is the additional safeguard of periodic reviews of that person's detention (section 40). These will be carried out by a 'review officer' who in the case of someone who has been arrested *and charged* is the custody officer. In the case of someone who has not been charged the review officer must be of at least the rank of inspector and must not have been directly involved in the case.

The first review must occur after six hours, or as soon as practicable thereafter, and the review officer must repeat the procedure carried out when the person was admitted to the police station (section 37(1) to (6)). He must satisfy himself that the person's continued detention is necessary to secure or preserve evidence or to obtain such evidence by questioning and he must make a written record of the grounds for the detention. If the review officer does not consider the detention conditions still apply the person must be released.

A second review must be held not later than nine hours after the first and subsequent reviews must occur at not more than nine-hourly intervals, until he is charged or released. If the person is kept in detention after being charged the custody officer must review the case at nine-hourly intervals (section 40) until the person is brought before a magistrates' court as soon as practicable (section 46) and if he is then committed to further detention at a police station periodic reviews as set out in section 40 must continue (section 48).

Obviously these stipulations may cause resource problems. The review officer must give the arrested person or his legal adviser the opportunity to make representations about the continued detention and, at a busy police station with the review deadlines for different people arising at varying times, the review officer may have time for little else. The inspectors so involved will inevitably have to sacrifice some of their other important duties.

One also needs to consider the role of superintendents, and those of chief inspectors who may be authorised under section 107 to perform superintendents' functions. The requirements in the Act for these officers to be consulted upon a wide range of operational matters, which will often occur at unsociable hours, will inevitably increase the burden upon them probably to the detriment of their general management role.

On a personal note, much attention has been given in the past three years in Northamptonshire to the role of the police manager in the efficient and effective use of resources. This is very much in accord with other central government initiatives designed to ensure that the police service provides the community with 'value for money', and it will be most regrettable if these developments are in any way jeopardised. Having said that, we accept the need for the detention reviews and several police forces, including my own, voluntarily introduced the provisions on reviews, as far as possible in line with the Act, before it came into effect.

It should be stressed that no person may be detained beyond 24 hours unless it is a serious arrestable offence, and then only if a superintendent or more senior officer certifies that the detention conditions still apply and the case is being dealt with expeditiously (sections 41 and 42). The suspect, or his or her legal adviser, also has a right to make representations to the superintendent on this issue. Even though the definition of a serious arrestable offence is necessarily widely drawn (section 116) most people will be released within the 24-hour limit.

Indeed, the Royal Commission recognised that only a very small percentage of suspects are detained beyond 24 hours, but that small percentage is made up of persons suspected of the most serious offences such as murder, rape, kidnapping and robbery. The Royal Commission found that three out of four suspects were dealt with in six hours or under and 95 per cent within the 24-hours period.[6] The detailed research carried out by Softley[7] and by Barnes and Webster[8] found no cases of detention without charge of more than 48 hours although the Metropolitan Police figures showed that in a three-month period in 1979 212 people (0·4 per cent) out of 48,343 were detained for 72 hours or more before charge or release.[9]

Under the provisions in the Police and Criminal Evidence Act the suspect must be released after 36 hours' detention unless a magistrates' court, at an *inter partes* hearing, issues a warrant of further detention (section 43). At or before 72 hours there must be a second court hearing if the police wish to detain the suspect further and no person may in any event be detained beyond 96 hours without being charged (section 44).

The provisions in practice

It is worth looking in a little more detail at the implications of the review procedure. If, for example, a person is arrested at midnight on a Friday the first review of his detention must take place under the Act's provisions at 6 a.m. Subsequent reviews must occur at intervals of nine hours and the detained person must appear before a magistrates' court after 36 hours if the police wish to detain him further without charge. As the three-day clock in figure 1 shows the 36-hour limit expires at 12 noon on the Sunday.

If a second arrest occurs at 6 a.m. on the Saturday the review sequence must take place as shown in figure 2. The detained person must be brought before a magistrates' court by 6 p.m. on the Sunday. If a third arrest is

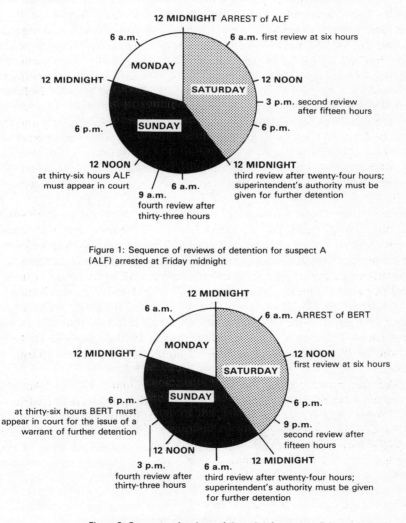

Figure 1: Sequence of reviews of detention for suspect A (ALF) arrested at Friday midnight

Figure 2: Sequence of reviews of detention for suspect B (BERT) arrested at 6 am on Saturday

made at 10 o'clock on the Saturday morning the reviews must take place as shown in figure 3 and this person must be taken before a magistrates' court for the issue of a warrant of further detention by the rather inconvenient time of 10 p.m. on the Sunday. And it is when the three cases are placed on the same three-day clock in figure 4 that the complexity becomes evident: clearly the review officers are going to be busy ensuring that each case is dealt with correctly.

It should be stressed that figure 4 shows the review sequences for only three cases. In many towns and cities in certain police stations it is not that

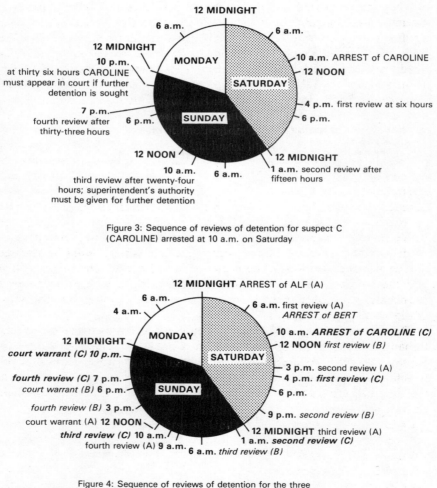

Figure 3: Sequence of reviews of detention for suspect C (CAROLINE) arrested at 10 a.m. on Saturday

Figure 4: Sequence of reviews of detention for the three suspects A, B and C arrested between Friday midnight and 10 a.m. on Saturday

unusual for five or six times this number of cases — perhaps 20 or more prisoners — to be involved at any one time.

The necessity for extended detentions

It is important to remember that police officers are not dealing with abstractions but with real cases and the changes brought in by the Act have all sorts of implications for the way crimes are investigated. I would like to give two real examples of police investigations to show the problems which may occur and the necessity on occasions to detain people without charge.

The first case occurred in May 1983 in Northampton when a three-year old boy was reported missing from his home. A full-scale search was mounted and tragically the little boy was discovered dead. He was found in a refuse cubicle close to his home and he had numerous stab wounds in his back, chest and abdomen. Following enquiries a 15-year old youth who lived two doors away from the deceased was arrested and detained. Whilst at the police station the youth had full access to legal advice and a solicitor was present at all interviews. Moreover, his mother and a social worker had unrestricted access and were with the youth at all times.

The youth denied any knowledge of the murder and at 36 hours after arrest the police had insufficient evidence to charge him and were awaiting the results of a forensic examination of his clothing. At this stage, of course, under the provisions of the Police and Criminal Evidence Act, operational from 1 January 1986, the youth would either have been released or would have been brought before a magistrates' court with a probability that he would have been released.

When further interviewed nearly 72 hours after his arrest, he made a full confession and gave a voluntary statement — again it should be stressed that at all times this was in the presence of his mother, the social worker and the solicitor. It was not until the following day that the forensic examination revealed that blood on the youth's clothing was the same group as the deceased.

The second case was a nationally prominent one involving the factional fighting of Hell's Angels' groups in Cookham, Thames Valley, in September, 1983. As a result of this fighting two men were killed, seven seriously injured and several others less seriously wounded. In addition to the deaths there were firearm wounds, knife and axe injuries and acid thrown into eyes.

Following the incident, 58 members of Hell's Angels' groups were arrested at 4.50 a.m. on 18 September and held at six separate police stations. Weapons discovered included a sawn-off shotgun, a pistol, ammunition, four axes, 36 knives and numerous metal stakes. Perhaps needless to say, there were no independent witnesses and many of the arrested persons refused to answer police questions.

It took the investigating team of 36 detectives three days of enquiries and interviewing before there was sufficient evidence to charge and take to court 26 persons. It is perhaps difficult to appreciate the resource and logistical problems experienced by the police, particularly in the early stages of the enquiry. There simply was insufficient evidence to charge any people before 36 hours and if they had been released it is most doubtful that subsequent enquiries would have led to more than a few of those arrested later appearing before a court.

From these two examples, of which there are many similar throughout the country, it can be seen that there are occasions in important cases when it is not possible to complete the enquiries and prefer charges within 36 hours. I wonder whether in the examples I have given a magistrates' court faced with the information that the police could provide at that time and hearing the arguments of an astute defence advocate, would agree to the issue of a warrant of extended detention? Even if they were prepared to do so, what damage would have been done to the police case by the requirement to 'declare their hand' at that stage of the investigation?

When mentioning the role of magistrates' courts, it should not be forgotten that magistrates and their clerks will also have a greater burden to bear. Although it has been agreed that they will not be asked to convene a court between 9.00 p.m. and 10.00 a.m., and I do not foresee too many occasions when a suspect will be detained as long as 36 hours, there will inevitably be occasions when courts will be required at inconvenient hours.

Access to legal advice

Another provision in the Act which will affect procedures in the police station is the entitlement of an arrested person to consult a solicitor at any time, subject to certain conditions (section 58). The Royal Commission on Criminal Procedure considered that the right to legal access, provided in the Judges' Rules and judicial decisions, is rarely exercised and is often refused by the police.[10] Whilst I do not necessarily accept that claim, it is an academic point now for the Act is specific in requiring the detainee to be informed both orally and in writing of this right and in requiring that when the detainee has asked for legal advice, no interviews or further interviews may be conducted until he has received it. A superintendent may delay access for up to 36 hours if certain stringent conditions apply but such cases are likely to be rare (section 58).

A further point worth note is section 59 which enables the provision of duty solicitors to attend people held in police stations. Strictly this is a matter for the legal profession but we anticipate that some difficulties will be encountered in finding sufficient solicitors willing to turn out at all hours to provide legal advice in police stations. Experiments to evaluate these difficulties took place in West Midlands, London and Northamptonshire, with mixed results. Section 56 of the Act gives a detained person the right to have someone informed of his arrest and location and so the picture which emerges from the legislation is one of a comprehensive range of rights and safeguards for a person held in police custody.

A host of stringent safeguards

If, then, there are so many safeguards for individuals' rights inside the police station, what of the other side of the equation identified by the Royal Commission — police powers to combat crime? What of the powers to pursue the objectives set out by the first Metropolitan Police Commissioners, Charles Rowan and Richard Mayne, and recently restated in modern language by the present Commissioner, Sir Kenneth Newman? The purpose of today's police remains the protection of life and property, the prevention and detection of crime and the preservation of public order, but what clearly defined and adequate powers are provided by the Police and Criminal Evidence Act which enable the police to pursue their objectives and warrant the considerable safeguards in the legislation?

First, let us consider the power to detain in part IV of the Act. Surely there can be no argument that the statute, in fact, limits and even reduces the length of time for which the police may lawfully detain a suspect whilst they carry out enquiries. In serious matters the time for which a suspect may be detained without charge has in the past been unclear and the only true limitation was determined in individual cases by the High Court through a writ of *habeas corpus*. During the debates as the Bill progressed into law, it was suggested that we should adopt the Scottish system, but for those with an appreciation of the system in Scotland, it is quite obvious that the Scottish criminal justice system is so very different from that in England and Wales that it cannot be properly compared.

Under the Act, not only will police powers of detention be severely limited, but a number of other difficulties will be created. For example, a suspect may indicate that he wants legal advice and may specify a particular solicitor, who then speaks to his client by telephone and advises him to say nothing, as he is quite properly entitled to do. If the solicitor tells the custody officer that he will attend the police station but then fails to do so within a reasonable time how long should the custody officer wait before informing the superintendent and obtaining permission for the interview to be conducted? This sort of delay in an investigation has all sorts of implications, and meanwhile the three-day clock mentioned earlier is moving round.

The rules contained in the Codes of Practice, which insist that a suspect is entitled to eight hours rest, free from interview, in every 24-hour period may also lead to delay (Code of Practice, paragraph 12.2). If the same solicitor represents more than one client in respect of the same matter this, too, is likely to delay the investigation. In some offences such as riot or other major disorder, or in crimes such as those involving the Hell's Angels at Cookham, such a large number of suspects may be being questioned that it is not possible to deal with the matter quickly.

Earlier proposals on the length of detention were for the *ex parte* intervention of a magistrate at 24 hours, and the Association of Chief Police Officers supported this proposal but it was rejected by the Magistrates' Association on the grounds that it would lead to suggestions that magistrates merely 'rubber stamp' decisions taken by the police. I suggest that even though that allegation might well have been made, it would be seen to be totally without foundation, and that system would have provided a truly independent supervisory element without creating the dangers which I believe exist in the *inter partes* hearings at 36 and 72 hours.

Some people have suggested that the Act grants an important 'new' power to the police giving them the right to search the premises of people who have been arrested, or the premises they were in immediately before being arrested (sections 18 and 32). Ole Hansen makes this point in chapter eight in this book. However, as is the case with virtually every power provided in the Act, this is really a codification of actions which the police have taken for many years, either with the consent of those involved or with a warrant.

Similarly, critics have pointed to sections 62 and 63 of the Act suggesting that the powers to take intimate and non-intimate samples represent an increase in police powers. Technically it appears to be correct to say that there have not in the past been specific powers physically to examine suspects or to take samples, but in my experience this has not caused the police any great difficulty as invariably suspects have given their permission. The introduction of the codified powers, after the various concessions made by the Government during the passage of the Bill, will result in the actions of the police actually being restricted.

Another contentious power, it seems, is the right to take fingerprints without the person's consent (section 61). The Act, though, makes it clear that this may only be done if it is authorised by a superintendent or above and so effectively the authority has been transferred from a magistrate to a senior police officer.

The more one examines the new legislation the more clear it becomes that a host of stringent safeguards has been introduced but it is not clear where the new police powers are which might justify these safeguards. The Royal Commission and Parliament determined that openness and account-ability were required, but this does not seem to have been balanced by giving the police extra powers and resources to investigate wrong-doers and bring them to justice. We must hope that the price to be paid by the victims of crime is not too great.

Tape-recording of interviews: encouraging trials

One major innovation in the Act is the requirement on the Home Secretary to make an order for the tape-recording of interviews in police stations (section 60). Field trials into the feasibility of tape-recording have been going on in six areas: Leicester; Wirral, Merseyside; Winchester, Hampshire; South Shields and Jarrow, Northumbria; Croydon, and Holborn, both Metropolitan Police. These have been monitored by the Home Office Research and Planning Unit, which has looked particularly at the impact of tape-recording on the length of interviews, the time taken by officers to prepare notes and statements, and the value of the evidence and criminal intelligence obtained.[11]

It is too early to reach any firm conclusions but the signs are encouraging. The police officers involved have accepted tape-recording and there is no evidence that they have attempted any systematic avoidance of it. The Home Office data show that interviews have become slightly less frequent and shorter, suggesting that interviewing techniques have become tighter using this method of recording. There is no evidence that recording inhibits either the suspect or the police:

> There appears to be no evidence to suggest that tape-recording inhibits suspects from confessing or making damaging admissions; nor do the results suggest any decrease in the amount of information about other offences obtained during interview.[12]

In fact, all the signs are that there has been very little change in the results obtained except that, of the few cases which have so far been dealt with by the courts, the guilty plea rate has been 100 per cent.

It may be recalled that on the grounds of costs and benefits, the Royal Commission on Criminal Procedure[13] recommended that tape-recording should be confined to the final stage of questioning, at least initially, but the Government are committed to include the whole interview, and the additional cost is to be offset by reducing to a minimum the need to transcribe the tapes. There will clearly need to be a degree of goodwill on all sides if the tape-recording safeguard — a safeguard for the police as much as for the person interviewed — is to work in the long term but we are very encouraged by the early response. It is my sincere hope that the legal profession will continue to be as enthusiastic about, and committed to, the practice of tape-recording as the police have so far shown themselves to be.

Protecting society and the individual

In this chapter I have been concerned primarily with the Act as it affects police procedures and citizens' rights *within* the police station. The Act, of course, also introduces innovations for policing on the streets and in various other areas. It must be recognised that these changes require extensive training for our officers and there is a need to train *all* officers. The instruction must be not only in the *detail* of the law but also in the *principles* behind the Act and the codes of practice and in the attitudinal changes that are required.

A national training package of videos and notes has been prepared by the police service's Central Planning Unit and it has been estimated that a minimum of three days per officer is needed to teach the basic package, with a further two days for officers who are required to carry out the duties of custody officer. This gives an indication of the commitment of the police service to ensuring the successful implementation of all that the Act and codes of practice entail. In this context it might be pertinent to ask how much extra training is intended for the legal profession.

So after a Royal Commission, endless hours of debate inside and outside Parliament, a vociferous and sustained campaign by special interest groups — often with exaggerated and erroneous claims of 'draconian' new police powers — the Police and Criminal Evidence Act, 1984 is now a reality. Insofar as it refers to actions within the police station those who are critical and who still say that the police have been given too many powers must be ready to say what powers *they* would give the police, or, alternatively, what further 'safeguards' they would have.

The vast majority of people in this country want to see those who commit crime, particularly serious crime, brought to justice. The police, of course, are society's mainstay at the commencement of this process and it is essential that public support and cooperation be forthcoming if the police are properly to fulfil their role. Quite clearly, this support will not be received by the police if the public feel we have too much power or that we abuse our position. But it is gratifying to note that the available evidence on public opinion shows that in general people do support the police and their fight against crime. Indeed, opinion polls and public attitude surveys[14] consistently put the police at the top of the list of organisations enjoying public confidence and esteem, above Members of Parliament, judges, the press and other worthy professions including, it might be added, lawyers.

Explicit in many of the innovations and changes brought about by the Act and codes of practice is a considerable administrative and record-keeping responsibility for the police. Indeed, some commentators have gone so far as to say that the Act will overwhelm the police with bureaucracy and thereby reduce their effectiveness. This may well prove to be a valid observation, but my main concern has always been, and remains, with the fundamental question of achieving the vital 'balance' to which I referred at the beginning of this chapter. I believe we all recognise that giving powers to the police without sufficient safeguards for the individual would be quite unacceptable — not only to society but also to the police themselves. Equally unacceptable, however, would be a situation of inadequate powers for the police and an over-provision of 'safeguards', which could be exploited by the criminal.

In my view, this Act is far from being the last word on the great debate, and perhaps books such as this one will increase our store of knowledge and appreciation of the issues involved. The final question to pose is whether Parliament has achieved the right balance in this Act and of course the answer is that only time and experience will tell. From the point of view of the ordinary citizen, I sincerely hope the law-makers have got it right for if the result is that the effectiveness of the police is reduced, where then will society turn for protection?

Notes

1. Royal Commission on Criminal Procedure (Chairman: Sir Cyril Philips), *Report*, London: HMSO, 1981 (Cmnd. 8092); see also the accompanying volume: *The Investigation and Prosecution of Criminal Offences in England and Wales: The Law and Procedure*, London: HMSO, 1981 (Cmnd. 8092–1).
2. The Royal Warrant is reprinted on pages iii–v of the Royal Commission's *Report*.
3. House of Commons Official Report, Parliamentary Debates (*Hansard*), Session 1983–84, Vol. 48, 7 November 1983, cols. 25–26.
4. See sections 66 and 67 of the Police and Criminal Evidence Act, 1984. Four codes of practice have been published: one deals with the exercise of statutory powers of stop and search; another outlines proper practice for the identification of people by police officers; a third stipulates the procedures for searches and seizures and the final code deals with the detention, treatment and questioning of people. This is the Code of Practice to which reference is made in this chapter. See: Home Office, *Police and Criminal Evidence Act 1984 (S. 66) Codes of Practice*, London: HMSO, 1985.
5. *The Brixton Disorders 10–12 April 1981: Report of an Inquiry by the Rt. Hon. The Lord Scarman, OBE*, London: HMSO, 1981 (Cmnd. 8427); see for example his comments on supervision and monitoring, paras. 5.33–5.40.
6. The Royal Commission on Criminal Procedure, *Report*, pp. 52–53.
7. Paul Softley, *Police Interrogation: An Observational Study in Four Police Stations* (Royal Commission on Criminal Procedure Research Study No. 4) London: HMSO, 1980.
8. J. A. Barnes and N. Webster, *Police Interrogation: Tape Recording* (Royal Commission on Criminal Procedure Research Study No. 8), London: HMSO, 1980.
9. Royal Commission on Criminal Procedure, *Report*, p. 53.
10. *Ibid*., pp. 97–98; see also Softley, *Police Interrogation, supra* note 7; J. Baldwin and M. McConville, 'Police interrogation and the right to see a solicitor', *The Criminal Law Review*, 1979, pp. 145–152; M. Zander, 'Access to a solicitor in the police station', *The Criminal Law Review*, 1972, pp. 342–350.
11. Carole F. Willis, *The Tape-Recording of Police Interviews with Suspects: An Interim Report*, London: HMSO, 1984 (Home Office Research Study No. 82).
12. *Ibid*., p. 32.
13. Royal Commission on Criminal Procedure, *Report*, pp. 77–79.

14. A ranking of the public's view of different groups is given in B. Whitaker, *The Police in Society*, London: Sinclair Browne, 1982, p. 212:

Percentage expressing a
great deal of confidence in:

Police	71
Medicine	67
Military	60
Law Courts	42
Education	39
Civil Service	26
Press	24
Parliament	19
Trade Unions	18

CHAPTER 13

Openness and accountability

GABRIELLE COX

A police authority is made up of one-third chosen from magistrates and two-thirds from the local authority and as such it can be seen as providing a voice for ordinary citizens. Unlike police officers, or lawyers or even sociologists and psychologists, the local authority members of a police authority do not have a professional interest to espouse, rather they are there to represent the wider community.

Perhaps it is possible to identify three roles and responsibilities which a police authority has. *First* it is charged with maintaining 'an adequate and efficient police force', *second* it can be seen as a watchdog, ensuring that money is well-spent and policing proprieties observed, and *third*, and arguably of increasing importance, it must promote improved relations between the police and the community. It is with these three aims in mind that I will examine the impact of the Police and Criminal Evidence Act, 1984.

An Act with few friends

The three roles of the police authority can be compared with two general aims which the Government claimed lay behind the new legislation. In the briefing guide issued by the Home Office on the second attempt at getting the Bill through Parliament, in November 1983, the two aims were outlined. First, the Government concluded that legislation was necessary to improve the balance of criminal justice and to ensure that the police have the means to deal with crime. Second, the measure was intended to underpin public confidence in the police and to achieve this practical steps were to be taken to protect the rights of individuals. These developments included the tape-recording of police interviews, the reform of the complaints procedures, the reinforcement of local arrangements for consultation and the establishment of a Crown Prosecution Service.

A fundamental question, then, is whether the Act achieves these aims — does it give the police the necessary tools to tackle crime effectively, and does it provide sufficient safeguards for ordinary citizens and an increase in public confidence? It certainly is striking how few friends and supporters the legislation seems to have. Civil libertarians, lawyers and police, alike, remain at best sceptical and more frequently openly critical of the Act.

On the one hand it is claimed that the additional police powers are too great, an encroachment on valued rights and difficult to supervise properly, on the other hand it is argued that there are too many safeguards which will prove onerous, time-consuming and costly and which create loopholes which will be exploited by professional criminals. No doubt the Home Secretary would argue that this shows the legislation has achieved the right balance, but I consider it is a matter of concern. There seems to be a worrying lack of confidence from different parts of the community that the Act is really going to bring about improvements.

I wonder, for instance, how stop and search powers really relate to the community's concern with crime. From the police authority point of view how do these powers relate to the three roles listed above? Do stop and search powers help to promote an adequate and efficient police force, can they be supervised properly and vigilantly, do they aid better relations between the police and their communities? The answers, I suspect, are 'no' on all counts.

If one looks, for instance, at the Home Office *Briefing Guide* it is claimed that in Scotland 27 per cent of people stopped and searched for offensive weapons in a 22-month period were subsequently convicted of carrying offensive weapons. But this tells us little except perhaps that by stopping people police officers may create crimes and hence criminals. In London, it has been argued on many occasions,[1] that often people who are stopped on the streets are actually charged with assaulting a police officer, or obstructing him, and so had they not been stopped no offence would have taken place.

The interesting statistics from the Scottish experience would be the effects that stop and search powers have on crime figures, and particularly on those which relate to crimes where offensive weapons are *used*, such as woundings. Only if these had dropped significantly would it be fair to say that stop and search powers 'are of great assistance in the detection and . . . prevention of crime'.[2] The evidence from the Metropolitan Police, where the clear-up rate is so low and where the use of stop and search is so high, suggests that these powers do not play an important part in the prevention and detection of crime.

Indeed the extensive study of the Metropolitan Police carried out by the Policy Studies Institute revealed that not only was there no specific reason to make a stop in 34 per cent of cases[3] but only 8 stops out of every hundred led to any sort of result in terms of the person being arrested and charged (3 per cent) or reported and summonsed (5 per cent).[4] From these figures it would not seem unreasonable to suggest that the stop and search powers are a waste of time, and cause unnecessary inconvenience to ordinary citizens.

The need for external reviews

If I have severe doubts about the usefulness of stop and search powers I wonder similarly about the provisions on detention. As others in this book point out, the extended powers also entail considerable form-filling and bureaucracy and these complex and onerous record keeping tasks may not mean an efficient use of resources. But the central question is surely whether we ought to have reached the position where people can be held without charge in a police station for up to 96 hours.

How important is this power of extended detention anyway? If, as the police claim and the Royal Commission research confirmed,[5] detention beyond 24 hours is needed on so few occasions was there not a simpler way of providing for this eventuality? When one considers the impact that the 96 hours provision has had on public confidence one begins to doubt even more strongly how successfully the Act is measuring up to the aims outlined earlier.

One of the false assumptions on which the Act appears to be based is that rules and procedures are always applied rationally, out on the streets or back in the police station. In real life, though, there is often a disparity between theory and practice. Complicated procedures, to protect citizens and police officers, which are devised in the quiet of an office may prove to be singularly ineffective when it is necessary to use them in practice.

Barrie Irving looks in detail at the difficulties which may occur, in chapter eleven in this book. Whether one's approach is that of a police officer attempting to handle tense or testing situations, or whether it is that of a civil libertarian concerned to ensure the protection of an individual's rights, one knows that it is not always possible to expect rational behaviour, or to follow complicated procedures, in difficult policing circumstances.

Furthermore, there seems to be considerable scepticism within the police service about the practicality, and perhaps the desirability, of many of the supposed safeguards in the Act. If there is a lack of real commitment to the procedures for recording stops and searches, and those for reviewing detention and allowing legal access and the various other safeguards, then they may not be performed in the way that the Act and the codes of practice intend.

In essence, I perceive two main problems with the way the legislation may operate in practice. *First*, the safeguards are basically internal. Thus, the checks on whether procedures are being implemented properly are internal to the system: it has to monitor its own working. My experience is that it will be rare for junior officers to question wrong decisions from above, and similarly it will be uncommon for those in supervisory positions to uncover those occasions when rules are being loosely applied.

Second, bearing in mind the three roles of the police authority, it is difficult to see how the Act and its impact can be evaluated in terms of adequacy and efficiency. Again there is a need for *external* evaluation of the Act and of police performance, for example to discover whether the use of the legislation and resources accords with public priorities. However, the police world tends to be relatively closed to external reviews of this kind, and there is little in the Act to bring about greater accountability and openness.

Lay visiting: negotiating access to police stations

The lack of provision in the legislation for increased openness and accountability is clear in an area of particular interest to me, that is lay visits to police stations. The Act does not even make reference to them even though Lord Scarman specifically recommended statutory provision

> for random checks by persons other than police officers on the interrogation and detention of suspects in the police station.[6]

The Greater Manchester Police Authority voted on 11 March 1983 to institute lay visitors and the scheme began in May of that year. My experience, though, was that it involved a process of *negotiating* oneself into the police station. This confirms the points made by Barrie Irving in his chapter, in relation to his own research, and adds weight to the view that the police service is reluctant to accept external reviews.

In general there are no rights for the community, even through its representatives on the police authority, to see what goes on in its own police force. Lay visiting of police stations is a low-key, small scale attempt to gain an insight and has been inhibited by many rules and regulations.

In the case of Greater Manchester, for example, we were originally only able to speak to detained people in the presence of a police officer. To the lay visitors it was clear that the officers' presence was an inhibiting factor in conversations with detainees. It took a process of persuasion and negotiation to extend the arrangement so that it is now 'in the sight but not the hearing of' a police officer. I am not seeking to criticise those with whom we are negotiating; I am merely stressing that it is the police officers who are very much in control and even when dealing with the police authority, it is the force which decides the extent to which non-police officers shall have access. The Police and Criminal Evidence Act is thus a missed opportunity, for had it incorporated certain basic rights of lay visiting it could have done something to break down the system which relies on internal checks of a closed institution.

Originally the scheme in my Authority area was limited just to members of the committee but this has been extended to include members of the police–community liaison panels. The scheme includes 24-hour access to police stations, and the three members from each liaison panel have the same rights as members of the Authority, except that they have access only to police stations in their own area, not across the whole of Greater Manchester.

It must be stressed that just as the success of the new position of custody officer created by the Act (sections 36–39) will depend greatly upon the character and personality of the police officers entrusted with that responsibility, so too the effectiveness of lay visitors depends upon the qualities of the individuals doing it, so although we provide training for them, ultimately it is up to the personality of individual lay visitors. It is sometimes difficult for an ordinary person to go into a police station and not be overawed by the system and those operating it. Some lay visitors will tend to accept the conditions imposed on them by the police officer, and different officers have different ways of interpreting procedures.

It is still early days and no doubt as suspicions are overcome and it is seen as less of a novelty, lay visiting will become an accepted feature of life in the police station. But if it is to become a really effective check, lay visiting needs to move out of its twilight zone of being seen as some sort of concession to the community. It should be a right of the community to inspect its own police stations, and this right should be backed up by proper resources, improved training and specific procedures.

Some benefits of lay involvement

Despite these reservations, the nascent lay visitors scheme in Greater Manchester has been generally successful. None of our visitors have been confronted by cases of assault but I would have expected the chances of this happening to be exceptionally rare. What is interesting is how often the lay visitors' reports include issues which are of importance in terms of the new Act and its codes of conduct. For example, a recent visit raised questions about the provision of meals and drinks, which are basic requirements raised in the *Code of Practice for the Detention, Treatment and Questioning of Persons by Police Officers* (paragraph 8.6).

Another issue which lay visitors' reports have raised is the sort of property and personal possessions which are taken away from people held in custody. It was discovered recently that spectacles are often removed from people in detention and this led to a discussion by the Police Authority, and within the force, on the arguments for and against confiscating possessions such as these. Clearly it is possible for a suspect to harm himself or others by using the glass from his spectacles, but on the other hand many people are unable to see without their spectacles, and to have them removed is a form of sensory deprivation. Discussion of questions such as this can lead to a more humane approach to detention, in accord with the Code of Practice.

Various improvements and benefits can occur if local communities are allowed to become involved in decisions which have been considered purely professional. For example, it is likely that members of the community would wish to ensure that information is provided, in a comprehensible form, for detainees in police stations. It seems ridiculous that a police authority should have to negotiate painfully and over many months to obtain the right to issue a leaflet setting out a detained person's rights — and to obtain this right in police stations which it maintains, staffed by officers for which it pays!

In short, accountability means more than being answerable to the law through the courts. Accountability should entail being responsible and responsive to properly elected representatives of the local community. Such a system not only brings benefits in terms of an adequate and efficient force and increased public confidence but it is also the foundation of democratic government, and as such should be evident in the way we run our police service.

Complaints: a missed opportunity

The notion of accountability — of being answerable for one's actions — brings into focus the question of complaints against the police. The Act is a missed opportunity for the establishment of an independent complaints system which would have commanded public confidence.

It is difficult to see how the new Police Complaints Authority, established in part IX of the Act, will enjoy any greater public confidence than its predecessor. Indeed, there is a strong argument that the new provisions will lead to a deterioration in investigation of complaints. Investigating officers will not know whether they are in charge of the case or not for on some occasions they may be subject to orders from the Complaints Authority, on other occasions they may *potentially* be subject to instructions and on other occasions they won't.

The new system does nothing at all about the waste of resources caused by the use of senior police personnel in the investigations when more profitably they should be managing their force. Many senior officers, and the Police Federation, believe an independent system would be less wasteful of precious resources and more likely to reassure the public. The only good thing about the new system is the provision for the informal resolution of relatively trivial complaints. This follows the suggestions made by Lord Scarman,[7] amongst others, and the introduction of conciliation for minor complaints is a welcome development.

There are those who state that an independent complaints system would be too expensive. I find this argument singularly unconvincing if only for the reason that the present system is already very expensive, but these costs are hidden within police budgets. In Greater Manchester each complaint cost on average £500 to investigate in early 1985 and the cost of course rises with inflation. It should be realised that this average cost includes that incurred for relatively simple investigations into complaints, for example, about a police car parked on double yellow lines or police incivility. This cost seems a high one to pay for a system which does not enjoy public respect, and were the money put into an independent system it would be more likely to bring value for money.

I was disappointed to hear the views recently of Mr. Harding from the Home Office, who implied that the resources for the Police Complaints Authority may well be insufficient. It was suggested that the Authority may have to choose between the superficial investigation of a lot of cases or the thorough investigation of just a few. It is time that the Home Office realised that public confidence must be secured, and any saving in this area will prove to be a false economy.

The Police Complaints Authority came into operation at the end of April 1985 and time will tell how effective it is. Personally I believe that a fully independent complaints system will have to be introduced eventually; as Lord Scarman observed:

> My own view is that if public confidence in the complaints procedure is to be achieved any solution falling short of a system of independent investigation available for all complaints (other than the frivolous) which are not withdrawn, is unlikely to be successful.[8]

It is regrettable that his advice was not adopted in the Police and Criminal Evidence Act.

The pathetic and derisory provision for consultation

Lord Scarman's recommendations have also not been implemented in the section of the Act which deals with arrangements for obtaining the views of local people. In my opinion this is the most pathetic and derisory part of the Act:

> Arrangements shall be made in each police area for obtaining the views of people in that area about matters concerning the policing of the area and for obtaining their co-operation with the police in preventing crime in the area (section 106(1)).

The way this is phrased makes it seem nothing more than a police public relations exercise. It is ridiculous to have a statutory obligation on police authorities to 'obtain the views of the people' and to 'obtain their co-operation with the police'. Councillors on the police authority are obtaining people's views all the time but there is more to consultation than this — far more.

This section of the Act totally distorts the view of consultation put forward by Lord Scarman. He stated:

> Community involvement in the policy and operations of policing is perfectly feasible without undermining the independence of the police or destroying the secrecy of those operations against crime which have to be kept secret.[9]

This concept of consultation entails a two-way process — a *real* dialogue. It was partly the absence of this process which led to the 'unwise' decision to launch Operation Swamp in Lambeth, which was the context within which the 1981 disorders occurred. Police officers have argued that discussions with public representatives could jeopardise their independence of judgement, but, said Lord Scarman:

> The proposition that it interferes, or may undermine, independence of judgement is a 'non-sequitur'; for consultation informs judgement: it does not pre-empt it.[10]

And Lord Scarman went further still. His view of consultation clearly involved the active participation of the community in policing decisions:

> . . . it is in my view essential that a means be devised of enabling the community to be heard not only in the development of policing policy, but in the planning of many, though not all, operations against crime.[11]

Section 106 of the Act is so far away from a meaningful approach to consultation that it is not just pathetic and derisory but it is also positively harmful, because in this guise 'consultation' is so worthless that people do not see any point in doing it.

The future success of policing and law and order policy surely lies in a common and cooperative approach across the whole community. The Police and Criminal Evidence Act does little or nothing to further such an approach and this is at least partly because its assumptions are based on, and in the context of, the Police Act 1964. The 1964 Act is increasingly being shown to be inadequate in the way it constituted accountability. The way in which the coal dispute was policed has raised enormous questions of accountability which have yet to be answered. To whom is a chief constable accountable for his force's policies and behaviour? The 1964 Police Act fails to answer this question satisfactorily and consequently we have not managed to find a non-polarised, non-conflict-ridden approach to law and order and policing.

If we are to avoid a continued drift towards coercive and imposed policing we must secure greater community involvement and support. Hence the need for not only genuine consultation but also proper accountability, and this will only be achieved by revision of the 1964 Police Act. We need a proper statutory structure of local accountability such as exists in every other area of public service provision at the local and county levels.

The Act's final irony

There is perhaps a final irony about the Police and Criminal Evidence Act. It is going to cost enormous sums of money to implement, not just in once-only costs like training every police officer and altering police stations to suit the new requirements but also in continuing costs such as additional personnel and the time-consuming nature of posts such as custody officers. The irony is that this comes at a time when spending on other local services is being drastically curtailed, and when public expenditure in general is being reined back. And yet whereas it is doubtful whether the expenditure on the Police and Criminal Evidence Act will significantly reduce crime, there can be little doubt that the creation of jobs and better housing, and higher standards of education, *would* cut crime.

It is wrong to consider the new Act out of context, and just as part of its context is the deficiencies of the 1964 Police Act and the role and powers of police authorities so another part of its context is the social deprivation in British cities. In the ward in which I live 50 per cent of men are unemployed. Crime in the inner city areas is considerably higher than elsewhere,[12] and not surprisingly when one looks at the rates of unemployment and the social and economic conditions there.

What does the new legislation do to tackle the *causes* of crime? As a member of a police authority I must stress that the Act gives me no reason to believe that the Government has done anything to tackle the very real problems which the police and local communities are facing.

Notes

1. See, for example, George Greaves, 'The Brixton disorders', in John Benyon (ed.), *Scarman and After*, Oxford: Pergamon, 1984, pp. 63–72; see also Benet Hytner *et al.*, *Report on the Moss Side Enquiry Panel to the Leader of the Greater Manchester Council*, Manchester, 30 September 1981.
2. Home Office, *Police and Criminal Evidence Bill Briefing Guide*, London: Home Office, 1983.
3. *Police and People in London*, Vol. IV: David J. Smith and Jeremy Gray, *The Police in Action*, London: Policy Studies Institute, November 1983 (PSI No. 621), p. 232.
4. *Police and People in London*, David J. Smith, *A Survey of Londoners*, London: Policy Studies Institute, November 1983 (PSI No. 618), pp. 114–117.
5. Royal Commission on Criminal Procedure (Chairman: Sir Cyril Philips), *Report*, London: HMSO, January 1981 (Cmnd. 8092), pp. 52–53; see also Paul Softley, *Police Interrogation: An Observational Study in Four Police Stations*, London: HMSO, 1980 (Royal Commission on Criminal Procedure Research Study No. 4).
6. *The Brixton Disorders 10–12 April 1981: Report of an Inquiry by the Rt. Hon. the Lord Scarman*, OBE, London: HMSO, November 1981 (Cmnd. 8427), paras. 7.7–7.10.

7. *Ibid.*, paras. 7.24–7.26.
8. *Ibid.*, para. 7.21.
9. *Ibid.*, para. 5.56.
10. *Ibid.*, para. 4.73.
11. *Ibid.*, para. 5.56.
12. Mike Hough and Pat Mayhew, *The British Crime Survey: First Report*, London: HMSO, 1983 (Home Office Research Study No. 76).

CHAPTER 14

The provisions in practice

TONY JUDGE

Sir Robert Mark said in the Dimbleby Lecture on BBC Television in November 1973 that the only power that a police officer possessed over his fellow citizens was the power to inconvenience them.[1] The Police and Criminal Evidence Act sets out for the first time in one comprehensive statute the precise limits of the inconvenience to which a citizen, who has become a suspect, may be subjected during the process of a ciminal investigation.

Abiding by the Judges' Rules

I have no idea who it was that first pointed out that one of the hallmarks of a civilised society is the way in which it treats those who are deprived of their liberty, but that sentiment has motivated penal reformers and simple humanitarians over the centuries. It is no coincidence that some of the great social reformers of British history, for example Colquhoun, the Fieldings, Fry,[2] and others saw that a professional police service, governed by men of integrity, was a necessary part of the radical reform of the criminal justice and penal system of eighteenth century Britain for which they were striving.

Elizabeth Fry, Charles Dickens, Henry Mayhew and others may well have been appalled at the treatment of convicted prisoners in the nineteenth century, but it was obvious to all observers, from the beginning of the New Police, that prisoners in police custody were treated with the decency and compassion which for example were not to be found in the prisons and the convict hulks bound for Australia.

In this century the treatment of suspects and persons in police custody has been governed, from 1912 until the Police and Criminal Evidence Act, by the Judges' Rules. And it is a remarkable tribute to the judges of the Edwardian bench that their statement of principles and practice should have survived on a non-statutory basis for more than seventy years, apart from changes brought about by administrative directions made in the light of experience and subsequent court rulings.

In passing, it is noteworthy that the Rules came into existence because, following some criticisms in the Court of Appeal, the Chief Constable of Birmingham asked the Lord Chief Justice to set out the judges' views on what policemen could, and could not, do when as the judges put it 'they were endeavouring to discover the author of a crime'.

Having for the past thirty years worked in daily contact with police officers and police matters, I have lost count of the number of times that I have heard critics of police behaviour insist that a stage has been reached where the Judges' Rules as a matter of habit are ignored by police officers when they are questioning suspects, and (worse still) that the superior officers of those police investigators condoned and encouraged breaches of the Rules. The reality, I believe, is that in the vast majority of investigations the Rules have been scrupulously observed, even though they have given to the guilty suspect with a knowledge of the ropes a distinct advantage over his interrogator. I also believe that there has been a significant minority of cases in which, sometimes inadvertently, but more often deliberately, detectives bent or broke the Rules.

That this behaviour was almost always prompted by a determination to convict a suspect whom the police were convinced was guilty, rather than a deliberate attempt to 'frame' a totally innocent party, cannot be accepted as an excuse for such cases. As time went on, and as we entered an era in which it was no longer taboo to criticise police witnesses in court, the retention of the Judges' Rules on a non-statutory basis[3] became a positive handicap to police investigations and certainly a handicap to the prospect of successful prosecution.

Police officers have a great regard for the force of statute law and the non-statutory nature of the Rules could, and sometimes did, lead detectives to believe that they were no more than advisory, and as such could be disregarded in the overriding interests of justice. But the result was that the ends of justice were defeated when palpably guilty men walked out of court[4] as a result of a judge's direction to a jury, or because the Court of Appeal found it unsafe to allow convictions to stand, in cases where the Rules had been breached.

Perhaps more to the point, an atmosphere has grown up in the criminal courts, particularly in inner city areas where tensions between the police and the public are greatest, in which it is virtually standard practice for defending barristers to base their strategies on all out attack on the integrity of the police witnesses.

The Act and unscrupulous lawyers

There are, practising in the criminal courts today, barristers who see their role as defenders of members of minority groups against their police oppressors. And although their tactics in court follow a predictable wearisome pattern, they operate in a climate of opinion where, whether or not such tactics incur judicial displeasure during a trial, it is sometimes enough merely to suggest that police witnesses are lying or that prisoners have been subjected to brutality in the police station, to persuade juries that they ought to acquit. It is apparently enough to convince juries that 'these things happen', to create that element of 'reasonable doubt' even in the face of ample corroborative evidence produced by the prosecution.

There was an increasing realisation of what was going on, both on the streets where police officers were facing the kind of difficulties to which Leslie Curtis refers in his chapter, and in the courts where the police were finding themselves under regular attacks of this sort. This prompted the Police Federation to urge upon the Royal Commission the need for statutory codes governing stop and search, detention and treatment, questioning and identification, and search and seizure.[5]

The success or failure of the Act will depend upon the extent to which the new statutory criminal investigation procedure is seen to have struck the right balance between the protection of the suspect against abuses in the process, and the need for society to have a system which aids the detection of crime and increases the chances of punishing the guilty. It will not be enough, therefore, to say of the Act in a few years' time that it has limited, or even curtailed altogether, the actuality of police malpractice — and I draw a distinction here between actual misconduct and the flights of fancy we hear from some sources. It will be just as important to note the extent to which the Act has trimmed the activities of those defence lawyers who have unscrupulously exploited doubts and even prejudices against police evidence.

The police will have to accept that what at first sight appears to be a bureaucratic nightmare of record keeping, and a mammoth load of personal responsibility and accountability heaped upon the shoulders of each police officer concerned with an investigation, may yet prove to be worthwhile if only it leads to criminal trials which are concerned with what actually happened, rather than trials which are no more than inquests into police activities. This could well happen if the mere existence of the custody records convinces defence lawyers that there is nothing to be gained from going down the avenues they have been exploring so profitably until now, and there is already some evidence to suggest that this may be the case.

For example, after initial hostility and suspicion, the police were persuaded to accept the principles of tape-recorded interrogations in the police station and although these are early days, preliminary reports on controlled experiments are encouraging. The same may be the case when the police and the courts become accustomed to the procedures laid down in the Act although this, admittedly, is an optimistic view which is not at this time shared by a number of very experienced crime investigators who are convinced that the Act has gone too far in protecting the rights of the suspect.

"Here's one aspect of police custody not catered for in the new 'Code of Practice', sarge — your prisoner's just hopped it."

What a performance! In this cartoon, which appeared in *Police* in March 1984, *Jedd* suggests that the complex procedures will be particularly onerous for the hard-pressed custody officer. Have we really got the balance right?

The position of custody officers

I must express the Police Federation's concern about the position of custody officers (the Act: Sections 36–39). There has always been a tradition in the police service of appointing a particular officer to have immediate responsibility for the custody and treatment of prisoners in police cells. As often as not, this has been the job of the uniformed officer of the rank of sergeant or inspector and in many stations it would be the responsibility of the station sergeant, who would combine it with general responsibility for the enquiry office during his tour of duty. In police stations where the number of prisoners can run into dozens, and often exceeds a hundred at busy weekends, then such officers have found that the care and custody of prisoners has been their sole responsibility.

The Police Federation's view is that the new procedures are so onerous in relation to the strict observance of time limits before various steps in the actual chain are activated, that it will become obvious that custody officers will have to be designated solely for that task. It is also our view that, save in exceptional circumstances, the custody officers should always be at least of the rank of sergeant, and indeed Section 36(3) of the Act stipulates this for designated police stations (Section 35).

However, it seems unlikely that this is going to be the case. Indeed, if we are to introduce designated custody officers of the rank of sergeant into the Metropolitan Police, there would be a shortfall of several hundred sergeants. Once again we have an example of the curse of legislation in the modern era: more and more duties and responsibilities are loaded onto the shoulders of overworked public servants, in this case the police, and the cost implications are just not taken into consideration. Worse still, wildly optimistic and absurdly underestimated assessments of the cost are put before Parliament.

The police service is at the moment going through a period of retrenchment after the comparative honeymoon period following the Edmund-Davies Report in 1978.[6] As evidence of this, notice that during 1984, even though thousands of officers had to be deployed in aiding other forces dealing with disorder on the striking miners' picket lines, the strength of the police service was deliberately allowed to fall by more than one thousand officers. This is nothing more than a cost-saving exercise, but the long-term implications for the police service are worrying.

I know of no professional assessment which disputes that the new procedures laid down in the Act are not more manpower intensive than their non-statutory and non-recorded predecessors. Yet there is no indication forthcoming from the Government that it is prepared to recognise the case for increased police manpower simply to deal with the requirements of the Act.

Our interest in this is not simply academic. It is not pleading a special case for more staff simply for the sake of building up empires. It is of a recognition that each and every sin of omission or commission committed against the manifold requirements of the codes of practice is, *prima facie*, a disciplinary offence which puts that police officer's job on the line.

As to the procedures themselves, let this be said. We must anticipate that, in the early years of implementation, the Act will be a happy hunting ground for the kind of lawyer to whom I have already drawn attention.

There are enormous possibilities of trials within trials seeking desperately to discover some procedural shortcomings which can be magnified into a case for throwing out an otherwise strong prosecution.

The danger points for police officers, particularly young and inexperienced, will be at the very outset of the investigation process: the first encounter with the suspect on the street, and these pitfalls are examined by Leslie Curtis in chapter seven. In the police station no amount of documentation is going to prevent allegations that records are not genuine and that procedures were not observed. After all, it would be foolhardy and flying in the face of experience to ignore what the lawyers and Her Majesty's judges were able to do with the apparently foolproof procedures established for dealing with drunken motorists.

Stout hearts, sturdy superiors and sane judges

I express the hope, which I know is shared by most police officers, that the officers who will bear the personal responsibility for taking decisions under the codes will not be tempted to take the easy option. That easy option follows the line of least resistance, requiring the metaphoric shrug of the shoulders, 'very well if that is what Parliament wants, who am I to argue?' And the danger is, of course, that officers will hesitate to take advantage of the provisions under the Act, for extended detention, for the denial of access to lawyers in the interests of justice, and so on, on the grounds that they would simply be running into an inevitable conflict when the case goes to trial.

These exceptions are there, although they were bitterly resisted by the opponents of the Act. They are not to be used habitually, and certainly not regularly, to a point where the whole purpose of disposing of cases as speedily as possible is lost. But the wider interests of justice, must transcend all other considerations, and police officers I am sure — and I am giving here a frank personal opinion — will have their worst fears about this Act confirmed if there is, in the early years, a flood of cases in which police officers are seen to have acted in good faith, but have their judgements rejected in the courts.

Young bobbies out on the streets, experienced detectives, custody officers, and others in the police station up to the chief superintendent rank are going to need stout hearts, sturdy superiors and sane judges. If any of these are lacking, then it will be a case of 'pass the valium and let them get on with it'.

Annex B of the *Code of Practice for the Detention, Treatment and Questioning of Persons* embodies sensible recognition of the need, in a small minority of serious cases, to go against the presumptions in favour of notifying a named person of someone's arrest, and granting access to legal advice. Always this must be done on the authority of a superintendent, and only on the grounds of the possibility of interference with witnesses or evidence, including physical harm to witnesses, alerting other persons or accomplices, or hindering the recovery of property (see the Act: Sections 56 and 58).

The limit of delay is thirty-six hours, and there is a requirement to bring it to an end as soon as such a reason no longer exists. There is nothing radically new in these exceptions for they were acknowledged in the Judges' Rules. What the Annex does is to put a grey area into black and white.

A code of practice without parallel

The Act and the Code govern every transaction between the police and the suspect throughout the custody period. It is clear that, as has always been the case, the decision on what happens to prisoners in a police station is not for the officer who is investigating the crime: it is for the custody officer, or the officer in charge of the police station (the Act: Sections 37–39). From the date of implementation (which was 1 January 1986) their responsibilities became statutory. For example, a request by an investigating officer to interview a detained person (charged or otherwise), requires a deliberate and recorded decision by the custody officer. Indeed, bearing in mind the comings and goings involving uncharged or charged prisoners, in a busy station one can conceive a nightmare in which the custody officer has spent all night running around checking everyone's 'starting clock' governing the various stages of detention, and trying to fulfil force requirements on the regular visiting of all the other prisoners, only to find in the morning that the drunk and incapable, thought to have been quietly sleeping it off, has choked to death on his own vomit.

The Code lays down a requirement for a continuous period of at least eight hours for rest (usually at night) in every twenty-four hours (the Code: paragraph 12.2). It says that interviews must take place in properly equipped rooms and the suspect must be allowed to sit (paragraphs 12.4 and 12.5). He must have regular meals and be given refreshment breaks during questioning at two-hourly intervals (paragraph 12.7, see also paragraph 8.6). If he makes a complaint — any complaint — about his treatment in custody, it must be, then and there, recorded (paragraphs 9.1 and 12.8).

The whole emphasis, the entire climate of opinion about this Act is undergoing a major shift: we are entering a new phase. Any day now there is going to be a bright light in the sky providing Damascusian illumination of the legal profession, social workers, police monitoring groups, Gabrielle Cox, Paul Boateng and all.[7] After two years of increasingly hysterical invective against the 'draconian extension of the police state', they are about to awaken to the stunning realisation that the Act enshrines a Code of Practice for prisoners and suspects against the abuse of police power which is without parallel in the rest of the world. As a result of this changed emphasis, the most fanatical enemies of this legislation, in its embryonic stage as the Bill, will now become its most devoted admirers following its metamorphosis into an Act.

But then, as with the Police and Criminal Evidence Act itself, there is nothing new about this. There was once a Bill presented to Parliament which so infuriated the guardians of our liberties, that they urged citizens to take to the streets. The police state of Napoleon and Vidocq was invoked to curdle the blood: it was the end of freedom as we knew it. The Duke of Wellington was appalled and Charles Fox's declaration was invoked that it was better to be governed by a mob than a standing army. I am referring of course to the Metropolitan Police Act of 1829.

Notes

1. The lecture is reprinted under the title 'Minority Verdict' in Robert Mark, *Policing a Perplexed Society*, London: Allen and Unwin, 1977, pp. 55–73; he actually said (p. 56): 'The only power we possess is the power to inconvenience by bringing people before the courts, and even then we are at risk if we use that power improperly, or unfairly. The fact that the British police are answerable to the law, that we act on behalf of the community and not under the mantle of government, makes us the least powerful, the most accountable and therefore the most acceptable police in the world'.
2. *Patrick Colquhoun*, 1745–1820, metropolitan police magistrate and author of *'Treatise on the Police of the Metropolis, explaining the various Crimes and Misdemeanours which are at present felt as a pressure upon the Community, and suggesting Remedies for their Prevention', by a Magistrate*; Henry Fielding, 1707–1754, the novelist who became Justice of the Peace for Westminster in 1748, and whose reforming work was carried on by his blind half-brother *Sir John Fielding* (d. 1780) from the Bow Street Offices: Elizabeth Fry, 1780–1845, prison reformer who undertook philanthropic work in Newgate and elsewhere, and campaigned energetically for social improvements.
3. It has been argued that some of the injunctions in Judges' Rules, for example the prohibitions on holding out hope of advantage and on threats, and the caution upon charging, have had some statutory force derived from the Administration of Justice (No. 1) Act 1848. Nevertheless, the Rules have not had a coherent statutory basis and indeed the Royal Commission on Criminal Procedure drew attention to 'their uncertain status': *Report*, London: HMSO, 1981 (Cmnd. 8092), paragraph 1.21.
4. A point made by the Criminal Law Revision Committee, *Eleventh Report: Evidence (General)*, London: HMSO, 1972 (Cmnd. 4991); see for example p. 12.
5. See the Royal Commission on Criminal Procedure, *The Investigations and Prosecution of Criminal Offences in England and Wales: The Law and Procedure*, London: HMSO, 1981 (Cmnd. 8092–1).
6. Committee of Inquiry on the Police (Chairman: Lord Edmund-Davies), *Reports on Negotiating Machinery and Pay*, London: HMSO, 1978 (Cmnd. 7283); see also *Report III*, London: HMSO, 1979 (Cmnd. 7633).
7. Gabrielle Cox chaired the Greater Manchester Police Authority and is the author of the chapter in this book on 'Openness and accountability'. Paul Boateng chaired the Police Committee of the Greater London Council and contributed a chapter entitled 'The police, the community and accountability' in John Benyon (ed.), *Scarman and After*, Oxford: Pergamon Press, 1984, pp. 152–159.

CHAPTER 15

Safeguarding the suspect

DAVID ASHBY

The major section of the Act with which this chapter is concerned is to be found in part IV, namely the safeguarding of the suspect during the detention and interrogation processes within the police station.

The basis of the Act is said to be founded on compromise, on a proper balance between sufficient powers for the police to interrogate coupled with sufficient safeguards for the detainee: a concept which I think we would all find laudable. In fact I am sure that we would all claim that this is an essential ingredient in such laws, but the real and only point is where to strike the balance. How far should we go in providing the police with extra powers and in doing so losing our liberties? Edmund Burke said:

> All Government, indeed every human benefit and enjoyment, every virtue and every prudent act, is founded on compromise and barter. We balance inconveniences, we give and take, we remit some rights that we may enjoy others.

Poles apart from other common law countries

There are some who argued vigorously for this Act on the *very* basis that it is a compromise, without looking to where that balance should be. There are others, including myself, who are disappointed that the one chance to get things right has not been taken. Indeed I recently attended a dinner with a number of distinguished American lawyers, including a Supreme Court Judge, who stood up and spoke upon civil and human rights and I turned to a former Solicitor General under the Labour Government and said: 'For God's sake don't mention the Police and Criminal Evidence Bill'. For it is absolutely clear to me that we are poles apart from the Americans and many other common law countries, in our concepts of human and civil rights and liberties.

Turning to the Act, the first detention of the suspect is on arrest, following which there is invariably a search. I must welcome the codification of the search laws whilst expressing my disappointment that evidence obtained by an illegal search should still be admissible in evidence. A 200-year-old wrong has not been put right and we are left with no safeguard for the suspect against the improper use of search warrants, save for a complaint against the police.

Before the passage of this Act, the law relating to detention in the police station was very obscure. Section 43(4) of the Magistrates' Court Act 1980, provides: 'Where a person is taken into custody for an offence without a warrant and is detained in custody, he shall be brought before a magistrates' court as soon as practicable.' That is as long as it is large.

Suspects had to resort to the ancient and powerful writ of *habeas corpus*, in order to seek their release from a detention which may be unlawful: in itself any detention could be unlawful. However, in practice the application for *habeas corpus* has been subject to financial means and the suspect's knowledge of the processes. In other words, the detained person has needed the wit to instruct a vigorous solicitor and the granting of the writ has been subject to the vagaries of the Lord Chief Justice of the day.

Under the Lord Chief Justice Parker the wholly improper practice, in my view, of adjourning applications grew up, thus giving the police additional time. Under the present Lord Chief Justice, Lord Lane, a much more judicial approach has evolved, starting with the case of Mr. Hudson (*R. v. Hudson* (1980) 72 Cr App R 163), and the case of *Sherman v. Apps* [1981] *Crim LR* 335 in which he stated that 48 hours was long enough in detention. However, the Lord Chief Justice may have got cold feet for in the case *R. v. Steel* (1981) 73 Cr App R 173 the Court resiled from the 48 hours, slightly afraid perhaps of the consequences in that particular case.

It follows therefore that the *fact that the Act prescribes a period of detention*, and limits that period, is in itself a substantial advance in the safeguarding of the suspect. The controversial issue must remain the *length* of that stay.

The first substantial safeguard of a suspect who is taken to the police station is the provision that there shall be a specific police officer of the rank of sergeant or above, whose duty it is to examine and decide whether a suspect should be released or detained for the purpose, as the Act says in section 37(2), of securing or preserving evidence or for questioning him. It is the custody officer who must authorise that detention and who must, therefore, have a responsibility thereafter for the detainee. No more, I hope, will we see the sorry spectacle of a solicitor phoning around trying to locate a detained client and being told that the officer in the case is away and will phone back. In other words, being given the 'run around' by experienced police officers.

Police powers 'to meet this modern challenge'?

The essence of detention will now be 'accountability' — and rightly so, for the liberty of the subject is at stake. The custody officer has to make a written record of his grounds for detaining and the suspect has to know those grounds. And he has to charge him if there is already sufficient evidence. Section 56 provides that a suspect is entitled to have a friend or relative informed of his arrest unless a delay of up to 36 hours is authorised by a police officer of the rank of superintendent, or above. After 36 hours there can be no delay and for a child or young person there can be no such delay, which is surely proper.

The Act basically divides detention into two sections, namely under 24 hours for less serious offences and over 24 hours and up to 96 hours for what are described as 'serious arrestable offences'. As the length of detention increases so a more senior police officer, and finally the magistrates' courts, have to decide whether the detention is justified. At the same time as the period of detention lengthens so the *rights* of the suspect, to consult and be represented by a solicitor, increase. The safeguards as will be seen are numerous and the duties laid upon the detaining authority and the police officer increasingly onerous.

The first review of detention must take place after six hours when an officer of the rank of inspector or above, who is independent of the investigation, must give an uncharged suspect or his solicitor an opportunity to make representations and he must decide whether the continued detention is necessary. If the suspect has been charged, it is the custody officer who carries out the review. The grounds for detaining the suspect are the same as for the original detention, namely 'to secure or preserve evidence relating to an offence or to obtain such evidence by questioning'. The second review which takes place nine hours later, that is 15 hours after the suspect first arrived at the police station, takes exactly the same format.

Although I deal only in outline, at all times there are the most stringent requirements for written records to be kept and for the reasons for detention to be given. If the reviews cannot take place at the prescribed times, for example if the suspect is being questioned, there are procedures for recording this. What then does one make of the first 24-hour period?

Perhaps the first point is to ask whether it is really necessary. The crimes envisaged in this period are not 'serious arrestable offences', since these are specifically reserved for the next period of 24 to 96 hours. In a speech, in October 1984, the Solicitor General, Sir Patrick Mayhew, justified this Act saying:

> How nice it would be if all the police had to investigate these days was the occasional scrumping of apples and the moonlit activities of the occasional Lincolnshire poacher. Unhappily we know that much graver crimes are committed by much more sophisticated people, backed by much more powerful resources, to the great danger of the public. . . . The police should not be denied the powers that they need to meet this modern challenge.

Leaving aside the fact that the last poacher I met was making £200,000 per year from his activities, I submit that the level of offences which are not serious arrestable offences, for which these powers are provided, are not the graver, sophisticated crimes envisaged by the Solicitor General and it follows that these powers are neither necessary nor reasonable. In Scotland, where everyone would agree there are both sophisticated criminals and sophisticated police, six hours is considered sufficient. What, one must ask oneself, is so special about England and Wales? Are the criminals more sophisticated or the police less able?

Furthermore, *after* 24 hours, as we shall see, the officer reviewing the detention has to consider the further point, namely, 'whether the investigation is being conducted diligently and expeditiously'. Why, I ask, is it not considered necessary to enquire the same of a police officer detaining some unsophisticated suspect charged with a lesser crime?

Warrants of further detention

Turning to the 24- to 96-hour detentions, the justifications, as I have stated, change. Not only must the detention be necessary to secure or preserve evidence, or obtain evidence by questioning, but the officer must also be satisfied that the investigations are being carried out, as I stated before, 'diligently and expeditiously' and the offence is a serious arrestable offence. These are defined in Section 116 and cover murder and all the serious acts of violence, serious sexual offences, firearm offences and the larger frauds and thefts.

At 24 hours the responsibility passes to a police officer of the rank of superintendent or above, who using the same procedures as at the six- and 15-hour reviews, may authorise an extension of up to 12 hours. At 36 hours, the safeguarding of the suspect passes to the magistrates' court who will hear evidence on oath on an application by a police officer for a *warrant of further detention.*

The Bench have to satisfy themselves of the same criteria as the superintendent at the 24-hour review and the suspect has the right to legal representation. Indeed if the suspect requests legal representation the courts *have* to *adjourn* the application until the solicitor appears and the legal aid schemes have been amended to allow legal aid for these applications. If the courts grant a warrant of further detention, this will be valid up to 72 hours from his arrest and a further and exactly similar application then has to be made to extend the detention up to 96 hours.

Of course in considering the safeguarding of the suspect over this long period we have also to consider the rights of the suspect to have access to legal advice. Where previously a suspect was allowed access to a solicitor by virtue of Home Office Rules and Directions, which were seldom honoured in their observance, the suspect now has his rights enshrined in section 58 of the Act, which says:

> A person arrested and held in custody in a police station, or other premises, shall be entitled, if he so requests, to consult a solicitor privately at any time.

This right is subject to the same sort of restrictions which prevailed in the pre-Act days under the Home Office Rules, namely that the request can be delayed, but now only on the authority of an officer of the rank of superintendent and above. He must have reasonable grounds for believing that allowing a solicitor will lead to interference with or harm to evidence connected with a serious arrestable offence or interference with or physical injury to other persons, or will lead to the alerting of other persons suspected of committing a serious offence or hinder the recovery of property connected with the offence. The delay can only be for up to 36 hours after arrest, so that the right to a solicitor at the 36-hour court application, as we have seen, is absolute.

It will be interesting to see how section 58 works in practice, since it is my experience that many police forces have frequently denied suspects access to a solicitor on spurious grounds. Now that it is in an Act of Parliament, how will they react? Certainly the Lords and others attempted to introduce clauses which would allow the sanction of excluding all evidence improperly obtained, contrary to the provisions of this Act, but those clauses were defeated.

Tape-recording: must be employed immediately

There is I believe a great need to safeguard the suspect who is detained on an extended warrant for a number of extra reasons. Firstly, although the justification is that it is a graver crime he is suspected of, he is also going to be dealt with more severely. If the crime is complicated, he needs more advice and less pressure in answering questions.

Secondly, the longer a person is detained, the less reliance can be placed on any confession and the greater the oppression, because of the very fact of being detained in the unpleasant surroundings of a police cell. The suspect, therefore, has the greater need for a solicitor's advice and for the accurate recording of his answers. The experimental tape-recording of interviews has been hailed as successful by lawyers and police alike. This Act provides for the universal tape-recording of all such interviews and it is a safeguard which must be employed immediately. The totally unsafe 'confession' at the 95th hour, which is neither signed to nor contained in any confessions statements, is no longer a permitted travesty of justice.

Since the avowed purpose of the extended periods of detention is that of obtaining evidence by further questioning, what happens if the suspect gives evidence to the magistrate on the application that he has answered *no* questions, relying on his right to silence, and that he will *not* answer any questions? Is there any right to detain where the purpose has been removed? During the course of the Bill the Home Secretary was asked this very question and his reply was that those grounds for extended detention would have disappeared and the suspect would either have to be charged or released.

If the courts interpret this section as it has been interpreted by the Home Secretary, then fears that this part of the Act would be used to 'break a suspect' will have been allayed. Most practising lawyers appreciate, as I have already said, that a confession obtained after a lengthy period may be suspect. As the means of interrogation become more sophisticated so the risk of saying what the interrogator appears to require becomes greater and the tired suspect is equally at risk from the misunderstood question or the sloppy answer.

There was a very real prospect of the courts refusing to admit evidence obtained after four days' detention before the Act and we only have to look at the case of *R. v. Hudson*, where 48 hours was held to be oppressive, for such an example. However, I cannot now see the courts refusing to admit evidence of confession obtained within 96 hours of detention since they will say 'if Parliament did not think 96 hours was oppressive for questioning, who are we to say it is oppressive?' There is also the further fear which many of us have that the periods of 24, 36 and 96 hours will become the *norms* for detention before charging.

An affront in a democratic society

To summarise, this legislation seeks to codify and control an area which lacked clarity and was becoming an increasing scandal. In that respect it is successful. Although it may be said that where the police had no restrictions they are now restricted, I believe that to be a gross over-simplification. Put more simply the Act *allows them to detain for very long periods indeed.*

At a time when many people are talking about a Bill of Rights, this surely was an opportunity to provide a comprehensive code of rights and duties in the criminal law? Such a code would form part of the constitution in almost every country in the world and would only be arrived at after a large measure of agreement amongst all parties had been reached. It is a disappointing feature of this legislation that there was not that agreement.

The safeguards contained in this Act are numerous and onerous. I remain convinced that every one of those safeguards is necessary. Equally I remain convinced that no number of safeguards could ever balance the *excessive* loss of that most precious and cherished *liberty* which the Act allows. I think this is an affront in a democratic society and it undermines that most precious of commodities, which is *justice*.

PART 4

In the Courts: Prosecution, Evidence and Admissibility

CHAPTER 16

Prosecution and criminal justice

COLIN BOURN

In this part of the book we are concerned with the changes which have been made to the process of prosecution and trial in the wake of the recommendations of the Philips Commission and the Eleventh Report of the Criminal Law Revision Committee. The Prosecution of Offences Act 1985 creates a national prosecution service independent of the police, whilst ss.73–81 of the Police and Criminal Evidence Act modify certain important rules of evidence.

The arguments for an independent prosecution service were accepted by the Philips Commission. The Royal Commission recommended a locally based system working within national guidelines, although the Prosecution of Offences Act has actually created a national system under the control of the Director of Public Prosecutions (DPP).

Our contributors have exposed a number of common themes in their discussion of the new Crown Prosecution Service. Whilst only Ron West is directly critical of the decision to separate police powers of investigation from the decision to prosecute, the form of the new service is clearly a matter for contention. There is considerable support for the proposition that a locally based service would have been preferable to a national one. The arguments deployed in favour of a local scheme include the view that it would have made co-ordination with local police forces much easier to achieve. Doubts about the concentration of so much power in the hands of the Attorney General and the Director of Public Prosecutions are expressed by several of our contributors. Clive Grenyer, along with other contributors, questions whether a national prosecution service may not prove to be an expensive and bureaucratic monolith. Great scepticism is expressed over the way in which the proposals have been costed and whether the anticipated savings in police manpower can be realised. It is feared that the result may be an under-funded service which cannot properly perform its function. Another structural issue which is of particular concern to Michael Hill is that of rights of audience before the Crown Court and the relation between the new Crown Prosecution Service and the Bar.

Another theme which is common is a concern as to how any discretion not to prosecute will be exercised in practice. The powers of the Crown Prosecutors only arise at the point where a charge has been preferred or an information laid. This leaves to the police a substantial discretion which is exercised at a point before the Crown Prosecutor is involved and which is incapable of review. The Crown Prosecutor may, however, either withdraw the prosecution or offer no evidence. There is considerable debate amongst our contributors as to the mechanics of such 'uncharging' and its consequences for the defendant. For Michael Hill this relates to a parallel question when counsel are instructed on an indictable offence. Will counsel be allowed in practice to retain a discretion to offer no evidence or to accept a lesser plea, if this decision does not accord with the views of the local Crown Prosecutor? Again there is an anxiety expressed particularly by Clive Woodcock as to the position of an 'uncharged' defendant in relation to costs, at least where he does not serve a notice requiring the proceedings to continue under s.23(7), with the result that he is formally acquitted.

In considering the exercise of this discretion to prosecute, the guidelines to be issued by the DPP are seen as very important. These will follow the example of the Attorney General's 1983 Criteria for Prosecutions. The publication of these guidelines in an annual report to Parliament on the new Service, which is to be made by the attorney general, should ensure that these decisions are made according to known criteria. Walter Merricks calls for the Attorney General's criteria to be fleshed out in relation to particular offences. Although the Attorney General will not be answerable to Parliament for decisions in individual cases, he will be accountable for the issue of any general guidelines. Whilst Robin White expresses some scepticism as to the searching nature of the public scrutiny which may thus ensue, decisions should be made according to known criteria.

The overall conclusion reached by Walter Merrick is that we are looking forward to a system which has the features of openness, fairness, accountability and modernness about it. Not all our contributors are quite so sanguine about the prospects for the Crown Prosecution Service but there is a general belief that the new arrangements mark a step forward for the criminal justice system.

The evidence provisions

The evidence provisions of the Police and Criminal Evidence Act are discussed by John Smith and Paul Sieghart.

As John Smith states, the evidence provisions are in the main based upon the recommendations of the Eleventh Report of the Criminal Law Revision Committee, although not all the recommendations of that Committee were adopted. The Act covers the admissibility of documentary evidence, computer records, the proof of previous convictions and acquittals, confessions and the exclusion of unfair evidence.

Attention has been focused primarily, upon the rules relating to confessions and unfair evidence. As John Smith observes, a great mass of old learning about voluntariness is displaced by s.76 of the 1984 Act. In place of this, s.76 renders inadmissible any confession obtained by oppression of the accused or in any way which might render the confession unreliable. John Smith reviews the interpretations which are likely to be given to these concepts, arguing that evidence of the whole course of the interrogation will be relevant.

The exclusion of unfair evidence is regulated by s.78, which as Paul Sieghart shows, is the form in which the Scarman Amendment finally became law. As it is the effect of the evidence in question on the fairness of the proceedings which will be central to the decision of the court, it is uncertain as to whether evidence obtained as a result of unfair or illegal methods of investigation will be excluded. Paul Sieghart sees the section as a strong restraining force upon police tactics, enforcing compliance with the other provisions of the Act and its associated codes of practice, whilst John Smith sees it as likely to be of more limited significance. Certainly both are in agreement that evidence obtained in unconscionable ways should be excluded, though beyond that there is clearly room for disparate interpretations.

CHAPTER 17

A public prosecution service for England and Wales

ROBIN C. A. WHITE

Introduction

In ancient times all prosecutions were private prosecutions. Indeed, the police have never enjoyed any special power in law to act as prosecutors. It has rather been the gradual evolutionary development of their functions which has resulted in their acting as prosecutors. In this way the chief officer of police became the person primarily responsible for the decision to institute criminal proceedings and the practice of the police acting as advocates in cases proceeding before magistrates' courts became widespread.[1] This primacy in practice of police prosecution of offences must be qualified by two developments. First, the creation of the office of Director of Public Prosecutions (DPP) in 1879 removed from the police the prosecution of certain, usually serious, offences the importance, difficulty or other characteristics of which made prosecution by the DPP appropriate.[2] Secondly, the statutes creating a number of offences made prosecution for them subject to the consent of the Attorney General, DPP or other designated authority.

In the investigation and prosecution of offences, four distinct areas of police discretion can be identified. First, it is clear that chief officers of police may determine the general disposition of their forces and the courts will not interfere with the judgement of chief officers of police in setting priorities for their forces, provided they do not amount to a decision not to enforce the law.[3] Secondly, police officers faced with incidents have a discretion as to how they respond to those incidents; this might best be thought of as the police officer's discretion 'on the streets'.[4] Thirdly, a police officer assigning to junior officers the investigation of an offence reported by the public has a discretion as to the resources to be devoted to the investigation of that offence.[5] Finally, the police enjoy a discretion as to whether to charge or to lay an information against a person against whom they believe there to be credible evidence of commission of an offence.[6] This is generally known as the decision to prosecute and it is with the discretion inherent in this decision that this chapter is primarily concerned in considering the structure and functions of prosecuting agencies. It should be stressed that the police have never been precluded from seeking legal advice at any stage of their decision-making. Obviously for many years the police have instructed lawyers to act for them in serious cases. From 1963 onwards, as a result of recommendations made by the Royal Commission on the Police,[7] the majority of police authorities established prosecuting solicitors' departments, but there are wide variations in the type and amount of work done for the police authority.[8] It is probably fair to say that prosecuting solicitors are not involved in the prosecution of the bulk of summary cases. All prosecuting solicitors are in a solicitor/client relationship with the chief officer of police and are subject to his instructions. Thus, in theory, a chief officer of police can instruct a prosecuting solicitor to undertake a prosecution even against the advice of that solicitor. The solicitor can only refuse to act where to do so would be unconscionable, that is, where the solicitor's duty to the court overrides the duty to act on the client's instructions. It seems that refusals to accept the advice of prosecuting solicitors are extremely rare. Prosecuting solicitors must also seek approval from the chief officer of police for any decision to withdraw a prosecution or to accept a plea of guilty to a lesser charge.

To summarise, the present position is that in the majority of cases heard before magistrates it is currently the police, who will have investigated the offence, collected the evidence and might naturally expect to see their efforts result in conviction, who make the decision to prosecute and conduct the prosecution in court. It has been suggested that the police cannot be expected to act impartially over the careful consideration of evidence and other non-evidential factors in deciding whether to proceed with the case.

The JUSTICE report[9]

The modern campaign for an independent prosecution service started with the 1970 JUSTICE report, *The Prosecution Process in England and Wales*. This report argued cogently for a complete separation of the responsibilities for the investigation of crime and for its prosecution. It was argued that independence of these functions was the best safeguard of fairness, objectivity and impartiality in the investigation and prosecution of offences. JUSTICE argued that the system obtaining in England and Wales was out of line with practice in other countries, including those with a common law tradition. JUSTICE also considered that an independent system was more likely to result in fair and proper disclosure of matters known to the prosecution which are relevant to the defence case.

JUSTICE recommended the introduction in England and Wales of a system similar to the Scottish system where the decision to prosecute and the conduct of the prosecution are undertaken by agencies independent of the police. Under the Scottish system[10] prosecutions at local level are supervised by procurators-fiscal appointed by the Lord Advocate. The police are required to report all cases to the fiscals who must examine each file and mark it with a decision whether or not to proceed. Fiscals have the power to direct the police to obtain fuller evidence if they think this is appropriate. They also conduct the prosecution of all lesser criminal offences; more serious offences are prosecuted by the Law Officers or an Advocate-Depute (one of six deputies to the Lord Advocate). JUSTICE argued that such a system would be convenient, economic, efficient and productive of greater uniformity of practice and procedure.

The Royal Commission's proposals

The themes of the JUSTICE report were taken up in evidence submitted to the Royal Commission on Criminal Procedure. Despite some strong evidence from the police, notably from the Metropolitan Police Commissioner, that existing arrangements were fair, economic and efficient, the Royal Commission seem to have had little difficulty in concluding that the time had come for the creation of some form of independent prosecution service. The Royal Commission accordingly recommended that there should be a clear separation between the investigation of offences and the responsibility for the conduct of the prosecution.[11] There is a hint in the Royal Commission's Report of a 'corporatist' approach: they clearly found the lack of consistency in arrangements within prosecuting solicitors' departments unattractive.[12] The new service would be built on the foundations of the prosecuting solicitors' departments in police authorities. Their proposed functions were to be:

(a)   the conduct of all criminal cases once the initial decision to prosecute has been taken by the police;

(b)   the provision of legal advice to the police, as and when requested, on matters relating to the prosecution of offences; and

(c)   the provision of advocates in magistrates' courts in all cases where proceedings are commenced by the police (apart from guilty pleas by letter under s.12 of the Magistrates' Courts Act 1980, which only require someone to read out the statement of facts) and the briefing of counsel in all cases tried on indictment which are not the province of the Director of Public Prosecutions.[13]

This list of functions makes clear that the police would retain the authority to make the initial decision to prosecute. The role of the new service prior to charge would be advisory only and the delivery of advice would be triggered by a request for advice from the police. The point at which the responsibility of the new service would arise was the point of charge or the laying of an information on which a summons was issued.[14] The Report stated explicitly that once responsibility had been transferred to the new service, the prosecutor 'may then on the information before him decide to proceed as charged, or to modify or withdraw the charges'.[15]

As to the form of the new service, the Prosecuting Solicitors' Society successfully argued before the Royal Commission for a locally based service with certain national features. The Royal Commission's recommendations[16] were in essence to enlarge and upgrade prosecuting solicitors' departments into a national network of local independent prosecutors. The local Crown prosecutor would be accountable to new police and prosecutions authorities, modelled on existing police authorities, for issues concerning management and resources and the efficiency and competence of staff. The Royal Commission favoured accountability to the Attorney General concerning issues of ethical and professional standards and national prosecuting policy. Finally, there would be Parliamentary accountability through the Attorney General, though in individual cases accountability was said to be to the courts.[17]

The overall result of the Royal Commission's recommendations was to split the decision to prosecute between the police and the new prosecution service. The initial decision to proceed taken by the police would be examined by the prosecution service who would be free to alter or drop the charges. Given this position, the basis upon which decisions should be made is extremely important. The Royal Commission undoubtedly expected some consistency between the approach adopted by the police and the new service and looked to the new service to provide the lead in the improvement of decision-making in this twilight zone of the criminal process characterised by the Royal Commission as not wholly fair, and as lacking in openness, accountability and efficiency.[18]

Immediate responses and second thoughts

One early response to the criticisms of the basis on which decisions to prosecute were made was the publication by the Attorney General of his 'Criteria for Prosecution' in 1983[19] which were also commended by the Home Secretary. The criteria are very similar to the existing criteria used by the DPP.[20] As a starting point there must be a sufficiency of evidence indicating a reasonable prospect of conviction; this has come to be known colloquially as 'the 51 per cent rule'. The criteria go on to state that factors about the offence, the offender and the circumstances of the victim will be relevant to any decision not to prosecute in a particular case. It is stressed that the more serious the offence, the more compelling must be the reasons for choosing not to proceed. Doubts should be resolved by choosing to prosecute and leaving the court to be the final arbiter of the matter. These criteria are not markedly different from those that appear to have been used by the police for some time,[21] but they are important because the Home Office envisages that the new service will be required to conform with guidelines produced by the Attorney General,[22] and it is unlikely that any revisions of the criteria will adopt a fundamentally different approach.

Just as the Royal Commission's decision to recommend the establishment of an independent service was uncontroversial, so too there was little controversy over the acceptance of the recommendation. But there has been much less agreement about the form the new service should take. The Royal Commission's choice of a local system with certain national features received much criticism,[23] and doubts were expressed about the feasibility of the Royal Commission's proposals.

The Government responded by setting up a working party to consider views of interested parties on the viability of three models:

(1)   an integrated national service;
(2)   a decentralised national service; and
(3)   a locally based service.[24]

Following this consultation the Government produced its White Paper, *An Independent Prosecution Service for England and Wales*[25] outlining its proposals. The Government came down in favour of an integrated national service with local Crown prosecutors responsible for the conduct of all cases now prosecuted by the police. The White Paper explained that this new service would have as its headquarters the office of the DPP, though there would be local offices of the service staffed by locally based Crown prosecutors. Despite this decentralisation, it is emphasised that all staff would be members of the national service with an integrated career structure. What was proposed was, in effect, an amalgamation of the office of DPP with prosecuting solicitors' departments to provide the new service. The White Paper agreed with the Royal Commission that the police will continue to make the initial decision to prosecute, though they will be free to consult the Crown prosecutor before doing so. Once a decision to prosecute has been made by the police, the matter will pass to the jurisdiction of the Crown prosecutor who may decide whether the charges should proceed, be amended or be dropped. Accountability of the new service would be through the Attorney General direct to Parliament, though only over general policy questions and not on individual cases. The proposals in the White Paper formed the basis of the Prosecution of Offences Bill introduced in the House of Lords on 16 November, 1984. The Bill received the Royal Assent on 23 May, 1985. It is expected that the Crown Prosecution Service will come into operation for the areas of the abolished metropolitan counties in April 1986 and for the rest of the country in October 1986.

The scheme of the Prosecution of Offences Act 1985[26]

Part I of the Prosecution of Offences Act 1985 establishes the Crown Prosecution Service which consists of the DPP as head of the service and of Chief Crown Prosecutors for areas which will be based on existing police force areas, though the report of the Home Office's management consultants does not envisage congruity in this regard. If the recommendations are accepted there will be fewer Chief Crown Prosecutors than chief constables. This will mean that some chief constables will 'share' a Chief Crown Prosecutor. The Director must be a barrister or solicitor of not less than ten years standing and will be appointed by the Attorney General. This removes the anomaly of appointment of the DPP by the Home Secretary though the Attorney General is answerable for the duties and acts of the DPP. The functions of the Director are to be:[27]

— the conduct of all criminal proceedings, other than proceedings specified by order made by the Attorney General,[28] instituted on behalf of a police force, including all binding over cases;
— to institute and have the conduct of criminal proceedings the importance or difficulty or other characteristics of which make it appropriate for the proceedings to be instituted by the DPP;
— to take over proceedings concerning the forfeiture of obscene articles under s.3 of the Obscene Publications Act 1959;
— to give advice to police forces on all matters relating to criminal offences;
— to appear for the prosecution on all criminal appeals;
— to discharge such other functions assigned from time to time by the Attorney General.

Barristers and solicitors employed by the service will be known as Crown Prosecutors and a Chief Crown Prosecutor will be appointed for each area. Without prejudice to functions assigned to them in their capacity as members of the service, every Crown Prosecutor 'shall have all the powers of the Director as to the institution and conduct of proceedings but shall exercise those powers under the direction of the Director'.[29]

The distribution of functions between the headquarters of the service (DPP's office) and local offices is elaborated in a White Paper, *Proposed Crown Prosecution Service* published in December 1984.[30] In essence the proposals are a share-out of the current consent requirements and intervention provisions applicable to the DPP and Attorney General between headquarters and the local offices. It is envisaged that most decisions will be taken in local offices in accordance with the guidelines produced by the Director. Indeed it is proposed that the bulk of cases currently requiring the consent of the DPP will be handled locally except for prosecutions for complicity in another's suicide. Two annexes to the

White Paper give examples of cases which will be handled locally and those where it is considered desirable that decisions should be taken by headquarters. The overall effect of these proposals is that only serious offences which experience has shown tend to create difficulties will be handled centrally. These include offences punishable by death, offences of attempted murder, abortion, grievous bodily harm where explosives are involved and major drugs offences. It is good to see that criminal proceedings involving questions of European Community law or where a reference has been made to the European Court of Justice will be handled by specialists at headquarters.

Crown Prosecutors, regardless of whether they are solicitors or barristers, will enjoy the rights of audience enjoyed by solicitors holding practising certificates including those rights granted by a direction of the Lord Chancellor extending the normal rights of audience of solicitors.[31] Section 4(3) allows the Lord Chancellor to make directions specifically extending the rights of audience of Crown Prosecutors.

The Act enables solicitors in private practice to be instructed to act as Crown Prosecutors if the need arises, though they must act under the Director's guidelines when so instructed. Nothing in the Act precludes the institution of private prosecutions. In such cases the DPP is under no duty to take over the conduct of the case, but may do so at any stage.[32] It seems that section 6 would enable a police officer to institute a private prosecution as an ordinary citizen where that officer disagrees with a decision by a superior officer not to proceed. But the Director will, of course, have the power to take over the conduct of the case and drop the charges if such action is considered appropriate.[33]

Section 10 imposes a duty on the DPP to issue a Code for Crown Prosecutors giving guidance on the general principles to be applied in exercising the decision whether or not to proceed with criminal cases begun by the police, on the choice of charges, and on the representations to be made to magistrates concerning mode of trial. The Director must make an annual report to the Attorney General,[34] who must in turn lay a copy before Parliament. The Attorney General can request the DPP to report on 'such matters as the Attorney General may specify'. The first annual report after the issue of the Code must contain a copy of it, and subsequent annual reports must set out any amendments to the Code.[35]

Section 8 enables the Attorney General to make regulations requiring chief officers of police to give to the DPP information about all offences of a kind specified in the regulations committed in the area in respect of which there appears to be a *prima facie* case for proceedings. This will enable the DPP and Crown Prosecutors to monitor the exercise of the discretion to prosecute which will remain with the police because they retain the initial decision as to whether to press charges or lay informations.

Section 23 overcomes the difficulty of court involvement in any decision by Crown Prosecutors to 'uncharge' those against whom the police have initiated criminal proceedings by enabling Crown Prosecutors to issue a notice of discontinuance of proceedings. Where the defendant has been charged after being taken into custody without a warrant but no magistrates' court has been informed of the charge, the notice of discontinuance ends the matter there and then. Once the court is seised of the matter, the procedure is more complex. Reasons must be given to the court, but need not be given to the defendant. The defendant on receiving a notice of discontinuance of proceedings may nevertheless elect to have the case proceed by serving a counter-notice. Service of a notice of discontinuance will not prevent the institution of fresh proceedings on the same offence.[36]

Finally, sections 11 to 14 deal with the administrative arrangements for the transfer of staff and protection of their interests on transfer, for the provision of premises and for the control of fees to be paid to witnesses attending to give evidence at the instance of the service.

Impacts: the structure of the new service

It is the writer's contention that the debate over the structure of the new service has detracted attention away from issues relating to the operational philosophy of the service. Institutional questions have dominated the discussion, both in and out of Parliament, almost to the total exclusion of discussion of operational questions. It is clear that the real meat of the issues faced by the new service is not contained in the Act's provisions, but will be found in the guidelines produced by the DPP once the service is up and running. In any case the current running beneath the debates about structure ultimately seem to be concerns about operational philosophy and who will shape it. Four factors seem to have bothered opponents of the central system with its devolution to local offices. First, it is said that there is a constitutional danger in concentrating the control of all prosecutions in the hands of one minister (Attorney General) and a leading civil servant (DPP). Secondly, it is argued that operating a national system will be cumbersome and involve unnecessary bureaucracy. Thirdly, it is suggested that legitimate local variations in the application of policy can not be accommodated. And fourthly, resort is made to the argument that prosecutions have always been locally based and decisions have been taken at local level which reflect the concern of the local community. All these issues could have been addressed in a detailed discussion of operational philosophies.

No voice in Parliament was heard to deny the need for a new service independent of the police. All who spoke referred to the necessity for complete and absolute independence of the service and several speakers stressed the need for the new service to be more than a reincarnation of the existing prosecuting solicitors' departments. One suggestion as to why a national system with powers devolved to local offices was preferred was that if a wholly local system had been adopted then there would seem to have been little alternative to a system of accountability similar to police committees. The present Government is keen to avoid any possibility that police committees might acquire any control over operational decisions. The same tensions would be likely to be present in relation to a prosecution service.[37] When all the arguments put by opponents of the Government's chosen system are considered, it does seem that the risks feared by advocates of a wholly local system are minimal. But this assumes that the new service takes great care to emphasise its new-found independence of the police and is not merely a reincarnation of the old system.

Impacts: the operation of discretion

The Crown Prosecution Service will share the decision to prosecute with the police. The police will begin criminal proceedings by charging suspects or laying an information to issue a summons. There is no doubt that proceedings are instituted at this stage and consequently the magistrates' courts acquire jurisdiction over the case before the jurisdiction of the Crown Prosecutor arises.[38] There is nothing in the Act to indicate how the police should in future exercise their discretion to prosecute. Will they confine their decision to charge solely to the issue of whether they believe there is enough evidence to support the decision or will they continue to exercise a discretion to charge on non-evidential grounds? What do we want them to do? Such questions are of some importance, because, although there is now a power to 'uncharge', the Crown Prosecutor does not appear to have to be advised of decisions by the police *not* to prosecute,[39] and as a consequence the Crown Prosecutor will not review such cases. A decision not to prosecute by the police is likely to be final.

Clearly the new service will be asking the same two principal questions that currently form the basis of the exercise of the decision to prosecute:

(a) is there enough credible and admissible evidence to support a prosecution in the case?
(b) is it socially desirable to prosecute in the case?[40]

What it is important to bear in mind is that the Crown Prosecutor will consider these questions only after criminal proceedings have been instituted.[41] There is a marked difference, if only psychologically, between a decision to start the ball rolling and one to stop it rolling after someone else has thought fit to start it. Additionally, where the court is already seised of the matter, the notice of discontinuance under section 23 requires an explanation to be provided to the court, though not to the defendant, as to why the proceedings are to be discontinued and the defendant may insist on their continuing and may ask for costs if the prosecution offers no evidence. These factors must operate as an inhibition to the exercise of the power to 'uncharge'. Indeed one commentator has already persuasively expressed grave reservations about the system, arguing that the Crown Prosecutor becomes involved too late to be an effective safeguard against weak and inadequate prosecutions.[42]

Unless Crown Prosecutors are bold in their decision-making and examine with some vigour the papers passed by the police there is a risk that they will simply become a 'rubber stamp' for police decisions. There is some empirical evidence that prosecuting solicitors do just that at present in relation to cases referred to them.[43] Since most Crown Prosecutors will be former prosecuting solicitors, this concern is therefore not purely speculative.

Impacts: accountability

Accountability is a fashionable concept. It is seen as a desirable quality by many agencies. Yet it is seldom defined with precision. The Royal Commission's discussion used accountability in two senses in its discussion of the issue.[44] In places the Royal Commission saw accountability as involving supervision of the operation of the system with supervisors able to veto decisions inconsistent with established policy guidelines and to direct action consistent with them. In others the Royal Commission saw a place only for explanation of the basis of decisions; where the decision was out of line with the views of the agency to whom the prosecutor was accountable, the consequence would only be advice and recommendations for the future. It is not always clear whether the Royal Commission saw these two types of accountability as part of the same system of accountability or as two different systems. The problem is compounded against the backcloth of the local system recommended by the Royal Commission. In twinning the two concepts or types of accountability, the Royal Commission was able to fudge the issue. The Commissioners appear to have wanted the general workings of the system to be subject to scrutiny in Parliament, but were not prepared to see individual decisions explained and justified in that forum, though they did envisage 'some formal channel of explanatory accountability to a local body'.[45]

Under the Act, the only form of accountability is through the Attorney General to Parliament, primarily by means of the annual reports the Attorney General is under a duty to lay before Parliament. Cynics will doubt whether reporting annually will give any kind of visibility to prosecuting policy in a busy parliamentary calendar. Under the proposed arrangements, it is difficult to envisage any real control being exercised by the ability of Members of Parliament to put questions to the Attorney General in Parliament.[46]

Impacts: the organisation of the legal profession

Aspects of this Act worry the Bar. The livelihood of many barristers is dependent upon a continuing flow of prosecution work.[47] The Law Society, smarting under the proposed loss of the conveyancing monopoly, chose to argue for an extension of rights of audience to allow Crown Prosecutors, whether solicitors or barristers,[48] a right of audience in the Crown Court. They backed up their case with argument normally persuasive to the Government — that costs would be reduced — and suggested that in two-thirds of the cases where counsel is presently instructed, 'it would be considered cheaper to use an employed prosecuting advocate'.[49] But such is the strength of the Bar's lobby that the Lord Chancellor has reassured the Bar, and repeated the assurance in Parliament[50] that the Government has no intention of extending the rights of Crown Prosecutors to include audience before the Crown Court. Despite these reassurances based on the belief that it was vital to have a strong independent Bar, the case for denying Crown Prosecutors at least extended rights of audience in the Crown Court[51] is difficult to sustain. It would at some time in the future be possible under Section 4(3) of the Act for a Lord Chancellor to achieve this by direction. It is difficult to see why solicitors should not be able to present the prosecution case on a guilty plea in the Crown Court. There is also the existing anomaly that permits defending solicitors a right of audience on appeal to the Crown Court where they have acted at trial in the magistrates' court. Is it not odd that a Crown Prosecutor should not enjoy the same extended rights of audience on the appeal? Extrapolating further, if Crown Prosecutors were granted further rights of audience, why should defence solicitors not enjoy the same rights? This would, of course, be a serious encroachment on the divided profession. These worries about the erosion of the distinction between solicitors and barristers were clearly in the mind of the Lord Chancellor in giving his assurance to the Bar. He described the controversy over extended rights of audience as 'damaging to the good relations between the two parts of the profession'. But the power to make a direction extending rights of audience remains in the Act. The section is not needed if the only objective is to allow Crown Prosecutors those rights of audience in the Crown Court enjoyed by solicitors in private practice; this is covered by Section 4(1) and (2). The only use to which Section 4(3) can be put is to extend rights to Crown Prosecutors which would not be enjoyed by other solicitors. As such, this sub-section, the sting of which is currently withheld by the assurance of the Lord Chancellor, may be another short step along the winding road to fusion of the two branches of the profession.

Impacts: a new deal for defendants

The Royal Commission concluded that existing prosecuting arrangements sometimes operated unfairly.[52] Occasionally prosecutions were brought where there was an inadequate and poorly prepared case. Occasionally prosecutions were brought where it was not in the public interest to do so. Occasionally the system displayed arbitrary and inexplicable differences in the treatment of apparently similar cases. In the light of these reasons for proposing change, it is right to ask whether the Crown Prosecution Service will represent a new deal for defendants. This largely remains to be seen. The DPP's Code for Crown Prosecutors will be based on the Attorney General's 'Criteria for Prosecution'[53] and it has already been noted that these do not differ markedly from existing criteria applied in the exercise of the discretion to prosecute. The Code will no doubt address the further issues of when it will be appropriate to drop, or add, charges, or to accept a plea of guilty to a lesser charge in exchange for dropping a more serious charge. No hint as to the content of these guidelines has been given.

A major question will be the relationship between the police and the Crown Prosecution Service. This takes on particular importance in a system which is police led: in the bulk of cases the Crown Prosecutor will be reviewing a decision to prosecute already made by the police. Too cosy a relationship will leave the *effective* decision to prosecute with the police. Andrew Sanders' research on prosecution decisions and the Attorney General's criteria for prosecution suggests that prosecuting solicitors do not currently throw out many cases and certainly feel constrained when a charge has already been preferred.[54] His papers also suggest that it is possible for the police to 'construct' the case to be presented to the prosecuting solicitor because the police have a monopoly over information in the case. In order to provide a real safeguard for defendants Crown Prosecutors will need to exercise the additional muscle given to them by their new independence from the police.

The new service also has the potential to 'police' the police. For example, if Crown Prosecutors adopted a policy of not prosecuting whenever the legality of the manner in which evidence has been obtained is doubtful, this would place pressure on the police to ensure complete fairness in the obtaining of evidence. This would be an additional safeguard to the safeguards of self-regulation by the police contained in the Police and Criminal Evidence Act 1984. But the writer ventures to suggest that it would be a supreme optimist who actually expected this type of supervision by Crown Prosecutors to arise, particularly when the conventional wisdom is that judicial discretion over the admission of evidence obtained in questionable circumstances is the main sanction.

Concluding comment

A major argument in this chapter has been that the focus on the form of the new service has directed attention away from the central issues for the reform of the conduct of the prosecution. Even when the debate has touched on such issues, it has soon been yanked back into the squabble over local versus national control. Our enthusiasm for the new service may need to be delayed pending research into the new system of prosecution decision-making. Indeed there is reason to be pessimistic. Though the new system is an improvement on the previous arrangements, it may be overly optimistic to believe that in the future the decision to prosecute in every case will be based on careful scrutiny of everything known to the police and on reasoned and principled guidelines.

It will be clear that the Crown Prosecution Service is markedly different from the much praised Scottish system. Yet even there recent research has shown that there is the gap we keep finding between the rhetoric of the protection offered by the system and what it actually delivers.[55] The research study showed that there is almost a presumption of prosecution which is only rebutted in a small number of cases. Furthermore the existence of fiscals does not seem to have resulted in any clearer understanding of the basis of decision-making in the exercise of the discretion to prosecute. Most decisions not to prosecute are based on an insufficiency of evidence or on the triviality of the offence. Decision-making is based on received wisdom learned in post rather than from the formulation and revision of prosecuting guidelines.

Given that the new system clearly builds on the traditions of the prosecuting solicitors' service and having regard to the research of Andrew Sanders discussed above, can we expect dramatic changes of practice from the Crown Prosecution Service? Might it not be the case that we simply have to accept that what is clearly to be an informal private process is incapable of any effective control, leaving us to fall back onto trust in the chosen decision-makers?

Notes

1. See generally Royal Commission on Criminal Procedure, *The Investigation and Prosecution of Criminal Offences in England and Wales: The Law and Procedure*, 1981, Cmnd. 8092–1, (cited in this paper as 'RCCP Procedure Volume'), paras. 3–7, 134–49.
2. See now Prosecution of Offences Act 1979 and Prosecution of Offences Regulations 1978 (SI 1978: 1357).
3. *R v. Commissioner of Police for the Metropolis, ex parte Blackburn,* [1968] 2 QB 118; [1968] 2 WLR 893, CA; *R v. Commissioner of Police for the Metropolis, ex parte Blackburn (No. 3),* [1973] QB 241; [1973] 2 WLR 43, CA; *R v. Chief Constable of Devon*

and Cornwall, ex parte Central Electricity Generating Board, [1982] QB 458; [1981] 3 WLR 967, CA.

4. *ibid.*
5. *ibid.*
6. *ibid.*
7. Cmnd. 1978.
8. See M. Weatheritt, *The Prosecution System: Survey of Prosecuting Solicitors' Departments*, 1980, (Royal Commission on Criminal Procedure Research Study No. 11).
9. JUSTICE, *The Prosecution Process in England and Wales*, 1970; for comments see Sigler, 'Public Prosecutions in England and Wales' [1974] *Crim LR* 642, and Bowley, 'Prosecution — A Matter for the Police' [1975] *Crim LR* 442.
10. See S. Moody and J. Tombs, *Prosecution in the Public Interest*, 1982.
11. *Report of the Royal Commission on Criminal Procedure* (Philips Commission) Cmnd. 8092 (cited in this paper as 'RCCP'), paras. 7.1–7.5.
12. See generally RCCP, chapter 6.
13. RCCP, para. 7.5. On (b), contrast the Prosecution of Offences Regulations 1978, which allow the DPP to give advice whether on application or on his own initiative. With regard to guilty pleas by letter the Magistrates' Court Rules will be amended to permit the clerk to the justices to read out to the court the prosecutor's statement of facts as well as any mitigation included in the defendant's written plea.
14. RCCP, para. 7.7.
15. RCCP, para. 7.7. See also para. 7.68 for the recommendations on the process of 'uncharging' because the courts acquire jurisdiction before the new service would take over responsibility for the conduct of the case. See also further comments later in this paper.
16. RCCP, paras. 7.25–7.32; see paras. 7.33–7.37 for the special arrangements for London.
17. RCCP, paras. 7.67 and 7.68.
18. RCCP, chapter 6.
19. Reproduced in *Justice of the Peace*, 9 April, 1983 at p. 228. For comment, see Sanders, 'Prosecution Decisions and the Attorney General's Guidelines' [1985] *Crim LR* 4.
20. Reproduced in RCCP Procedure Volume, Appendix 25.
21. See Written Evidence of the Commissioner of Police for the Metropolis to the Royal Commission on Criminal Procedure, 1978, pp. 1–10 and A. Wilcox, *The Decision to Prosecute*, 1972.
22. *An Independent Prosecution Service for England and Wales*, Cmnd. 9074, para. 10.
23. Silkin, 'The Shape of Prosecutions to Come', *The Lawyer*, October 1983, at p. 4; Silkin, 'The Prosecution Process' [1984] *PL* 6; see also comments in Working Party on Prosecution Arrangements — The Organisation of an Independent Prosecution Service: Discussion Paper, 1982, reproduced as an Annex to *An Independent Prosecution Service for England and Wales*, Cmnd. 9074. The arguments against the Royal Commission's proposals are well put in J. Edwards, *The Attorney General, Politics and the Public Interest*, 1984, at pp. 98–104 and 107–19.
24. Working Party on Prosecution Arrangements — The Organisation of an Independent Prosecution Service: Discussion Paper, 1982, reproduced as an Annex to *An Independent Prosecution Service for England and Wales*, Cmnd. 9074.
25. Cmnd. 9074.
26. The Prosecution of Offences Act 1985 is cited in this paper as 'the Act'. For a series of detailed comments on the Act, see [1986] *Crim LR* 3–44; see also Prosecution of Offences Act 1985 (Commencement No 1) Order 1985, (SI 1985: 1849).
27. Section 3 of the Act.
28. The Solicitor-General hinted in Parliament that minor motoring cases will be included in such an order: HC Deb. Vol. 79, No. 116, col. 145, 13 May, 1985; see now Prosecution of Offences Act 1985 (Specified Proceedings) order 1985, (SI 1985: 2010).
29. Section 1(6) of the Act.
30. Cmnd. 9411.
31. Such directions are made under s.83 of the Supreme Court Act 1981. Currently a direction applies to certain Crown Courts because of a shortage of barristers in the area.
32. Section 6 of the Act.

33. But acting in this way might well get the case before the Crown Prosecutor when otherwise it might never get out of the police station; see below.
34. Section 9 of the Act.
35. Section 10(3) of the Act.
36. See also discussion below.
37. See Silkin, 'The Shape of Prosecutions to Come', *The Lawyer*, October 1983, at p. 14; see also comments of Lord Elton at HL Deb. Vol. 458, No. 28, cols. 1092–3, 17 January, 1985.
38. See Section 15(2) of the Act.
39. Save under Section 8 (see above) which seems to concern only an overall monitoring function.
40. This seems a better formulation that the more usual, 'Is it in the public interest to prosecute?'
41. Save in those cases where the Crown Prosecutor will institute proceedings under Section 3(2) (b); these are cases formerly requiring the intervention of the DPP.
42. Sanders, ' "Arrest and Charge", Its Meaning and Significance', *New Law Journal*, 31 August, 1984, at p. 741; Sanders, 'Prosecution Decisions and the Attorney-General's Guidelines' [1985] *Crim LR* 4; Sanders, 'The Uncertain Powers of Crown Prosecutors', *New Law Journal*, 29 March, 1985 at p. 313 and 5 April, 1985 at p. 352; Sanders, 'An Independent Crown Prosecution Service?' [1986] *Crim LR* 16.
43. Sanders, 'Prosecutions Decisions and the Attorney-General's Guidelines' [1985] *Crim LR* 4.
44. See RCCP, paras. 6.48–6.60, 7.67 and 7.68.
45. RCCP, para. 6.55.
46. But see *contra* J. Edwards, *The Attorney General, Politics and the Public Interest*, 1984, at 113–19, esp. at p. 119.
47. Wright, 'The Independent Prosecution Service: The Opinion of the Bar', *The Lawyer*, November 1984, at p. 2.
48. Employed barristers have no right of audience in either magistrates' courts or the Crown Court, though magistrates frequently exercise their discretion to allow employed barristers to act as advocates before them.
49. Law Society Paper presented to the Home Office, 'Rights of Audience in the New Prosecution Service' reproduced in the *Law Society's Gazette*, 31 October, 1984, at p. 3004. See also Hoole, 'The Independent Prosecution Service: The Law Society's View', *The Lawyer*, November 1984, at p. 3.
50. HL Deb. Vol. 458, No. 28, cols. 1143–4, 17 January, 1985. The assurance was also given by Lord Elton on behalf of the Government on the Second Reading of the Bill: HL Deb. Vol. 457, No. 12, col. 1017, 29 November, 1984. See also the statement of the Solicitor-General to the House of Commons: HC Deb. Vol. 77, No. 97, cols. 215–16, 16 April, 1985.
51. Perhaps initially only for guilty pleas and committals for sentence.
52. RCCP, paras. 6.14–6.48.
53. See statement by Lord Elton, HL Deb. Vol. 458, No. 28, col. 1118, 17 January, 1985.
54. Sanders, 'Prosecution Decisions and the Attorney-General's Guidelines' [1985] *Crim LR* 4 and Sanders, 'An Independent Crown Prosecution Service?' [1986] *Crim LR* 16.
55. See S. Moody and J. Tombs, *Prosecution in the Public Interest*, 1982.

CHAPTER 18

A prosecuting solicitor's view

CLIVE WOODCOCK

The Prosecuting Solicitors' Society of England and Wales has over 800 members who are solicitors and barristers engaged full time in prosecuting criminal offences on behalf of the police and other public bodies. The Prosecution of Offences Act represents not only a fundamental change and challenge for our Society and its members, but a profound constitutional change in the administration of justice. The Society has for 20 years been campaigning with what I hope may be described as restrained vigour for an independent prosecution system in this county, has worked diligently to assist the Royal Commission in its deliberations and it has participated keenly in the subsequent discussions.

Many issues of the greatest importance are raised in this Act: I propose to offer a view upon some of the more important ones. On some of these issues I shall be writing on behalf of my Society and representing its views: on others, I shall be representing no one but myself. By refraining from being precise as to which are which, I hope to avoid later recrimination!

Organisation: central or local?

The first and main decision the Government had to take, once it was decided that the introduction of an independent system was necessary, was whether that system should be nationally organised and centrally based, or locally organised with an element of central coordination and regulation. The Royal Commission strongly favoured the latter solution, with Crown Prosecutors accountable to a locally appointed and elected prosecutions authority. That was a view very strongly supported by the Prosecuting Solicitors' Society. Since time immemorial the administration of justice in courts of summary jurisdiction, which will remain the much greater part of the prosecutor's work in the independent system, has been the responsibility of the local community. Those of us who work in the provinces are aware of a keen desire abroad in public and civic life for the local involvement and responsibility of elected members in the prosecution process or its administrative supervision to be retained.

211

This debate now appears to have been lost and the Act provides simply for a greatly enlarged Directorate of Public Prosecutions to operate as a uniform national system throughout England and Wales.

The framework for the conduct of criminal prosecutions in this country may be summarised in this way:

(a) Under s.2 the Attorney General appoints the DPP. (This is a new provision, the DPP having hitherto been appointed by the Home Secretary.)

(b) Under s.3 the Attorney General superintends the DPP in the discharge of all his functions.

(c) Under s.1 the DPP appoints Crown Prosecutors for areas which the Government has announced will largely coincide with existing police force areas.

(d) The DPP will appoint all the staff of the new service: those who are solicitors or barristers will have the full powers of the DPP but will exercise them 'under his direction' (s.1(6)); and

(e) The Director and his staff will have the duty under s.3(2) (a) to take over all criminal proceedings instituted on behalf of a police force.

It therefore follows that on the day that this Act is brought into effect, all police prosecutions in England and Wales will be controlled by two persons, one of whom is appointed by the other. I here tread with great diffidence on ground which would more appropriately be occupied by constitutional lawyers, but are there not great dangers in placing such a large measure of control over our criminal process in such few hands? Of course, the present holders of those high offices are of the utmost distinction and unquestioned integrity, as have been their predecessors. Lord Rawlinson, formerly Attorney General himself, said:

> The whole of this service will come under the umbrella of the quasi-judicial role which is the great and proud tradition of all Attorneys General whose aim is to make sure and maintain that they are wholly outside the influence of politics.

Is it not, however, possible to discern a gradual polarisation in political life as decades pass and is it that unreasonable to suggest that in the future a day might well come when the holders of those offices might be of a different stamp and the powers of the state become less separate as a result? Lord Simon in the House of Lords in January 1985, addressing himself to this question, said (quoting Mr. Justice Langton):

> I am not really impressed by forensic foreboding of indeterminate future disasters.

Others were not so sanguine. Baroness Faithfull put it in this rather direct way:

May I pose the hypothetical question: in the future . . . might a future Attorney General veer towards wearing a political hat?

The Government Minister, Lord Elton, replied as follows:

As to the question of political influence, I have to ask my noble friend whether her aspersions cast in a purely hypothetical way against the Attorney General who is a Law Officer of the Crown are any less reprehensible than the aspersions which by inference I suppose we may be said to cast against local government by seeking to take control of this machine away from local authorities? Recent history in the current coal strike suggests to me that we have perhaps fractionally more basis for our anxiety than does my noble friend. I urge her to read the cuttings of local papers.

Was that barbed reply entirely fair? There have been press reports (the substance of which is difficult to evaluate) of difficulty over *resources* being made available for police operations and prosecutions but I should have thought that resource supply could be protected without great difficulty. I have to say that so far as I am aware, despite all the very high feelings that were present during the coal dispute to which the Minister was referring, none of my colleagues reported a single instance of interference by local elected representatives with the professional conduct of a prosecution once it was instituted.

We have to recognise, however, that the decision to base the new system on a unified national directorate has been taken and is now not going to be reversed. My Society's present objective is therefore to ensure that as much autonomy as is possible is reposed in the local Crown Prosecution Offices. When the Bill was first published we were greatly alarmed and dismayed at the lack of any indication of the intention to give local prosecutors any freedom from central direction or to delegate tasks or functions to them.

Clause 1(4) provided at that time:

The Director may, for any area specified by him, designate a prosecuting officer (i.e. any solicitor or barrister on his staff) as senior officer for that area and any person so designated shall be known as a Crown Prosecutor.

This of course amounted to no more than permission to the Director (not even a requirement) to confer on a member of his staff a courtesy title unsupported by any duty or function. At the Second Reading of the Bill on 29 November 1984 Lord Diplock delivered the following rebuke to the draftsmen of this Clause:

If I were construing the Bill, I would say that the reference in Clause

1(4) as it stands at present to a 'Crown prosecutor' is meaningless window dressing.

The Government quickly took that admonition to heart, and in the Committee Stage introduced its own amendment to Clause 1 (this amendment following very closely a draft amendment submitted by my Society) making the post of Crown Prosecutor a statutory office as head of the service in each area and giving the holder of that post the statutory function of taking responsibility for the operation of the service in his or her area.

Furthermore, since the publication of the Bill a number of assurances have been given by Ministers (including the Attorney General) and by the Director to the effect that it is intended to delegate full responsibility to the local Crown Prosecutor not only for the management of his office but for the conduct of most cases arising in his area, including categories of cases at present conducted by the Director's staff. Flesh has been put onto these assurances by the publication of the White Paper on the 'Proposed Crown Prosecution Service' (Cmnd. 9411) in which is set out the proposed distribution of functions between the Headquarters and Local Offices of the new service.

There will of course be policy guidelines promulgated by Headquarters designed to secure consistency of approach throughout the country, but that is clearly in the interests of fairness and therefore a fulfilment of one of the three main objectives set by the Royal Commission for any new service.

In summary, the community of prosecuting solicitors would greatly have preferred a locally accountable system but recognises that a contrary decision has been taken which we will do our best to implement. Some of our fears of over-centralisation have been removed by the amendments to s.1 of the Act by the assurances of Ministers and by the publication of the White Paper on the distribution of functions.

The areas

S.1(4) of the Act as amended imposes on the Director the duty of dividing England and Wales into areas, each area to be the operational unit of the new service. We would have preferred the Act to specify each police force area (with special arrangements for the Metropolitan Police Area and the City of London) as the 'area' for this purpose, but assurances which very nearly meet our view were given by the Minister of State, Lord Elton, as follows (*Hansard*, 17 January 1985, vol. 458, 1084):

> The intention is, subject to the advice which we shall have from consultants about the best way to operate this in administrative terms, that the areas shall coincide with existing police force areas. There may

be cases where smaller police force areas could, with advantage, be amalgamated. I cannot give a hard and fast undertaking that they will be the same, but they will be approximately the same.

Juveniles

There is no special provision in the Act for the conduct of prosecutions in the Juvenile Court: indeed, there is no reference at all to juveniles in the Act. A considerable number of peers forcefully led by Baroness Faithfull has proposed and supported a number of amendments designed to secure within the new prosecution service a specialist attached to each Juvenile Court who would be expert in the problems and treatment of juvenile offenders and who would perform a function similar to that performed by the Reporter in the Juvenile Courts of Scotland.

So convincing were the arguments put forward in this regard that at the conclusion of the debate on Baroness Faithfull's amendment, the Minister gave this undertaking:

> We have in fact adopted the approach recommended . . . of ensuring that we rely on the development of specialisation and specialists within the service — people who have direct experience of children. I can undertake at the Box at this moment that in areas where there is sufficient Juvenile Court work to justify specialisation, whether whole time or part time, officers of the Crown Prosecution Service will be assigned and trained specially to deal with Juvenile Court cases.[1]

This is a proposal which we welcome with great warmth. The only comment we would offer from our experience is that part time specialisation in the prosecution of juvenile offenders is preferable to whole time specialisation. Not only will this be more practicable outside the very large conurbations, since in most towns Juvenile Courts do not sit with sufficient frequency to occupy the services of a full time specialist prosecutor, but also it is in the interests of balanced presentation that the prosecutor in the Juvenile Court should act in the context of knowledge and experience of the adult Courts.

Withdrawal of prosecution

One of the main objectives of the Act is to provide a system under which there is an independent review by lawyers of every prosecution at an early stage after its commencement by charge or information giving the opportunity (as it was put in the 1983 report of the Working Party on Prosecution Arrangements) for ensuring that 'cases which are unlikely to succeed should be weeded out at an early stage'.

S.3(2) (a) provides that it shall be the duty of the Director (and therefore the duty of all his professional staff) to take over the conduct of all criminal proceedings (other than proceedings to be specified later by regulation) instituted on behalf of a police force. This means that from the moment of the preferment of the charge or the laying of the information all prosecution decisions are to be taken by the Director and his staff, and this of course includes the decision as to whether the prosecution is to proceed.

The question immediately arises as to how the Director or a Crown Prosecutor is to proceed when he decides that a prosecution should be discontinued.

The position is that in every case in which the prosecutor wishes to withdraw he must give notice to the court under s.23, giving reasons for not wanting the proceedings to continue. Such a notice may only be given at the preliminary stages, i.e. before evidence is heard in a summary trial or before commitment in a trial on indictment. There is no necessity for reasons to be given to the accused for the withdrawal of proceedings (s.23(b)) but the accused may require the proceedings to be continued. (The position in Scotland may be contrasted where the Procurator Fiscal as 'master of the instance' is empowered simply to abandon a prosecution without giving his reasons.)

As Walter Merricks pointed out as soon as the Bill was published, if the power to discontinue (which is central to the whole fabric of the independent system) was to operate effectively it may be very undesirable that formal applications to withdraw should remain necessary. Section 23 was a late amendment to the Bill introduced to take account of the following conflicting considerations.

On the one hand the prosecutor, having decided that a prosecution should not proceed, should not be impeded in giving effect to that decision by obstacles of court procedure. From the defendant's point of view also, if the decision to withdraw is taken before the first appearance he would no doubt prefer there to be no proceedings in court in which it is revealed that he has fallen under sufficient suspicion for him to be charged. On the other hand, it is no light matter for a citizen to be charged and then not proceeded against and there ought to be a measure of openness and accountability when such an event occurs. It might also be argued that there may be occasions when the decision to withdraw is quite simply wrong and *should* be reviewed by the court. (An example of the Crown Court directing the prosecutor to proceed with the trial of a defendant against whom he was seeking to discontinue, the trial then resulting in conviction is *R v Broad* (1979) 68 Cr App R 281.)

There are cases in which the prosecutor would have great difficulty in giving his reasons for withdrawal in open court. Examples are:

(a) a witness or the defendant himself is dangerously ill and has not been told;

(b) circumstances not amounting to evidence of a criminal offence have

led the prosecutor to conclude that a witness's word can simply not
be relied upon;
(c) a witness has been charged with a similar offence, where to
announce publicly that his evidence is not worthy of belief would
clearly prejudice that witness's own trial.
Other examples can no doubt be thought of without difficulty.

The answer has been to insert a provision in the Act (s.23) along the
lines of the proposal made by the Royal Commission at para 7.68 of their
Report in which the Crown Prosecutor would (by submission of a
document rather than in open court) notify the court of his withdrawal,
such notification to be accompanied by reasons in writing.

There are three further difficulties of fundamental importance which the
Act has not resolved in this vital matter of discontinuation:
(i) There do not appear to be any provisions for a defendant against
whom proceedings are commenced and then discontinued to recover
any costs he has incurred, other than by serving a notice requiring the
proceedings to continue under s.23(7). Normally costs would only be
payable following a formal dismissal in open court: there are
provisions in s.16 for costs to be ordered where a prosecution is not
proceeded with but the section provides no mechanism for costs orders
to be made otherwise than on the defendant's appearance at court.
(ii) Some attention should have been given to the effect on the
prosecutor's decision-making process of the rights under civil law of a
defendant against whom process is withdrawn. A proportion of such
defendants are likely to claim damages against the police for false
imprisonment or malicious prosecution. If the police defend such
proceedings, as in most cases they surely will, the correctness of the
Crown Prosecutor's decision to withdraw is likely to be a central issue
in the proceedings. Will the Crown Prosecutor be a compellable
witness in such proceedings? Will not in any event the prospect of his
decision becoming a central issue in civil proceedings to which he is not
even a party be an unhealthy restraint upon the making of that
decision?
(iii) It is clear that the Government is anxious not in any way to interfere
with the rights of private citizens to bring prosecutions and the right of
private prosecution remains untouched by the Act (s.23(9)). If the
Crown Prosecutor withdraws proceedings against a defendant, there is
nothing in the Act to prevent a complainant or indeed any other
private citizen from bringing his own prosecution. Section 3(2) (b)
would of course permit the Director in such a case to take over that
prosecution also for the purpose of dropping it, but in order to prevent
yet another citizen from proceeding on the same charge the matter
would have to be brought before the court for a formal dismissal, and
any intention there may have been to protect the defendant from the

publicity of attending court would then be completely frustrated. In addition, the defendant would have by then undergone two separate criminal proceedings on the same charge to no purpose, a possibility that our legislature ought surely to prevent.

The answer to some of these problems might have been to provide that any withdrawal or discontinuance of the charge by the Director or his staff shall have the same effect as a formal dismissal of that charge, so entitling the defendant to indemnification for his costs and preventing any further proceedings.

Rights of audience

S.4 of the Act provides that in the new system Crown Prosecutors (whether solicitors or barristers) shall have the same rights of audience in any court as those enjoyed by solicitors. The power of the Lord Chancellor to make directions under s.83 of the Supreme Court Act 1981 extending these rights of audience is preserved.

This provision in s.4 in fact technically extends the rights of audience of barristers since at present employed barristers (other than those appearing in performance of a statutory function, e.g. barristers in the existing DPP Department) have to apply for the Justices' permission before they can advocate in a magistrates' court.

The Government have announced that they have no intention of giving Crown Prosecutors rights of audience in the Crown Court, and this announcement has of course been greatly welcomed by the Bar. I should make it clear that the Prosecuting Solicitors' Society has, with one exception, never sought rights of audience in the Crown Court. Indeed, in the context of the new prosecution service it would be quite unrealistic to do so since the withdrawal of police officers as advocates will mean that the service will have its work cut out providing advocate coverage for magistrates' courts.

The one exception arises from the fact that, though it has been little used, *defending* solicitors have at present a right to appear in the Crown Court in committals for sentence, and appeals against conviction or sentence, where they appeared in the court below. *Prosecuting* solicitors have no such right and, while again it is a right which if granted would be little used, it has always seemed to us wrong in principle (particularly in the solicitor/client relationship which at present exists between prosecuting solicitors and Chief Constables) that the legal representatives of one party to proceedings should have less advantage than those of the other party and that one party should have greater choice of representation than the other.

Reports and publication of guidelines

S.9 provides that as soon as practicable after 4th April each year the

DPP shall make to the Attorney General a report on the discharge by him in that year of his functions. The Attorney General must then lay that report before Parliament. Under s.10(3) a copy of any guidelines issued by the DPP to Crown Prosecutors shall be included in the DPP's report for the relevant year. The Government were reluctant to commit the Director to an obligation to include such guidelines in his report, while acknowledging that there might be occasions when he would wish to do so, either in part or in whole.

It was felt that there could be many matters affecting investigation, preparation or prosecution which would be legitimately contained in such guidelines while it would not be in the public interest for them to be generally known.

If some defect in the criminal law suddenly becomes apparent, it was felt that it would not be in the public interest for the criminally-inclined to be made aware of the loophole. Similarly, if pressure on the courts or other good reason caused guidelines to be issued to the effect that henceforth (perhaps for a temporary period) people of a certain age or people committing offences below a certain value of property would be cautioned rather than prosecuted, this again would be material which it was felt would clearly not be in the public interest to make generally known.

The Attorney General's guidelines on the criteria for prosecution and the further guidelines on the disclosure of evidence have been made public, and clearly rightly so since these are matters of general public interest which give reassurance by their disclosure. Even though other guidelines may touch on more delicate and dangerous matters, s.10(3) nonetheless requires that the Code for Crown Prosecutors and any subsequent amendments to that Code, shall be set out in the DPP's report for the year concerned.

Counsel's fee

Arrangements for the remuneration of the Bar closely affect the independence of the Bar in this country, that independence being frequently described as essential to the protection of our freedoms. At present the fees of prosecution counsel in the great majority of cases are taxed by Crown Court officials (with provision for appeal). While prosecuting solicitors play a part in negotiating with Crown Court taxing officers appropriate fees for the counsel they have instructed, the final assessment is made by the taxing officer.

Section 14 proposes that all taxation functions in respect of prosecution counsel shall be removed from the Crown Court staff and reposed in the new prosecution service. The section provides for regulations to be made by the Attorney General prescribing scales or rates of fees, costs or expenses of both counsel and witnesses and (as I understand the Government's intention) counsel's fees will be assessed by the Crown

Prosecutor's staff in accordance with these regulations before being paid direct to counsel from budgets previously provided. Mr. David Mellor, Parliamentary Under Secretary of State, has I am sure to everyone's relief confirmed in correspondence that there will be no question of prosecutions having to be aborted or delayed at the end of a financial year because the budget for that year has been exceeded. However, other causes for slight unease remain.

First, to place in the hands of the prosecutor the responsibility for payment of counsel may lead to a suspicion in the mind of the public (and perhaps in the mind of young or inexperienced counsel) that there is an element in the arrangement of 'payment by results'. It seems to us that however keenly we seek to preserve our independence and integrity, such suspicions may form in the minds of those who do not fully understand our traditions.

Secondly, at present the fees of both prosecution and defence counsel in a particular case are settled by the same authority. If, as is now proposed, the Crown Prosecutor becomes responsible for the assessment and payment of prosecution counsel's fees while the clerk of the Crown Court remains responsible for the same matters in respect of defence counsel, the need for such fees to bear a relation to each other is not going to be met. This, it seems to us, is bound to lead to unsatisfactory anomalies and harmful resentments. It may also lead to a proliferation of appeals by one side or the other.

It may be that some of these fears may be found to be unwarranted when the regulations and full details of the proposals in this regard are published. Let us hope so, because harmonious relationships between the Bar and the staff of the new service will contribute much to the success of the system.

Costs

The position regarding costs under the Act does not differ greatly from the previous statutory arrangements.

S.16 in summary provides for the defendant to receive his costs out of central funds when any charge in the magistrates' court or the Crown Court is not proceeded with or results in an acquittal and for costs out of central funds likewise to be paid to a defendant who succeeds in the Divisional Court, the Court of Appeal or the House of Lords. As I have mentioned earlier, it remains unclear by what procedure the defendant is to receive costs if the proceedings are withdrawn by the Crown Prosecutor before any appearance in court. The same consideration applies with summary offences.

My Society, alongside the Magistrates' Association and the Justices' Clerks' Society, has for many years campaigned for the view that all costs incurred by acquitted defendants, in whatever court and whether an indictable or summary offence is involved, should be paid out of central

funds. It is very difficult to see why in the opportunity provided by the new
prosecution service, it has been necessary to retain the distinction between
on the one hand 'costs out of central funds' for indictable offences and
'costs payable by the prosecutor' for summary offences. There was a long
debate on this point in the Committee Stage in the House of Lords, with a
number of distinguished and learned peers arguing for an amendment
which would make costs in summary cases awarded to a defendant payable
out of central funds, this argument being stoutly resisted by the Lord
Chancellor. Very nearly at the conclusion of the debate Lord Simon of
Glaisdale put the rather obvious question that since the new prosecution
service would be entirely funded from central funds, what would be the
difference between 'costs out of central funds' and 'costs payable by the
prosecutor'? The two notions, he implied, were surely different ways of
expressing exactly the same thing? To this he received a reply from the
Lord Chancellor that, not yet being civil servants, none of my colleagues is
able to understand. Explanation would be greatly appreciated. It went as
follows:

> It matters in Government out of which pocket you pay the taxpayers'
> money . . . I think it is probably not purely an accounting matter: it is a
> question of accounting discipline, which is not quite purely an
> accounting matter. Perhaps we could leave it there for a moment, while
> hope dawns eternal.

(Postscript: In the Third Reading provisions were inserted by amendment
to Clause 16 making it possible for any court to order costs out of central
funds to any accused person who is acquitted or against whom a
prosecution of any offence, whether summary or indictable, is not
proceeded with.)

Attorney General's reference on sentence

Clause 22 of the Bill proved almost as intractable as Catch 22: it was
finally ejected from the Bill by a large majority in the House of Lords. The
Lord Chancellor was, however, defiant in defeat, telling his opponents that
they were 'grandees' out of touch with public opinion.

Clause 22 made provision for the Attorney General to refer to the Court
of Appeal any case in which a person had been tried on indictment and
convicted of an offence before the Crown Court for the Court of Appeal's
opinion as to whether, having regard to all the circumstances of the case
which were known to the Crown Court, a different (i.e. more severe)
sentence ought to have been imposed on the offender and, if so, what that
sentence should have been.

This provision was of course similar in its machinery to that enacted in
s.36 of the Criminal Justice Act 1972 enabling the Attorney General to
refer points of law to the Court of Appeal where the defendant is acquitted

in the Crown Court. In neither case is the defendant in jeopardy at any stage of the reference of having his acquittal reversed or his sentence increased.

Clause 22 attracted as much attention as any other provision of the Bill. It is certainly not a provision which has ever been sought by my Society and we have serious doubts as to whether its enactment would have served any useful purpose.

It would of course constitute a fundamental departure from one of the oldest traditions of our criminal justice arrangements, namely the complete detachment of the prosecutor from all questions of sentence. The length of a tradition is not necessarily a sufficient reason for prolonging it, but the onus of proving the need for a change rests heavily on those proposing it.

For a Crown Prosecutor (and it is upon the staff of the new service that the invidious task of reporting cases for reference would fall) to report a sentence to the Director with a view to the Attorney General making a reference would involve both that Crown Prosecutor and prosecution counsel in forming and articulating a view as to the appropriate sentence in a case they have presented. The articulation of such a view after a sentence is only a short step from the preparation of a view before the sentence and that is a road down which I suspect that most prosecutors, both members of the service and counsel whom they instruct, will not wish to travel or even take the first step.

The prosecution of course have a duty to present to the court all facts which may mitigate the seriousness of the offence. It is interesting to contemplate the mental, philosophical and professional contortions through which prosecutors would have to go if, having brought mitigating circumstances to the attention of the court, they were to find themselves under a kind of statutory duty to report that court to the Attorney-General for having taken *too much notice* of those circumstances.

It must also be borne in mind that no prosecutor sees the social enquiry or medical reports which the court considers when sentencing; he is therefore generally in no position to comment upon sentence even if he wished or were required to do so.

The proposal furthermore seemed to be defective in logic. There are many ways in which sound sentencing policy is promulgated to judges. The Lord Chief Justice's sentencing guidelines, the growing body of sentencing decisions, the Judicial Studies Board and the frequent judicial sentencing seminars are all means whereby judges are trained and tutored in sentencing policy. If discipline is the aim, there are surely far less cumbersome and more discreet ways of achieving it.

If the reassurance of the public is the aim, it seems to us that the provision would have had the opposite effect. In all punishments for serious crime there is, or there is perceived by the public to be, an element of public protection in the imposition of a custodial sentence. For it to be publicly announced in the Court of Appeal that an unidentified defendant, who sentencing policy required should receive a custodial sentence of five years for the protection of the public, will in fact be walking the streets in six months is hardly likely to be reassuring in any quarter.

For this reason logic would dictate that such a reference should not operate in theory but in reality so that the sentence itself could be altered. This would seem to be the view of no less an authoritative criminologist than Professor Nigel Walker who, in a letter to *The Daily Telegraph* on 24 January, 1985 said:

> It would make more sense to amend the Clause so that the sentence itself could be altered. This is especially desirable when a dangerous offender has received a sentence which will set him free too soon for the safety of others.

Professor Walker proceeded to point out that in most European countries, and in some Commonwealth countries such as Canada, there is a two-way system which allows both defence and prosecution the right of appeal against verdict and sentence. My own view is that our tradition of prosecution detachment from sentencing considerations is important in its restraint and humanity and is worthy of careful preservation.

Time limits

S.22 gives power to the Secretary of State to set time limits for all preliminary stages of criminal proceedings, so as to produce acquittals where the limits are exceeded. Not much can be said about this section in the absence of the regulations to be made under it. One point is, however, worth emphasising. The concept of time limits acting as guillotines is an import from Scottish criminal procedure. The Scottish procedure is fundamentally different from that obtaining in England and Wales, particularly in the matter of committal proceedings. The Scots have no equivalent to the s.6(1) committal under which witnesses are called to give their evidence to examining justices. Where this procedure is opted for by defence in preference to committal without consideration of the evidence under s.6(2) of the Magistrates' Courts Act 1980, delays inevitably ensue. If we are to have time limits, they should be accompanied by a review of our present arrangements for s.6(1) committals.

This is an Act the central proposition of which, the need for an independent prosecution service, we warmly welcome. Those of us who are privileged to serve under its provisions intend to make it a success in which all participants in our criminal justice system can have full confidence.

Note

1.   It was stated in Parliament (HC Vol. 77, col. 150) that the guidelines in the Code for Crown Prosecutors will contain special provision on juveniles.

CHAPTER 19

Police superintendents and the prosecution of offences

RON WEST

The Police Superintendents' Association of England and Wales represents the senior management of the police service, of whom there are nearly 2,300 members, holding the ranks of chief superintendent or superintendent. Our particular strength in stating a viewpoint is that we speak as those undertaking an investigative and prosecuting function, through our position in the management structure, where our members are and have been directly concerned in prosecution policy in divisions and sub-divisions in all police forces in England and Wales.

As the Philips Commission's report shows[1] the prosecution of offenders is a process which raises many issues and in this chapter it is only possible to touch upon a few of them. My intention is to look at some of the advantages and disadvantages of an independent prosecution service and to summarise the sort of system which the superintendents would most prefer. Our initial stance in which we sought to retain the responsibility for prosecution policy has been overtaken by the Government's proposals in the Prosecution of Offences Act, which should enable a new Crown Prosecution Service to be fully operational from October 1986. To that extent our original viewpoint is academic but I would be wrong not to state our reservations about the format of the new system.

In 1979, in evidence to the Royal Commission on Criminal Procedure,[2] the Police Superintendents' Association registered strong disagreement with the proposal that a solicitor should be able to reverse decisions of the police. It was generally considered that the ultimate responsibility for decision making should remain at the local level. We welcomed the establishment of separate prosecution departments in all forces where they did not already exist and although believing that the ultimate responsibility for decisions to prosecute should remain with the police, we felt that disagreements between chief constables and prosecuting solicitors' departments would be rare, although retaining our solicitor/client relationship.

We are, if nothing else, flexible and although some of our reservations

224

persist, I am sure we shall come to terms with the new system and make it work in an operational context. The Superintendents' Association has worked with the Home Office on the content and submission of case papers to the prosecutor once the new service is introduced, and we are adjusting to the many changes which have occurred in the police service during recent years, not least the ramifications of the Police and Criminal Evidence Act 1984.

The advantages and disadvantages of an independent prosecution service

I can see as many counter arguments as there are views in support of the Crown Prosecution Service, operating on an integrated national system. It is perhaps worth looking closely at three arguments which have been offered in support of the changes, and the responses which we in the police service have made:

1. *The prosecution service has to be, and be seen to be, independent of the police. There must be a clear division between the police investigative functions and the responsibility for a prosecution policy.*

The response. During discussions between the police staff associations, the Home Office and the Director of Public Prosecutions, one of our fears related to the word 'independent' in the title of the new service. We wondered whether it signified a bar to contact prior to the presentation of the case between the police and the solicitor. Fortunately we have received reassurances on this question and these are evident in working party papers and to some extent further confirmed in the distribution of functions between the headquarters and the local offices of the service. All point to the fact that our fears are without substance and that the advisory features of the prosecuting solicitors' role to the police will in no way be diminished.

Why, though, must there be this *division*, between investigation and prosecution, at all? For many years the notion of separating police investigative powers from prosecution decisions has been gaining momentum; but where has it been seen to be so manifestly improper in operation? Our prosecution policy has been hedged in by safeguards and the most recent were the Attorney General's guidelines, in his 'Criteria for Prosecution', issued in February 1983. Critics should realise that the hierarchical, disciplined structure of the police service has prevented decisions being taken in an arbitrary manner: accountability to the chief constable has been coupled with the fact that every decision has been the subject of advice tendered by a number of experienced people including, where necessary, qualified lawyers. I would suggest that very careful consideration has gone into prosecution decisions and, far from being motivated by a 'conviction lust', the police service has taken great care to make a balanced judgement on each case. It is also of interest to note that the system has been in operation since the inception of the police service and during this long period it has apparently operated with public confidence and that of the judiciary. Finally, in defence of the existing system one should realise that before moving into superintendent ranks most members will have cut their teeth as prosecuting chief inspectors, and I known of no more certain way to ensure that prosecution decisions are not taken lightly.

2. *The structure of the prosecution service will promote greater consistency of policy across the country and provide public confidence in the fairness of prosecution arrangements.*

The response. In all honesty police superintendents doubt whether the general public will be terribly concerned whether there is a national or local prosecution service. We appreciate that uniformity in prosecution policy seems attractive, but in practice we believe it is neither possible nor desirable. One of the principal strengths of the existing system is the responsiveness to local conditions. It is true it has vested a large measure of discretion in the chief constable, but will this be so different with an area Crown Prosecutor? The law enforcement and investigative roles of the police mean they are uniquely well-fitted to exercise this discretion in a way which is genuinely in accord with public opinion and local conditions. Although the Crown Prosecutor will be in touch with the police and could accordingly take account of such factors, albeit indirectly, conferring on him responsibility for the decision to prosecute must reduce the number of agencies involved and remove the checks and balances inherent in the present system. Machinery already exists to keep variations between areas within reasonable limits: for example the conferences of the Association of Chief Police Officers, and within each force extensive consultation occurs, particularly through staff associations. We would favour the extended use of prosecuting solicitors' departments on a force basis, where experience reveals few disagreements occur.

3. *The proposals will produce a workable, effective and fair system which consumes the minimum of public resources and has an essential degree of control of cost and efficiency.*

The response. We are not convinced that the surveys undertaken truly reflect a cost-saving in the prosecution function, of the equivalent of 608 police officers who (it is claimed) will be released for operational duties.[3] Certainly Government emphasis has sought effectiveness and efficiency in police operations and non-operational officers have returned to patrol duties. However, from my own experience, I do not think the inception of a Crown Prosecution Service will release so many police officers. Without being unduly cynical it makes it sound an attractive proposition, but how many officers will still be required to spend time on case preparation and administration? Much of the time police officers are in the courts they are present not as an alternative to the prosecuting solicitor but as a necessary addition to his presence. It will also need careful consideration about the extent to which police officers will still be involved in tasks such as warning witnesses. Furthermore, no quantification was given in the White Paper[4] on the level of expenditure which will be required for accommodation to house the Crown Prosecution Service.

It appears that the county councils will have to meet additional costs in those areas which are left unfilled by the Crown Prosecution Service. It is stated by the Government that it would be inappropriate for the independent prosecution service to represent police officers who were being sued, or to become involved in advising the police on matters relating to complaints. Nor is it envisaged that the independent prosecutor will be involved in civil proceedings as a joint tortfeasor: he would not share the vicarious liability of the chief constable.

Problems and pitfalls with the new system

Despite the opinions of those in the police service and elsewhere the Government has decided to create a national Crown Prosecution Service. We have forcefully expressed our reservations but we will now do our best to work with the new system and to make it a success. However, there are ten problems and pitfalls which we have to face and it is worth briefly listing these.

First, the Prosecution of Offences Act, in s.3, deals with the functions of the Director of Public Prosecutions in taking over the conduct of all criminal proceedings instituted on behalf of a police force (other than specified proceedings), but remains silent on the implications of other difficult areas where legal advice is required. At present prosecuting solicitors' departments advise in complex cases where there are problems relating to licensing matters, which may need representation at Licensing Sessions. Such areas include opposition to renewal of Justices' Licences, for example, and advice to chief officers on matters where opposition is considered to renewal of firearms certificates. These are complex issues where hitherto police have referred to prosecuting solicitors for advice which has been readily forthcoming. These areas are not within the functions of the Crown Prosecuting Solicitor. Where will the funds be found to finance this expenditure?

Second, what avenue is now open to the police to appeal against a decision by the prosecutor not to proceed with a case? *Third*, should there be some form of formal mechanism by which an appeal can be made to the office of the Director of Public Prosecutions?

Fourth, has sufficient thought really been given to extending the work of existing prosecuting solicitors' departments and a localised form of Crown Prosecution Service rather than the integrated national system? *Fifth*, have the new measures in the Act taken away from each police officer some of his responsibilities as an officer bearer, under the Crown?

Sixth, because there is no natural distinction between a police officer's private and official capacities, should a constable be able to institute proceedings in a case where the prosecutor has declined to proceed? *Seventh*, s.6 of the Act preserves the right of any person to institute criminal proceedings but is it right that this seemingly exempts a constable? *Eighth*, how far, if at all, will the Crown Prosecution Service relieve police officers of their responsibilities for warning witnesses at court?

Ninth, will the current practice of taking offences into consideration be workable once decisions for prosecution lie with the new service? At present a standard of proof lower than the Director of Public Prosecution's standard of a greater chance of conviction than acquittal is applied to these offences, which are taken into consideration with the agreement of the defence. *Tenth*, will the scale at which the fully-integrated national prosecution service is to be conducted lead to arguments for a national police force?

Prosecutions in the public interest

This brief canter over a very wide field leaves many questions unasked as well as unanswered. I have only managed to touch on some of the issues in this complex area.[5] Police superintendents have been strongly opposed to the loss of the prosecuting function, but we have had to accept this is to go. However, we still greatly favour the *locally based* system, which could be achieved by providing every police area with legally qualified prosecuting staff. Based on police authority areas, and administered by local councils, this flexible structure could cater for extra responsibilities where necessary and there would be fewer problems in funding such a service. The local system would have served the public interest at least as well if not better than a national system and at lower cost *and* with less fear ultimately of a bureaucratic, monolithic structure. In this way an overall national role could be fulfilled yet retaining local identities.

We shall be closely monitoring the effects the new proposals have on the workload of the police after the introduction of the service in late 1986. Will it increase or decrease individual officers' time spent on cases and will the independent prosecution service follow the way of other bureaucracies and generate even more paper which can only be supplied by the police officers dealing with cases? I do not think there is any great cause for concern but as was recognised by Mr. Michael Partridge, Deputy Under Secretary of State at the Home Office, in a speech he made on 31 May, 1984:

> We know that the new service, if it places undue demands on the police service, or if it fails to take account of the needs of the courts, could, far from enhancing the overall effectiveness of the criminal justice system, actually inhibit it.[6]

I am sure none of us wants that, least of all the police service.

Notes

1. Royal Commission on Criminal Procedure (Chairman: Sir Cyril Philips), *Report*, London: HMSO, 1981 (Cmnd. 8092), see especially chapters 6–9.
2. See Royal Commission on Criminal Procedure, *The Investigation and Prosecution of Criminal Offences in England and Wales: The Law and Procedure*, London: HMSO, 1981 (Cmnd. 8092–1).
3. For estimates of the resource implications of an independent prosecution service see David R. Kaye, *The Prosecution System: Organisational Implications of Change* (Royal Commission on Criminal Procedure Research Study No. 12) London: HMSO, 1980.
4. *An Independent Prosecution Service for England and Wales*, London: HMSO, October 1983 (Cmnd. 9074).
5. There is a growing literature on the issues raised by the Prosecution of Offences Act. Some recent articles worth attention include: 'Criteria for prosecution', *Justice of the Peace*, 9 April 1983; 'Prosecution for the public', *Police Review*, 2 September 1983; R. Kinsey, 'Taking the worst and leaving the best', *New Statesman*, 12 August 1983; 'Enter the state prosecutor', *Justice of the Peace*, 10 December 1983; 'Prosecution: Let's have evolution not revolution', *Police Review*, 8 June 1984; 'The independent prosecutor', *Justice of the Peace*, 20 October 1984; 'Prosecution of Offences Bill', *Justice of the Peace*, 17 November 1984; 'Independent, nationally and locally', *The Times*, 7 December 1984.
6. Speech on 31 May 1984 to a conference organised jointly by the Association of Chief Police Officers, the Association of Metropolitan Authorities and the Association of County Councils.

CHAPTER 20

An independent prosecution service:
a view from the shires

CLIVE GRENYER

The Association of County Councils represents the non-metropolitan county councils in England and Wales. At the present time a prosecuting solicitors' department is employed to conduct police prosecutions in all but some six counties of England and Wales. In some cases the department is directly in the employment of the county council and the chief prosecuting solicitor is a chief officer. In other cases the department forms part of the county secretary's department. In others the department is employed by the police authority — where for example there is a joint police authority covering more than one county.

The Association of County Councils is not in favour of the Government proposals embodied in the Prosecution of Offences Act 1985. We feel that the structure of an organisation has a major effect on the efficiency of its operation. We agree that there is a case for the prosecution service to be entirely independent of the police. That is just as well because public opinion demands it. We therefore accept that prosecutors should be freestanding and with a responsibility equal to that of the chief constable.

What we do not agree is that the prosecution service should be centrally controlled. We have the same fear that central Government has about local control — that the prosecution service will be the subject of political interference. We are also concerned that the prosecution of juveniles is not the subject of special statutory arrangements.

During the Committee Stage in the House of Lords, Lady Faithfull put down a number of amendments that would have retained a degree of overall central control, but would have ensured the independence of Crown Prosecutors and their staff. What was suggested was that Crown Prosecutors should be appointed and paid by county councils, but they should hold office rather than be employed, and should only be dismissed by the Director of Public Prosecutions. Although such a system sounds a bit of a camel, it is one that is adopted in a number of areas where total independence is important. It is the basis of the Coroners' Service, the

Registration Service and the Rent Officer Service.

Lady Faithfull's proposals were not, however, accepted by the House of Lords although I doubt, judging from the debate, that their Lordships really understood the implications of the proposals.

I have three main intentions:

1. To try and establish how and why the present proposals came into existence.
2. To ascertain the effect of the implementation of the proposals on the operation and cost of the prosecution service.
3. To ascertain the effect of the implementation of the proposals on the police service.

Let us look first at why the present proposals are before us. The Royal Commission reviewed the existing arrangements back in 1981.[1] They recommended the establishment of a prosecutions service independent of the police. In summary the arguments for a national system were firstly that there is a single official who would be responsible for every decision to prosecute. Secondly there is a direct line of management leading to an integrated career structure; and thirdly that the result would be consistent prosecution policies leading to improved performance nationally.

The arguments against were:

1. The large bureaucratic structure would automatically lead management to be in the hand of administrators rather than solicitors. We have seen this in most branches of the civil service.
2. There would be a very substantial cost; and
3. forces would be at work tending to promote the interests of those at the centre rather than of those on the periphery where the service is basically to serve and work with the local community.

The Commission added that they knew of no common law jurisdiction in which the equivalent of a national prosecuting system covered an area anything like that as large as was proposed, and that a centrally directed national prosecutions system for England and Wales was neither desirable nor necessary.

In 1982, the Home Secretary asked an inter-departmental working party to advise on the form that an independent service might take. It is interesting to compare the constitution of the Royal Commission with that of the inter-departmental working party. The Commission had sixteen members of whom eleven had current experience of the practical operation of the legal system in the courtroom. In contrast, the working party which consisted of fifteen civil servants had not a single member who had any current courtroom experience. Evidence was taken by the working party from a number of sources, but no indication was ever issued that that evidence expressed a balance of opinion in favour of one system or another.

It is no reflection upon the members of that working party that the outcome of their report was predictable and predicted. Because of the Government's anxiety about the risk of local political influence, particularly in certain areas, and because of the Government's general lack of confidence in local government which underlies so many of its proposals today, minds were made up before the working party set to work that a locally based system simply was 'not on'.

Evidence of this preconceived conclusion to the working party's report abounds. One has only to look at the discussion paper issued by the Home Office in November 1982. Paragraph 24 of that paper states, 'the proposal for a local supervisory body, whether by extension of the police authority into a police and prosecutions authority or the establishment of a separate body, is generally regarded as introducing an unacceptable risk of interference in prosecution decisions'. On what factual or evidential grounds could such a statement possibly be made? Clive Woodcock[2] mentions that in his experience there has never been any political interference with the prosecution system once a decision to prosecute has been made. This is a point with which I totally agree, and I am glad it has been made so strongly by him. 'Generally regarded' by whom? Much professional and informed opinion was substantially contrary to the view expressed in paragraph 24.

In due time the working party reported. It is difficult to resist the feeling that its recommendation in favour of a national integrated system is against the weight of much of the argument. The Government published the White Paper which in a mere fifteen paragraphs endorsed the recommendations of the working party.[3] The Government also managed to reach its decision without giving the local authority associations or any other national organisation the opportunity to comment on the working party's conclusions.

That, then, is the background to the new Act and I think we should now look at what is likely to be the effect of implementation of the proposals on the operation and cost of the prosecutions service nationally. Firstly, the operation of the service. For this it is necessary to look at the second White Paper that was issued by the Government in December 1984.

The White Paper[4] indicates that decisions will be taken in the local offices of the service. However, the Director of Public Prosecutions will prepare guidance on policy and practice — and we now know that he is to have a new political master.

In 'cases of particular importance or difficulty', decisions will be taken at headquarters. A list of likely offences is set out on the back of the White Paper. But inside, in paragraphs 13–15 that specific list is substantially widened. For example cases involving Members of Parliament are to be dealt with at headquarters as are 'other cases of difficulty or exceptional public concern'. And paragraph 14 ends: 'in addition it will be open to the

Director or his senior staff at headquarters to call for the papers in any case handled locally'.

Incidentally what does 'senior staff' mean? Can it be that the prosecution service locally, headed by a practising lawyer, will no longer have the final say, and that a non-practising non-lawyer administrator will be issuing guidelines and calling in papers for examination?

Another effect intended by the Government is that there will be more consistency and uniformity in prosecution policies across the country. We are not convinced by that argument. Consistent perhaps but surely not uniform. There are many services administered by county councils and of interest to the Home Secretary where consistent levels of application are necessary. The fire service, and indeed, the police, are examples. Consistency in these cases is ensured by the inspectorate system. But there is no need for uniformity in the delivery of the service. We would be most reluctant to see the role of the private practitioner eliminated completely. Some authorities may continue to feel this to be the most cost effective way in some parts of their area. In the more remote rural areas, local flexibility in prosecution arrangements fits in with maintaining local courts and keeping the administration of justice as accessible as possible to the people.

Consistency can only be achieved by central guidelines, and it is here again that we have misgivings. It is too easy for such guidelines to be used for secondary purposes. One can see little objection in guidelines which say that there is too much robbery and prosecutors should be prepared to take on more cases. But what about guidelines that might say 'too many prosecutions for technical electoral offences — people are being discouraged — reduce the numbers of cases taken' or, 'the number of small company fraud cases and cases under the employment and health and safety at work legislation is too high and small businesses are being discouraged. So only take on the open and shut cases'.

Such guidelines are not beyond the realms of possibility. There's an internal government inquiry being undertaken that is looking at the legal and administrative burdens of small businesses. One of the possibilities being examined is a suggestion that small businesses should be exempt from some of the criminal provisions of the Trade Descriptions Act.

It is difficult to be specific about the effect of the proposals on efficiency. This however, brings us to the question of cost because my perception of efficiency is bound up with value for money.

The costs of the proposals have only been glossed over. The first White Paper, when it looked at the disadvantages of the proposed system, blandly said: 'it may also be difficult under this system to secure the most efficient and cost effective use of resources; so it seems likely to cost more than either of the other options'.

The explanatory and financial memorandum to the Bill was better on quantity but worse on quality. It started off by saying that the financial effect could not yet be quantified and went on to say that 2,500 new civil servants would be needed to take over work currently undertaken by 1,670 local authority and police staff. No surprises there? However, it then went on to say that this would result in a saving of £3·2m. *excluding the continuing costs of police manpower.*

Now where does all that come from? Home Office Research and Planning Unit Paper 22 is entitled *The Staff Resource Implications of an Independent Prosecution System.* The summary indicates that, provided solicitors in the new service achieve eight half-day sittings per week, 788 new staff will be needed. About the same as the financial memorandum to the Bill. But it goes on to say that serious consideration must be given to the possibility that eight half-days will not be achieved. This is for four reasons:

1. Only six half-day sittings per week can be achieved by solicitors.
2. The Metropolitan Police (which is controlled by the Home Office) having unique problems, is not susceptible to targetting.
3. The problems of court scheduling where there are more morning than afternoon sittings make it difficult to achieve productivity in terms of half-days.
4. When 41 per cent of magistrates' courts have morning sittings that extend at least one hour into the afternoon a half-day system becomes very difficult.

The Association believes that prosecuting solicitors' departments have become highly efficient under the impetus of successive government stringency policies together with the continuing pressure of the Manpower Watch System. If you accept that, then on the basis of the Home Office's own research one can say that the savings they expect will not accrue.

You will recall that the financial memorandum to the Bill estimated savings of £3·2m, excluding the continuing costs of police manpower. The Home Office Research Department estimated £3·3m savings, *excluding the costs of the police released from prosecution work.* Both estimates of savings therefore assume that police will be released to do 'proper police work'. Those who ought to know doubt this. There will still have to be all the leg work connected with prosecutions, the preparation of evidence, the other preparatory work. Much of the police costs, on the best available evidence, will continue. They therefore cannot be excluded. And given the commitment to law and order can it be said that the police forces will shed manpower to accommodate those who are released from prosecution work? The truth is that the police will continue to be employed and the actual cost of the Crown Prosecution Service, according to the Home Office figures, would therefore not decrease £3·3m.: they will increase by

£4·9m. This particular prediction of the Home Office Research Department has so far not received very much publicity.

And if it is found that solicitors can only achieve six half-day sittings per week instead of the projected eight, then the increase in the number of solicitors required from the present 767 will not be to the Home Office proposals of 1,345, but will amount to 1,793. This is an increase of 1,026 solicitors to run the service.

That would, using the Home Office estimate of the cost of a solicitor of £11,900 per annum, result in a further increase in cost of £5·3m. The total additional cost to the country of the Government's proposals will then be of the order of £10·2m.

I should emphasise that these are Association estimates based on Home Office research. Much more detailed work has been carried out by the Sussex Police Authority.[5] This research shows that the increased cost of the new service in Sussex would be 17 per cent.

If a service is expensive, there is inevitably government pressure to reduce costs. The reduction of costs, as we all know, results in the reduction of quality. So the effect of the Government's proposals in our estimation would be that the quality of the prosecution service will decline.

The only other point on the question of cost is that of new premises. The new service clearly has to quit the police premises which it currently occupies. Offices do not come cheap.

We have looked at why this system is being foisted upon us and what its effect will be on the service. Let me consider what effect it will have on the police.

It will result in 608 extra policemen being released for proper police duties. These are Home Office figures. I would ask whether Britain wants 608 more policemen. If we do not, will there be reductions in the police forces? This is unlikely — HM Chief Inspector of Constabulary would not wish to see that. So the police service, as a proportion of total law and order expenditure, will cost more. But there will not be more policemen really. We mentioned before that the police think that they will have considerable administrative tasks to perform in connection with prosecutions. So in real terms policing will be more expensive.

What happens when things get more expensive? There is political pressure to reduce the costs and in particular pay levels. The Official Side of the Police Negotiating Board is already concerned about the level of police pay. So there will be possible industrial unrest unless the inevitable increase in policing costs is contained. Far more importantly however, the Association thinks that the tendency will be towards a national police force. The arguments that have been advanced in support of a national prosecutions service mirror absolutely the arguments that lead to a national police force. The arguments are that there will be a single official who will be responsible for every decision; that there will be a direct line of management leading to an integrated career structure; and that there would be consistent policies leading to an improved national performance. The case for one leads inexorably and logically to the other. When you look at all the other straws in the wind, such as the need for the National Reporting Centre, the Home Office guidelines that have just been issued relating to security and terrorism, the pressures that are being brought on police to be more accountable to some, but not all, police authorities, and the need to review the mutual aid guidelines. I am prepared to bet that if we have a national prosecutions service, a national police force is not ten years behind. And the difference between a national police force and the army is difficult to define.

Notes

1. R.C.C.P. 1981, Part II, paras. 6.1–9.13.
2. See chap. 18. p. 213
3. *An Independent Prosecution Service for England & Wales.* London: HMSO, 1983 (Cmnd. 9074).
4. *Proposed Crown Prosecution Service.* London: HMSO, December, 1984 (Cmnd. 9411).
5. *Independent Prosecution Service for Sussex.* Brighton: Sussex Police Authority, May 1984.

CHAPTER 21

The Criminal Bar and the prosecution service

MICHAEL HILL

There are three things I want to say as a preliminary to a more detailed discussion of the operations of the independent prosecution service in relation to the work of the Bar.

First, can I ask you to consider the situation in which those of us who were then involved in the practice of the criminal law saw ourselves in the late 1960s and early 1970s? We might have had some intimation of what was to happen to us through the 1970s into the 1980s, but I doubt whether we could have had any conception of the plethora of enquiries, of Commissions, of Reports on the criminal justice system or of the statutory changes or delegated legislation which have occurred.

Those of us who have been involved, as I have been, really since about 1974, in the formulation of Bar views upon the various proposals designed to amend or to improve the criminal judicial process, have found these last ten to fifteen years both exciting and totally exhausting. Exciting, because the kinds of topic which were being discussed, of which the creation of an independent prosecution service was but one, were long overdue. Exhausting, because, as these discussions proceeded, those of us at the Bar who were concerned with these matters were confronted with a blinkered approach to the problems of the criminal judicial process. We faced proposals for change which, whilst they might be justified in their own terms, were being put forward without proper regard to their consequences upon the system as a whole.

The last fifteen years have been marked, also, by a lack of regard for the fundamental principles of the Constitution. I venture to suggest that the proposals for an integrated national independent prosecution service, which are contained in the Prosecution of Offences Act, very clearly illustrate that lack of regard for the constitutional position. The Criminal Bar Association, and the Bar Council with it, has always maintained that the idea of wholly autonomous local Crown Prosecutors, independent of the police but controlled by local political organisations, was wrong. To that extent we agreed with the Government. We have, also, maintained that the proposals for an integrated national service were wrong because they give too much power to a monolithic organisation which, although it may be directed by people whom we all currently trust, is far too easily distorted if the political balance in this country moves from some semblance of consensus politics into extremism. I state, as a fundamental stance, that whilst the Bar as a whole has long wanted, for reasons of principle and of practical experience, a prosecution service which is independent of the police, we are opposed to the system which the Government is currently propounding.

Secondly, whilst I am very reluctant to get myself involved in an argument about Bar sectional interests in the context of the proposals that are contained in the Act, there are certain things that need to be said. Most particularly, of course, the Bar is concerned with s.4(3) which gives the Lord Chancellor the power to make Directions which would result in professional officers of the Crown Prosecution Service having rights of audience in the Crown Court.

Can I remind those of you who are minded to support the principle contained in sub-section 3, and this includes the Law Society, of the comments contained in paragraph 18.45 of the Benson Report.[1] That paragraph discussed the proposition that a division was beginning to appear in the magistrates' courts between solicitors who are always identified as being on the side of authority and solicitors who are always identified as being against authority. This is castigated as an unpalatable development, pointing to experience outside the United Kingdom which indicated that it *would be* an unpalatable development. Having had some experience of working outside the United Kingdom in criminal judicial systems which have institutionalised prosecutions conducted wholly by legal departments, having had some experience of looking at other systems where such departments exist, though not having had to work in them, I am prepared to say that what Benson said in paragraph 18.45 of his Report is an understatement of the danger. That is what is really wrong with s.4(3). It is intended to bring into the Crown Court if it is ever put into operation (which I doubt, in the light of what the Lord Chancellor had to say at the Committee Stage) professional prosecutors who ought not to be there at all. But I foresee much more serious problems befalling the relationship between the Crown Prosecutor, in this independent prosecution service, and the Bar, whom I hope it will continue to instruct, which are the main burden of my comments in this chapter.

Thirdly, I am particularly concerned, as are all of those at the Bar who are involved in prosecution work, with the proposals which are contained within the Act, and in various policy statements, with regard to the remuneration of counsel when counsel is instructed. I shall return to this at the end.

It is axiomatic in our system of criminal justice that the prosecution, whilst a party to criminal litigation, is a party with very special responsibilities. Whether you describe those special responsibilities as being a minister of justice, or you try to find more modern phrases, matters little. But those responsibilities, to be fair, to conduct proceedings as a party, but also as a detached party, are ones that have crucially to be maintained. Because if they are not, whether we have a national, a regional or a local service, whether we have professional officers in the Crown Court or the Bar conducting proceedings in the Crown Crourt, are irrelevances, if ever we move away from the situation where the prosecution regards it as a duty to give and give and give in the pursuit only of *proper convictions upon the evidence*. If this is not maintained, we will have destroyed a fundamental part of our system which is admired and envied abroad.

Why do I raise that now? My concern arises from a series of complaints or questions which the Bar Council received during the early part of the 1980s from barristers who were seeking to determine what really was the nature of their relationship with those who instructed them when they were conducting prosecutions.

The professional responsibility of the Bar

It is generally accepted that the barrister has responsibility for the conduct of the case, but from what point in time does he assume that responsibility and to what extent does that responsibility allow him to override the express instructions which he receives from the prosecuting solicitor or from the departmental solicitor or from the Director of Public Prosecutions? To what extent, when counsel has made a decision, is he really empowered to speak on behalf of the prosecution if there is dispute behind him as to whether he has made the right decision when he is relating to the court?

The discussions that arose out of those problems that were being posed to the Bar Council developed into a discussion of the relationship between prosecution counsel and the court. Did counsel have to ask leave to withdraw or stop a prosecution by offering no evidence? Did counsel have to ask leave if he was prepared to accept a plea of 'guilty' to a lesser offence, if that was an offence for which the defendant could be convicted on the charge or the indictment then before the court?

In 1983, the Bar Council drafted some guidelines, the effect of which was to say, without answering the question as to when the responsibility actually started, that counsel was responsible for the conduct of the prosecution in relation to all those matters that I have just mentioned. He could ask for the court's approval, but he did not have to and, insofar as there was a dispute between him and those who instructed him, once the moment has arisen that his responsibility has to be exercised, then he is entitled to override instructions.

Those guidelines were presented to the Lord Chief Justice. Judges work, of course, remarkably quickly and nine months later we got a letter back saying, 'I think we may have found an answer'. There turned out to be one particular area of dispute, which was in relation to the acceptance of lesser offence pleas. At that stage Michael Wright, who was then Chairman of the Bar, and I decided that it was time that we involve those who would be responsible for the new prosecution service, which we knew by then was going to come.

Since the summer of 1984 there has been a committee chaired by Mr. Justice Farquharson, upon which the Bar is represented by Igor Judge and myself and upon which the new service is represented by Michael Chance from the Director of Public Prosecutions Office. I think we may at last have found a way in which we can resolve the conflicting interests involved in that particular discussion. But the point of conflict, between the new service and the Bar, is not so much about the time counsel's responsibilities arise, nor is it about whether we have responsibility for matters which could be properly described as evidential, even if those who sit behind us do not happen to agree with us, but about those decisions which could be described as policy decisions. It arises directly out of the statutory duty that will be imposed upon the Crown Prosecution Service for the conduct of all prosecutions initiated by police charge or through police inquiry.

The Attorney General has issued guidelines as to the institution of prosecutions which reflect policies which have been operated for some time, without being wholly articulated, by those responsible for the initiation and conduct of prosecutions on behalf of the Director of Public Prosecutions. The essence of those guidelines is that you have to ask two questions: (1) evidentially, is there any evidence which if accepted would establish the commission of the offence? and (2) if yes, is that evidence of sufficient strength and cogency to provide a better chance than not of a conviction being recorded?

There have long been arguments about that particular policy, but the policy, by and large, has been operated by the Director, the Metropolitan Police Commissioner and his solicitor and by counsel acting on their behalf, for a very long time indeed. That particular method of approaching the initiation or continuation of prosecutions will clearly, now, be adopted by the Crown Prosecution service.

That is not the area of contention. The area of contention in relation to policy matters goes back to that phrase that was used earlier, 'is it socially desirable', which ultimately will come down to such questions as do we think it is right to prosecute a seventy-five year old woman for shoplifting, do we think it right to prosecute a particular politician who has been found in the wrong lavatory at the wrong time?

Those are matters of policy, as are the questions which arise when confronted with a case where a defendant can be shown to have committed a series of robberies, but who says, 'well I'll plead to one and three, but I won't plead to number two'. Is the decision, as to whether to take that plea, of the same calibre as the decision as to whether we prosecute the seventy-five year old or the poor unfortunate M.P.? If it is of the same category, what is the position of counsel who is asked to advise or to conduct a case on behalf of the new Crown Prosecutor, and who says, 'All right, there is evidence, but my view, in relation to the application of your known policy guidelines, is that we should or we should not be doing this'? That has been an area of quite considerable conflict between the impending service and the Bar, about which I have expressed my own views in that committee time and time again.

These are matters of public policy, as to the initiation of prosecutions, upon which we can advise, but upon which in my view the Bar has no final responsibility for decision. Much more important, in the practical workings of the court and the application of our function as counsel, is the decision as to the accepting of pleas, and ultimately the offering of no evidence. It seemed at one stage that it was and, I believe, still is intuitively felt by those who are concerned with the new service that these ought to be regarded as matters of policy. My profound hope is that we have avoided the conflicts that will arise out of that situation and that it will now be the position that, once counsel has been instructed and the case has got beyond the point where it will be impractical to withdraw the instructions but before the case gets into court, the Bar will be responsible for decisions as to whether pleas should be accepted or whether evidence should be offered or not. This will be the case even where the instructions from behind are not to accept a plea, or to go on with the prosecution.

If I am right as to what is going to happen in regard to the Bar's relationship in these areas with the new service, there has got to be a close relationship and a close understanding between the prosecution service and the counsel it instructs.

There has been too much of a tendency, I suspect, in recent years, for those who are responsible for the conduct of prosecutions at directorial level, to regard a lot of the work which they handle as being mere fodder to be parcelled out. I have been very conscious of the fact that people are being allowed to prosecute who have no real understanding of what the relationship really ought to be between the instructor and the instructed and of the relationship that really ought to exist between the prosecution counsel and the court. I hope, although it is perhaps a pious hope, having regard to the enormous size of this new service and the amount of counsel's work that it is going to control (perhaps as much as 40 per cent by volume) that, when the new service comes into existence, the work that is done by the Bar will be done by people who actually understand what it is they are doing and why they are doing it.

Prosecution fees

There is one aspect of the funding of counsel's fees that I do want to refer to, and for these purposes it matters not whether the centrally-funded Crown Prosecution Service is required to mark our fees in advance or whether we have some kind of internal *post-facto* assessment by the Service, or however it is organised. The Criminal Bar since 1974 has gone through a period of such deterioration in its rates of remuneration that it needs to be faced and faced very quickly that the morale of that specialist section of the Bar has been damaged almost beyond recall. It needs to be understood that we are in very grave danger of producing a Bar where people will cut their teeth on criminal work and leave it as soon as they possibly can. As matters stand at the moment, I can see no reason, save that by the time that situation arises they are so locked in to criminal practice that they cannot get out, why any competent young barrister should specialise in crime beyond about the seventh year of his call. The position was well illustrated at a recent meeting of the Criminal Bar Association at which a youngish member of the Bar was telling us that, although she and her husband had comparable degrees and similar experience, he was earning between three and four times as much as she was. He specialises in common law work, whilst she is in a criminal chambers with a certain amount of family law work. The reason is that ninety per cent or more of the criminal barrister's work is publicly-funded, for which there is no market rate, unless you are lucky enough to get to the level where, as silk, you do a fair amount of private work.

The whole of the Criminal Bar's remuneration has been controlled by central Government, effectively since 1960, but damagingly since 1971 or 1972. Insofar as any of you have a;.y control or influence in respect of the way in which the Bar's remuneration is going to be structured with regard to prosecution work for the new Crown Prosecuting Service, I do ask you to bear in mind that if this Service acts in regard to remuneration in the way that the Lord Chancellor's Department has acted in regard to central funds and legal aid fees, then we may actually get the situation where the Lord Chancellor will need to make th/se directions under s.4(3) if the work is actually to be conducted at any level of competence at all in the Crown Court. And you know my view about that eventuality.

Note

1.   The Royal Commission on Legal Services (the Benson Report) Cmnd. 7648-1, 1979.

CHAPTER 22

An independent prosecution service: principles and practice

WALTER MERRICKS

The Philips Commission[1] attempted to formulate three principles, fairness, openness and efficiency, as standards by which to judge proposals for a new prosecutions service. By fairness we meant that only defendants against whom an adequately prepared case could be launched should be prosecuted. Only those whom it was in the public interest to prosecute should be prosecuted, and there should be no arbitrary or inexplicable inconsistencies across the country.

As far as openness was concerned, a matter which we linked with accountability, we intended that those who made the key and crucial decisions on matters of prosecution policy should be able to be called to account in some way for the exercise of their power. Efficiency was in our terms of reference; no enquiry is set up these days without being required to consider the issue of efficiency and the use of resources, and so we naturally devoted some time to that.

A central or a local system

I have often been asked since the Commission Report whether I am disappointed at the decision of the Government not to adopt the recommendations that we put forward for a local system. Although I am disappointed, I am sufficiently inured to the political reality to recognise that if the Government was going to go ahead with any kind of independent prosecutions system in the present context, it was not going to be a locally based system. When you have a Government which has abolished large chunks of local government, it would have been very surprising had they entrusted a sensitive issue like prosecutions to it. For all the arguments that I saw in principle, and still see both in principle and in practicality, for having a locally based service I am also interested in getting on with an independent prosecution service. The reality of the matter is that unless there is a national service, we will not get a service at all. Therefore I was concerned not to participate too much in the debate about whether it is right or wrong to be discussing national versus local systems. I think that that debate has been sensibly played out, but that in any national system there can be many local features, and in any local system there can be very many centralising features.

The real question is how one gets the balance right between those, and not necessarily the question of whether we have constitutionally a local or a national system. I think the debate needs to proceed from here to see how that balance can really be struck within the context of what is inevitably a national system.

There was one other factor which seemed to me to point overwhelmingly towards the inevitability of a national service; that was the difficulty of structuring any local service in London. The Royal Commission pointed out that some different structure of accountability would have to be devised for London, where there is no police authority other than the Home Secretary, and desirable though it might have been to establish a new police authority in London, that was clearly not going to happen. It would certainly have been odd to have had a prosecutions authority for London in advance of a proper police authority.

One should perhaps congratulate the Government. Against the advice of the Royal Commission, against the advice of the Bar, against the advice of the prosecuting solicitors, against the advice of the local authorities, against the advice of the police organisations, it has actually gone ahead with a national service, which is going to cost[2] some £10 million or so of additional annual expenditure to that which is being incurred at the moment, on something which nobody in their right minds could say was a great vote-winner.

This is a relatively insignificant area of national life as far as most people are concerned, I am afraid. It would be convenient for the Government to be able to present this as a part of its law and order programme, but I do not think it would be right to do that, and nor does the Government seek to make great political capital out of it in that way. So I am pleased to see that something has emerged from our recommendation, even if it was not in the form in which we originally envisaged it.

There are, of course, going to be particular difficulties about account-ability in a national system, although we accepted that such difficulties would arise even in a local system. Either in a local system with accountability to a local committee, or in a decentralised national system, which is what many people now seem to be suggesting, how do you provide that Crown Prosecutors are to be independent constitutionally and free to run their own services, whilst remaining accountable, and to whom?

The model that has been adopted is that the Attorney General should be answerable to the House of Commons for general policy decisions taken by the Director of Public Prosecutions, at least those in the central office. One has to expect that it really is very unlikely that the Attorney is going to be able to answer in any detailed way about decisions taken in the local areas in accordance with the distribution of functions which is set out in the White Paper.[3] He is more likely simply to say (if he says anything) that he has examined the case, perhaps, and is satisfied that correct principles have been applied. Or really is it going to be simply that he is satisfied that justifiable principles were applied? Or perhaps, he may say that he is not satisfied and he is going to do something about it. That seems to me even less likely.

National consistency is not easy to combine with sensitivity to local and regional conditions. How is the Attorney who is answerable for prosecution policy, to explain away what may be justifiable local variations within the context of a national policy aimed at national consistency? I leave this question to those devising the new service.

The other feature that is emerging in the national service is that managerially the system can be operated through consistent models from London. A new principal establishment officer is already working in the DPP's office, considering the way in which the new system should be structured in managerial terms.

It seems to me inevitable that central headquarters will need to have management information fed back into London. What is that management information going to consist of? Apart from the number of pencils used and number of typewriter days or ribbons used, it is also going to consist of acquittal and conviction rates. Those bald statistics are so obviously capable of being misused that people will want to qualify them in all sorts of ways. They could not conceivably, by themselves, be a real guide to the efficiency or effectiveness or the quality of the work that has been carried out in Crown Prosecutors' Departments. Nevertheless they must be some indication. But what other measures of effectiveness, what measures of quality can we or should we apply to the new service? How should it be evaluated?

The new service is to be a national service, and naturally that is a disappointment to all those who gave advice that it should not be. One of the serious matters that concerns me is the morale of not only those who are to work in the new service — the existing prosecuting solicitors, who have made it so demonstrably clear that they are unhappy with the way that the service is being set up, but also the remainder of the legal and police community who all seem to have their reservations about it.

It does seem particularly unfortunate in a situation where that entire community has been pressing for a general change of this kind for so long, that there should now be a feeling of dissatisfaction, particularly I think in relation to money. 'Penny pinching', people are saying; if they are going to set this system up we really must be adequately funded. That seems to me a really severe handicap.

If this system is to be able to present itself confidently to the public as a new service which is capable in its own right of dealing fairly with prosecutions; if it is going to be able to present itself to the police service in a confident way saying, 'We are not just removing opportunities from you, we are trying to improve on the service which we offer you and the public'; then it seems to me that a head of morale has got to be built up within that service — something which does not seem to be happening so far in any measure. After all this service has got to attract a large number of new lawyers and other officers, somewhere between 600 and 800 extra lawyers according to the latest estimates. There may be no obvious shortage in the sense that the legal professions are turning out lawyers at quite a high rate at the moment, something like two-and-a-half to three thousand solicitors a year. That rate of production may well exceed the rate at which they can find or retain satisfactory employment in the private and other employed sectors. So there may be no shortage of people who could possibly work in the new service. The question is whether they are going to be attracted to work in it. Is it going to be something which people are going to want to do? I think that that is partly going to depend on the image that this new service is going to be able to project, which will depend to a certain extent on the smiles on the faces of those who currently work in it.

The police and the Crown Prosecution Service

One of the other principles on which our proposals were predicated was that there should be a division between the investigative functions of the police and the conduct of prosecutions which we saw as essentially different roles. But although it was necessary to make that case, and although it has a great deal of validity in itself, it should not be overstated. It does seem to me that the investigation and the prosecution always merge into each other at different points and the attempt, the undoubtedly justifiable attempt, to divide these two should not be done with such a rigidity that would give rise to difficulties.

After all the police are necessarily going to be involved in the preparation of the case after charge. (Or are they? I should perhaps ask.) Will they want to be? Or will they say, 'You now have responsibility for this case, according to the Prosecution of Offences Act, we don't have to go out and interview more witnesses just because you think more witnesses should be interviewed. You send somebody out to interview the witnesses'.

How far should solicitors working for the prosecution service act in the way that defence solicitors do, investigating their own cases, or satisfying themselves at least that witnesses do come up to proof, in the same way that Scottish solicitors and procurator fiscals do by interviewing, or as they call it precognosing. Who is going to carry out that function? Is it not part of improved preparation? Who is going to warn witnesses and defendants of the fact that their case is about to come on?

All that is to a certain extent linked to the point that has already been developed about the degree of disclosure and information-transfer which must take place between the police and the prosecutor at an early stage. Full case files, semi case files, abbreviated case files — the important thing is obviously that the prosecutor is capable of making judgements with the level of information which is necessary to decide whether or not the right charges have been laid, or whether the prosecution should proceed at all.

And, of course the prosecutor is going to have to fulfill this function. Linked to this is his obligation to disclose more information to the defence, under the new rules introduced under the Criminal Law Act 1977, Section 48. But at the moment the prosecutor may feel that the thing that he first wants is disclosure to the prosecutor, before he can contemplate disclosing anything to the defence.

Once the prosecutor is in possession of all this information (and I query how he gets it all, and if he thinks he needs more, how he gets that) he has a continuing responsibility for the case, throughout the proceedings. He has to review the case and see whether or not the charges are appropriate, whether in the light of any changed circumstances the case should proceed as originally planned or whether it should change course. It was in that context that I was particularly pleased to see the Government responding favourably to Lord Mishcon's Amendment in the House of Lords about the withdrawal of proceedings (*Hansard*: Lords Vol. 458 Col. 1125: 17 Jan. 1985). I should say at this point that I am certainly not willing to let Lord Mishcon take the entire claim to fame for that amendment, and I am pleased that the Government has taken on board the point, because it would have been difficult and wholly improper, in my view, to leave the prosecutor with the obligation to explain to a court, during an application for leave to withdraw, the reasons why it was necessary to withdraw proceedings. The Government has left it open as to exactly the way in which this will work, and I think some consideration and careful judgement will have to be given to this. The last thing one wants to do is to shower a defendant against whom the prosecutor is going to withdraw proceedings with papers of confusing legality which frighten the life out of him by telling him first that he is entitled to appear before the court and apply for costs, when he probably has not incurred any, and secondly that he may yet be prosecuted if the prosecutor decides to proceed again. The important thing is that he should feel reassured that the matter is now over.

Criteria for prosecution

Michael Hill has made a distinction between the legal aspects of the decision to prosecute and the social or policy element.[4] Those who have re-read the Royal Commission Report in recent years will remember that we discussed that matter, and whether or not it would be a possible point of division of function between the police and the new prosecution service. We rejected it. We said there was no conceivable way in practical life in which it would be possible to divide the legal or evidential decision about a prosecution from the social and other factors which were implicit in the decision to go ahead. The facts that somebody, in a shoplifting case perhaps, is elderly, was taking drugs which affected their memory or affected their capacity to form an intention, are relevant to the question of whether or not the prosecution should proceed on legal grounds. They are also relevant to the social factor as to whether or not it is right and in the public interest in all those circumstances that such a case should go ahead. So we rejected that distinction and I am very interested to hear that an attempt is now being made to revive it albeit in a slightly different context.

I am certain that the Criteria for Prosecution that the Attorney General has issued are a first step on the road, but only a first step. They need a good deal of fleshing out in relation to specific offences. Great play was made when the Attorney General issued these guidelines in 1982, but frankly, they were only a re-hash and a rather limited re-hash of the evidence that the Director of Public Prosecutions had given to the Royal Commission and which is published in an appendix to our Law and Procedure volume.[5] So there was nothing new in them, indeed they were a rather weaker version of that evidence. Prosecutors who are really going to be expected to apply consistent policies across the country are going to need criteria which spell things out a little more clearly for them in relation to particular offences. I am particularly concerned with the wide variations which can occur in attitudes, for instance to motoring offences which, as we known, constitute a large volume of offences. Many people are inclined to put these at the bottom of their particular pile and say, 'Well those are only motoring cases', but they are of immense interest to a large number of individuals and they are often the only contact that those individuals will have with the criminal justice system.

It is also important therefore whatever guidelines are issued should be open, as part of our policy of openness and accountability. But any criteria which effectively state that cases in a particular category will not be prosecuted must surely be open to inspection. If there comes a time when it is decided that people who drive at, say thirty-five miles an hour in built-up areas should not be prosecuted; or should only be prosecuted if they drive in particular ways; or to take a different example if it is necessary to give a general guidance on robbery or rape cases; it seems to me of overwhelming importance that those guidelines are made available for public inspection and that the Attorney General, if necessary, justifies them.

The courts and the prosecution service

It seems to me inevitable that the courts, and justice's clerks in particular, must be brought in to a closer relationship with the prosecution service.

There will inevitably be tension between those courts which are not willing to sit in the afternoon, because their magistrates do not wish to sit in the afternoon, or have jobs which mean that it would be very inconvenient for them to sit in the afternoon, and those prosecutors who wish to keep their staff employed in the afternoon and would therefore wish for the courts to sit in the afternoon. This tension therefore has to be resolved in a way which does not mean that magistrates who can only a spare a limited time are effectively precluded from participating in the justice system.

Future developments

Looking forward to further developments, I hope that the institution of the Crown Prosecution Service might lead to a further evolution within the system. The Crown Prosecution Service may well eventually be extended to take over other prosecutions, particularly in the public arena, and I would not be unhappy to see that. It seems to me that the Crown Prosecution Service might eventually be given the responsibility at least for the issue of summonses and, I hope, we might see some tidying up of the bizarre system of issuing summonses by the laying of informations, charges and then of indictments. It does seem to me that at some future time, if not now, the Government could consider the recommendations that the Commission made for an integrated system, and for a single procedure for the institution of criminal proceedings. A further possibility, in the future, would be fixed penalties issued by prosecutors. After all this has been contemplated in Scotland by the Stewart Committee, although it has not yet been implemented.

As for the police — they have to see how they can take advantage of the new system. There will be some extra work for them in some areas, but there will certainly be some officers who will be released from prosecution work. The police need to think well in advance how they are going to take advantage of this opportunity because I do not suppose that any of their officers will be sacked or made redundant. I hope they take advantage of the opportunity and make efficient use of those extra resources which will be made available to them.

So we are looking forward to a system which has these features of openness, fairness and accountability and, I would add, modernness about it. We need a system which can present an identifiable image to the public, and that is going to be not easy for a civil service operation. It will want to present an image of humanity and responsiveness when people normally associate prosecutions with the exercise of unthinking state power. We need a system which is going to be efficient in its management, and which will play a full part within the criminal justice system.

Notes

1. Royal Commission on Criminal Procedure (R.C.C.P.), *Report* London: HMSO, 1981, (Cmnd. 8092).
2. See chapter 20, pp. 234–235.
3. *Proposed Crown Prosecution Service*, London: HMSO, December, 1984, (Cmnd. 9411).
4. See chapter 21, pp. 240–241.
5. *The Investigation & Prosecution of Criminal Offences in England and Wales: The Law & Procedure*, London: HMSO, January 1981, (Cmnd. 8092–1).

CHAPTER 23

The new rules of evidence*

JOHN SMITH

The evidence provisions in the Police and Criminal Evidence Act 1984 are in the main based on the *Eleventh Report* of the Criminal Law Revision Committee (*Evidence* (*General*), Cmnd. 4991, 1972). They do not incorporate by any means all of the recommendations of that Committee. The more controversial are left out. Someone has made a careful selection, but there are some surprising omissions.

Hearsay Evidence

The Committee made quite radical proposals as to the reform of the rule against hearsay, but those proposals are not adopted. Instead Section 68 of the Police and Criminal Evidence Act 1984, the first section that we are concerned with, makes a more modest, but nevertheless important, reform. It enlarges the scope of the exception to the hearsay rule which was created by the Criminal Evidence Act 1965. That Act is now repealed. The 1965 Act itself was passed, of course, in consequence of the decision in *Myers v DPP* [1965] AC 1001 which remains the basic authority on the rule against hearsay evidence. It is authority for the proposition that a document is not evidence of a fact stated therein unless that document comes within the terms of Section 68 of the Act, or some other statutory or common law exception to the hearsay rule.

In *Myers* the prosecution needed to prove, in order to establish their case, that a particular engine (say, number 123) went with a particular chassis (say, number 456) of a car. They tendered in evidence a document, produced by an official of the makers of the car and made by some unknown, and now quite undiscoverable, workman years ago, in which the workman recorded (in effect). 'I put engine number 123 into chassis number 456'. It looks excellent evidence that engine number 123 was installed in chassis number 456; but it was not admissible because it was hearsay. It was not a statement by a witness in the witness box. It was a

---

statement by a person not called as a witness, tendered to prove the fact asserted in that statement. It was hearsay evidence; and it did not come without any established exception to the hearsay rule. The House of Lords declared that they were not going to create any new exceptions to that rule. So it was inadmissible. The Criminal Evidence Act 1965 was passed as a stop-gap measure to deal with that particular case, pending the report of the Criminal Law Revision Committee. That stop-gap measure has lasted for twenty years (as seems so commonly to happen) but now at least it will be superseded.

Section 68, like the 1965 Act, is limited to documentary evidence. It applies only to a statement in a document, but both 'statement' and 'document', adopting the provisions of the Civil Evidence Act 1968, are defined widely. These definitions, so far as the criminal law is concerned, are new. 'Statement' is defined to include words and other means of conveying information, and 'document' includes such things as a disc, tape, film, etc. This evidence must be a 'statement in a document'. It must also be a 'record' if it is to be admissible under this provision. 'Record' is not defined but there is a certain amount of case law on the meaning of that word which is also used in the 1965 Act. Particularly useful is the case of *Tirado* (1974) 59 Cr. App. R. 80 at p. 90 —

> That means the keeping of a book or a file, or a card index, into which information is deliberately put in order that it may be available to others another day. A cash book, a ledger, a stock book: all these may be records because they contain information deliberately entered in order that the information may be preserved. (See also *Archbold, Criminal Pleading Evidence and Practice* (41st ed.) 111–28).

You will see that the essence of a record appears to be that it is a document containing information deliberately recorded in order that the information may be preserved.

The 1965 Act was confined to records compiled in the course of a trade or business. It was intended only to reverse the decision in *Myers* on its particular facts and to deal with similar cases. It did not go beyond that; but the new provision in Section 68 is much wider. This is the main change made in the law. It extends to any record compiled by a person acting under a duty. The Act tells us that this includes a person acting in the course of any trade, business, profession or other occupation in which he is engaged or employed or for the purposes of any paid or unpaid office held by him. It *includes* those cases, but it is not an exclusive definition. Also included will be National Health Service records, medical records, armed forces records and police records (all of which were outside the scope of the 1965 Act). The only test is, was the record compiled by a person acting under a duty? The log kept by a certain submarine officer in the course of his duty will be admissible evidence (provided the other conditions are satisfied) as to when the torpedo was fired; but his private diary, which he wrote at the same time, will not, because that is not compiled in the course of the duty.

The second condition, as in the 1965 Act, is that the record must be compiled 'from information supplied by a person (whether acting under a duty or not) who had, or may reasonably be supposed to have had, personal knowledge of the matters dealt with in that information'. So, for example, an ordinary citizen witnesses a robbery and sees the number of the getaway car. He tells a police constable who writes the number down in his notebook. Assuming that the notebook is a record it will, if the other conditions are satisfied, be admissible evidence of the number of the car.

The record may be compiled from information of which the compiler himself had personal knowledge. In the *Myers* case itself it was presumably the workman who installed the engine who made the note. He knew that engine 123 had gone into chassis 456 so that this was not a case of the supply of information by one person to another; the compiler himself had the information. Curiously enough, you have to turn to Schedule 3, paragraph 1, to find that this case is covered. Under the 1965 Act, the information might be supplied indirectly. That allows the possibility of the admission of second, third or fourth hand hearsay. So does the new provision. But the law is tightened up in one respect. Where the information has been passed from one person to another in this way, the Act provides that the resulting record will be admissible in evidence only if any intermediary was acting under a duty — a duty, that is, to pass on the information. For example, if the citizen who spotted the number of the getaway car tells a constable who, in the course of his duty, tells a sergeant, who, likewise in the course of his duty, tells an inspector who, in the course of his duty, writes it down, the record made by the inspector is admissible in evidence provided that the other conditions are satisfied. But, if citizen A sees the number of the car and tells citizen B, who tells the sergeant, then this may not be so. Though citizens are, no doubt, under a moral duty to give information regarding crimes, they are generally speaking under no legal duty. And I think the Act, when it refers to 'duty', must be referring, not to moral duties, but to duties recognised by the law. So in that case I take it that the record will be inadmissible in evidence under the provision unless, for example, the crime in question is not a robbery but treason. The difference is that all citizens are under a duty to report what they know about treasonable activities, otherwise they may commit the offence of misprision of treason.

The third condition of admissibility is that the person with the personal knowledge, the supplier, or the compiler, if he himself had personal knowledge, cannot testify to the matter for one of the reasons stated in Section 68(2). If the person with personal knowledge is available and able to testify to the matter, then he must be called. The principle is that testimony in the witnesses box is the best evidence and must be produced if possible. But if the person with personal knowledge is dead; or unfit to attend as a witness; or outside the United Kingdom and it is not reasonably practicable to secure his attendance; or if he cannot reasonably be expected to have any recollection of the matters dealt with in that information (as for instance the workman in *Myers*, even if he could have been found, could not reasonably have been expected to remember the number of the engine that he put into the chassis); or reasonable steps have been taken to identify the person who supplied the information and he cannot be identified; or he can be identified but, after taking reasonable steps, he cannot be found — in any of these cases the record is admissible in evidence and the record establishes the fact which has been stated in it. Of course, the party relying on the record and putting it in evidence must satisfy the court that one of these conditions is satisfied and, if it is the prosecution, they will have to satisfy the court beyond reasonable doubt: *Nichols* (1976) 63 Cr. App. R. 187.

There is one exception, and that is in the case of a statement by a prospective witness. A statement which is prepared for use in court may not be admitted under Section 68 without the leave of the court. This is because it has been prepared for the purpose of giving evidence. The court is not to give leave unless it is satisfied that the document ought to be admitted in the interests of justice.

The Act (Sch. 3, para. 3(a)), again following the provisions of the Civil Evidence Act 1968, provides means by which the credit of the supplier of the information may be impeached. Any evidence which could have been called to impeach his credit, if he had been called as a witness, may be given. If the supplier of the information had himself been called it would have been possible under the rules stated by the House of Lords in *Toohey* [1965] AC 595 to call, for example, a medical witness who would swear that this person was suffering from a mental abnormality of some kind which made his evidence unreliable. Even if the supplier does not give evidence for one of the reasons stated in section 68(2), a medical witness can be called who will swear to that fact. He might be an oculist (an example given in *Toohey's* case), who will swear that he knew about the condition of the person's eyesight and that it was quite impossible for him to have seen what he claimed to have seen.

When a witness is called and cross-examined as to his credit (i.e. he is cross-examined as to matters which have nothing to do with the present case but go to show that he is not likely to be a witness of truth) his answers are generally final. It is put to him that he has done such and such a discreditable thing in the past, nothing to do with the present case, and if he denies it, then his answer must be accepted as final. The Act (Sch. 3, para. 3(b)) allows evidence to be called of a matter which could have been put to the supplier in cross-examination, although his answer to that would have been final, but here the leave of the court is required. The Act also permits evidence to be given of either an earlier or a later inconsistent statement by the supplier of the information. That evidence may be put in for the purpose of showing that the record is unreliable and not to be believed. Notice that where evidence of an earlier or later inconsistent statement is admitted under this provision, that statement is not evidence of the facts asserted. It only goes to destroy the validity of the statement made in the record. It does not have any positive effect; it only has a negative effect. That is the common law rule. It is one of the rules which I would have thought could happily have been abolished by this Act, as indeed the Criminal Law Revision Committee recommended and as is the case now in the civil law of evidence. Under the Civil Evidence Act 1968, when an inconsistent statement is proved in these circumstances, it is evidence of the fact stated in it. But not so in the criminal law.

Now, of course, it may be that the compiler of the information, or the intermediary, was lying or mistaken; but the Act makes no provision about any attack on their credit. They might be called, of course, and, if they are called, they may be cross-examined like any other witness. But, whether they are called or not, any incentive which the compiler (but not, apparently, any intermediary) had to misrepresent the facts may be proved. That is allowed by the terms of Schedule 3. In this Schedule para. 7 also gives some guidance as to the weight to be given to the statement contained in the document. It tells us that the court is to have regard to the question whether the supplier supplied the information contemporaneously with the facts. Obviously the longer the interval between the occurrence of the event and the supply of the information, the less the weight. This is really only common sense but it is a bit of common sense which is stated in the Act. Likewise the question of whether the supplier or the compiler had any incentive to conceal or misrepresent the facts.

The Act contains provisions in Section 71 about proving the contents of documents by copies.

Computer records

Section 69 deals with computer records. There was a provision in the Bill introduced in 1983 about this which I thought was really very unsatisfactory. Under that Bill a document produced by a computer might have been admissible in evidence although the information on which it was based was hearsay or otherwise inadmissible. The only matter to be proved was that the computer was working properly. Although the information given to the computer would have been inadmissible, once the computer had processed it, provided the computer was working properly, it would be admissible. That, incidentally, is the position under the Civil Evidence Act of 1968. One small contribution which I may have made to this Act was to help to persuade the Home Office that that was nonsense and that, if what is put into the computer is so unreliable that it should not be admitted in evidence, what comes out of the computer cannot be any better. That argument appears to have prevailed and so Section 69 does not render admissible any evidence which would otherwise be inadmissible. Instead, it provides an additional test which a computer record must pass and the effect, as I see it (because this is my interpretation, not actually the words of the Act), is that a computer record is admissible, first, if it is not hearsay and not excluded by any other general rule and it complies with Section 69; and secondly, if it is hearsay, but is within Section 68 or any other statutory or common law exception to the hearsay rule, and it complies with Section 69.

In the case of *Pettigrew* (1980) 71 Cr. App. R.39 the question was as to the admissibility of a document produced by the Bank of England's computer. The computer operator presented this clever computer with a pile of bank notes. The computer was able to recognise defective notes and rejected them. It then tied the good ones up into bundles of one hundred and made a record of the serial numbers in each bundle. The question was whether that record (which appears to be very attractive evidence) was admissible in evidence. It was held that it was not. The Court of Appeal thought the conditions of the 1965 Act must be satisfied. They held that there was no supplier of information with personal knowledge. Only the computer 'knew' the numbers of the notes that went into the bundles. The person who gave the notes to the computer did not know which ones were going to be rejected. So there was no one with personal knowledge. If that decision was right, it is still right because the 1984 Act, like the 1965 Act, requires that the supplier of the information have personal knowledge. I have argued in the *Criminal Law Review* ([1981] *Crim LR* 387) and continue to argue that *Pettigrew* was wrongly decided because it was not concerned with hearsay evidence at all. This was simply a case of a machine itself 'observing' facts. When a machine observes and records facts, the record that it makes is not hearsay. Hearsay only arises where information goes through a human mind and is stated by some person. To take a simple example, the thermometer. The thermometer observes the temperature; no one would suggest that the reading on the thermometer is hearsay evidence. Or a camera takes a photograph, a radar machine plots the course of a ship: as in *The Statue of Liberty* [1968] 2 All ER 195. The radar machine observes and makes the plotting: the outline plotted is admissible in evidence. Similarly with the computer in this case. The legal principle is no different from that of the thermometer. The physics, of course, are very different. We do not require any evidence that thermometers work because we all know that and the courts can take judicial notice of it. Computers differ only in the sense that it is not common knowledge that a computer programme 'works'; but, if it does work, then there is no question of hearsay. So my conclusion is that if statements admissible under Section 68, or any other exception to the hearsay rule, are processed by a computer the statement produced by the computer is admissible, if Section 69 is complied with. But, if statements constituting inadmissible hearsay are processed by a computer then any resulting statement produced will be inadmissible.

What are the requirements of Section 69? The onus is on the party tendering the document to prove the negative — that there are no reasonable grounds for believing that the statement is inaccurate because of improper use of the computer. The onus is on him to show that the computer was operating properly and that any requirements of rules of court (which are yet to be made) are satisfied. But these matters may be proved by a certificate in which it is sufficient for the declarant to state a matter to the best of his knowledge and belief (Sch. 3, para. 8). So I suppose what will happen is that the person in charge of the computer will state that, to the best of his knowledge and belief, (a), (b) and (c) of Section 69 are satisfied and that will normally settle the matter. There is a provision in the Act allowing the court to call oral evidence on this issue if it is disputed. So if there is a dispute about it the computer operator may be called to give evidence.

The Act gives us some guidance on the weight to be given to a computer statement: regard is to be had to all the circumstances and in particular the contemporaneity of the supply of information to the computer and whether there was any incentive to conceal or misrepresent facts.

Convictions and acquittals

That brings me to Part VIII and the question of convictions and acquittals. We can deal very briefly with Section 73 which provides for the proof of convictions and acquittals by certificate. This simply replaces provisions in the Criminal Procedure Act 1865 s.6 and I do not think it makes any substantial changes. But Section 74 presents us with rather more substantial problems. This section relates, of course, to the decision of the Civil Court of Appeal in *Hollington v Hewthorn* [1943] KB 587 where it was held that a criminal conviction was not evidence in a subsequent case that the defendant committed the offence of which he was convicted. In that case the defendant's conviction of careless driving was not admissible evidence in the later civil action that he drove carelessly at that time and place. It was generally recognised that the rule in *Hollington v Hewthorn* applied to criminal as well as to civil proceedings. The rule was repealed for civil cases by the 1968 Civil Evidence Act, but it has remained the law so far as crime is concerned.

Section 74 (1), however, repeals that rule so far as the conviction of a person other than the accused is concerned. Under this section the conviction of that third party is evidence that the third party committed the offence of which he has been convicted, and it throws the onus of proof on to the party denying that. Now, of course, either the defendant or the prosecution may wish to rely, for one reason or another, upon the conviction of a third party. If the defendant relies upon it then it will be for the prosecution to prove, beyond reasonable doubt, that the third party was not guilty of the offence of which he has been convicted. Whereas, if it is the other way around, the onus on the defendant will clearly be proof only on a balance of probabilities. That is quite clear from the terms of the Act and it follows from the rather surprising recommendation of the Criminal Law Revision Committee. That Committee was generally very much against putting the burden of proof on the defendant but they agreed that it should be on him in this case. Their reason was that the matter has already been tried by a criminal court, the matter has already been proved beyond reasonable doubt so why should the prosecution have to prove it again? I think there are several possible answers to that question, but that is the way the Criminal Law Revision Committee saw it.

This is how I understand that it will work. Our accused is charged with handling goods which it is alleged were stolen by the third party, T. The prosecution, of course, on a charge of handling stolen goods has to prove that the goods were stolen and they say they were stolen by T. T has been convicted of stealing the goods in question. His conviction can be proved whereupon it must be taken that the goods are stolen goods unless and until the accused can prove, on the balance of probabilities, that T did not steal them. It is an easy way for the prosecution on a handling charge to prove that the goods were stolen. Take another case, aiding and abetting. Our accused is charged with aiding and abetting T to murder P. If T has already been convicted of murdering P his conviction can be put in evidence and it must be taken that T murdered P unless the accused can prove that he did not.

It appears that it makes no difference that the third party's conviction was on a plea of guilty (though I draw attention to the fact that the Civil Evidence Act 1968 says so expressly and the 1984 Act does not); a conviction is a conviction whether it is on a plea of guilty or not guilty. It does not make any difference that it was on a confession, or that it took place in a Magistrates' Court when the present trial is on indictment.

Now there is a controversy under the 1968 Civil Evidence Act about the effect of the corresponding provision. There are two views about it which are to be found in the case of *Stupple v the Royal Insurance Company* [1971] QB 50. In that case Lord Justice Buckley said the only effect of this provision is to shift the onus of proof. It shifts the onus of proof to the party who says the conviction was wrong, and that is all it does. Once it has done that, its effect is spent. But Lord Denning took the view that the conviction itself was a weighty piece of evidence to be put in the scales. The 1984 Act does nothing to resolve that conflict. I have my own view about who is right. I think Lord Justice Buckley is right because you get into the most appalling difficulties if you have to decide what weight should be given to a conviction. Do you give less weight to a conviction in the Magistrates' Court? Do you give less weight to a conviction where there was a majority verdict or where the whole of the case was based on a confession? These are insuperable difficulties, and so I hope the courts will say that the only effect of this provision is to shift the burden of proof.

That concerns the conviction of a third party. Section 74(3) goes further because it deals with the convictions of the accused himself. It provides that, *where evidence is admissible that the accused has committed an offence on another occasion*, his conviction of that offence establishes that he committed it, unless he proves on a balance of probabilities that he did not. Notice that whether evidence is admissible that the accused committed this other offence depends on the general law of evidence and not on the Act. There is nothing in the Act to make evidence that the accused has committed an offence on another occasion admissible, when previously it would not have been. Sometimes, under the general law of evidence, it may be permissible to prove that the accused has committed an offence on another occasion. For example, our accused is charged with murder. We will suppose that the murderer, whoever he was, arrived at the scene in a car, registration number XYZ 123. Suppose the accused stole the car XYZ 123 the day before the murder. This would be relevant and cogent evidence connecting him with the murder: the murderer arrived in that car and the accused stole that car only the day before. So that is a case, I think, where, under the ordinary law of evidence, it would be possible to prove that he committed that offence. This is an unlikely sequence of events, but suppose he has been convicted of stealing the car. The conviction may now be proved and it establishes that he did steal the car on that day, unless he proves the contrary on a balance of probability.

There is, however, an exception to this rule. I think this is one of the more difficult parts of the Act. I found some difficulty in construing this sub-section. The exception is that section 74(3) does not apply where the commission of the offence is admissible because of its tendency to show in the accused a disposition to commit the kind of offence with which he is charged. Now, of course, generally the fact that the accused has a disposition to commit a particular kind of offence, for example burglary, is inadmissible and it remains so. In this respect the law is unchanged. If a man is charged with burglary you cannot set about convicting him by proving that he has committed thirty previous burglaries. But, where the accused's disposition has a very high degree of cogency to show that he committed the offence charged, then under the so called 'similar facts rule' evidence may be admissible of his disposition. Suppose, for example, that the burglary with which he is charged was committed in a very unusual or striking way, not at all the usual way of committing a burglary, and the defendant has committed ten previous burglaries in this very unusual way. You may then prove that he committed those other burglaries in order to identify him as the burglar on this occasion. It is very cogent evidence because it is a very peculiar burglary and he has committed ten similar peculiar burglaries in the past. So you may, under the general law, prove that he committed those burglaries. Now what the exception says, as I understand it, is that even so, even though you may prove his commission of those earlier burglaries, Section 74(3) does not apply. His convictions are not admissible evidence to prove the commission of the burglaries and to throw upon him the onus of proving that he did not commit them. It is for the prosecution to prove by other evidence that he did commit the burglaries on those other occasions.

Confessions

The admissibility of a confession against the accused person is no longer regulated by the common law but by Section 76 of the Police and Criminal Evidence Act and so a great mass of old learning, in some cases quite ancient learning, about 'voluntariness' and about who is 'a person in authority' disappears. 'Confession' is widely defined in the Act and includes an admission of particular facts as well as a full admission of guilt. It includes what we usually call 'admissions' rather than confessions. Any statement wholly or partly adverse to the person who made it and whether made in words or otherwise is a confession. So where an accusation is made in the accused's presence and he, by conduct of some kind, acknowledges its truth, that operates as a confession. It is his acknowledgement of the truth of the allegation made in his presence which is evidence against him. That, I take it, is a confession for the purpose of the Act and the rules about its admissibility will have to be satisfied. Authorities such as *Christie* [1914] AC 545 and *Chandler* (1976) 63 Cr. App. R. 1, remain valid but they are subject to the conditions of admissibility stated in the Act.

It appears that a confession is admissible against the accused unless he challenges it, or the judge or a magistrate challenges it. When the admissibility of a confession is challenged in a trial on indictment there must, as now, be a 'trial within a trial' (*voir dire*). There is no change as far as the procedures are concerned. We will have to have the same trial within a trial as we do now in the Crown Court. The same procedures to be followed in Magistrates' Courts continue to be those described in *F* (an infant) *v the Chief Constable of Kent* [1982] *Crim LR* 682, DC. As at present in a trial on indictment, there are distinct questions for the judge and the jury to answer. The prosecution must prove to the judge (or the magistrates) beyond reasonable doubt (and the Act expressly states that proof beyond reasonable doubt is required) that the confession, notwithstanding that it may be true, was not obtained (a) by oppression of the person who made it or (b) in consequence of anything said or done which was likely, in the circumstance existing at the time, to render unreliable any confession which might be made by him in consequence thereof. As now, the confession is excluded only if there is a causal relationship between the oppression, or the thing said or done, and the confession. Confessions are excluded if they *result* from oppression and if they *result* from something said or done. This is the law as stated by the House of Lords in *DPP v Ping Lin* [1976] AC 574, HL which also continues to be authority for the proposition that the confession may be rendered inadmissible although there is no impropriety in the thing said or done. The fact that a confession is excluded does not necessarily mean that the police or anybody else have necessarily behaved improperly.

The Act tells us the confession may be inadmissible notwithstanding that it may be true. As now, the judge is not to be concerned with its truth or untruth when he is determining admissibility. The accused may not be generally cross-examined on the *voir dire* as to its truth because that is not in issue. If he makes admissions on the *voir dire*, they, as under the present law, will be inadmissible at the trial unless they were irrelevant to the issue on the *voir dire*. The theory is, of course, that the defendant must be free to say anything which is relevant to the issue of admissibility. If what he says could be used against him at the trial he could not do that. In *Brophy's case* [1981] 2 All ER 705, in Northern Ireland, the defendant on the *voir dire* stated that he had been a member of the IRA for six years. That was relevant to the issue because, if he had been a member of the IRA for six years, it was very likely that the police knew about it. If the police knew about it then they were more likely to have treated him in the rather rough way which he said they had. They would expect him to have been trained to resist the extraction of a confession and would react accordingly. So his statement on the *voir dire*: 'I have been a member of the IRA for six years', was relevant to that issue and it followed that it was inadmissible against him at the trial. That, I think, will continue to be the case.

Section 76(8) tells us that 'oppression' includes torture, inhuman or degrading treatment and the use or threat of violence, whether or not amounting to torture. That is not an exclusive definition and I think it is clear that oppression extends beyond this. It is a concept which first appeared in the case of *Callis v Gunn* [1964] 1 QB 495, 501 and is fully described in the case of *Prager* (1971) 56 Cr. App. R. 51, 161 to which I would refer you. A failure to comply with the Code of Practice, will not, I think, necessarily constitute oppression. It may be evidence of it, depending upon the nature of the failure. For example, the accused says that he was questioned for seventeen hours without the breaks for meals prescribed in the Code of Practice and that he was required, contrary to the Code of Practice, to stand for long periods. If he says that, the prosecution have got to prove either that this did not happen, that he is lying, or that if it did happen, it did not constitute oppression — which might be quite difficult.

Even though there was no oppression, the confession will still be excluded by the judge if it was made in consequence of anything likely to render unreliable any confession made in consequence of it. The Criminal Law Revision Committee were the originators of this test. This is how they described it in para. 65 of the *Eleventh Report*: (HMSO, 1972; Cmnd. 4991):

> The essential feature of this test is that it applies not to the confession which the accused in fact made but to any confession which he might have made in consequence of the threat or inducement.
>
> On this scheme the judge should imagine that he was at the interrogation and heard the threat or inducement. In the light of all the evidence given he will consider whether, at the point when the threat was uttered or the inducement offered, any confession which the accused might make as a result of it would be likely to be unreliable. If so, the confession would be inadmissibile. For example, if the threat was to charge the suspect's wife jointly with him, the judge might think that a confession even of a serious offence would be likely to be unreliable. If there was a promise to release the accused on bail to visit a sick member of his family, the judge might think that would be unlikely to render a confession of a serious offence unreliable but likely to do so in the case of a minor offence. We do not suggest that at the trial within the trial the evidence should stop short at the point where the threat was uttered or the inducement offered. For the judge will usually require evidence of the whole course of interrogation in order to enable him to gauge the likely effect of the threat or inducement at this point, especially as there will usually be conflicting accounts of what happened at the interrogation. Even the terms of the confession may have to be considered. For although the fact that a particular confession seems clearly to be true will not make it admissible if the threat or inducement was of a sort likely to cause the accused to make an unreliable confession, yet evidence of the terms of the confession may throw light on the facts concerning the interrogation. As mentioned above, the provision will not apply to confessions obtained as a result of oppression. These will remain inadmissible.

The Committee's view was that the judge has to imagine that he was present at the interrogation and that he heard all that went on and knew of all the circumstances up to the time when the confession was made. He has to decide whether anything said or done would render unreliable *any* confession, not just this confession. Should you believe a confession after all that has happened? Only if he is satisfied that it would not render unreliable any confession should he admit it. He will require evidence, it is said, of the whole course of the interrogation and he may look at the terms of the confession, but only for a limited purpose and only insofar as they cast light upon the events which led up to the making of it. It will be very interesting to see how that works out.

If the confession is admitted, the next question is for the jury and this of course is: is the confession true? As under the present law, witnesses who have been examined in the absence of the jury may be examined again in their presence and on the same matters for the purpose now of showing that the confession should not be believed. If the jury is satisfied beyond reasonable doubt that the confession is true they should act on it, otherwise not. This is so even if they think there was oppression. That is not a matter for them, it is a matter for the judge. The question for them is, are we satisfied it is true?

The Act solves some problems for us about inadmissible confessions. It provides that facts discovered as a result of an inadmissible confession are admissible in evidence if relevant. So, for example, after the defendant has confessed in consequence of oppression, a policeman goes to the hollow tree in the defendant's garden and finds the stolen goods where the defendant confessed that he had hidden them. The constable may testify that: 'I went to the accused's garden and looked in the hollow tree in his garden and there I found the stolen goods', even though he had got the information which led him to the stolen goods from an inadmissible confession. But evidence that the fact was discovered as a result of an inadmissible confession or the excluded part of a partly inadmissible confession, cannot be given, unless evidence of how the fact was discovered is given by the accused or on his behalf. So the police constable may *not* say, '*In consequence of what the accused said*, I went to his garden and there I discovered the goods concealed in the hollow tree'. That would be breaking that rule in Section 76(5).

So much of an inadmissible confession as is relevant to show that the accused speaks, writes or expresses himself in a particular way may be approved. That is specifically to cater for a case like *Voisin* [1918] 1 KB 531, where a murdered body was discovered with a note attached to it on which was written 'bladie Belgiam'. The accused person was asked if he would mind writing out the words 'bloody Belgian', and he obliged by writing those words in that highly individual way. This was, of course, relevant evidence connecting him very closely with the particular murder.

There are special rules in Section 77 about a confession by a mentally handicapped person. Where the case against a mentally handicapped person depends wholly or substantially on a confession by him not made in the presence of an independent person (a police officer or person engaged on police purposes is not an independent person: s.77(3)) the judge must warn the jury of the special need for caution: s.77(1).

Unfair evidence

That brings me to Section 78 which gives the court a discretion to exclude unfair evidence. This section is the result of an amendment inserted at a fairly late stage following an earlier amendment proposed by Lord Scarman. (See the next chapter by Paul Sieghart for a full account of 'the Scarman amendment.') Section 78(1) provides that in any proceedings the court may, in its discretion, refuse to allow evidence, on which the prosecution proposes to rely, to be given if it appears to the court that, having regard to all the circumstances, including the circumstances in which the evidence was obtained, the admission of the evidence would have such an adverse effect on the fairness of the proceedings that the court ought not to admit it. I think there is going to be a good deal of controversy as to how far this discretion goes, but we can get a certain amount of help from the Act. The Act provides that the Sub-section does not prejudice any existing discretion to exclude evidence. Any discretion which the judge has had, he continues to have now that the Act has come into force. In particular the discretion approved in *Sang* [1980] AC 402, HL still applies. Unfortunately the extent of that discretion is uncertain. But I think we can say with conviction that the judge may certainly exclude admissible evidence: first where in his opinion its prejudicial effect outweighs its probative value; secondly, where the evidence in question is tantamount to a self-incriminatory admission, obtained from the defendant after the commission of an offence, by means which would justify a judge in excluding an actual confession in the exercise of his discretion. The stock example is where the defendant is tricked into handing over a document and by doing so incriminates himself or is tricked into submitting to a medical examination which proves adverse to his interests. The *Sang* discretion allows the judge to exclude evidence of that kind and that certainly continues. Equally I think it will remain the law (although perhaps the Section 78 does not make this as awfully clear as it might have been) that the judge may not exclude evidence of the commission of an offence on the ground that the defendant was trapped into committing it. In *Sang* the court was concerned with the question whether the evidence of the commission of the offence should be excluded because the defendant has been tricked into committing it. The decision that there is no direct or indirect defence of 'entrapment' in English law is, I am sure, not intended to be affected and I think will be held not to be affected.

What I find to be less clear is whether the judge may now exclude evidence which was obtained after the commission of an offence by illegal force or by an illegal search without the defendant's consent. There is no element of self-incrimination. In *Sang*, Lord Dilhorne thought there was no discretion to exclude whereas the other judges left open the possibility. That is the common law but it will no longer be the whole story. It will now be a question of the interpretation of this section. Of course, it does not need any argument to show that it is unfair to obtain evidence by force or illegality, it is not only unfair, it is illegal. The question is now, does the admission of that evidence which has been obtained by force or illegality, affect *the fairness of the proceedings*. That matter was actually considered in *Sang* and Lord Fraser and Lord Scarman thought it did. But I think another view might be that, provided the evidence which is tendered at the proceedings is relevant evidence and entirely reliable evidence, it does not affect *the fairness of the proceedings* to admit it. It is the fairness of the proceedings we have to look at. Are the proceedings rendered unfair because this very cogent, reliable evidence was obtained in an unfair way? I think that is an open question.

Notice again that we have to read the Act as a whole (though it was not written as a whole). This amendment got in at a late stage, but still I think we have to read the Act as a whole. We can discern from the Act that the admission of evidence discovered as a result of oppression does not *necessarily* have such an adverse affect on the fairness of the proceedings that the court ought not to admit it. If it did Section 76(4) (a) (evidence may be admitted which is discovered as a result of an inadmissible confession) would be nugatory. It would be redundant. The suggestion would have no function if evidence which was discovered as a result of oppression *necessarily* had such an adverse effect on the fairness of the proceedings that it ought to be excluded. So I think we can at least say that the admission of evidence discovered as a result of oppression does not necessarily have that adverse effect. That leaves the possibility that no such evidence has that effect. Or secondly, some evidence does and some does not, depending on how outrageous was the violation of the defendant's rights. Was it, in the words of Justice Frankfurter in a famous American case, 'conduct that shocks the conscience?' In that case the police got the evidence by stuffing a tube down the accused's throat and extracting it from his stomach. Mr. Justice Frankfurter thought that was conduct that shocks the conscience and the contents of the stomach were not admissible in evidence. Well, I rather suspect that that is how it will be and that it will depend on how outrageous was the conduct in question.

Competence and compellability of the accused's spouse

Finally I might deal briefly with the question of the competence and compellability of the accused person's spouse. It was at one time regarded as a deep seated constitutional principle (I think they were the words of the House of Lords) that the defendant's spouse should not be allowed to give evidence against him. But that rule has gone, deep-seated constitutional principle or not, without any fuss following the recommendation of the Criminal Law Revision Committee. The accused's spouse under the Act is generally a competent though not compellable witness for the prosecution (s.80(1) (a)). So, if a wife is willing to give evidence against her husband on a murder charge, or vice versa, she or he may do so. The Criminal Law Revision Committee's view was, if the spouse is prepared to give evidence, the law would be showing an excessive regard for the preservation of matrimonial harmony if it prevented him or her from doing so. If he (or she) wants to, let him (or her); and so the Act provides.

The defendant is not only competent but compellable for the prosecution or for a person jointly charged with the accused, when the defendant is charged with an assault on, or injury, or threat of injury to, the spouse. Thus far, the effect is merely to reverse *Hoskyn v Metropolitan Police Commissioner* [1978] 2 All ER 136, HL. *Hoskyn* joins that long line of decisions of the House of Lords which have within a few years been reversed by Parliament, a phenomenon which prompted me to speculate in the *Criminal Law Review* some time ago whether we could really afford the House of Lords as an appeal court in criminal cases. The Act, however, goes further than the common law as we understand it before *Hoskyn*. The spouse is also compellable where the defendant is charged with assault on, or a sexual offence against, a person under sixteen. That follows, but goes further than, a recommendation of the Criminal Law Revision Committee. The Committee thought that the reasons of expediency which justified making the spouse a compellable witness, extended also to children of the same household. The problem is one of getting evidence. Parliament has gone beyond the Committee's recommendation and has extended the compellability of the spouse to any case where the defendant is charged with an assault on any person under sixteen, not necessarily of the same household (s.80(3)). The example was given of a fifteen-year-old baby-sitter in the house being raped by the husband when there was nobody else there, except the members of the family who could provide the corroboration which will be required in practice because she is fifteen years old and it is rape. How are you going to get a conviction unless you can call the spouse? So we will make the spouse compellable. 'Sexual offence' is very widely defined in Section 80(7), to include virtually all the existing sexual offences against a person under sixteen, or attempting or conspiring to commit, or aiding and abetting, such an offence. There is an exception, of course, where the spouses are jointly tried.

The incompetence of the spouse at common law extended to a former spouse by a dissolved marriage or a marriage which had been annulled, where that former spouse would testify to some matter which occurred during the marriage. For instance in *Algar's* case [1954] 1 Q.B.279 the defendant was charged with forging his former wife's cheques at a time when they were married. The marriage had been annulled but he had forged her cheques, it was alleged, during the continuance of the marriage. The judge allowed her to be called as a witness against him and his conviction had to be quashed because she was not competent to testify.

That was an absurd rule and Section 85(5) reverses it.

Finally the defendant's spouse is to be compellable for the defence (s.80(2) and (4)) except when they are jointly charged. So if the wife is charged with murder and she thinks the husband can give evidence in her defence and he declines, he can now be required to do so.

Privilege

There are certain minor and unimportant rules of privilege which are abolished. Privilege no longer attaches to communications between husband and wife or to evidence by a spouse that marital intercourse did or did not take place between them (s.80(9)).

CHAPTER 24

Reliable evidence, fairly obtained

PAUL SIEGHART

Let me start with a word about JUSTICE, a society of lawyers concerned, in the words of its constitution, with 'the maintenance of the liberties of the subject and the highest standards of the administration of justice in those territories for which the Westminster Parliament is directly responsible'.

When the society was first founded 30 years ago, these territories extended rather further than they do today. Today they are the United Kingdom of Great Britain and Northern Ireland, Gibraltar, Hong Kong, Bermuda, and the few small islands, including the Falklands, for which the Westminster Parliament still legislates. But that still provides a lot of work for us. Perhaps the most important thing to be said about JUSTICE is that it is an all-party society. We have on our Council, and we have had since the beginning, distinguished lawyers of all political parties, including many peers and MPs. We have had two former Lord Chancellors, and I think I am right that since JUSTICE was founded there has not been an Attorney General or Solicitor General who was not a member of the society before his appointment.

In all the years that I have sat on the Council, I cannot remember a single matter ever being taken to a vote. This gives an idea of the concern which the society has for the two things in its constitution, the liberties of the subject and the administration of justice, on which it is often easy to agree regardless of your party-political starting point.

The work of JUSTICE

Since its foundation, JUSTICE has taken a very wide ranging interest in all aspects of the law of these islands: civil law; administrative law, in which it has done a great deal; industry; the establishment of the Ombudsman; and inevitably also the criminal law. In its concern with the administration of criminal justice it has basically done two things; it has tried to promote reforms, and it has also undertaken a fair amount of individual casework, because it is only through individual casework that you can see where the system can occasionally go wrong, and discover the loopholes that need to be plugged.

In criminal law reform, JUSTICE has a superb track record. Somewhere around three-quarters of all the reforms that JUSTICE has ever proposed have already reached the statute book. This is not bad in a country where law reform requires the patience of Job and the persistence of a fox terrier. For example, we have pioneered substantial changes in the procedures of the Court of Criminal Appeal (as it was) and the Court of Appeal, Criminal Division (as it has since become). The Criminal Injuries Compensation Scheme was entirely invented by JUSTICE; it was the result of an early JUSTICE report and that system now distributes more than £20 million a year to the victims of criminal violence.

The independent element in the investigation of complaints against the police was pioneered by JUSTICE, even-handedly with the introduction of an independent element into the investigation of complaints against solicitors. Whenever Robert Mark used to say: 'You lawyers always forget that there are not only bent coppers; there are also bent lawyers', we were able to say: 'Quite so, and that is why we want an independent element in the investigation of both of them'. And it was in 1970 that JUSTICE published a report called *The Prosecution Process* recommending, I think for the first time in England, the establishment of an independent Crown Prosecution Service. This I am happy to say is yet another one of JUSTICE's reforms that has reached the statute book.

As for casework, I think in an average week the JUSTICE office must get something like thirty or forty letters from Her Majesty's prisons, all of them from convicted persons who allege that they were totally innocent of the offence of which they were found guilty. Having only a very small staff and working on a shoestring, it is not possible to investigate them all fully, and we can only take up comparatively few. By the superb intuition of Tom Sargant, who was our secretary for many years and has now retired, he managed to winkle out the ones which had a whiff of genuine injustice about them. His average record was one man a year who had been convicted of a serious offence and given a very substantial sentence and who, either on a Home Secretary's reference to the Court of Appeal, or by way of early release, or by way of pardon, or in some other way, was eventually released — it having been positively established that he was totally innocent.

One a year is pretty good in a criminal justice system with a million or so indictable offences coming before the courts every year. The number that are sent to prison must run into some tens of thousands, and if the system only misfires once a year, that must be pretty good. Mind you, that is the one a year that we can affirmatively establish; I think it must be the case that it happens in fact a few more times than that each year. Yet, whenever it happens, it is a major blot on the system of justice for two reasons. Not only the obvious one that you have sent an innocent man to prison, which is dreadful enough and ought in theory never to happen, but there is a second reason. Whenever an innocent man is sent to prison, the guilty perpetrator of that crime goes free; he stays around committing further offences; and therefore society's concern to ensure that guilty men are convicted is identical with society's concern that innocent men should not be convicted. These concerns are not in fact antithetical; they point in the same direction. This is not perhaps as widely known or appreciated as it ought to be.

The Philips Commission and the Bill

JUSTICE of course took a great deal of interest in the appointment of the Philips Commission. Several members of the Commission were themselves members of JUSTICE. JUSTICE gave evidence to the Commission, both in the form of a written memorandum as well as orally. We all looked forward greatly to the Philips Commission's Report and when it came out we were, needless to say, delighted to find that in many respects our evidence had been accepted, and many of the Report's recommendations followed our suggestions.

However, there was one striking exception, which was that the entire Report manifestly did not contain any sanction for the performance of the rules which it recommended should be laid down for the conduct of the police in the exercise of their powers. When we read chapter 4 and paragraphs 117–135 under the heading of 'Methods of enforcing the rules', we found that the Commission — after what had obviously been a great deal of debate — had come to the conclusion that the best and the only way to ensure that, when all police powers had at last been codified in a single statute, those rules would actually be obeyed, would be by the internal disciplinary procedures of the police. There I fear we collectively parted company with the Philips Commission and we said so, out loud, and quite often.

When the Police and Criminal Evidence Bill was first presented before the 1983 election we said it again, because the Bill likewise contained no sanction of any kind to ensure that the police would conform with the rules which the Bill was going to lay down. We very much welcomed the Bill. Unlike some other civil liberties organisations, we said that we greatly welcomed the fact that there would finally be on the statute book one single Act of Parliament which would lay down, one hoped in the simplest possible language, precisely what the powers of any policeman are in any circumstances, what the safeguards are, what the limitations on the powers are, and so forth. That must be a good thing. Of course one can argue about the details; about whether the powers should be enlarged or restricted. But they should obviously all be together in a single statute —

provided that one can be sure that they will be obeyed. It is quite pointless putting a statute on the statute book if it is not going to be obeyed: quite apart from anything else, it merely brings the law into disrepute.

So we began to press for the addition of sanctions, and one in particular to which I shall come in a moment. We of course did the usual work that we always do on these occasions. Our Standing Committee on Criminal Justice spent many many evenings drafting many amendments with supporting notes to Members of Parliament and to peers. We had meetings with Home Office ministers and their officials. As a result of that, when the Bill came back after the 1983 election, with a new Home Secretary who made it his first task to take it all back and look at it again, it came forward with quite a number of substantial changes, some of them of the kind which we were proposing at the time.

At that point it became plain to us that, in the years that we had been around, this was probably the single most important Parliamentary Bill which we needed to scrutinise. I should explain that we are all volunteers. The members of our Council and our Executive Committee are all either practising or teaching lawyers; very busy people, wholly unpaid; and we only have a minute staff because we have virtually no money.

It is really very difficult to get busy people to give the amount of time that is required for this, so we created a special Emergency Committee of just five people for this Bill. I chaired it, and the other members were Sir Denis Dobson KCB, QC, who used to be Permanent Secretary of the Lord Chancellor's Office; and three solicitors with great experience in the criminal courts: Charles Wegg-Prosser who had been on the Council of the Law Society, Stanley Clinton-Davis who had been a Member of Parliament, and Gavin Mackenzie, younger than the rest of us and with current active experience of the sharp and dirty end of the criminal process. I should like to take this opportunity of paying tribute to the members of that Committee who worked enormously hard and spent a vast amount of time thinking, planning, discussing, drafting, briefing Members of Parliament, and briefing peers of the realm; most of all perhaps to Charles Wegg-Prosser who sat through all the 59 Committee days that this Bill took up in the House of Commons. At the end of this the Committee had one of those badges printed with a '59' on it and they gave one to Charles Wegg-Prosser, the only non-parliamentarian to be given one.

Sanctions for abuse of police powers

I have already made it clear that, apart from a lot of detail, our principal concern was sanctions and incentives for compliance with the rules which this Act lays down. The classic answer that you always get — and it is the one which the Royal Commission in our view mistakenly adopted — is that there are already sufficient sanctions in the law. If a police officer breaks the rules, you are told, the aggrieved citizen already has a choice of remedies. He can prosecute the officer in the criminal courts if the breach of the rules constituted a criminal offence, such as an assault. He can bring a civil action against him for trespass, or false arrest, or false imprisonment or even malicious prosecution. Or he can use the statutory procedure for complaints against the police.

We came to the conclusion that all these are hollow remedies. In particular, they are quite hollow for any person of moderate intelligence or articulacy; even more so for juveniles; and totally so for anyone who has already been unfortunate enough to collect a criminal record — at which point, if his evidence is tested against that of a police officer, there is hardly ever a court that is likely to prefer it.

Moreover, relationships between the police and the citizen do not take place in a vacuum; they take place within a community, usually quite a small community. Abuses of power are usually the result of pre-existing ill-will. If there is somebody in a particular community who has been getting up the nose of the local constabulary for some time, with the result that the local constabulary (to continue with these homely metaphors) have got their knife in him a bit, and are therefore liable to go to the limits (and sometimes even beyond the limits) of their statutory powers when investigating him for a possible offence, is it really likely that he is going to expose himself to even greater hostility by bringing a private prosecution against the officer in the magistrates' court, suing him in the county court (let alone the High Court) or even troubling to complain against him — knowing that in the last case the investigation will be conducted entirely by other police officers? On top of that, if he uses the complaints procedure, he will now be exposed to a libel action on the part of that police officer, supported by the funds of the Police Federation, with the Home Secretary's permission by Regulation, when he himself is debarred by law from getting legal aid in defending a libel action.

I ask, not at all rhetorically, is it likely that the ordinary citizen will use any of these remedies? Besides, even if an ordinary citizen of more than modest articulacy, intelligence and determination were to decide to use one of them, what are the prospects of his success? According to the Director of Public Prosecutions (DPP), it is much more difficult to get a conviction against a police officer than against anybody else. If the DPP finds that difficult, do you not think that the ordinary citizen would find it more difficult still? Or take civil litigation. It is notorious that civil litigation is a lottery. It is also extremely expensive; unless you are very poor indeed, you are not going to get legal aid; and unless you are very rich indeed, you are not going to be able to afford it. If you look in the books, you will see what happens to cases like *Glinski v. McIver*, [1962] AC 726, where the jury found a senior police officer guilty of malicious prosecution. The Court of Appeal affirmed that, but the House of Lords finally decided it was not quite right on some point of law. Who is going to undertake civil litigation in these circumstances?

But then let us take it even further. Suppose by some miracle one of those remedies were to succeed. What good does it do the man who has already been convicted as the result of an abuse of police powers? He remains languishing in his cell. What kind of damages is he likely to get in a civil action? In the event of a complaint against the police under the new Act, he is very unlikely even to discover whether the outcome of the complaint has brought up anything in his favour, because section 98 of the Act now says that all these things should remain confidential to the Police Complaints Authority.

So we came to the view that there was really only one possible sanction which would ensure compliance with the rules, and that was the obvious one that if you break the rules you fail to achieve your objective, because you are likely to lose your case. You will recall paragraph 4.130 of the Royal Commission's *Report*, where they describe what they call the 'protective principle'. There is a splendid passage there which I quote:

> Where certain standards are set for the conduct of criminal investigations, citizens can expect, indeed they have a right, to be treated in accordance with those standards. If they are not so treated, then they should not be put at risk nor should the investigator gain an advantage. The courts have the responsibility for protecting the citizen's rights. The most appropriate way to do so in these circumstances is to remove from the investigator his source of advantage and from the accused the cause of his risk, that is to exclude the evidence.

Now I am not suggesting that that was the Royal Commission's recommendation, that was only their restatement of the protective rule, and if I may say so I think they re-stated it extremely well. However, the Government from the start objected to anything of this kind. The Home Office *Briefing Guides* from 1983 onwards had this passage in paragraph 11.10. 'It would be contrary to the interests of justice to exclude relevant evidence solely because it was obtained following a breach of the rules. Breaches are more suitably dealt with by police complaints and disciplinary procedures or separate criminal (or civil) proceedings when these are appropriate. It would be a deviation from the main purpose of the original criminal trial to use it as an instrument for disciplining the police.'

The Scarman amendment

So that was the position when the Bill was before Parliament. What is perhaps most surprising is that it was not until after the 1983 election, when the Bill came before Parliament in its second version, and then only at the Report Stage after the 59 days in Committee, that there was first put forward a reasoned clause which was designed to introduce what, for the sake of brevity, I will call a discretionary exclusionary rule. I emphasise the word 'discretionary' because you obviously cannot have an *absolute* exclusionary rule. One has seen what happens with that kind of absolute rule in the United States; one need only imagine a police officer making some minor mistake in applying for a search warrant as a result of which the search that he actually carries out is unlawful, even though he discovers a store of explosives and machine guns. It would be a lunacy if that evidence were rendered inadmissible simply because of a mistake in applying for the search warrant.

Equally well, at the other end of the scale, it is at least arguable that if, in an extreme case, the police in a particular district really have got their knife into somebody, with the result that, without a search warrant or perhaps with a search warrant obtained by fraud, they come ten strong and break down the door, tear up the floorboards, behave in the most disgraceful fashion, and finally find three milligrams of cannabis, then the magistrates' court ought to have the power to say, 'we will not admit that evidence, it was unlawfully obtained'.

In a pragmatic system like ours there is a great deal to be said for judicial discretion in these matters, and therefore JUSTICE prepared an amendment, a new clause to the Bill, designed to be a discretionary exclusionary rule. I will not write it out in full, but in effect what it said was that, once it is put to a court that some evidence might have been unlawfully obtained, the court has three options. First of all, it can invite the prosecution to prove beyond reasonable doubt that the evidence was lawfully obtained, in which case that would be the end of the matter. Or, the court can come to the conclusion that although there was some unlawfulness in obtaining it, this was trivial and can therefore safely be ignored. Or, if the court comes to the conclusion that it was not trivial, it could still have a discretion to say, 'Well, never mind; it was unlawfully obtained and the unlawfulness was not trivial; but in the interests of justice we are still going to let the evidence in'.

That particular amendment was first put forward by Alliance members at the Report stage in the House of Commons, and it was interesting that despite the fact that this was the first time that this had come forward, the Minister of State's reply to it was not perhaps quite as firm as one might have expected in the light of the past history. What he said was this: 'It is [a matter] in which I think the debates in the House of Lords, in which senior judiciaries' (it says in *Hansard*, though I am sure that cannot be right) 'will have the chance to play a part, that will be particularly interesting'. Now that proved to be prescient on the part of the Minister, because in the House of Lords the judicial members amply fulfilled his expectations. Lord Scarman put down the JUSTICE new clause, which then became rightly known as the Scarman amendment. (By the time that the Bill became an

Act there were two Scarman amendments; the other was about racism and police discipline, which is not my concern here.) He put down this particular amendment at the House of Lords Committee Stage and was magnificently supported by Lord Edmund-Davies, Lord Fraser of Tullybelton, Lord Denning, and learned and less learned peers on all sides of the House.

But of course the proposal predictably ran into considerable opposition from the Lord Chancellor on behalf of the Government. So Lord Scarman withdrew it, which is always a sensible thing to do at the Committee Stage in the House of Lords, and re-presented it at the Report Stage, where again it was very fully debated. By this time Lord Denning had changed his mind, because he had meanwhile had lunch in Oxford with the Chief Justice of the United States Supreme Court, and the Chief Justice of the U.S. Supreme Court had obviously told Lord Denning how dreadful the absolute exclusionary rule was in the United States. Unfortunately, Lord Denning did not have the Scarman clause with him to show the Chief Justice, but he came back and said: 'Well, on second thoughts, perhaps exclusionary rules are a bad idea'.

Notwithstanding the advice of the Lord Chancellor and Lord Denning, Lord Scarman pressed the matter to a division, and won by 125 votes to 118. Now that is a pretty good turnout in the House of Lords at the Report Stage of a bill. (I may add it was fortunate that it was before dinner; had it been after the dinner adjournment I doubt that there would have been more than fifty peers left in the House.)

We then ran into some procedural confusion, because Lord Hailsham had a Government amendment down later on the Order Paper which conceded the JUSTICE principle, because it was the precursor of what is now Section 78 of the Act, which allows judicial discretion to exclude evidence unlawfully or improperly obtained in certain circumstances, though without all the specifics that were in Lord Scarman's clause. After a great deal of confusion, the Lord Chancellor gracefully decided not to move his clause, as the House had already passed Lord Scarman's version. However, when the Bill went back to the Commons the Government was not willing to accept defeat at the hands of the judicial and other members of the Upper House, but advised the House of Commons to reject the Scarman clause. Instead it decided to put forward an improvement on Lord Hailsham's clause.

There was a long debate about the new amendment, but needless to say a three-line whip was on. Again, there is one man to whom I would like to pay tribute on that occasion for his courage: Sir Edward Gardiner, QC, Chairman of the Select Committee on Home Affairs of the House of Commons. Alone of all his party — perhaps partly because he is a long-standing member of the Council of JUSTICE — he spoke and voted against the Government, in favour of Scarman and against Hailsham.

However, Hailsham was carried, and Hailsham is now Section 78 of the Act.

Old rules and new

What the result of all this will be is, I think, almost anybody's guess. I was very interested to see what Professor Smith writes about it in chapter twenty-three. When you look at the cases there have been on this issue in recent years, you will find that in *Jeffrey v. Black* [1978] 1 All ER 555, Lord Widgery, when he was Chief Justice, had a pretty wide idea of judicial discretion. He was in that respect following the great Lord Goddard, admittedly in the Privy Council, in a case called *Kuruma son of Kaniu* [1955] 1 All ER 236. He had also been echoed by Lord Parker in *Callis v. Gunn*, [1963] 3 All ER 677.

So three Lords Chief Justice with enormous experience in these matters all took the view that the discretion was pretty wide, and was not limited to the 'more prejudicial than probative' test or to the other lines still left open by the decision in *R. v. Sang* [1979] 2 All ER 1222. *Sang* undoubtedly narrowed what had previously been conceived of as a very wide discretion, though how much *Sang* actually narrowed it is still very much a matter of academic dispute. *Sang* has itself been sometimes followed, sometimes distinguished, in a variety of cases.

Now all that has gone overboard and we have these statutory words; and perhaps we might just for a moment remind ourselves of what Section 78 of the Act stipulates: 'In any proceedings the court may refuse to allow evidence on which the prosecution proposes to rely to be given if it appears to the court that, having regard to all the circumstances, including the circumstances in which the evidence was obtained, the admission of the evidence would have such an adverse effect on the fairness of the proceedings that the court ought not to admit it'. The marginal note, which is not available for anything other than a last resort on construction, calls this 'Exclusion of unfair evidence'.

How the courts will interpret that over the years is still anybody's guess. I would hope that Professor Smith is right, and that in any case which really shocks the conscience and where the court is faced — and I hope it will not be too often — with evidence which has been obtained in a grossly improper fashion by trickery, deception, malice and so on, it will apply that rule and not admit that evidence. There is a real problem about whether one should be more careful about this kind of thing in a serious case where the offence is particularly grave — say, for example, terrorism, or professional robbery.

One could argue that in such cases we do not want to be too conscience-stricken about how the evidence was obtained; and yet one could argue it the other way and say that the graver the offence, the graver the peril in which the accused finds himself, and the more careful the court ought therefore to be to not admit evidence which has any taint about it. All these things, I have no doubt, will provide splendid material over the years to come for the columns of the *Criminal Law Review*, and I very much hope that there will be a lot of academic discussion about it. I also hope that by the time the House of Lords first becomes seized of this in its judicial capacity, certain principles about the application of this rule will have evolved, and will have become sufficiently established and supported by the Court of Appeal, so that the House of Lords will not wish to overthrow them too lightly.

The legislative process

I just want to stress one more thing, which goes perhaps a little beyond my brief. When you consider what a very important section this is — some would argue that it is perhaps the *most* important section, because it is the only one that provides any real teeth for this Act, it seems an extraordinary way to legislate that it should be first put forward by Alliance members on Commons Report; that it should be the accident of the time of day when it is debated on Report in the Upper House which decides that there will be a majority against the Government; and that it should be a whole variety of accidents which determine that the original Hailsham version was substantially changed before it was re-presented in the Commons. Do we really have to go about our legislation in this way in matters as important as this for the two most important liberties of the ordinary citizen, namely the liberty to be free from people who want to hit him over the head or steal from him, and the equally important liberty not to be unnecessarily harassed by the police?

I cannot think of any other country in Europe that legislates in this fashion. Were such a Bill to be presented in France, Germany, Italy, Spain or anywhere else that I can think of, it would have been published many months before it went to Parliament, in order that everybody would have ample time to consider it, write memoranda, consult experts, hear evidence, and so forth. It would have been scrutinised by opposition members who would have had a good deal of help, not only from voluntary organisations in the outside world, but from full-time and well-paid staff. This is the system all over Europe, and it is the system in the United States.

Let me just make one last suggestion about this. In matters of this kind which will profoundly affect what we nowadays no longer call 'the liberties of the subject', but 'human rights' and 'fundamental freedoms', ought it not to become a constitutional or parliamentary convention that any such Bill should automatically be referred to a Select Committee of both Houses for a thorough professional examination of their compatibility with the international obligations of Her Majesty's Government under the European Convention of Human Rights, by which we have been bound for over 35 years? After all, if we get it wrong in this country, somebody will go to Strasbourg, where the European Court of Human Rights will tell us several years later that we have to legislate again. Would it not be a lot simpler to make quite sure that we get it right in the first place, by procedures substantially different — and if I might say so more professional — than those which I have described in this chapter?

PART 5

In Perspective: the Police, the Acts and the Public

CHAPTER 25

Conclusion: the police, the Acts and the public

COLIN BOURN

The Police and Criminal Evidence Act 1984 has its origins in the decision of the Labour Government in 1977 to authorise a comprehensive review of the criminal justice system. The growing crime rate gave force to those who argued that the police were hampered in their efforts to combat crime by the restraints of the criminal justice system. On the other hand it was argued that existing police powers were capable of being abused, endangering individual liberties and putting community relations in jeopardy.

The result was the Royal Commission on Criminal Procedure (the Philips Commission)[1] which was required to have regard 'to the interests of the community in bringing offenders to justice and the rights and liberties of persons suspected or accused of crime' in its investigation of criminal procedure. The Royal Commission recognised the difficulties which are inherent in endeavouring to strike a balance between the rights of the individual and the claims of the community.[2]

Since the mid 19th century it is the police which have been responsible for investigating crime and bringing accused persons to trial: in this task they seek adequate powers, a demand we see articulated at several points during this book.[3] Increased investigative powers have been necessary in the face of a rising crime rate and the emergence of a more professional class of criminal. Yet civil liberties groups remain uneasy about the way in which police powers are used and of the effects of those putative abuses on community relations. The power and eloquence of the advocates of these rival positions caused the Police and Criminal Evidence Act to consume an unprecedented amount of parliamentary time and gave rise to widespread public debate.

Stop and search

The growth of burglary, street crime and drugs offences has given rise to much public anxiety. One avenue open to the police in dealing with these types of offences is to intensify the use of stop and search powers. It was the perhaps heavy-handed use of these powers[4] which was said to have sparked off the riots of 1981. The purpose of Part I of the Act is to provide a national statutory framework for the exercise of these powers which were hitherto not equally available to all police forces.

The exercise of stop and search powers poses the problem of balance between the need to combat crime and any adverse impact on community relations which the overuse or abuse of these powers can create. The evidence is that a disproportionate number of the people who were stopped by the Metropolitan Police in 1982 were young males, especially black males.[5] The fear is that by codifying these powers the Act is endorsing a police practice which some would see as being inimical to good community relations.[6]

But the Act does not merely grant powers to stop and search persons and vehicles, it also provides, via the associated codes of practice, guidance as to the manner in which these powers should be used. S. 67(8) provides that police officers shall be liable to disciplinary proceedings for failure to comply with the provisions of the codes whilst s. 67(11) provides that wherever the codes are relevant in criminal proceedings they shall be taken into account, though they do not in themselves create any criminal liability. The Code on Stop and Search stipulates that an officer must have reasonable grounds to suspect that a person whom he proposes to search is carrying stolen property[7] or a prohibited article and that these powers must be used sparingly and responsibly.[8] Further details are given as to how the search may be carried out and what constitutes grounds for reasonable suspicion i.e. such suspicion must have an objective basis and not consist merely of the fact that the person falls into a particular social group or ethnic category.[9]

The provisions of the Code have been criticised as being unnecessarily restrictive and wholly unrealistic in the conditions encountered by police officers out on the beat, especially in the requirement to make a written record of which the subject has a right to a copy.[10] The codes are not themselves statutory provisions and are not intended to be construed as such but provide practical guidance and set standards of good practice. The question is whether they will, as Professor Zander contends, [11] come to be the norm: 'the routine method of dealing with suspects. What is routinised becomes internalised and accepted as the ordinary way of doing daily business'. If that happens the provisions of the Code will become what David Smith defines as 'working rules . . . internalised by police officers to become guiding principles of their conduct'.[12]

The fear is that the Code on Stop and Search will tend to be used as a camouflage, invoked by officers to conceal and re-present the true nature of their conduct in circumstances in which direct checks are almost impossible to apply. Much depends, as Professor Zander observes,[13] on the attitude of senior officers. It is at least not certain that the fears expressed by Ole Hansen[14] that 'the net result is likely to be a further deterioration in relations between the police and many communities' will prove to be justified. It remains possible that the conditions now surrounding the use of stop and search provisions will prove to be so irritating and irksome to the policeman out on the streets that stops will in fact be confined to those cases where there *are* grounds for reasonable suspicion, with a consequent rise in the proportion of those which lead to some further action.

The relationship between police and young people has been characterised by one writer[15] as one in which

> taut limits tend to be accepted. There may be some conflict about the control and ownership of public space, adolescents and police contending with one another, but a conventional order has been constructed. Young, working class policemen and young, working class males have built something of a symbiotic relationship. It is inherently precarious and unstable. But both sides have found it amusing and useful enough.

Rock contends that this precarious balance can be upset by aggressive patrol tactics, especially when these are conducted by officers from outside the area. It may be that the renewed emphasis on foot patrols and community policing which has emerged in the wake of the Scarman Report will ensure that the guidelines set down in the Stop and Search Code will be observed and the precarious balance between police and young working class communities restored.

It is less easy to be so confident about the most sensitive area of community relations, that between the police and young blacks. The lack of underlying bonds has tended to create a situation in which a substantially unemployed young black population has clashed with the police, seeing them (just as the police tend also to see themselves) as an agency dedicated to upholding the social order as it now exists, an order from which many young blacks feel alienated. Unemployment delays the completion of adolescence for many young people, frustrating their movement towards adult status and responsibilities. This can only make the situation less tractable. Set against this background one cannot be optimistic that the provisions of the Code will act as anything more than an *inhibitory rule* in David Smith's sense,[16] restraining abuses, perhaps reinforcing a withdrawal from the confrontational attitudes which characterised police–public relations within these specific communities in the period which led towards the riots of 1981.

Powers of arrest

Whilst there are grounds for cautious optimism on the question of stop and search. Part III of the Act on powers of arrest is not the subject of a parallel code. Under this Part the basic definition of arrestable offence (an offence which could be the subject of a five year sentence) is maintained and many specific powers of arrest are repealed. There is also a wider power of arrest provided in s.25, under which a constable can make an arrest for an otherwise non-arrestable offence or attempted offence, if it is impracticable or inappropriate to proceed by way of a summons because one of the certain 'general arrest conditions' is satisifed.

The general arrest conditions in s.25(3) are that the name of the person is unknown or cannot be readily ascertained or the constable has reasonable grounds for doubting that the name given is correct (and similarly for a person's address). Further a constable may make such an arrest if the person concerned is causing physical injury to himself or others, damage to property, committing an offence against public decency, causing an unlawful obstruction of the highway or that arrest is necessary to protect a child or other vulnerable person. Whilst these powers are clearly of great practical utility to the police officer out on the street, they leave a great deal of discretion in his hands. The Royal Commission noted[17] that the proportion of indictable offences in which an arrest is made varies greatly from one force to another, thus showing the level of discretion which is open to the police.[18]

The legislation gives little firm guidance and as Ole Hansen argues,[19] the power contained in s.18 to search without a warrant the premises of a person under arrest may provide a significant incentive for the police to make an arrest, subject only to the safeguard that an inspector or more senior officer must authorise the search. S.32(2) also provides that police officers may similarly search any premises in which a person was present immediately before the arrest. Whilst these provisions leave considerable discretion in the hands of the police, and the possibility remains that they may on occasion be used in an oppressive manner against individuals, their potential for causing communal disturbances is less.

Treatment in the station

The second main concern of the Act is the treatment of suspects held in the police station. The powers of the police prior to the Act were unclear, governed by the uncertain effects of case law and the Judges' Rules.
  Whilst the Magistrates' Court Act 1980 provided that 'where a person is taken into custody for an offence without a warrant and is detained in custody, he shall be brought before a magistrates' court as soon as possible', there was little statutory guidance as to how long a person could

be detained for questioning. In those cases where a well advised suspect felt that he had been detained for an excessive period a writ of *habeas corpus* could be obtained. And yet, as David Ashby[20] makes clear, there was little certainty in the outcome as to how long was an excessive period. A figure of 48 hours was held to be a long enough period in detention in (*Sherman v Apps* [1981] *Crim LR* 335) but the later case of *R v Steel* (1981) 73 Cr. App. R.173 cast doubt on using this figure as a rule of thumb.

Yet the available statistics show that three quarters of suspects are either released or charged within six hours and 95 per cent within 24 hours.[21] It is only in exceptional circumstances that suspects are detained for long periods e.g. Metropolitan Police figures showed that for a three month period in 1979 only 0.4 per cent of those detained were held for 24 hours or more before charge or release. The need for more certain standards which did not hamper police investigations was apparent. The question is whether the regime of reviews at regular intervals is needlessly long, as some contend,[22] barely sufficient[23] or about right.[24] There seems a consensus at least that the certainty of the new regime is preferable to the uncertainty of the previous situation.

This controversy is paralleled by the controversy concerning the role of the custody officer and the keeping of full records of a suspect's detention. It is admitted by all concerned that the burden of record-keeping and administration will be considerable and may pose a substantial managerial problem for the police. It will draw experienced sergeants away from supervision in the field. Yet some fear that the records will be only a bureaucratic burden without offering real safeguards that suspects will not be detained for excessively long periods of time. The police fear[25] that there will frequently be trials within trials, when the defence attempts to establish that the provisions of the Act and the accompanying Code have been in some respect breached. These are all legitimate fears but must await the test of experience.

Tape-recording

Many of these fears as to the oppression of suspects on the one hand or the distortion of legitimate police practice will be stilled by the practice of tape-recording interviews sanctioned by s.60. The initial experiments carried out at six centres prior to the full implementation of the scheme have been greeted with enthusiasm by both police and defence lawyers. Even though a tape-recording will not capture facial expressions or informal chats held off the record, there can be little doubt that they will provide a far more positive record of what happened in the police station than it is possible to obtain from note taking. The public nature of such a record promises to be a more effective check on the veracity of suspects' statements and the use of overbearing or tricky tactics by the police. It makes the police accountable to the courts for the conduct of the investigation of suspects in a much more direct fashion than has previously been possible but it will also substantially remove the possibility of any accusation that a defendant's admissions were unreliable or obtained unfairly.

Accountability

On one view the police have been given few, if any, new powers (certainly not *draconian new powers*) whilst their operations will now be subject to more precise limits and inhibited by a new weight of bureaucracy.[26] The question is really how the restrictions with which the police will be hedged about will operate in practice and in what ways the police can be called to account for any lapses in the procedures. Only if the restrictive provisions of the Act have an impact in the real world are the fears of the police about their effects justified. By implication if these are effective mechanisms which will make the restrictive provisions of the Act a reality, the fears of those concerned about civil liberties may prove to be unfounded.

If the provisions of the Police and Criminal Evidence Act 1984 and the codes of practice are to be effective in influencing police behaviour, some means of enforcement is necessary. Without such means of enforcement there would be little incentive for the police to take the new safeguards seriously. The Philips Commission[27] canvassed the most effective means of securing compliance with the new provisions. It saw the two main alternative, though not mutually exclusive, methods as being review after the event or contemporaneous controls and supervision. Review after the event meant review by the courts whereas contemporaneous controls and supervision meant the use of the police discipline code.

Review by the courts

There are three forms in which the courts might come to review breaches of the provisions of the Act and the codes, namely if they (1) constitute criminal offences, (2) give grounds for an action in the civil courts or (3) because there is a question as to the admissibility of the evidence gathered as a result of the breach.

Criminal prosecutions

A criminal prosecution could only be brought by a member of the public if the policeman concerned has committed a crime such as assault. To bring such charges successfully it is necessary to be able to identify the individual policeman. It is not easy to substantiate such charges, as by their very nature there are unlikely to be any witnesses present who can speak about the actions of the alleged victim and the officer concerned. It is common knowledge that courts tend to prefer the evidence of police officers, especially where that evidence contradicts the testimony of someone with a criminal record.

The nature of the requirements introduced by the new legislation makes it unsuitable to constitute a breach of either the Act itself or the Codes, as criminal offences in themselves. Consider the position of the custody officer otherwise!

Civil Actions

It remains open to a complainant who believes he has suffered a civil wrong, a tort, to bring an action in the civil courts. This is the only avenue of complaint which is capable of yielding financial compensation. The chief constable is vicariously liable for the torts of his officers and may recoup himself out of police funds, thus providing a substantial source of compensation to successful civil litigants. Whilst an individual who has been detained for an undue time may have such a remedy, there are substantial difficulties in his path. Not only is there the expense of civil litigation, for which only the very poor can claim legal aid, but there are the difficulties of proof with little certainty about the outcome. There can be few cases in which an action in the civil courts will prove to be a feasible and attractive remedy for the person who believes he has suffered as a result of police actions.

The exclusion of evidence

It has been argued[28] that it is only when matters are so arranged that breaches of the new regime cannot bring an advantage to the police officers concerned, that there is any sanction capable of effectively upholding the provisions of the Act. If a breach of the Act or the codes leads to the exclusion of the relevant evidence and the prosecution consequently fails, it is argued that there can be no incentive to take short cuts or trespass upon the rights of the suspect. This was the reasoning behind the Scarman amendment, which in somewhat changed form is now contained in s.78 of the Act.[29] But it has also been argued that this amendment is unlikely to change the law substantially.[30]

Confessions. The Act deals with both confessions and the exclusion of unfair evidence. Confessions are not admissible (whether true or not) unless the prosecution can prove beyond reasonable doubt that they were not obtained by oppression (s.76(2)(a)) or because, in the circumstances existing at the time of the confession, nothing was said or done which might render any confession unreliable (s.76(2)(b)). These rules displace the previous position in which the test was whether or not a confession was voluntary in that it had not been procured as a result of a threat or inducement made by a person in authority.

Oppression has been defined as 'questioning which by its nature, duration, or other attendant circumstances (including the fact of custody) excites hopes (such as the hope of release) or fears, or so affects the mind of the subject that his will crumbles and he speaks when otherwise he would have stayed silent'.[30a] Further it was held that 'what may be oppressive as regards a child, an invalid, an old man, or somebody inexperienced in the ways of the world may turn out not to be oppressive when one finds that the accused person is of a tough character and an experienced man of the world'.

It is unlikely therefore that a simple breach of the rules on meal breaks or a delay in reviewing the case of a suspect will prove to constitute oppression. Would it, however, render unreliable any confession so obtained. Professor Smith[31] sets out the way in which the test was first formulated by the Criminal Law Revision Committee, which stressed that it is the task of the judge to imagine himself present throughout the interrogation and to consider whether any confession extracted under those circumstances would be unreliable. The question is not whether the particular confession is true but whether any confession obtained under these circumstances could be relied upon.

It is interesting to speculate about the effects of tape-recording on these provisions, which will enable the judge or the magistrates to have a far more intimate and immediate sense of the occasion on which the confession was made. Tony Judge[32] and Maurice Buck[33] both emphasise that since initial police suspicion was overcome in the preparatory experiments on tape-recording, the police have come to believe that tape-recording of interviews will reduce the opportunities for questions to be raised as to the reliability (or the truth) of alleged confessions. The statutory custody record will have similar effect, although no doubt there will be many detailed questions to be settled in the courts about the form and content of these records. Thus in relation to confessions it is the combination of the new custody records and the tape-recording of interviews, in the light of the provisions on confession, which may prove both a restraint and an asset to the police in securing convictions.

Unfair evidence. What of the exclusion of unfair evidence. The introduction of this provision, known as the Scarman amendment, is extensively discussed by Paul Sieghart.[34] who takes the view that such a discretionary exlusionary clause is a vital sanction in the whole scheme of the Act. The Philips Commission[35] discussed both absolute and discretionary exclusion clauses. An absolute exclusion clause, as operates in the

U.S.A., was seen as likely to defeat the purpose of justice and to lead to the failure to convict on a technical breach of the rules, suspects against whom there is a considerable weight of evidence. The Commission proposed an automatic exclusion of evidence obtained through oppressive methods of interviewing but only a discretion to exclude evidence obtained in consequence of other breaches of the rules.

Section 78 provides for a judicial discretion to exclude evidence where to admit the evidence would, in the circumstances in which the evidence was obtained, have an adverse effect on the fairness of the proceedings. What are the circumstances which would have such an adverse effect on the fairness of the proceedings? It is not sufficient that the evidence was found as a result of an inadmissible confession under s.76, for sub-section 4 provides otherwise. Any existing judicial discretion to exclude evidence is also preserved by s.78(2), so that the discretion approved in *R. v Sang* [1980] AC 402, HL, still applies. In that case it was held that evidence might be excluded if its prejudicial effect outweighed its probative value or if a self-incriminatory admission was obtained from the defendant by means which would have resulted in the exclusion of an actual confession. What further discretion is provided by the new section is uncertain[36] and is fully discussed by Professor Smith.

Two points should perhaps be made in the context of the use of such an exclusionary rule as a sanction against police misconduct. Firstly the section is concerned only with the fairness of the proceedings and the circumstances in which evidence was obtained, perhaps illegally obtained, may not be relevant (*Kuruma v. R* [1955] AC 197, PC and *Jeffrey v. Black* [1977] 3 WLR 895, CA). Secondly the House of Lords in *Sang* held that:

> It is no part of the judge's function to exercise disciplinary powers over the police or prosecution as respects the way in which evidence to be used at the trial is obtained by them. If it was obtained illegally there will be a remedy in civil law; if it was obtained legally but in breach of the rules of conduct for the police, this is a matter for the appropriate disciplinary authority to deal with.

It is unlikely, therefore, that s.78 will operate consistently as a new and substantial sanction on the operations of the police. Evidence obtained in breach of the rules laid down in the Act or the Code, may not be held to prejudice the fairness of the proceedings. Only if such a breach is gross and obvious is it likely to result in the exclusion of the evidence so obtained.

Contemporaneous controls

The Philips Commission concluded that it was through day-to-day supervision within the police service, backed up by the provisions of the

Police Disciplinary Code[37] that control over police behaviour was exercised most effectively.

The Police Disciplinary Code has been revised to include within the general offence of *disobedience to orders*, the case where 'a member of a police force, without good and sufficient cause fails to comply with any requirement of a code of practice for the time being in force under section 60 or 66 of the Act 1984'. The Code also includes a wide range of controls over the day-to-day actions of policemen including, for example, discreditable conduct and abuse of authority. The latter offence includes oppressive behaviour by a police officer towards any person in the execution of his duty and in particular where he conducts a search without good and sufficient cause, requires a person to submit to any test or procedure or makes an arrest.

This offence also includes the use of unnecessary violence or threats of violence towards prisoners or other persons or acting in an abusive or uncivil manner to any member of the public. These provisions would be quite adequate to make sure the codes were observed, if they were accepted as guiding principles of conduct, as *working rules* in the terms of David Smith,[38] conscientiously enforced by the senior officers of the police service.

In addition the offence of racially discriminatory behaviour has been introduced by S. 101(1)(b) of the 1984 Act. This is translated into the Discipline Code as acting towards a person in consequence of that person's colour, race, nationality or ethnic origin in a manner which would constitute an abuse of authority (as defined above) or in any way treating such a person improperly on those grounds whilst on duty. The provisions of the Discipline Code are thus comprehensive in respect of the changes made by the 1984 Act.

The question is whether if there are deviations from the practice specified in the Act or its associated codes action will be taken. Such action may be taken on the initiative of superiors or in consequence of complaints made by members of the public.

The Act has itself introduced substantial changes in the police complaints procedure, which are designed to increase public confidence. Under the *previous* complaints procedure investigations were conducted by a member of the police service, but not from the branch or force in which the accused officer works. The investigating officer would report his findings to the chief constable who sent a copy to the Director of Public Prosecutions, if there was any possibility of criminal charges being brought. Otherwise the chief constable would decide whether disciplinary charges were to be brought. If the accused admitted the charges it would be for the chief constable to decide on the appropriate penalty ranging from dismissal, through demotion to a reprimand or caution. If the charges were not admitted the chief constable would hear the charges. At the hearing the officer could be represented by another member of the force and the complainant could be present. The complainant could put questions to the witnesses through the chief constable.

An independent element was introduced in 1976 with the setting up of the Police Complaints Board. If on completion of the investigating officer's report, the papers had not been forwarded to the DPP, and neither had disciplinary charges been brought and admitted nor had the complaint been withdrawn, the report would be forwarded to the Police Complaints Board. The Board could then recommend and direct charges to be brought. If there were exceptional circumstances or if the Board had issued a direction that charges be brought, the case would be heard before a three man tribunal rather than the chief constable. The other two members of the tribunal were to be members of the Board, but if the charges are upheld, punishment was for the chief constable alone to decide.

In 1982–1983 there were 22,970 complaints against the police of which 1,180 were substantiated (approx 5 per cent). These resulted in 149 disciplinary proceedings and 32 criminal charges other than for traffic offences. Eighty-four per cent of substantiated complaints were dealt with other than by disciplinary or criminal charges i.e. usually by advice being given by a senior officer.[39]

There was considerable pressure to amend this procedure because it was felt in certain quarters that the investigation of complaints against the police by the police, albeit subject to the independent element supplied by the Police Complaints Board (some of the members may be serving or former police officers), was unlikely ever to command public confidence. Others took a contrary view that a wholly independent procedure would be excessively bureaucratic and impractical.

This controversy was resolved by Part IX of the 1984 Act which created a new Police Complaints Authority and institutes a new complaints procedure. The new procedure provides for the informal resolution of complaints under s.85 where this is suitable. Whilst the majority of cases will be investigated as before by police officers from another branch or force, in those cases where the complaint relates to conduct which it is alleged led to death or serious injury, the matter shall be referred to the Police Complaints Authority (s.87). The Home Secretary may by regulation prescribe that certain other classes of case are also referred to the Authority and although no Regulations have been issued at the time of writing it is anticipated that complaints relating to corruption will be similarly referred to the Police Complaints Authority.

A case may also be referred to the Authority where it appears that a criminal offence of exceptional gravity may have been committed, although it is not the subject of a complaint (s.88). The new Authority will supervise the investigation, and must approve the choice of investigating officer and oversee the question as to whether disciplinary charges are preferred. A police officer may not be punished by dismissal, requirement to resign or demotion unless he has been given the opportunity for legal representation at the disciplinary hearing (s.102).

The independent element in the complaints procedure has been strengthened by the new procedure, so that the sanctions ultimately upholding the provisions of the Act and the code may now be applied with greater rigour and consistency. None the less Paul Sieghart[40] is sceptical about the value of the complaints procedure, especially to those complainants with a criminal record. Yet if it were the case that an officer was the subject of persistent complaints, even though they were not all substantiated, his career prospects must be adversely affected. The complaints system must, if no more, at least operate as an *inhibitory rule*.[41] discouraging overt conduct which transgresses the new stop and search, arrest, detention and interrogation provisions.

Community accountability

A police authority, according to Gabrielle Cox,[42] has three main roles, that of maintaining an adequate and efficient police force, checking that money is well spent, and the promotion of improved relations between the police and the community. The importance of this third role is recognised in s.106 of the Act which provides for arrangements to be made for obtaining the views of the people in an area and for obtaining their co-operation with the police in preventing crime. Such arrangements shall be made by the police authority after consulting the chief constable.[43] The Metropolitan Police Commissioner shall make such arrangements in London, following guidance to be issued by the Home Secretary. Gabrielle Cox is critical of these arrangements,[44] contending that they fall short of true consultation and are merely a public relations exercise.

The basic reason for the difficulty felt by some police authorities in fulfilling their role lies in the constitutional position of the police force.[45] Since *Oldham v Fisher [1930]* 2 KB 364 it has been well accepted in law that a chief constable is the holder of a public office and not an employee of his police authority. A chief constable is thus answerable neither to the courts nor to his police authority for the operational control of his force, including both policy decisions and decisions in individual cases.[46]

As questions of law enforcement can involve choices between competing interests and policies (e.g. a choice on occasion between preserving public tranquillity and the prevention or apprehension of crime) it can be argued persuasively that it is elected bodies such as police authorities that should exercise such choices. This is the essence of the demand for the democratic accountability of the police[47] which has been expounded by many local politicians in recent years, especially in the wake of the Brixton, Toxteth and Tottenham riots. Such views have not prevailed and chief constables have resisted any sharing of operational control with their police authorities. It is for this reason that such lay visitor schemes as exist, have come into being only by negotiation between police authorities and chief constables. Gabrielle Cox argues that such schemes have a valuable humanising role to play and should have been put on a statutory footing.[48]

Yet there are those who see a positive role for community consultation of the type proposed by the Act,[49] believing that it is a vital means of feeding back to the police the views of the community which they are policing and thus in many cases influencing the formulation of policy. Although it may be argued that community involvement of the type proposed in s.106 lacks any sharp teeth, such consultation may nonetheless be helpful and influential in modifying the rough edges which may exist to police activity. It is true though that such consultative mechanisms will fall into neglect and disuse if they are not taken seriously and the views expressed recognised and listened to.

The role of consultation is perhaps complementary to that of the external discipline of a force and the use of the complaints procedure. It would be insufficient on its own or removed from the context of a wider concern over police matters, but may be a valuable adjunct to other controls. For example police authorities have a power to call for reports from their chief constables on matters of concern to them. This would be a way of following up and strengthening the role of local consultative groups.

The independent prosecution system

The Prosecution of Offences Act 1985 introduces a reform which was proposed in a somewhat different form by the Royal Commission,[50] namely a separation of the prosecution process from the process of investigation. Under the new system responsibility for prosecution will be transferred to a new independent Crown Prosecution Service at the point where charges are preferred or an information laid before the magistrates. From this point on the responsibility for the conduct of the prosecution falls to the Crown Prosecutors, who will prepare all cases and conduct those which are heard before the magistrates. Rights of audience in the Crown Court are still reserved to counsel, who will be instructed by the Crown Prosecutors. The conduct of cases on indictment in the Crown Courts remains the preserve of counsel,[51] including the withdrawal of charges.

The Crown Prosecutors will form part of a national service responsible through the Director of Public Prosecutions (DPP) to the Attorney General and ultimately to Parliament. Whilst the Attorney General is responsible to Parliament for the general conduct of the service, he will not be answerable on decisions on individual cases. The Crown Prosecutors will operate according to the guidelines on prosecution policy to be issued by the DPP[52] although serious and sensitive cases may be reserved to the DPP's office.

What will be the impact of these provisions on the police? One question which remains to be sorted out in practice is the division of work between the Crown Prosecutors and the police over the need to interview witnesses and check evidence after charges have been formulated and the matter has become the responsibility of the Crown Prosecutors' Office.[53]

More to the present point will be the influence of the independent prosecution service on the way in which evidence is collected and used by the police. Will the Crown Prosecutors exercise independent judgement reviewing both the social and evidential bases of prosecutions or will they tend automatically to endorse police decisions to prosecute, as Robin White fears?[54] The evidence is that the Scottish Procurators Fiscal do not exercise a power of independent judgement to a very significant extent.[55]

The Crown Prosecutors will be operating under guidelines issued by the DPP which will be similar to the criteria for prosecution issued by the Attorney General in February 1983.[56] The criteria for prosecution include the requirement that there must be a reasonable prospect of conviction and that the circumstances of the offender be taken into account but doubts should be resolved in favour of prosecution, especially for more serious offences. The question will be whether the need to submit evidence to the Crown Prosecutors Office will act as any sort of control over the extent to which the police abide by the requirements of the codes of practice and the provisions of the 1984 Act.

If the Crown Prosecutors act only on an evidential basis and base their decision on a better than fifty per cent chance of conviction, bearing in mind the limited discretion to exclude evidence which is likely to be exercised by the courts,[57] it must be doubted that the interposition of an independent prosecution service will have a very substantial effect. Bearing in mind the possibility that the accused may ask for costs if a charge is withdrawn[58] and that once a process has started and acquired impetus, it is more difficult to stop and reverse it than it would have been not to begin it in the first instance, it seems unlikely that Crown Prosecutors will exclude cases because some of the proprieties have not been observed in the collection of the evidence.

Conclusions

The 1984 and 1985 Acts together form an elaborate new code of criminal procedure. Fears have been expressed that the liberties of the individual will be eroded whilst others fear that the investigation and prosecution of offences will be hindered and inhibited. The latter can only be the case if the safeguards set upon the investigation and prosecution process are observed. The possibility of them not being observed arises either from a lack of commitment by the police service or because there are no effective external checks upon police practice.

We have reviewed the whole range of those checks, namely action in the civil and criminal courts, the exclusion of unfair or improper evidence, the operation of the police discipline code, the complaints procedure, accountability to police authorities and the community and the operation of the new independent prosecution service. Whilst none of these checks seems on its own to be of overwhelming deterrent power, the range of pressures and sanctions seems impressive by its extent and variety. Taken as a whole, it is possible that the safeguards will operate as intended and become the normal way of doing police work. Yet unless police officers are committed to the spirit which lies behind the new procedures there may not be any improvement in relations between the police and the public in those areas where difficulties have occurred. It is particularly important that the spirit behind the Code of Practice on Stop and Search Powers is honoured, for the indiscriminate use of these powers has been shown to create baleful attitudes towards the police amongst those groups in the population which are at most risk of being stopped.

Yet we cannot expect the police to take community relations more seriously than they are taken in political life generally: we can only expect the police to mirror the general tone of public opinion. Nor can we expect the reform of police practice or criminal procedure to solve social problems. So long as the Government continues to signal that its approach to economic and social discontent is to adopt a tougher attitude towards all who break the law and especially towards those who in any way threaten public order, there will be little *political pressure* on the police to become more sensitive towards their relations with dissenting minorities.

We have a long tradition of police impartiality in political matters, a tradition which is bolstered by the constitutional position of Chief Constables as the holders of a public office. In the more highly charged political atmosphere of the 1980's this tradition is one which is becoming more and more difficult to maintain. We may expect to see the political ambitions of minority groups expand to encompass some form of influence or control over policing in at least certain parts of our inner cities, especially if the safeguards which are built into the 1984 Act are not widely and fully observed, or if the mechanisms for consultation are not implemented effectively.

The other question is whether the safeguards will inhibit effective police work? The most valuable resource open to the police is information supplied by the community. This makes good relations with the public, and even with minority groups within the public, a very salient consideration in policing policy. If the Act imposes limitations on those aspects of policing which have been felt to harm relations with certain sections of the public, such as the widespread use of stop and search powers is said to have done, there may paradoxically be an increase in the quantity and quality of information supplied, rather than a diminution in police effectiveness. Likewise the anticipated effect of tape-recording is the reverse of that which was originally feared by the police and may turn out to enhance their reputation, as well as securing a very satisfactory proportion of guilty pleas and a reduction in the number of occasions on which the credit of police witnesses is impugned. It would, though, be naive to imagine that some 'professional' or experienced criminal justice system, may not be able to take some advantage of the new procedures.

Only future research and monitoring of the ways in which the Acts are implemented will show whether the fears which have been expressed about police effectiveness or community relations have any justification in reality.

Notes

1. Royal Commission on Criminal Procedure (Chairman: Sir Cyril Philips), *Report*, London: HMSO, 1981 (Cmnd. 8092); hereafter referred to as R.C.C.P.
2. R.C.C.P. para. 1–12.
3 See particularly chaps. 4, 8 and 12, in this book; all chapter references below refer to contributions in this book.
4. See chap. 5, p. 77.
5. See chap. 5, p. 77.
6. See chap. 8, p. 104.
7. *Code of Practice for the Exercise by Police Officers of Statutory Powers of Stop and Search* Annex B.
8. *Code of Practice — Stop and Search*, para. 1(A).
9. See chap. 3, p. 55 for a further discussion of the standard of reasonable suspicion.
10. See chap. 7, pp. 97–100.
11. See chap. 10, pp. 123–124.
12. See chap. 6, p. 89.
13. See chap. 10, p. 124.
14. See chap. 8, p. 111.
15. Paul Rock 'Rioting' in London Review of Books, *Anthology Two*, Junction Books, London, 1982.
16. See chap. 6, p. 89.
17. R.C.C.P. pp. 42–43.
18. See chap. 6, p. 93.
19. See chap. 8, p. 110.
20. See chap. 15. p. 184.
21. See chap. 12, p. 154.
22. See chap. 15
23. See chap. 12 and chap. 14.
24. See chap. 10.
25. See chap. 14, pp. 176–178.
26. See chap. 12, p. 150 et seq.
27. The R.C.C.P., paras. 4.115–4.134.
28. See chap. 24, p. 273 et al.
29. See chap. 24.
30. See chap. 23, pp. 264–265.
30a. *R v Prager* (1971) 56 Cr App R 151, 161.
31. See chap. 23, p. 262.
32. See chap. 14, p. 177.

33. See chap. 12. p. 161.
34. See chap. 24.
35. R.C.C.P., paras. 4.126–128.
36. C.f. chap 23, p. 265.
37. *Police Disciplinary Regulations* 1985 S.I. 618–620 (as amended)
38. See chap. 6, p.89.
39. *Report of the Police Complaints Board 1984.*
40. See chap. 24, pp. 271–273.
41. See chap. 6, p. 89.
42. See chap. 13, p. 165.
43. S.106(2).
44. See chap. 13, pp. 171–173.
45. See for example *Government & Law*, T. C. Hartley & J. A. G. Griffith, London: Weidenfeld & Nicholson, 1981. pp. 116–127.
46. This was confirmed in *R. v. Commissioner of the Metropolitan Police ex parte Blackburn* [1968] 1 All ER, 763 at p. 769 where Lord Denning said:

    Although the chief officers of police are answerable to the law, there are many fields in which they have a discretion with which the law will not interfere. For instance, it is for the Commissioner of Police, or the chief constable, as the case may be, to decide in any particular case whether enquiries should be pursued, or whether an arrest should be made, or a prosecution brought. It must be for him to decide on the disposition of his force and the concentration of his resources on any particular crime or area. No court can or should give him direction on such a matter. He can also make policy decisions and give effect to them, as, for instance, was often done when prosecutions were not brought for attempted suicide; but there are some policy decisions with which, I think, the courts in a case can, if necessary, interfere. Suppose a chief constable were to issue a directive to his men that no person should be prosecuted for stealing any goods less than £100 in value. I should have though that the court could countermand it. He would be failing in his duty to enforce the law.

47. See Paul Boateng in John Benyon (ed.), *Scarman & After*, Oxford: Pergamon Press, 1984, p. 155 *et seq*.
48. See chap. 13. pp. 168–170.
49. See the views of George Greaves, Member of Lambeth Consultative Committee in chap. 5. pp. 79–81.
50. R.C.C.P. 1981 (Cmnd. 8092) paras. 6.1–9.13.
51. See chap. 21, pp. 239–242.
52. See chap. 20, p. 232.
53. See chaps. 18 and 19.
54. See chap. 17, p. 205.
55. See S. Moody & J. Toombs, *Prosecution in the Public Interest*, 1982.
56. Reproduced in R.C.C.P. 1981 *Law & Procedure Vol.* Appendix 25, (Cmnd. 8092–1).
57. See chap. 23 and 24.
58. See chap. 18, p. 217.

Select Bibliography

There is a large and growing literature on the topics covered in this volume, and a comprehensive bibliography would probably merit a book of its own. The following selection of books and articles includes some published in America and elsewhere, and the attention of readers is also drawn to sources referenced at the end of many of the chapters.

Ackroyd, C., Margolis, J., Rosenhead, J. and Shallice, T., *The Technology of Political Control*, Harmondsworth: Penguin, 1977.

Adorno, T. W. *et al.*, *The Authoritarian Personality*, New York: Harper & Row, 1950.

Alderson, J. and Stead, P., *The Police We Deserve*, London: Wolf, 1973.

Alderson, J., *Policing Freedom*, Plymouth: Macdonald & Evans, 1979.

Alderson, J., 'Police leadership in times of social, economic turbulence', *Police Journal*, **49**, 2 (1976).

Alderson, J., *Law and Disorder*, London: Hamish Hamilton, 1984.

Alex, N., *New York Cops Talk Back*, New York: Wiley, 1976.

Anderton, J., 'Accountable to whom?', *Police*, **13**, 6 (February 1981).

Angell, J. A., 'Towards an alternative to the classic police organisational arrangements: a democratic model', *Criminology*, **2** (1971), pp. 185–206.

Anning, N., 'How the police swamped Brixton', *The Leveller*, **63** (August 1981).

Antunes, G. and Scott, E. S., 'Calling the cops', *Journal of Criminal Justice*, **9**, 2 (1981).

Archer, P., *The Role of the Law Officers*, London: Fabian Society, (Fabian Research Series, 339), 1978.

Ascoli, D., *The Queen's Peace*, London: Hamilton, 1979.

Association of Metropolitan Authorities, *Policies for the Police Service*, London: AMA, 1982.

Atkins, S. and Rutherford, A., 'The police and the public: in search of new styles of accountability', *Public Law* (Summer 1983).

Aubrey, C., *Who's Watching You? Britain's Security Services and the Official Secrets Act*, Harmondsworth: Penguin, 1981.

Bailey, V., *Policing and Punishment in the 19th Century*, London: Croom Helm, 1981.

Baldwin, J. and Bottomley, A. K., (Eds.) *Criminal Justice: Selected Readings*, London: Martin Robertson, 1978.

Baldwin, J. and McConville, M., *Negotiated Justice*, Oxford: Martin Robertson, 1977.

Baldwin, J. and McConville, M., *Jury Trials*, Oxford: Oxford University Press, 1979.

Baldwin, R. and Kinsey, R., *Police Powers and Politics*, London: Quartet, 1982.

Baldwin, R. and Leng, R., 'Police powers and the citizen', *Howard Journal of Criminal Justice*, **23**, 2 (June 1984).

Ball, J., Chester, L. and Perrott, R., *Cops and Robbers: an Investigation into Armed Bank Robbery*, Harmondsworth: Penguin, 1979.

Banton, M., *The Policeman in the Community*, London: Tavistock, 1964.

Banton, M., *Police–Community Relations*, London: Collins, 1973.

Banton, M., 'Police', *The New Encyclopaedia Britannica*: *Macropaedia*, 14, London: Encyclopaedia Britannica, 1974.

Banton, M., 'The keepers of the peace', *New Society*, **5** (December 1974), p. 635.

Banton, M., 'Crime prevention in the context of criminal policy', *Police Studies*, **1** (1978).

Baxter, J. and Koffman, L., 'The Confait inheritance — forgotten lessons?', *Cambrian Law Review*, **14** (1983).

Baxter, J. and Koffman, L., (Eds.), *Police, The Constitution and the Community*, Abingdon: Professional Books, 1985.

Baxter, J., Rawlings, P., Williams, J., 'Police Bill codes of practice', *Justice of the Peace News*, **148** (September 1984), pp. 595–597 and 612–614.

Bayley, D., *Forces of Order*, Berkeley: University of California Press, 1976.

Bayley, D., (Ed.), *Police and Society*, Beverly Hills: Sage, 1977.

Bayley, D. and Mendelsohn, H., *Minorities and the Police*, New York: Free Press, 1968.

Bean, R., 'Police unrest, unionisation and the 1919 strike in Liverpool', *Journal of Contemporary History*, **15**, 4 (1980).

Belson, W., *The Police and the Public*, London: Harper & Row, 1975.

Bennett, T., 'The social distribution of criminal labels', *British Journal of Criminology*, **19** (1979).

Bennett, T., (Ed.), *The Future of Policing*, Cropwood Papers, **15**, Cambridge: Institute of Criminology, 1983.

Bent, A., *The Politics of Law Enforcement*, Lexington, Mass.: D. C. Heath, 1974.

Benyon, J., (Ed.), *Scarman and After*, Oxford: Pergamon, 1984.

Benyon, J., 'The policing issues', *in* J. Benyon (Ed.), *Scarman and After*, Oxford: Pergamon, 1984, pp. 99–113.

Benyon, J., 'The riots, Lord Scarman and the political agenda', *in* J. Benyon (Ed.), *Scarman and After*, Oxford: Pergamon, 1984, pp. 3–19.

Benyon, J., 'The riots: perceptions and distortions', *in* J. Benyon (Ed.), *Scarman and After*, Oxford: Pergamon, 1984, pp. 37–45.

Benyon, J., 'Scarman and After', *in* J. Benyon (Ed.), *Scarman and After*, Oxford: Pergamon, 1984, pp. 233–243.

Benyon, J., *Legitimacy, Conflict and Order: Urban Disadvantage and Political Stability in Britain*, Colchester: European Consortium for Political Research, 1985.

Benyon, J., 'Going through the motions: the political agenda, the 1981 riots and the Scarman inquiry', *Parliamentary Affairs*, **38**, 4 (Autumn 1985).

Benyon, J., 'Spiral of decline: race and policing', *in* Z. Layton-Henry and P. Rich (Eds.), *Race, Government and Politics in Britain*, London: Macmillan, 1986.

Benyon, J., 'Turmoil in the cities', *Social Studies Review*, **1**, 3 (January 1986), pp. 3–8.

Benyon, J., *A Tale of Failure: Race and Policing*, Coventry: Warwick University Centre for Research in Ethnic Relations, 1986.

Bethnal Green and Stepney Trades Council, *Blood on the Streets: A Report on Racial Attacks in East London*, London: The Trades Council, 1978.

Bevan, V. T. and Lidstone, K., *The Police and Criminal Evidence Act 1984*, London: Butterworth, 1985.

Bieck, W., *Response Time Analysis*, Kansas City: Kansas City Police Department, 1977.

Binder, A. and Scharf, P., 'Deadly force in law enforcement', *Crime and Delinquency*, **28** (1982).

Bittner, E., 'The police on skid row: a study in peacekeeping', *American Sociological Review*, **32** (1967).

Bittner, E., *The Functions of the Police in Modern Society*, Chevy Chase, Maryland: National Institute of Mental Health, 1970.

Blaber, A., *The Exeter Community Policing Consultative Group*, London: NACRO, 1979.

Black, D. and Reiss, A., 'Police control of juveniles', *American Sociological Review*, **35** (February 1970).

Blake, N., *The Police, the Law and the People*, London: Haldane Society, 1980.

Block, P. B. and Bell, J., *Managing Investigations: the Rochester System*, Washington, D.C.: Police Foundation, 1976.

Blom-Cooper, L. and Drabble, R., 'Police perception of crime: Brixton and the operational response,' *British Journal of Criminology*, **22**, 1 (April 1982).

Blom-Cooper, L., 'Criminal justice in 1984', *Criminal Justice*, **2**, 2 (June 1984).

Blumberg, A., *Criminal Justice*, New York: Franklin Watts, 1979.

Bogolmony, R., 'Street patrol: the decision to stop a citizen', *Criminal Law Bulletin*, **12**, 5 (1976).

Boateng, P., 'The police, the community and accountability' *in* J. Benyon (Ed.), *Scarman and After*, Oxford: Pergamon, 1984.

Boostrom, R. and Henderson, J., 'Community action and crime prevention', *Crime and Social Justice*, **19** (Summer 1983).

Bordua, D. (Ed.), *The Police: Six Sociological Essays*, New York: John Wiley, 1967.

Bottomley, A. K., *Decisions in the Penal Process*, Oxford: Martin Robertson, 1973.

Bottomley, A. K. and Coleman, C., 'Criminal statistics: the police role in the discovery and detection of crime', *International Journal of Criminology and Penology*, **4** (1976).

Bottomley, A. K. and Coleman, C., *Understanding Crime Rates*, Hants: Gower, 1981.

Bowden, T., *Beyond the Limits of the Law*, Harmondsworth: Penguin, 1978.

Bowes, S., *The Police and Civil Liberties*, London: Lawrence and Wishart, 1966.

Box, S., *Deviance, Reality and Society*, London: Holt, Rinehart and Winston, 1981.

Box, S., *Power, Crime and Mystification*, London: Tavistock, 1983.

Box, S. and Russell, K., 'The politics of discreditability', *Sociological Review*, **23**, 2 (1975).

Boydstun, J. E., *San Diego Field Interrogation Study: Final Report*, Washington, D.C.: Police Foundation, 1975.

Bridges, L., 'Policing the urban wasteland', *Race and Class* (Autumn 1983).

Bridges, L., 'Extended views: the British left and law and order', *Sage Race Relations Abstracts* (February 1983).

Bridges, L. and Bunyan, T., 'The Police and Criminal Evidence Bill in context', *Journal of Law and Society* (Summer 1983).

Bristol T.U.C., *Slumbering Volcano? Report of an Enquiry into the Origins of the Eruption in St. Paul's, Bristol on 2 April 1980*, Bristol: T.U.C., 1981.

Brodeur, J. P., 'High policing and low policing: remarks about the policing of political activities', *Social Problems*, **30**, 5 (June 1983).

Brogden, A., ' "Sus" is dead but what about "Sas"?', *New Community*, **9**, 1 (Summer 1981).

Brogden, M., 'A police authority — the denial of conflict', *Sociological Review*, **25**, 2 (1977).

Brogden, M., *The Police: Autonomy and Consent*, London: Academic Press, 1982.

Brogden, M., 'The myth of policing by consent' *Police Review*, **22** (April 1983).

Brogden, M., 'From Henry VIII to Liverpool 8: the complex unity of police street powers', *International Journal of Sociology of Law* (Winter 1983).

Brogden, M. and Wright, M., 'Reflections on the social work strikes', *New Society*, **53**, (1979).

Brooks, T. R., 'New York's finest', *Commentary*, **40** (August 1965).

Brown, D. W., 'Arrest rates and crime rates: when does a tipping effect occur?', *Social Forces*, **57** (1978), pp. 671–682.

Brown, J., *Shades of Grey*, Cranfield: Cranfield Police Studies, 1977.

Brown, J. and Howes, G. (Eds.), *The Police and the Community*, Farnborough: Saxon House, 1975.

Brown, J. and Howes, G. (Eds.), *The Cranfield Papers*, London: Peel Press, 1979.

Brown, M., *Working the Street*, New York: Russell Sage, 1981.

Browne, D. G., *The Rise of New Scotland Yard*, London: Harrap, 1956.

Bunyan, T., *The Political Police in Britain*, London: Julian Friedman, 1976.

Bunyan, T., 'The police against the people', *Race and Class* (Autumn 1981–Winter 1982).

Bunyan, T. and Kettle, M., 'The police force of the future is now here', *New Society*, 21 August 1980.

Bunyard, R. S., *Police: Organisation and Command*, Plymouth: Macdonald & Evans, 1978.

Burrows, J. and Tarling, R., *Clearing Up Crime*, London: HMSO, 1982 (Home Office Research Study No. 73).

Butler, A. J., *Police Management*, London: Gower, 1984.

Butler, A. J. P., 'Police "professionalism": what do we mean?', *Police*, **12**, 5 (January 1980).

Butler, D. and Halsey, A., (Eds.), *Policy and Politics*, London: Macmillan, 1978.

Byford, L., 'Hands off the police authorities', *Police*, **16** (March 1975).

Cain, M., 'Police professionalism: its meaning and consequences', *Anglo-American Law Review*, **1** (1972), pp. 217–31.

Cain, M., *Society and the Policeman's Role*, London: Routledge & Kegan Paul, 1973.

Cain, M., 'The general practice lawyer and the client: towards a radical conception', *International Journal of the Sociology of Law*, **7**, 4 (November 1979).

Cain, M., 'Trends in the sociology of police work', *International Journal of Sociology of Law*, **7**, 2 (1979).

Cain, M. and Sadigh, S., 'Racism, the police and community policing', *Journal of Law and Society*, **9**, 1 (Summer 1982).

Canetti, E., *Crowds and Power*, Harmondsworth: Penguin, 1981.

Carlen, P. and Collison, M., (Eds.), *Radical Issues in Criminology*, London: Routledge, 1980.

Carr-Hill, R. and Stern, N., *Crime, the Police and Criminal Statistics*, London: Academic Press, 1979.

Carr-Hill, R. A. and Stern, N. H., 'Crime and the dole queue', *Police*, **15**, 5 (April 1983).

Carter, A., 'The wonderful world of cops', *New Society*, 23 September 1982.

Carter, D., 'Complaints against the police', *Legal Action*, **37** (1984).

Cashmore, E. and Troyna, B., (Eds.), *Black Youth in Crisis*, London: Allen & Unwin, 1982.

Chaiken, J. M., Lawless, M. W. and Stevenson, K. A., *The Impact of Police Activities on Crime: robberies in the New York City subway system*, Santa Monica, California: The Rand Corporation, 1974.

Chaiken, J. M., 'What is known about the deterrent effects of police activities', *in* Cramer, J. A., (Ed.), *Preventing Crime*, Beverley Hills, California: Sage Publications, 1978.

Chambliss, W. and Mankoff, M., (Eds.), *Whose Law, What Order?* New York: Wiley, 1975.

Chapman, B., *Police State*, London: Macmillan, 1970.

Chapman, D., *Sociology and the Stereotype of the Criminal*, London: Tavistock, 1968.

Chatterton, M., 'Police in social control', *in* King, J. F. S., (Ed.), *Control Without Custody?*, Cambridge: Institute of Criminology, 1976.

Chibnall, S., *Law and Order News*, London: Tavistock, 1977.

Chief Constable of Avon and Somerset, *The Disturbances in the St. Paul's Area of Bristol, 2 April 1980*, Unpublished Report to the Home Secretary, 1980.

Chippindale, P., 'Countryman in trouble with the DPP', *New Statesman*, **99**, 2556 (14 March 1980).

Christensen, J., Schmidt, J. and Henderson, J., 'The selling of the police: media, ideology and crime control', *Contemporary Crises*, **6** (1982).

Christian, L., *Policing by Coercion*, London: GLC Police Committee and Pluto Press, 1983.

Clarke, A.,'Holding the blue lamp: television and the police in Britain', *Crime and Social Justice*, **19** (Summer 1983).

Clarke, D., 'Blue murder', *The Leveller*, **32** (November 1979).

Clarke, J., Critcher, C., Jefferson, T. and Lambert, J., 'The selection of evidence and the avoidance of racialism: a critique of the Parliamentary Select Committee on Race Relations and Immigration', *New Community*, **3**, 3 (Summer 1974).

Clarke, R. and Hough, M., *The Effectiveness of Policing*, Farnborough: Gower, 1980.

Clarke, R. and Hough, M., *Crime and Police Effectiveness*, London: HMSO, 1984 (Home Office Research Study No. 79).

Clarke, R. and Mayhew, P., (Eds.), *Designing Out Crime*, London: HMSO, 1980.

Clarke, R., 'Situational crime prevention: theory and practice', *British Journal of Criminology*, **20**, (1980), pp. 136–145.

Clayton, R. and Tomlinson, H., 'Can police authorities give orders to chief constables', *New Law Journal*, **134**, 6173 (12 October 1984), pp. 880–882.

Cloward, R. A. and Piven, F. F., *The Politics of Turmoil: Essays on Poverty, Race and the Urban Crisis*, New York: Pantheon 1974.

Clutterbuck, R., *Britain in Agony*, Harmondsworth: Penguin, 1980.

Coatman, J., *Police*, London: Oxford University Press, 1959.

Cobb, R., *The Police and the People*, London: Oxford University Press, 1970.

Cohen, P., 'The "effective force" of a fatal blow', *New Statesman*, 6 June 1980.

Cohen, S., (Ed.), *Images of Deviance*, Harmondsworth: Penguin, 1971.

Cohen, S., *Folk Devils and Moral Panics*, St. Albans: Paladin, 1973.

Cohen, S., 'The punitive city', *Contemporary Crises*, **3**, 4 (1979).

Cohen, S. and Scull, A., *Social Control and the State*, Oxford: Martin Robertson, 1983.

Coleman, C. A. and Bottomley, A. K., 'Police conceptions of crime and "no crime" ', *Criminal Law Review*, 1976.

Colman, A. and Gorman, L. 'Conservatism, dogmatism and authoritarianism in British police officers', *Sociology*, February 1982.

Colquhoun, P., *Treatise on the Police of the Metropolis*, 1795.

Commissioner of Police of the Metropolis, *Written Evidence to the Royal Commission on Criminal Procedure*, Parts I and II, London: New Scotland Yard, 1978.

Committee of Inquiry on the Police (Chairman: Lord Edmund-Davies), *Reports on Negotiating Machinery and Pay*, London: HMSO, 1978 (Cmnd. 7283).

Committee of Inquiry on the Police (Chairman: Lord Edmund-Davies), *Report III*, London: HMSO, 1979 (Cmnd. 7633).

Communist Party, *Black and Blue: Racism and the Police*, London: Communist Party, 1981.

Coulter, J., Miller, S. and Walker, M., *State of Siege: Miners' Strike 1984*, London: Canary Press, 1984.

Cowell, D., Jones, T. and Young, J. (Eds.), *Policing the Riots*, London: Junction, 1982.

Cox, B., Shirley, J. and Short, M., *The Fall of Scotland Yard*, Harmondsworth: Penguin, 1977.

Cranfield Papers, *The Proceedings of the 1978 Cranfield Conference on the Prevention of Crime in Europe*, London: Peel Press, 1978.

Critchley, T. A., *The Conquest of Violence*, London: Constable, 1970.

Critchley, T. A., *A History of Police in England and Wales*, London: Constable, 1978.

Cronin, J. E. and Schneer, J. (Eds.), *Social Conflict and the Political Order in Modern Britain*, London: Croom Helm, 1982.

Croft, J., *Crime and the Community*, London: HMSO, 1979 (Home Office Research Study No. 50).

Davey, B. J., *Lawless and Immoral: Policing a Country Town 1838–57*, Leicester: Leicester University Press, 1983.

Davis, K., *Discretionary Justice*, Urbana, Ill.: University of Illinois, 1969.

Davis, K., *Police Discretion*, St. Paul, Minn.: West Publishing, 1975.

Dean, M., 'The finger on the policeman's collar', *The Political Quarterly*, 1982.

Deane-Drummond, A., *Riot Control*, London: Royal United Services Institute, 1973.

Demuth, C., *'Sus' — A Report on the Vagrancy Act, 1824*, London: Runnymede Trust, 1978.

Denning, Lord, *The Discipline of Law*, London: Butterworth, 1979.

Denning, Lord, *The Due Process of Law*, London: Butterworth, 1980.

Ditton, J. and Duffy, J., 'Bias in the newspaper reporting of crime news', *British Journal of Criminology*, **23**, 2 (April 1983).

Donajgrodzki, A. P., *Social Control in Nineteenth Century Britain*, London: Croom Helm, 1977.

Douglas, J., (Ed.), *Crime and Justice in American Society*, New York: Bobbs Merrill, 1971.

Dromey, J. and Taylor, G., *Grunwick: the Workers' Story*, London: Lawrence and Wishart, 1978.

Edgar, J. M., Marcus, M. M., Wheaton, R. J. and Hicox, R. C., *Team Policing*, Washington, D.C.: LEAA, 1976.

Emsley, C., *Policing and its Context 1750–1870*, London: Macmillan, 1983.

Ericson, R., *Making Crime: A Study of Detective Work*, Toronto: Butterworth, 1981.

Ericson, R., *Reproducing Order: A Study of Police Patrol Work*, Toronto: University of Toronto Press, 1982.

Evans, P., *The Police Revolution*, London: Allen & Unwin, 1974.

Ferdinand, T. and Luchterhand, E., 'Inner city youths, the police and justice', *Social Problems*, **17** (Spring 1970).

Field, S. and Southgate, P., *Public Disorder*, London: HMSO, 1982 (Home Office Research Study No. 72).

Fielding, H., *An enquiry into the late increase of robbers*, 1751.

Fielding, N., 'Police socialisation and police competence', *British Journal of Sociology* (December 1984).

Fienberg, S., Kinley, L. and Reiss, A. J., 'Redesigning the Kansas City preventive-patrol experiment', *Evaluation*, **3** (1976), pp. 125–131.

Fine, R., Hunt, A., McBarnet, D. and Moorhouse, B., (Eds.), *Law, State and Society*, London: Croom Helm, 1981.

Fine, R., Kinsey, R., Lea, J., Picciotto, S. and Young, J., (Eds.), *Capitalism and the Rule of Law*, London: Hutchinson, 1979.

Fisher, C. and Mawby, R., 'Juvenile deliquency and police discretion in an inner-city area', *British Journal of Criminology*, **22**, 1 (January 1982).

Fogelson, R., *Big-City Police*, Cambridge, Mass.: Harvard University Press, 1977.

Foster, J., *Class Struggle in the Industrial Revolution*, London: Methuen, 1974.

Foucault, M., *Discipline and Punish*, Harmondsworth: Penguin, 1977.

Fox, I., 'Is there a need for a Third Force?' *Police Journal* (1978).

Franey, R., *Poor Law*, London: Campaign for Homeless People, Child Poverty Action Group, Claimants' Defence Committee, National Association of Probation Officers, National Council for Civil Liberties, 1983.

Freeman, M., 'Law and order in 1984', *Current Legal Problems*, 1984.

Friedman, M., *Capitalism and Freedom*, Chicago: University of Chicago Press, 1962.

Gash, N., *Mr. Secretary Peel*, London: Longman, 1961.

Gilbert, T., *Only One Died*, London: Kay Beauchamp, 1975.

Gilroy, P., 'The myth of black criminality', *Socialist Register 1982*, London: Merlin, 1982.

Gilroy, P., 'Police and thieves', *in* Centre for Research on Contemporary Cultural Studies, *The Empire Strikes Back*, London: Hutchinson, 1983.

GLC Police Committee, *A New Police Authority for London: A Consultation Paper on Democratic Control of the Police in London*, Discussion Paper No. 1, London: GLC, 1983.

GLC Police Committee Support Unit, 'Royal Commission on Criminal Procedure — Home Office Consultative Memorandum — Suggested Response by the Council,' *Paper PC, 23, Item 5*, London: GLC, 1982.

GLC Police Committee Support Unit, 'Police & Criminal Evidence Bill — A Response,' *Paper PC, 78A, Item 1*, London: GLC, 1982.

Goldstein, H., *Police Corruption: a Perspective on its Nature and Control*, Washington D.C.: Police Foundation, 1975.

Goldstein, H., *Policing a Free Society*, Cambridge, Massachusetts: Ballinger, 1977.

Goldstein, H., 'Improving policing: a problem-oriented approach', *Crime and Delinquency*, **25** (1979), pp. 236–258.

Goldstein, J., 'Police discretion not to invoke the criminal process: low-visibility decisions in the administration of justice', *Yale Law Journal*, **69** (1960).

Goodson, A., 'Police and the public' *in* J. Benyon (Ed.), *Scarman and After*, Oxford: Pergamon, 1984.

Gordon, P., *White Law*, London: Pluto Press, 1983.

Gordon, P., 'Community policing: towards the local police state', *Critical Social Policy*, **10** (Summer 1984).

Gorer, G., *Exploring English Character*, London: Cresset, 1955.

Graber, D. A., *Crime News and the Public*, New York: Praeger, 1980.

Greenwood, P. W., Chaiken, J. M., Petersila, J. and Prusoff, L., *The Criminal Investigation Process*, Lexington, Mass.: D. C. Heath, 1977.

Griffith, J., *The Politics of the Judiciary*, London: Fontana, 1977.

Griffiths, B., 'One-tier policing' *in* J. Benyon (Ed.), *Scarman and After*, Oxford: Pergamon, 1984.

Grigg, M., *The Challenor Case*, Harmondsworth: Penguin, 1965.

Gross, B., 'Some anti-crime proposals for progressives', *Crime and Social Justice*, **17** (Summer 1982).

Gwyn, W. B., *The Meaning of the Separation of Powers*, The Hague: Martinus Nijhoff, 1965.

Hain, P., (Ed.), *Policing the Police*, volume 1, London: John Calder, 1979.

Hain, P., (Ed.), *Policing the Police*, volume 2, London: John Calder, 1980.

Hain, P., *Political Trials in Britain*, Harmondsworth, Penguin, 1984.

Hall, S. and Jefferson, T., (Eds.), *Resistance through Rituals*, London: Hutchinson, 1976.

Hall, S., Critcher, C., Jefferson, A., Clarke, J. and Roberts, B., *Policing the Crisis: Mugging, the State and Law and Order*, London: Macmillan, 1978.

Hall, S., *Drifting into a Law and Order Society*, London: Macmillan, 1980.

Halloran, J., Elliott, P. and Murdock G., *Demonstrations and Communication*, Harmondsworth: Penguin, 1970.

Hargreaves, F. and Levenson, H., *A Practitioner's Guide to the Police and Criminal Evidence Act 1984*, London: Legal Action Group, 1985.

Harring, S., *Policing a Class Society*, New Brunswick: Rutgers University Press, 1983.

Harris, J., 'What the police committee member needs to know', *Local Government Review*, **148** (1984), p. 27.
Hart, J. M., *The British Police*, London: Allen & Unwin, 1951.
Hay, D., (Ed.), *Albion's Fatal Tree*, Harmondsworth: Penguin, 1975.
Heal, K. and Morris, P., *Crime Control and the Police*, London: HMSO, 1981 (Home Office Research Study No. 67).
Hebdige, D., *Subculture: the Meaning of Style*, London: Methuen, 1979.
Henricson, C., 'Civil liberties undermined', *Legal Action Group Bulletin* (March 1985).
Hewitt, P., *The Abuse of Power*, Oxford: Martin Robertson, 1982.
Hingeland, M. J., *Criminal Victimisation in Eight American Cities*, Cambridge, Mass.: Ballinger, 1976.
Hines, V., *Black Youth and the Survival Game in Britain*, London: Zulu Publications, 1973.
Hiro, D., *Black British, White British*, Harmondsworth: Penguin, 1973.
Hirst, P., *On Law and Ideology*, London: Macmillan, 1979.
Hobsbawm, E., *Primitive Rebels*, Manchester: Manchester University Press, 1959.
Hobsbawm, E., *Labouring Men*, London: Weidenfeld & Nicolson, 1964.
Holdaway, S., 'Changes in urban policing', *British Journal of Sociology*, **28**, 2 (1977).
Holdaway, S., (Ed.), *The British Police*, London: Edward Arnold, 1979.
Holdaway, S., *Inside the British Police*, Oxford: Basil Blackwell, 1983.
Home Office, *Racial Attacks*, London: HMSO, 1981.
Home Office, *Criminal Statistics (England and Wales)*, London: HMSO, published annually by Command.
Home Office, *Research Bulletin* (published twice a year).
Hough, J. M. and Heal, K. H., 'Police effectiveness: some popular misconceptions', *Home Office Research Bulletin*, 7, London: Home Office, 1979.
Hough, M., *Uniformed Police Work and Management Technology*, London: Home Office, 1980 (Research Unit Paper No. 1).
Hough, M. and Mayhew, P., *The British Crime Survey*, London: HMSO, 1983 (Home Office Research Study No. 76).
Hough, M. and Mayhew, P., *Taking Account of Crime: Key Findings from the Second British Crime Survey*, London: HMSO, 1985 (Home Office Research Study No. 85).
House of Commons, *Police Complaints Procedures: Fourth Report from the Home Affairs Committee, Session 1981–82*, HC 98, London: HMSO, 1982.
Howard, G., *Guardians of the Queen's Peace*, London: Odhams, 1957.
Humphry, D., *Police Power and Black People*, London: Panther, 1972.
Ignatieff, M., *A Just Measure of Pain*, London: Macmillan, 1978.
Ignatieff, M., 'Police and people: the birth of Mr. Peel's blue locusts', *New Society* (1979), pp. 443–445.
Institute of Race Relations, *Police Against Black People*, London: IRR, 1979.
Jacob, H. and Rich, M., 'The effects of the police on crime; a second look', *Law and Society Review*, **15**, 1 (1980).
Jacob, H. and Rich, M., 'The effects of the police on crime; a rejoinder', *Law and Society Review*, **16**, 1 (1980).
Jacobs, J. and Cohen, J., 'The impact of racial integration on the police', *Journal of Police Science and Administration*, **6**, 2 (1978).
Jefferson, T., 'Review article', *British Journal of Criminology*, 1 (1979), pp. 76–79.
Jefferson, T. and Grimshaw, R., 'The problem of law enforcement policy in England and Wales: the case of community policing and racial attacks', *International Journal of the Sociology of Law*, **12** (May 1984).
Jefferson, T. and Grimshaw, R., *Controlling the Constable: Police Accountability in England and Wales*, London: Muller, 1984.
Johnson, T., *Professions and Power*, London: Macmillan, 1972.
Jones, D., *Crime, Protest, Community and Police in 19th Century Britain*, London: Routledge, 1982.
Jones, J. M., *Organisational Aspects of Police Behaviour*, London: Gower, 1980.
Jones, J. M. and Winkler, J., 'Policing in a riotous City', *Journal of Law and Society*, **9**, 1 (Summer 1982).
Joshua, H., Wallace, T. and Booth, H., *To Ride the Storm: The 1980 Bristol 'Riot' and the State*, London: Heinemann, 1983.

Judge, A., *A Man Apart*, London: Arthur Baker, 1972.

Judge, A., 'The police and the coloured communities: a police view', *New Community*, **3**, 3 (Summer 1974).

Judge, A., 'Alderson's law', *Police*, October 1981.

Judge, A., 'Scarman: police responses', *New Community*, **9**, 3 (Winter 1981/Spring 1982).

Judge, A. and Reynolds, G., *The Night the Police Went on Strike*, London: Weidenfeld, 1968.

Kahn, A., 'Police Complaints under the 1984 Act', *Solicitors Journal*, **129**, 4 (January 1985), pp. 56–58.

Keeton, G. W., *Keeping the Peace*, Chichester: Barry Rose, 1975.

Kelling, G. *et al.*, *The Kansas City Preventive Patrol Experiment*, Washington, D.C.: Police Foundation, 1974.

Kelling, G., 'Police field service and crime: the presumed effects of a capacity', *Crime and Delinquency*, **24** (1978), pp. 178–184.

Kelman, A., 'Computer evidence and the Police & Criminal Evidence Bill', *New Law Journal*, **134**, 6145 (1984).

Kettle, M., 'The police take a political road', *New Society*, **51** (1980).

Kettle, M., 'A conflict of evidence', *New Society*, 1 January 1981.

Kettle, M., 'Controlling the police', *New Society*, 8 January 1981.

Kettle, M., 'The march of black outcast London', *New Society*, 12 March 1981.

Kettle, M. and Hodges, L., *Uprising!, The Police, the People and the Riots in Britain's Cities*, London: Pan, 1982.

King, J. F. S., (Ed.), *Control Without Custody?*, Cambridge: Institute of Criminology, 1976.

Klug, F., *Racist Attacks*, London: Runnymede Trust, 1982.

La Fave, W., *Arrest*, Boston: Little, Brown, 1965.

Lambert, J., *Crime, Police and Race Relations*, Oxford: Oxford University Press, 1970.

Lambeth Council Working Party, *Final Report of the Working Party into Community/Police Relations in Lambeth*, London: Borough of Lambeth, 1981.

Landau, S., 'Juveniles and the police', *British Journal of Criminology*, **21**, 1 (January 1981).

Landau, S. and Nathan, G., 'Selecting delinquents for cautioning in the London Metropolitan Area', *British Journal of Criminology*, **23**, 2 (April 1983).

Lane, T., 'Liverpool: City in crisis', *Marxism Today*, **22** (1978).

Larson, R., *Urban Police Patrol Analysis*, Cambridge, Mass.: MIT Press, 1972.

Larson, R., 'What happened to patrol operations in Kansas City?' *Journal of Criminal Justice*, **3**, 4 (1976).

Laugharne, A., *Skelmersdale Co-ordinated Policing Experiment*, Paper presented at the Cranfield Conference, Bedford, England: Cranfield Institute of Technology, 1980.

Laurie, P., *Scotland Yard*, London: Penguin Books, 1970.

Lea, J. and Young, J., *What Is To Be Done About Law and Order?* Harmondsworth: Penguin, 1984.

Leigh, L., 'The Police Act 1976', *British Journal of Law and Society*, **4**, 1 (Summer 1977).

Leigh, L., 'The Royal Commission on Criminal Procedure', *Modern Law Review*, May 1981.

Leigh, L., *Police Powers in England and Wales*, London: Butterworth, 1975.

Levenson, H., 'Democracy and the police', *Poly Law Review*, **6**, 2 (Spring 1981).

Levenson, H. and Hargreaves, F., 'The Police and Criminal Evidence Act 1984: stop & search without arrest', *Law Society Gazette*, **82**, 13 (April 1985).

Levenson, H. and Hargreaves, F., 'The Police and Criminal Evidence Act 1984: the new law on arrest', *Law Society Gazette*, **82**, 15 (24 April 1985).

Levi, M., *Bureaucratic Insurgency*, Lexington, Mass.: D. C. Heath, 1977.

Levi-Strauss, C., *The Savage Mind*, London: Wiedenfeld and Nicolson, 1966.

Lidstone, K., 'Investigative powers and the rights of the citizen', *Criminal Law Review*, July 1981.

Lidstone, K., 'Magistrates, the police and search warrants', *Criminal Law Review*, August 1984.

Littlejohn, G. *et al.* (Eds.), *Power and the State*, London: Croom Helm, 1978.

Loveday, B., 'The role of the police committee', *Local Government Studies*, **9** (January/February 1983).

Loveday, B., 'The role of the police committee: constitutional arrangements and social realities, a reply to Dr. P. Waddington', *Local Government Studies*, **9** (September/October 1984).

Lundman, R., (Ed.), *Police Behaviour*, New York: Oxford University Press, 1980.

Lyman, J. L., 'The Metropolitan Police Act of 1829', *Journal of Criminal Law, Criminology and Political Science*, **55** (March 1964).

McBarnet, D. J., *Conviction: Law, the State and Construction of Justice*, London: Macmillan, 1981.

McBarnet, D., 'Balance and clarity: has the Royal Commission achieved them?', *Criminal Law Review*, July 1981.

McBarnet, D., 'The Royal Commission and the Judges' Rules', *British Journal of Law and Society*, **8**, 1 (Summer 1981).

McBarnet, D., 'Legal form and legal mystification' *International Journal of the Sociology of Law*, **10** (1982).

McCabe, S. and Sutcliffe, F., *Defining Crime: a Study of Police Decisions*, Oxford: Blackwell, 1978.

McClure, J., *Spike Island: Portrait of a Police Division*, London: Macmillan, 1980.

McClure, J., *Cop World*, London: Pan, 1985.

McConville, M. and Baldwin, J., *Courts, Prosecution and Conviction*, Oxford: Oxford University Press, 1981.

McConville, M. and Morrell, P., 'Recording the interrogation: have the police got it taped?', *Criminal Law Review*, 1983.

MacDonald, I., 'The creation of the British police', *Race Today*, **5**, 11 (December 1973).

MacDonald, K., 'A police state in Britain?, *New Society*, 8 January 1976.

MacDonald, L., *The Sociology of Law and Order*, London: Faber, 1976.

McNee, D., 'The Queen's police keepeth the peace', *The Guardian*, 25 September 1979.

McNee, D., *McKnee's Law*, London: Collins, 1983.

Manning, P., *Police Work*, London: MIT Press, 1977.

Manning, P. and Van Maanen, J., (Eds.), *Policing: A View From the Street*, Santa Monica, Cal.: Goodyear, 1978.

Manwaring-White, S., *The Policing Revolution*, Sussex: Harvester, 1983.

Mapplebeck, J., 'The strange death of Liddle Towers', *New Statesman*, 29 July 1977.

Mark, R., *Speech given to the Institute of Journalists on 30 November 1971*, London: New Scotland Yard, 1971.

Mark, R., *Report to the Home Secretary from the Commissioner of the Metropolitan Police on the actions of police officers connected with the case of Kenneth Joseph Lennon*, HC 251, London: HMSO, 1974.

Mark, R., *Policing a Perplexed Society*, London: Allen & Unwin, 1977.

Mark, R., *In the Office of Constable*, London: Constable, 1978.

Marshall, G., *Police and Government: the Status and Accountability of the English Constable*, London: Methuen, 1965.

Marshall, G., 'The government of the police since 1963', *in* Alderson, J. and Stead, P., (Eds.), *The Police We Deserve*, London: Wolfe, 1973.

Marshall, G., 'Police accountability revisited', *in* Butler, D. and Halsey, A. H., (Eds.), *Policy and Politics*, London: Macmillan, 1978.

Martin, J. P. and Wilson, G., *The Police: a Study in Manpower*, London: Heinemann, 1969.

Matza, D., *Becoming Deviant*, Englewood Cliffs, New Jersey: Prentice Hall, 1969.

Mawby, R., *Policing the City*, Farnborough: Saxon House, 1979.

Mawby, R. and Batta, I. D., *Asians and Crime*, London: National Association for Asian Youth, 1980.

Maxfield, M., *Fear of Crime in England and Wales*, London: HMSO, 1984 (Home Office Research paper No. 78).

Merricks, W., 'How we drew the thin blue line', *New Statesman*, 9 January 1981.

Michalowski, R., 'Crime control in the 1980s: a progressive agenda', *Crime and Social Justice*, **19** (Summer 1983).

Miliband, R., *Capitalist Democracy in Britain*, Oxford: Oxford University Press, 1982.

Miller, W. R., *Cops and Bobbies*, Chicago: University Press, 1977.

Minto, G. A., *Thin Blue Line*, London: Hodder & Stoughton, 1965.

Mirfield, P., 'The future of the law of confessions', *Criminal Law Review*, February 1984.

Mitchell, B., 'Confessions and police interrogation of suspects', *Criminal Law Review*, 1983.

Mitchell, B., 'The role of the public in criminal detection', *Criminal Law Review*, August, 1984.

Moore, C. and Brown, J., *Community versus Crime*, London: Bedford Square Press, 1981.
Moore, M. and Kelling, G., ' "To serve and protect": learning from police history', *The Public Interest*, **70** (Winter 1983).
Moore, R., *Racism and Black Resistance*, London: Pluto, 1975.
Morgan, R. and Maggs, C., *Following Scarman?*, Bath University, 1984.
Morris, P. and Heal, K., *Crime Control and the Police*, London: HMSO, 1981 (Home Office Research Paper No. 67).
Morrison, C., 'Why PC Plod should come off the beat', *The Guardian*, 30 July 1984, p. 8.
Mount, F., 'From Swing to Scarman', *The Sepectator*, 26 November 1981.
Muir, Jr., K. W., *Police: Streetcorner Politicians*, Chicago: Chicago University Press, 1977.
Muncie, J., *'The Trouble with Kids Today'*, London: Hutchinson, 1984.
National Advisory Committee on Criminal Justice Standards and Goals, *Police*, Washington: US Government Printing Office, 1973.
National Youth Bureau, *Young People and the Police*, London: NYB, 1979.
Newman, G. F., *Law and Order*, London: Granada, 1983.
New Society, *Social Studies Reader: Race and Riots '81*, London: New Society, 1982.
Nicholas, E. R., 'The police: a unique group in society', *Police Review*, 22 May and 19 June, 1981.
Niederhoffer, A. and Blumberg, A., (Eds.), *The Ambivalent Force*, Hinsdale, Ill.: Dryden Press, 1976.
Norris, D. F., *Police–Community Relations: a Programme that Failed*, Lexington: Lexington Books, 1973.
Nott-Bower, W., *Fifty-Two Years a Policeman*, London: Edward Arnold, 1926.
Oxford, K., 'Policing by consent' *in* J. Benyon (Ed.), *Scarman and After*, Oxford: Pergamon, 1984.
Palmer, J., 'Evils merely prohibited', *British Journal of Law and Society*, **3**, 1 (Summer 1976).
Pate, T., Ferrara, A., Bowers, R. and Lorence, J., *Police response time: its determinants and effects*, Washington, D.C.: Police Foundation, 1976.
Pearson, G., *Hooligan*, London: Macmillan, 1983.
Perkin, H., *The Structured Crowd*, Brighton: Harvester Press, 1981.
Perrier, D., 'Is policing a profession?', *Canadian Journal of Criminology*, **21** (1979), pp. 52–70.
Philips, C., 'Politics in the making of the English police', in *The Home Office*, London: RIPA, 1982.
Philips, D., *Crime and Authority in Victorian England*, London: Croom Helm, 1977.
Philips, D., 'A just measure of crime, authority, hunters and blue locusts; the 'revisionist' social history of crime and the law in Britain 1780–1850', *in* Cohen, S. and Scull, A., (Eds.), *Social Control and the State*, Oxford: Martin Robertson, 1983.
Philips, O. H. and Jackson, P., (Eds.), *Constitutional and Administrative Law*, London: Sweet & Maxwell, 1978.
Pillavin, I. and Briar, S., 'Police encounters with juveniles', *American Journal of Sociology*, **70** (1964).
Platt, T. and Takagi, P., (Eds.), *Crime and Social Justice*, London: Macmillan, 1981.
Plehwe, R., 'Police and government: the Commissioners of Police for the Metropolis', *Public Law*, 1974.
Police Complaints Board, *Triennial Review Report*, London: HMSO, 1980 (Cmnd. 7966).
Police Complaints Board, *Triennial Review Report*, London: HMSO, 1983 (Cmnd. 8853).
Police Training Council, *Community and Race Relations Training for the Police*, London: Home Office, March 1983.
Pollard, B., *A Study of the Leicestershire Constabulary Highfields Community Policing Scheme*, Bedford: Cranfield Institute of Technology, 1979.
Pope, D. and Weiner, N., (Eds.), *Modern Policing*, London: Croom Helm, 1981.
Porter, D., *The Pursuit of Crime*, New Haven: Yale, 1981.
Powell, G. and Magrath, C., *The Police and Criminal Evidence Act 1984*, London: Longman, 1985.
Powis, D., *The Signs of Crime: A Field Manual for Police*, London: McGraw Hill, 1977.
Pratt, M., *Mugging as a Social Problem*, London: Routledge, 1980.
President's Commission on Law Enforcement and Administration of Justice, *Task Force Report: the Police*, Washington, D.C.: Government Printing Office, 1967.

Price, C. and Caplan, J., *The Confait Confessions*, London: Marion Boyars, 1977.
Pulle, S., *Police-Immigrant Relations in Ealing*, London: Runnymede Trust, 1973.
Punch, M., *Policing the Inner City*, London: Macmillan, 1979.
Punch, M., (Ed.), *Control in the Police Organisation*, London: MIT Press, 1983.
Punch, M., *Conduct Unbecoming: The Social Construction of Police Deviance and Control*, London: Tavistock, 1985.
Punch, M. and Naylor, T., 'The police: a social service', *New Society*, **24** (1973).
Radzinowicz, L., *A History of the English Criminal Law and its Administration from 1970: Cross Currents in the Movement for the Reform of the Police*, **3**, London: Stevens and Sons, 1956.
Ramsey, M., 'Mugging, fears and facts', *New Society*, 34 March 1982.
Rawls, J., *A Theory of Justice*, London: Oxford University Press, 1972.
Rees, T., Stevens, P. and Willis, C., 'Race, crime and arrests', *Home Office Research Bulletin*, **8**, London: Home Office, 1979.
Regan, D. E., 'Enhancing the role of police committees', *Public Administration*, **61**, 1 (Spring 1983).
Reiner, R., *The Blue Coated Worker*, Cambridge: Cambridge University Press, 1978.
Reiner, R., 'The police in the class structure', *British Journal of Law and Society*, **5**, 2 (Winter 1978).
Reiner, R., 'Fuzzy thoughts: the police and law and order politics', *Sociological Review*, **28**, 2 (March 1980).
Reiner, R., 'Political conflict and the British police tradition', *Contemporary Review*, April 1980.
Reiner, R., 'Black and blue: race and the police', *New Society*, 17 September 1981.
Reiner, R., 'Who are the police?', *The Political Quarterly*, **53**, 2 (April–June 1982).
Reiner, R., 'Bobbies take the lobby beat', *New Society*, 25 March 1982.
Reiner, R., 'Is Britain turning into a police state?, *New Society*, 2 August 1984.
Reiner, R., *The Politics of the Police*, Brighton: Wheatsheaf, 1985.
Reiss, Jr. A. J., *The Police and the Public*, New Haven: Yale University Press, 1971.
Reith, C., *The Police Idea*, Oxford: Oxford University Press, 1938.
Reith, C., *Police Principles and the Problem of War*, Oxford: Oxford University Press, 1940.
Reith, C., *British Police and the Democratic Ideal*, London: Oxford University Press, 1943.
Reith, C., *A Short History of the British Police*, London: Oxford University Press, 1948.
Reith, C., *The Blind Eye of History*, London: Faber, 1952.
Reith, C., *A New Study of Police History*, London: Oliver & Boyd, 1956.
Report of Her Majesty's Chief Inspector of Constabulary, London: HMSO, annually.
Report of the Commissioner of Police for the Metropolis, London: HMSO, annually.
Report of the Committee on Police Conditions of Service (The Oaksey Committee), London: HMSO, 1949 (Cmnd. 7831).
Roach, L., *The Metropolitan Police Community Relations Branch*, Police Studies, **3** (1978).
Roberts, D., 'Tape-recording the questioning of suspects', *Criminal Law Review*, September 1984.
Roberts, R., *The Classic Slum*, London: Penguin, 1973.
Robertson, G., 'Lennon: a case to answer', *New Statesman*, 15 November 1974.
Robinson, C., 'The deradicalisation of the policeman', *Crime and Delinquency*, **24**, 2 (1978).
Robinson, C., 'Ideology as history', *Police Studies*, **2**, 2 (Summer 1979).
Robson, P. and Watchman, R., (Eds.), *Justice, Lord Denning and the Constitution*, Hants: Gower, 1981.
Rogaly, J., *Grunwick*, Harmondsworth: Penguin, 1977.
Rolph, C. H., (Ed.), *The Police and the Public*, London: Heinemann, 1962.
Rosenhead, J., 'The technology of riot control', *New Scientist*, 23 July 1981.
Royal Commission on Police Powers and Procedure, *Report*, London: HMSO, 1929 (Cmnd. 3297).
Royal Commission on the Police, *Interim Report*, London: HMSO, 1960 (Cmnd. 1222).
Royal Commission on the Police, *Final Report*, London: HMSO, 1962 (Cmnd. 1728).
Royal Commission on Criminal Procedure, *Report*, London: HMSO, 1981 (Cmnd. 8092).
Rubenstein, J., *City Police*, New York: Ballantine, 1973.
Ruchelman, L., (Ed.), *Who Rules the Police?*, New York: New York University Press, 1973.
Rude, G., *The Crowd in History*, New York: Wiley, 1964.

Russell, K., *Complaints against the Police*, Leicester: Milltake, 1976.
Sanders, W., *Detective Work*, Glencoe: Free Press, 1977.
Savage, S., 'Political control or community liaison?', *The Political Quarterly*, **55**, 1 (January–March 1984).
Scarman, Lord, *The Brixton Disorders 10–12 April 1981: Report of an Inquiry by the Rt. Hon. the Lord Scarman, OBE*, London: HMSO, November 1981 (Cmnd. 8427).
Schaffer, E. B., *Community Policing*, London: Croom Helm, 1980.
Select Committee on Home Affairs, *Race Relations and the 'Sus' Law: Second Report from the Home Affairs Committee, Session 1979/80*, HC 559, London: HMSO, 1980.
Select Committee on Race Relations and Immigration, *Report on Police/Immigrant Relations*, HC 71, London: HMSO, 1972.
Shaw, M. and Williamson, W., 'Public attitudes to the police', *The Criminologist*, **7**, 26 (1972).
Shearing, C., (Ed.), *Organisational Police Deviance*, Toronto: Butterworths, 1981.
Shearing, C. and Stenning, P., 'Private security: implications for social control', *Social Problems*, **30**, 5 (June 1983).
Sherman, L. W., *Scandal and Reform: Controlling Police Corruption*, London: University of California Press, 1978.
Sherman, L., Milton, C. and Kelley, T., *Team Policing*, Washington, D.C.: Police Foundation, 1983.
Silberman, C., *Criminal Violence, Criminal Justice*, New York: Vintage, 1978.
Silver, A., 'The demand for order in civil society', *in* Bordua, D., (Ed.), *The Police*, New York: Wiley, 1967.
Sim, J., 'Scarman: the police counter-attack', *Socialist Register 1982*, London: Merlin, 1982.
Simey, M., 'Partnership policing' *in* J. Benyon (Ed.), *Scarman and After*, Oxford: Pergamon, 1984.
Skolnick, J., *Justice Without Trial*, New York: Wiley, 1975.
Skolnick, J., *The Politics of Protest*, New York: Bantam, 1969.
Sloan, P., *Public Order and the Police*, London: Police Review Publishing Co., 1978.
Smith, A. T. H., 'Breaching the peace and disturbing the public quiet', *Public Law*, Summer 1982.
Smith, D. A. and Klein, J. R., 'Police control of interpersonal disputes', *Social Problems*, **31**, 4 (April 1984).
Smith, D. A. and Visher, C. A., 'Street-level justice: situational determinants of police arrest decisions', *Social Problems*, **19**, 2 (December 1981).
Smith, P. and Hawkins, R., 'Victimisation types of citizen–police contacts and attitudes toward the police', *Law and Society*, **8** (1973), pp. 135–152.
Smith, S., *Race and Crime Statistics*, Church House, London: Board for Social Responsibility, 1982.
Smoker, B., 'The Challenor Case', *British Journal of Criminology*, **6** (January 1966).
Softley, P., *et al.*, *Police Interrogation*, London: HMSO, 1980 (Home Office Research Study No. 61).
Southall Rights, *23 April 1979: A Report*, Southall: Southall Rights, 1980.
Southgate, P., *Police Probationer Training in Race Relations*, London: Home Office, 1982 (Research and Planning Unit Paper No. 8).
Southgate, P. and Ekblom, P., *Contacts Between Police and Public*, London: HMSO, 1984 (Home Office Research Study No. 77).
Sparks, R. F., Genn, H. G. and Dodd, D. J., *Surveying Victims: A study of the measurement of criminal victimisation, perception of crime, and attitudes to criminal justice*, Chichester: John Wiley, 1977.
Spitzer, S. and Scull, A., 'Privatisation and social control', *Social Problems*, **25** (1977).
State Research, 'Policing the 80s: the iron fist', *State Research Bulletin*, **19** (August–September 1980).
Stead, P., (Ed.), *Pioneers in Policing*, New Jersey: Patterson Smith, 1977.
Steedman, C., *Policing the Victorian Community*, London: Routledge, 1984.
Steer, D., *Police Cautions: A Study in the Exercise of Police Discretion*, Oxford: Blackwell, 1970.
Steer, D., *Uncovering Crime: the Police Role*, Royal Commission on Criminal Procedure Research Study, 7, London: HMSO, 1980.

Stevens, P. and Willis, C. F., *Race, Crime and Arrests*, London: HMSO, 1979 (Home Office Research Study No. 58).

Stevens, P. and Willis, C. F., *Ethnic Minorities and Complaints Against the Police*, London: Home Office, 1982 (Research Unit Paper No. 5).

Storch, R. D., 'The plague of the blue locusts', *International Review of Social History*, **20** (1975).

Storch, R. D., 'The policeman as domestic missionary', *Journal of Social History*, **9**, 4 (Summer 1976).

Storch, R., 'Crime and justice in 19th-century England', *History Today*, **30** (1980).

Sumner, C., (Ed.), *Crime, Justice and the Mass Media*, Cambridge: Institute of Criminology, 1982.

Sweeney, T. J. and Illingsworth, W., (Eds.), *Issues in Police Patrol*, Washington D.C.: Police Foundation, 1973.

Taylor, I., *Law and Order: Arguments for Socialism*, London: Macmillan, 1981.

Taylor, I., Walton, P. and Young, J., *The New Criminology*, London: Routledge, 1973.

Taylor, L., *In the Underworld*, Oxford: Basil Blackwell, 1984.

Taylor, P., 'How Hendon police cadets are wooed away from racialism', *Police*, August 1983.

Thompson, E. P., *The Making of the English Working Class*, London: Penguin, 1968.

Thompson, E. P., *Whigs and Hunters*, Harmondsworth: Peregrine, 1977.

Thompson, E. P., *Writing by Candlelight*, London: Merlin, 1980.

Tittle, C. R. and Rowe, A., 'Certainty of arrest and crime rates. A further test of the deterrent hypothesis', *Social Forces*, **52** (1974), pp. 455–461.

Tobias, J. J., *Crime and Police in England, 1700–1900*, London: Gill & Macmillan, 1979.

Traini, R., 'Police and the press', *Police Review*, 15 June 1979.

Tuck, M. and Southgate, P., *Ethnic Minorities, Crime and Policing*, London: HMSO, 1981, (Home Office Research Study No. 70).

Tumber, H., *Television and the Riots*, London: British Film Institute, 1982.

Unofficial Committee of Enquiry, *Report: Southall 23 April 1979*, London: NCCL, 1980.

Unofficial Committee of Enquiry, *The Death of Blair Peach*, London: NCCL, 1981.

Unsworth, C., 'The riots of 1981', *Journal of Law and Society*, **9**, 1 (Summer 1982).

Vennard, J., 'Disputes within trials over the admissibility and accuracy of incriminating statements', *Criminal Law Review*, 1984.

Waddington, P. A. J., 'Racism and the police — the making of a myth', *Police*, **15**, 2 (October 1982).

Waddington, P. A. J., 'Why the "opinion-makers" no longer support the police', *Police*, December 1982.

Waddington, P. A. J., 'Conservatism, dogmatism and authoritarianism in the police: a comment', *Sociology*, November 1982.

Waddington, P. A. J., *Are the Police Fair?*, Research Paper 2, London: Social Affairs Unit, 1983.

Waddington, P. A. J., 'Beware the community trap', *Police*, March 1983, p. 34.

Waddington, P. A. J., 'The role of the police committee: constitutional arrangements and social realities', *Local Government Studies*, **10** (September/October 1984).

Walker, S., *A Critical History of Police Reform*, Lexington, Mass.: D. C. Heath, 1977.

Walker, S., *Popular Justice*, New York: Oxford University Press, 1980.

Walker, S., *Police in America*, New York: McGraw Hill, 1983.

Wallington, P. and McBride, J., *Civil Liberties and a Bill of Rights*, London: Cobden Trust, 1976.

Warren, K. and Tredinnick, D., *Protecting the Police*, London: Conservative Political Centre, 1982.

Webb, J., *The Badge: The Inside Story of the Los Angeles Police Department*, London: W. H. Allen, 1959.

Westley, W., *Violence and the Police: a Sociological Study of Law, Custom and Morality*, Massachusetts: MIT Press, 1970.

Whitaker, B., *The Police*, London: Eyre Methuen, 1964.

Whitaker, B., *The Police in Society*, London: Sinclair Browne, 1982.

Whitelaw, W., 'The police and the public: the James Smart memorial lecture', *Police Review*, 26 September 1980.

Whyte, W. F., *Street Corner Society*, Chicago: University of Chicago Press, 1955.

Willis, C. F., *The Use, Effectiveness and Impact of Police Stop and Search Powers*, London: Home Office, 1983 (Home Office Research and Planning Unit Paper 15).

Wilson, J. Q., *Varieties of Police Behaviour*, Cambridge, Massachusetts: Harvard University Press, 1970.

Wilson, J. Q., *Thinking About Crime*, New York: Vintage, 1975.

Wilson, J. Q. and Boland, G., 'The effects of the police on crime', *Law and Society Review*, **12**, 3 (1978).

Wilson, J. Q. and Boland, G., 'The effects of the police on crime: a response to Jacob and Rich', *Law and Society Review*, **16**, 1 (1981).

Wilson, O. W. and McLaren, R. C., *Police Administration*, New York: McGraw-Hill, 1963.

Wolmer, C., 'Neighbourly nosing', *New Statesman*, 21 September 1984.

Wren-Lewis, J., 'TV coverage of the riots', *Screen Education*, **40** (Autumn/Winter 1981–82).

Zander, M., 'Acquittal rates and not guilty pleas: what do the statistics mean?', *Criminal Law Review*, 1974, pp. 401–408.

Zander, M., *A Bill of Rights?*, London: Barry Rose, 1979.

Zander, M., 'What is the evidence on law and order?', *New Society*, 13 December 1979.

Zander, M., 'The investigation of crime: a study of cases tried at the Old Bailey', *Criminal Law Review*, 1979.

Zander, M., 'Police powers', *The Political Quarterly*, **53**, 2 (April–June 1982).

Zander, M., *The Police and Criminal Evidence Act 1984*, London: Sweet & Maxwell, 1985.

Zellick, G., 'The purpose behind an arrest', *Criminal Law Review*, **94** (1984).

Index

(i) Index to contributors

(Page references in bold indicate main contributions)

(ii) Table of statutes

(iii) Table of cases

(iv) Main index